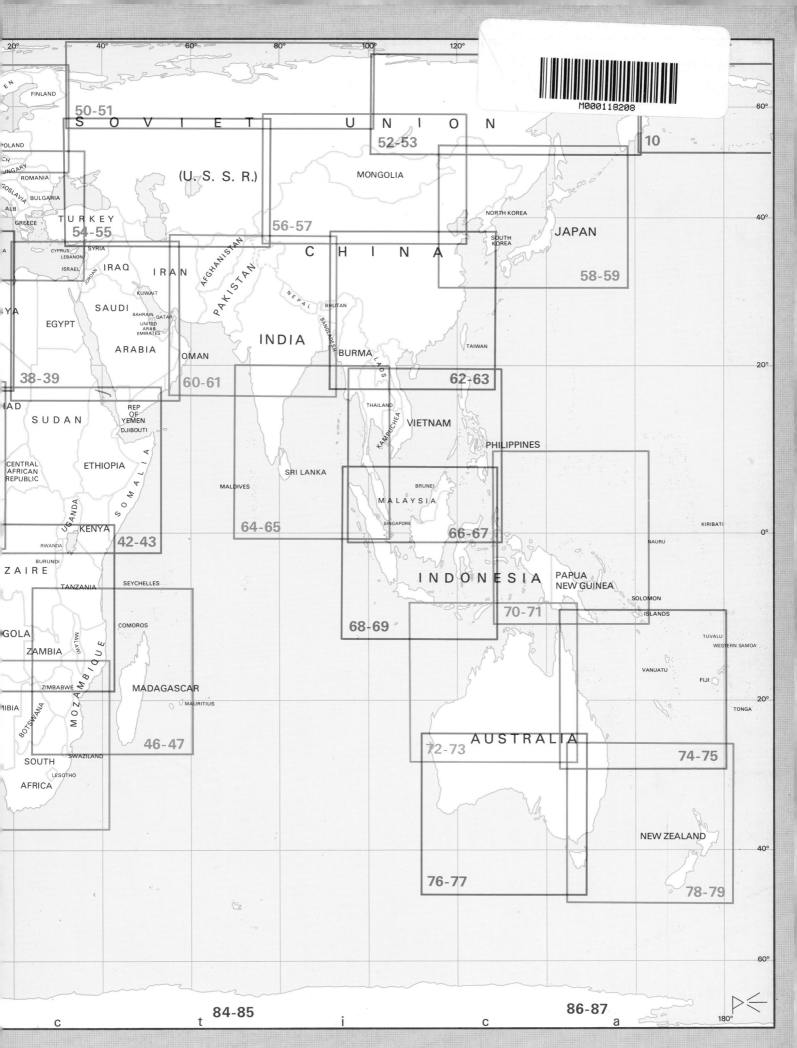

TOPOGRAPHIC MAPS

COMPACT PETERS ATLAS OF THE WORLD

Longman ⊞

Cartography:
Kümmerly + Frey, Bern (graticules, coastlines, borders, seas, rivers and lakes)
Oxford Cartographers (topographic and thematic maps)

Longman Group UK Limited,
Longman House, Burnt Mill, Harlow,
Essex CM20 2JE, England
And Associated Companies throughout the world.

First published 1991

British Library Cataloguing in Publication Data
Peters, Arno
Compact Peters atlas of the world.
I. Title
912

ISBN 0582089565

Photography: Clyde Surveys Ltd, Oxford Litho Plates Ltd
Scanning: Rapidagraphics Ltd, London
Typesetting: Oxford University Press, Getset (BTS) Ltd
Machine Proofing: Colourproof (UK) Ltd
Printing: Neue Stalling, Oldenburg
Binding: Neue Stalling, Oldenburg

FOREWORD

In 1493 – one year after Columbus's first voyage to America – the Pope apportioned the non-European world among the most powerful nations of his own continent. By the time Mercator completed his Atlas 100 years later, European domination had spread across the world, and Mercator's Atlas was the embodiment of Europe's geographical conception of the world in an age of colonialism.

Since then thousands of atlases have been published. They differ in many respects from Mercator's, but all adhere to the principle of a Eurocentric view of the world. The country and continent of origin are represented at a larger scale than the non-European countries. If, together with the age of colonialism, the view of the world that underpinned it is to come to an end, we need a new geography - one that is based on the equal status of all peoples.

This Atlas represents all countries and continents at the same scale. Their actual size and their position in the world can thus be taken directly from the map. This equal presentation is the expression of the consciousness that is gradually replacing our conventional ways of thinking about the world.

The use of a single scale for all topographic maps; the principle of fidelity of area; and a new, universally applicable presentation of relief; together, these now make possible a fundamental change in our conception of the world. All 246 thematic maps are also equal-area world maps. The comprehensive presentation in these thematic maps of man, nature and society is based on the same principle of equality as that underlying the topographic maps.

This Atlas, therefore, offers a way of understanding the background to, and causes of, the North-South divide as well as the tensions between East and West – so often the outcome of the gulf which separates rich and poor. In so doing, it throws new light on the profound changes of our times.

Arno Peters

CONTENTS

THE WORLD IN 43 MAPS AT THE SAME SCALE

NATURE, MAN AND SOCIETY IN 246 THEMATIC WORLD MAPS

CARTOGRAPHIC INTRODUCTION

It may come as a shock to realise that all of the atlases we have known until now present a distorted picture of the world. The nature of this distortion, and the reason for it, are now so obvious that it seems hardly possible to have overlooked them for over 400 years. The distortion caused by attempting to represent the spherical earth on flat paper is more or less unavoidable, but the distortion caused by the use of inconsistent scales, which has acquired the unquestioned sanction of habit, is not.

We have come to accept as "natural" a representation of the world that devotes disproportionate space to large-scale maps of areas perceived as important, while consigning other areas to small-scale general maps. And it is because our image of the world has become thus conditioned, that we have for so long failed to recognise the distortion for what it is – the equivalent of peering at Europe and North America through a magnifying glass and then surveying the rest of the world through the wrong end of a telescope.

There is nothing "natural" about such a view of the world. It is the remnant of a way of thinking born even before the age of colonialism and fired by that age. Few thinking people today would subscribe to a world-view of this kind. Yet, until now, no atlas has existed which provided the undistorted picture of the world which seems so long overdue.

A single scale
All topographic maps in this atlas are at the same scale: each double-page map shows one-sixtieth of the earth's surface. This means that all the topographic maps can be directly compared with one another. Among the many surprises this unique feature offers may be, for some users, the relative sizes of Great Britain (page 32) and the island of Madagascar (page 47); or, perhaps, the areas respectively covered by Europe (pages 32–33) and North Africa (pages 36–37). For most people it will soon become apparent that their hazy and long-held notions of the sizes of different countries and regions are, in a lot of cases, quite drastically wrong.

But what do we mean by scale? The scale indicator that appears on reference maps only shows distance scale. It enables the user to calculate the factor needed to multiply distances so as to compare them with those on other maps. This is a complex and somewhat tedious exercise that the great majority of users understandably neglect to carry out. Moreover, the number of different scales in our atlases is surprisingly high, in general between twenty and fifty. The concept of relative scale must become increasingly vague in the user's mind. What is generally not mentioned is that, because it is impossible to transfer the curved surface of the globe correctly to a flat plane, the scale indicator on a map is only valid for a single part of the map, such as a line of latitude.

Distance is only one aspect of the scale. Area has also to be considered. Whereas there can be no maps with absolute fidelity of distance, there can be maps with fidelity of area. The maps in this atlas preserve fidelity of area, a feature never previously achieved in an atlas. In the Peters Atlas all topographic maps have equal area scale: 1 square centimetre on the map is equal to approximately 7,400 square kilometres in reality.

But there is a price to pay for the introduction of this innovation. This atlas is unsuitable for some purposes. A world atlas like this one is not designed to guide the motorist, or to replace the inexpensive detailed road map; nor is it intended as an aid for local geography. It offers, instead, a comprehensive global view.

A single symbology
This equality of scale offers further advantages besides direct comparability. The basis of any map compilation is the simplification of reality, which cartographers call "generalisation". This transfer of the real character of the earth's surface into a system of lines and symbols, which can be graphically represented, has to be adapted to the scale employed. Thus a river or road with all its turns and windings on a scale of 1:100,000 can be drawn nearer to reality, (that is, with more detail) than on a scale of 1:1,000,000. Symbols also vary for different scales. Thus the same symbol can mean a town with 50–100,000 inhabitants on one scale, but a city with 1–5 million inhabitants on another. The same elevation may be differently coloured on maps of different scale. All such difficulties vanish in this atlas, which by way of its single scale has only one level of generalisation and a single set of symbols.

Topographic map colours
The green/brown colouring of most current atlases represents the topographic relief of the region; green stands for low-lying areas, brown for mountainous country, with different shades of the two colours for different elevations. Since, however, both colours (as also the blue of the sea and the white of snow-covered mountains) are borrowed from nature, the user of the atlas may be forgiven for assuming the green parts on the map to represent areas with vegetation and the brown parts to be the barren land. Although this is broadly true in Europe it may not be so elsewhere. For example, in North Africa the lower areas, even those below sea level, are usually deserts, and it is only above a certain height in the mountains that vegetation begins. The green/brown colouring is thus unsuitable for representing relief in a genuine world atlas. So in this Atlas green represents vegetation, brown barren land, and a mixture of the two colours represents thin or scattered vegetation. Global vegetation data were obtained from 1985–86 satellite photography with the help of the Remote Sensing Unit at the Department of Geography of Bristol University. The resolution of this imagery down to individual units of 20 square kilometres, and its conversion to the Peters base maps by the Remote Sensing Unit, makes this the most up-to-date statement available of the distribution of world vegetation.

Topographic map relief
To give the impression of relief the Peters Atlas has combined two techniques: shading by hand, which has developed to an advanced art in recent years, and the technique less often used because of its high cost – that of making relief models of the terrain and then photographing them. Although model photography is unsurpassed in its three-dimensional effect, it presents two difficulties. Because the light source has to come primarily from one

direction, relief features running directly along the line of the light source are under-represented. At the same time, relief features running at 90 degrees to the light source and close to it sometimes lose detail, becoming either uniformly light or shadowed. To overcome both of these in the Peters Atlas, the relief features on the model photograph have been enhanced by hand. At the same time, more intense shading has been added to the highest mountains, so that the relative height of the mountains on any map can be judged at a glance. The addition of spot heights for selected peaks and other points on the map lends accuracy to this technique.

The Peters Projection
Anyone who has ever tried to peel an orange and press the peel into a continuous flat piece without tearing will have grasped the fundamental impossibility that lies at the heart of all cartographic endeavour: that fidelity of shape, distance and angle are of necessity lost in flattening the surface of a sphere. On the other hand it is possible to retain three other qualities: fidelity of area, fidelity of axis and fidelity of position. Fidelity of area makes it possible to compare various parts of a map directly with one another, and fidelity of axis and position guarantee correct relationships of north-south and east-west axes by way of rectangular grid.

In 1973 Arno Peters published his world map, which unites in a single flat map all three achievable qualities – fidelity of area, fidelity of axis and fidelity of position. In this way the real comparative sizes of all countries in the world are clearly visible. For this Atlas Arno Peters has generalised the projection principle upon which his World Map was based, so that now each regional map represents the maximum possible freedom from distortion. Since map distortions through a projection decrease in proportion as the area represented becomes smaller, the forty-three topographical maps in this Atlas are considerably closer to reality than in the Peters World Map. In particular these individual maps correct the distortions which are unavoidable on the Peters World Map in the equatorial and polar regions. An indication of how this has been applied can be seen from the shapes of the page areas on the Map Finder (front endpaper). In the North they are long and thin while towards the Equator they are nearly square. The degree of departure from the normal page proportion is a guide to the amount of shape correction applied to the regional maps.

The eight polar maps on pages 80–95 have the same scale as all the other topographical maps. They also have fidelity of area, and represent one-sixtieth of the Earth's surface on each double page. Thus the size of the countries and continents shown on them can be directly compared with all the other 35 topographical maps. The fidelity of position and axis which is necessarily lost on polar maps is also not present on these maps.

The thematic maps
The second part of this Atlas directs attention to the whole earth. The author has collected data for 246 individual world thematic maps under 45 subject headings. Each of these subject headings is given a double page spread, but if more than one topic is covered under any subject, separate maps are given. Thus under the subject heading "Life Expectancy" only one topic is covered so the double spread comprises a single map, whereas the subject heading "Domestic Animals" requires sixteen topics and therefore displays sixteen individual maps. The principle of one topic per map also enables all the maps to be represented by simple grades of colour, with, usually, a single hue chosen for each topic. Within this hue the range from light to dark colour represents low to high values of the topic. In this way all the thematic maps can be understood at a glance, without the necessity for complicated symbols or explanations.

The graticule
The traditional zero meridian running through Greenwich was adopted worldwide in 1884, when Britain was the strongest European colonial power and ruled over a quarter of the world. After the ending of colonialism and with the closure of Greenwich Observatory, there is no reason other than custom for retaining this zero meridian. The International Dateline, which is dependent upon the zero meridian, also needs correction, since over its whole length it has been partially diverted where it cuts an inhabited area. The retention of the division into 360 degrees is also, it can be argued, an anomaly in the age of worldwide decimalisation.

Arno Peters has therefore proposed a new decimal grid in which the zero meridian and the International Date Line would become a single line placed in the middle of the Bering Strait, and the earth is divided into 100 decimal degrees east-west and north-south. While for practical reasons the Greenwich system is retained throughout the bulk of the Atlas, the new decimal grid is shown on pages 230–231.

The Index
Someone consulting an index in search of a district, town or river has until now had to memorise, besides the page number, at least two grid figures, two letters, or a letter and a number. There can be few users of an atlas who have not experienced the irritation of forgetting at least one item in this unwieldy string of digits by the time the relevant map has been located, and the time-consuming exercise of turning back to the index to recall this information. In the Peters Atlas there is, apart from the page number, only a single letter, which can easily be remembered. This innovatory and simple indexing system is explained on page 188.

Computer cartography
Computer cartography now makes it possible to keep maps up to date with the latest results of worldwide research. At the same time, however, pure automation can rob the map of its best characteristics – the handcrafted workmanship of the cartographer.

The Peters Atlas combines both of these approaches. The base maps have been recentred from the world projection using Europe's most modern Scitex computer installation in Berne, with geographic data from the Erdgenössische Technische Hochschule. Satellite data for vegetation has been tailored by computer to fit these bases. The rest of the cartography for the topographic and thematic maps has remained in the hands of traditional cartographic craftsmen in Oxford. The Peters Atlas therefore reconciles these two approaches. We have used as much mechanisation as necessary and as much handcraft as possible.

Terry Hardaker

Chief Cartographer
Oxford Cartographers

ACKNOWLEDGEMENTS

Contributors and Consultants
Dr. E. C. Barrett
Professor Ulrich Bleil
Michael Benckert
Wolfgang Behr
Professor Heinz Bosse
Professor Walter Buchholz
Dr. Nicola Bradbear
Carol Claxton
Professor Heinrich Dathe
Hellmuth Färber
Jean Fernand-Laurent
Kurt Ficker
Professor Fritz Fischer
Karlheinz Gieseler
Professor Manfred Görlach
Professor Ulrich Grosse
Arnulf Hader
Max Hann
Dirk Hansohm
Dr. Günther Heidmann
Professor Wolf Herre
Karl-Heinz Ingenhaag
Dr. Andreas Kaiser
Professor Gunther Krause
Dr. Manfred Kummer
Daniel Lloyd
Konrad G. Lohse
Wolfgang Mache
Dr. Udo Moll
Georg Möller
Dr. Aribert Peters
Birgit Peters
Werner Peters
Thomas Plümer
D. H. Reichstein
Hellmut Schlien
Professor Hermann Schulz
Professor Axel Sell
Eduard Spescha
Jürgen Wendler
Professor Adolf Witte
Professor Karl Wohlmuth
Siegfried Zademack
Madeleine Zeller

Cartographic Editor
Terry Hardaker

Editorial Coordination
Penny Watson

Computer Programmer
H. Morelli

Topographic Map Compilation
Katharine Armitage
Claire Carlton
John Hall
Hazel Hand
Sheila Hodson
Christine Johnston
Jean Kelly
Tanya Lillington
Angela Morrison
Kay Roberts
Fiona Sutcliffe

Editorial Checking
Ann Leleu
Georg Möller

Technical Coordination
John Dawson
John Wilders

Draughting
Gerhard Engel
Bob Hawkins
Ben Hill
Sally Horn
Robert Hundley
Jeff Jones
David Lewis
Sue Lovell
Colin McCarthy
Michael Oakley
Piet Summerfield

Estimating
Peter Langran
John Williams

Terrain Modelling
David Angus

Terrain Colouring
Terry Hardaker

Indexing
Barbara Croucher
Duncan Croucher
Betty Döppl
Petra Faltermeier
Karin Geier
Franz Huber
Ingrid Kampfhenkel
Hermann Lechner
Lothar Meier
Anton Sommer
Iris Sommer
Margret Suhr

THE WORLD IN 43 MAPS AT THE SAME SCALE
EACH MAP SHOWS ONE-SIXTIETH OF THE EARTH'S SURFACE.

The colours used on the maps simulate those found in nature.

Water (Lakes, Seas, Oceans)

Ice Shelf

Vegetation (Plains)

Barren Land (Plains)

Continental Ice (Plains)

Vegetation (Hills)

Barren Land (Hills)

Continental Ice (Hills)

Vegetation (Mountains)

Barren Land (Mountains)

Continental Ice (Mountains)

Spot Heights:

· *1236*   1236 Metres above Sea Level

· *-25*   25 Metres below Sea Level

Communications:

——————   Railway

——————   Road

══════   Motorway

═ ═ ═   Motorway in Tunnel

∿∿∿   River

⊢⊢⊢⊢⊢   Canal

Boundaries:

▬ ▬ ▬   International Boundary

∿∿∿   International Boundary on River

▬ ▬ ▬   Disputed International Boundary

▪ ▪ ▪   State Boundary

On each double page the 1000 largest and most important cities and towns are shown; if the double page shows sea as well as land, there are proportionally fewer:

  o   fewer than 100,000 inhabitants

  ◉   100,000 – 1,000,000 inhabitants

  ◼   1,000,000 – 5,000,000 inhabitants

  ☁   over 5,000,000 inhabitants

Adjoining map indicator:

    Map of adjoining area is on page 25.

Other physical features:

⚓   Waterfall

≡≡≡   Swamp, Marsh

◯   Salt Lake

▬ ▬ ▬   Coral Reef

Other man-made features:

∴   Archaeological Site

⌐⌐⌐⌐   Great Wall of China

Latitude and Longitude:

25°E   25 degrees Longitude East

50°W   50 degrees Longitude West

—30°N—   30 degrees Latitude North

—60°S—   60 degrees Latitude South

— — —   Tropics

Type styles:

Mato Grosso   Physical Features

Kolhapur   Cities and towns (capital cities underlined)

BELGIUM   Countries

T E X A S   States

INDIAN
OCEAN   Oceans, Seas

    Peters Projection (fidelity of area, axis and position)

165°E   170°E   175°E   180°   175°W   170°W   16

A R C T I C

1097

Wrangel Island

De Long Strait

C H U K C H I

S E A

70°N ○Ambarchik   *Cape*
                                                                                                        Lisburne
    ○Mal.   ○Point
  ○Cherskiy Baranikha   ○Pevek ○Krasnoarmeyskiy   Hope

North Anyuskiy Mts.   ○Retkucha   ○Mys
  Little Anyuy ○Ostrovnoy .1641   Shmidta
         ○   ○Plamennyy   ○Iultin
South Anyuskiy Mts.   2300
                                              .1707   ·1508
Great Anyuy S O V I E T   U N I O N

Arctic Circle   *Chukot Peninsula*   ○Uelen ○Shishmaref
                                                                              1250
Oloyskiy Mts. .1313   (U. S. S. R.)   .1504   ○Egvekinot Krasnaya   Sewo
                   ○Petushkova   Yaranga   ○Wales
                                                                                    Little
65°N   ○Yeropol ○Morokovo ○Ust'-Belaya   ○Uel'kal   ○Akkani *Diomede*○ ○Teller
Kolymskiy Mts. .2200
                                ○Anadyr' ○Anadyr'   ○Nunligran
              ○Markovo   ○Provideniya   N
                                Gulf of Anadyr
                  ○Penzhino *Velikaya*   ○Gambell *Saint Lawrence Island*
                                        ○Tumanskiy   *(U.S.A.)*
              ○Berezovo
                                                            ○Beringovskiy   *Alakanu*
  ○Kovrizhka ○Manily *Koryak Mountains*
                                      ○Maynopil'gyn *Cape Navarin*   *Hooper*
  ○Dana *Gulf of Penzhinskaya*   ○Khatyrka   Bay
                                    .2562   *Saint Matthew*
  Penzhinskiy Mts. .1285 ○Vatyna
                    Verkh. ○Apuka   *Nunivak*
                 ○Pakhacha Chukotskaya
                      ○Olyutorskiy   *Saint Matthew*
60°N ○Il'pyrskiy ○Korf   *Nunivak*
53   *Cape Olyutorskiy*

          .1700 ○Ossora
              ○Ostrovnoy
          Karaginskiy Island

                                              B E R I N G
Kamchatka
                                                                              Pribilof Islands

                              S E A

  ○Kamchatsk

  .2412

55°N   ○Podutesnaya
  .1327   *Komandor Islands*   *Uni*
                   (U.S.S.R.)
                                                                                              Unima

                                                                                      Dutch
                                                                          ○Unalaska ○Harbor
                                                                      Umnak *Fox Islands*
                        Attu
                  Near Islands   *Andreanof Islands* Atka *Aleutian Islands*
                     (U.S.A.)

              Kiska   ○Adak
            Rat Islands   *Amchitka* *Adak*
               (U.S.A.)   *Aleutian Islan*

165°E   170°E   175°E   180°   175°W   170°W   16

This map shows 1/60 of the earth's surface.

a b c d e f g h i j k l m

160°W 155°W 150°W 145°W 140°W 135°W 130°W

O C E A N

B E A U F O R T S E A

Cape Barrow
Barrow
○ Wainwright
Cape Dalhousie

Prudhoe
Bay
Deadhorse ○
○ Kaktovik
● Herschel
○ Tuktoyaktuk
70°N

Colville
Mount
Chamberlin
2749
2286
Mackenzie
Bay

Misheguk
Mountain
1289
B r o o k s R a n g e
Anaktuvuk
Pass
2319
• *2438*
○ Arctic
Village
Porcupine
● Old Crow
Fort
McPherson •1981
Aklavik
Inuvik ○
NORTHWEST

Baird Mountains
E n d i c o t t M o u n t a i n s
○ Wiseman
Arctic
Red River

Kotzebue ○
Kobuk ○
Fort
Yukon
Eagle
Plain ○
Mackenzie
TERRITORIES

Noorvik ○
A L A S K A
Eagle

1372
Hughes ○
Circle ○
Yukon
Clinton
Creek
1874
Keno •2088
2975

Koyuk ○
U.S.A.
Tanana ○
Manley
Hot Springs
Eagle Summit
1611
Sixtymile ○
Dawson ●
2499
Mount
Campbell
Y U K O N
Barlow
Mayo
Stewart
Keele
Peak
65°N

Galena ○
Fairbanks
Stewart ●
Pelly
Crossing
Stewart
Crossing
Macmillan

Kaltag ○
Ruby ○
Nenana ○
Richardson ○
Big Delta
1291
1374
T E R R I T O R Y

Unalakleet
Delta Junction
Tok ○
Carmacks ○
Faro ●

○
Holy
Cross
McGrath ○
Cantwell ○
Mount McKinley
6194
Tanacross ○
Mount Kimball
3155
Northway
Junction
Snag ○
Little
Salmon
•2399
Ross River ○

Aniak ○
Stony
River ○
Talkeetna ○
Paxson ○
Slana ○
Beaver
Creek
Koidern ○
C A N A D A

Lime
Village ○
Mount Torbert
3479
Willow ○
Glennallen ○
Gulkana ○
Mount Blackburn
4996
Braeburn ○

Kwethluk ○
Palmer ○
Copper
Center
Burwash
Landing
Haines
Junction
Whitehorse ●

Port
Alsworth ○
Anchorage ●
3108
Tonsina ○
Chitina ○
501
Mount Logan
6050
•4785
2213
Johnsons
Crossing

Kwigillingok ○
Kenai Peninsula
Valdez ○
Mount
Witherspoon
3665
Carcross ○
Jakes
Corner
Teslin ○
60°N

Iliamna
Lake
Kenai ○
Seward ○
Cordova ○
Lake
Atlin
Morley
River ○

Goodnews
Bay ○
Yakutat ○
Skagway ○
BRITISH
2301

Togiak ○
G u l f
Haines ○
COLUMBIA
Cassiar ○

Dillingham ○
o f
Mount Fairweather
4670
Juneau ○
Dease
Lake ○

Bristol
Bay
Naknek ○
King
Salmon ○
A l a s k a
•3882
Telegraph
Creek ○

Ugashik ○
Kodiak ○
Sitka ○
Mount Ratz
3136

Kodiak
Baranof
Island
•3049
Wrangell ○

Chignik ○
P A C I F I C
Mount
Pattullo
2729
Stewart ○

Mount Veniaminof
2507
Prince
of
Wales
Island
Ketchikan ○

Alaska Peninsula
(U.S.A.)
O C E A N
Dixon
55°N

Squaw
Harbor ○
Queen
Charlotte
Islands
Prince
Rupert ○

Entrance

Hecate
Strait

160°W 155°W 150°W 145°W 140°W 135°W 130°W

n o p q r s t u v w x y z

89

125°W 120°W 115°W 110°W 105°W 100°W

80°N

ARCTIC

OCEAN

E l i z a b e t h   I s l a n d

Meighen Island

Q u e e n

Borden Island

Prince Gustav Adolf
Sea

S v e r d r u

Ellef Ringnes Island

•457

Magnetic
North Pole (1991)

Amund Rin
Island

BEAUFORT

Prince Patrick Island

Mackenzie-King Island

Lougheed Island

Bathurst Island

•320

○ Mould Bay

P a r r y   I s l a n d s

SEA

75°N

Cape
Prince Alfred

McClure Strait

•1067

M e l v i l l e   I s l a n d

Dundas Peninsula

V i s c o u n t   M e l v i l l e   S o u n d

•457

•248

Corn
Re

Peel

Banks Island

Prince of Wales Strait

Prince Albert
Peninsula

•640

Hadley Bay

Stefansson
Island

Storkerson
Peninsula

McClintock Channel

Prince of Wales Island

Franklin
Strait

○ Sachs Harbour

•762

Minto Inlet

V i c t o r i a

Victoria Strait

King William
Island

70°N

Cape
Bathurst

○ Cape Parry

Amundsen Gulf

Cape Baring

○ Holman Island

P r i n c e   A l b e r t   S o u n d

I s l a n d

Kitikmeot   Region

Adelaide
Sherm
Basin
Peninsula

○ Paulatuk

•366

Wollaston
Peninsula

•518

Read Island ○

Dease Strait

•221
Cambridge Bay ○

N

O

R

T

H

Inuvik

Bluenose Lake
•609

Dolphin and Union Strait

C o r o n a t i o n   G u l f

Queen   Maud   Gulf

○ Colville Lake

Coppermine ○

Perry Island ○

•460

•518

Arctic Circle

•244
MacAlpine
Lake

Bathurst
Inlet

•823

Back

○ Fort Good
Hope

Region

Great Bear Lake

○ Port Radium

Takijuk Lake

Contwoyto
Lake

Garry Lake

Aberdeen Lake

Franklin Mountains

○ Norman
Wells

•1003

○ Fort Franklin

Hottah Lake

•704

65°N

11

○ Fort Norman

•2164

Rae Lakes ○

Warburton
Lake

Aylmer Lake

Clinton
Colden
Lake

Thelon

•413

Ke

•122

Lac
La Martre

Snare River

T   **E**   **R**   **R**   **I**   **T**   **O**

Wrigley ○

•1577

Mackenzie Mountains

Lac la Martre

Artillery Lake

Dubawnt
Lake

Fort

Edzo ○ ● Rae

•221

Reliance ○

Region

Yathkyed
Lake

Mount
Sir James
McBrien
2762

C

Yellowknife ○

Smith

A

Whitefish
Lake

N

Mount
Hunt
2743

Fort Simpson ○
•1548

Mackenzie

Fort
Providence ○

Snowdrift ○

•354

Nonacho
Lake

○ Nahanni Butte

**Great
Slave
Lake**

○ Fort Resolution

Ennadai
Lake

R

○ Hay River

Dawson Landing ○

Wholdaia
Lake

Kasba Lake

**YUKON
TERRITORY**

Enterprise ○

•594

Nueltin Lake
•349

○ Watson
Lake

Tathlina
Lake

Slave River

Fort Smith ○

60°N

•1763

Liard

○ Nelson Forks

Caribou
•1036

•236

Uranium ○ ☐ Eldorado
City

Stony Rapids

○ Caribou

Mountains

Peace River

Fort Chipewyan ○

Lake
Athabasca

Wollaston
Lake

○ Rabbit Lake

Steamboat ○

○ Fort Nelson

Hay River

High Level ○

•340

Churchill Peak
3049

○

Athabasca

•674

Cree Lake

Reindeer
Lake

BRITISH

3048

ALBERTA
•859

•672

SASKATCHEWAN

○ Kinoosao

Southern
Indian
Lake

MANI

COLUMBIA

Manning ○

Frobisher Lake

Peter
Pond
Lake

Churchill
Lake

Southend ○

○ Lynn Lake

•1094

○ Thompson

Mount Pattullo
2729

Mount Burden
1324

○ Fort
St. John

Fort McMurray ○

Buffalo
Narrows ○

•390

•2047

Dawson Creek ○

○ Peace River

○ Fort Black
•553

Lake
La Ronge

Churchill

○ Island Falls

Lake
Williston

Chetwynd ○
869

Rycroft ○ ○ McLennan

○ Flin Flon

○ Wabowden

○ Mackenzie

McLeod Lake ○

○ Tupper

High Prairie ○

Lesser Slave Lake

○ Hazelton

○ McLeod Lake

○ Grande Prairie

Valleyview ○
1259

○ Slave Lake
Smith ○

55°N

125°W 120°W 115°W 110°W 100°W

14

15

This map shows 1/60 of the earth's surface.

130°W   125°W   120°W   115°W

55°N

Dixon Entrance

Prince
Rupert

*Hecate
Strait*

*Queen
Charlotte
Islands*

Hazelton

Skeena Terrace Walcott
1981 Kitimat

Endako

McLeod
Lake

R

Prince
George

BRITISH

Sinclair Mills

869

Grande Prairie

Grande Cache

Valleyview   Slave Lake   Smith

Whitecourt   Barrhead   Westlock

Edson   Leduc

Athaba

Athabasca

Edmonton

Ocean Falls

Nechako
Reservoir

COLUMBIA

Quesnel

1000·

Williams
Lake *2543*   Blue River

Mt. Robson
Red *3953*
Pass

C

Jasper

Rocky Mountain
House

Olds

·3394

Vegrey

Wetaskiwin

A

Red Deer

ALBERT

Drumhel

Mount Waddington
·4042

Queen Charlotte Strait

Port Hardy

·1749

Blackpool

Cache Creek

Beavermouth

Golden

Revelstoke

Banff

Calgary

M
o
u
n
t
a
i
n
s

Vancouver

Campbell River
1966

Powell River

2500·

Fraser

Kamloops

Armstrong

·2537

High River

·100

50°N

Island

Nanaimo

Strait of Georgia

Vancouver

Hope

Chilliwack

Kelowna

Penticton

·2304

Nelson   Cranbrook

Trail

Fort
Macleod

Lethbr

Milk R

Victoria

Bellingham

Oroville

Omak

Bonners Ferry

Libby

Browning

Strait of Juan de Fuca

Cape Flattery

Mount Vernon

Everett

Sandpoint

Coeur
d'Alene

Kalispell

Lake
Flathead

Polson

Chotea

Port Angeles

Seattle

Bremerton

Tacoma

WASHINGTON

Wenatchee

Spokane

Thompson Falls

Wallace

M

Wolf C.

Missoula

Hele

PACIFIC

Aberdeen

Olympia

Mt. Rainier
4392

Centralia

Astoria

Longview

Ellensburg

Yakima

Richland

·822

Moses Lake

Pullman

Snake

Lewiston

Moscow

Pierce

Hamilton

Anaconda

45°N

Tillamook

Vancouver

Portland

columbia

The Dalles

John Day

·1018

Heppner

Pendleton

La
Grande

Grangeville

Riggins

New
Meadows

Salmon

B
l
u
e

Salmon

Dubo

OCEAN

Salem

Albany

Eugene

Madras

Bend

OREGON

John Day

Hampton
2441

Baker

Columbia

2420·

Weiser

Ontario

IDAHO

Salmon River

Mountains

Hyndman Peak
3682

Borah Peak
3857

Arco

Ida
Fa
14

Coos Bay

Roseburg

Chemult

·1982

Wagontire

*Malheur
Lake*

Caldwell

Boise

Mtn

Pocatell

Grants
Pass

Medford

Klamath Falls

Lakeview

Burns

Burns
Junction

Snake
·1000

Owyhee

Riddle

Glenns
Ferry

Twin Falls

Gooding

Crescent City

Yreka

Mount Shasta

Mount Shasta
4317

Alturas

McDermitt

Orovada

North Fork

Contact

Wells

·3263

Malad City

Great
Salt
Lake

Ogd

40°N

Eureka

Cape Mendocino

Burney

Redding

Susanville

Winnemucca

2390·

Humboldt

Battle
Mountain

Elko

Wendover

Salt Lake

Eu

Garberville

Red Bluff
2465

Sacramento

Chico

Oroville

C

Pyramid
Lake

Lovelock

Great

NEVADA

Delta

Richfie

Ukiah

Yuba
City

Reno
1369

Fallon

Basin

Austin

Eureka

Ely

Wheeler Peak
3980

Milford

Santa
Rosa

A

Sacramento

Carson
City

Hawthorne

Currant

2620·

Vallejo

Stockton

Oakland

Oakland
San Francisco

Modesto

Boundary Peak
4007

Goldfield

Tonopah

Caliente

Cedar C

San Jose

Santa Cruz

Merced

·100

Bishop

Beatty

St. George

Kanab

Monterey

Salinas

Fresno

Mount Whitney
·4418

*Death
Valley*
·-86

Las
Vegas

Lake
Mead

2449·

Co

35°N

·1346

King City

Visalia

Boulder
City

Searchlight

Kingman

San Luis
Obispo

Avenal

Delano

Ridgecrest

Baker

Cottonw

Prescott

Bakersfield

Mojave

Ludlow

Lake Havasu
City

Santa Barbara

Barstow

Lancaster

AR

Ventura

130°W   125°W   120°W   115°W

This map shows 1/60 of the earth's surface.

a   b   c   d   e   f   g   h   i   j   k   l   m

12

95°W   90°W   85°W   80°W   75°W

Hudson Bay

MANITOBA
55°N

Shamattawa
Fort Severn
Winisk
Cape Henrietta Maria
Point Louis XIV
Belcher Islands
Great Whale
Kuujjuarapik
.168
Kanaaupscow

Gods Lake
Bearskin Lake
Big Trout Lake
Winisk Lake
Lake River
James Bay
Akimiki Island
Chisasibi
La Radisson
Sakami
.195

Island Lake
Sandy Lake 276
North Caribou Lake
Wunnummin Lake
.88
Hannah Bay
Eastmain
Eastmain
.100
La

Pipangikum Lake .396
Cat Lake
Attawapiskat Lake
Fort Hope
Attawapiskat
Ogoki
Fort Albany
Moosonee
Fort Rupert
Rupert

Red Lake .359
268
Lac Seul
Lake St. Joseph
Albany
Abitibi
Lake Evans .232

Pinawa .317
Middleboro
Kenora
Dryden
Sioux Lookout
358
Armstrong
Nakina
Longlac
Geraldton
Hearst
Fraserdale
Kapuskasing
Cochrane
Monts Deloge .533
Lake Abitibi
Matagami
Chibougamau
.556 Chapais

ONTARIO
OCEAN
QUA
50°N

Lake of the Woods
Trans Canada Highway
English River
.500
Nipigon
Lake Nipigon
Schreiber
Marathon
White River
390.
Timmins
Noranda
Kirkland Lake
Val-d'Or
.609
Cabonga Reservoir

International Falls
Rainy Lake
Atikokan
Thunder Bay
Isle Royale
Wawa
Chapleau
.640
New Liskeard
.693
Sturgeon Falls
Témiscaming
Mont Laurier
Maniwaki

Thief River Falls
358
Lower Red Lake
Upper Red Lake
Grand Marais .646
Copper Harbor
Lake Superior
Sault Ste. Marie .665
Blind River
Espanola
Sudbury
.196
North Bay
Ste-Agathe-des-Monts .960
Buckingham
Hull
Montréal

Bemidji
Hibbing
436.
Grand Rapids
Virginia
.471
Duluth
Superior
Apostle Islands
Houghton
.603
Marquette
Seney
322
Little Current
Manitoulin Island
Parry Sound
Huntsville
Bancroft .419
Pembroke
Smith's Falls
Perth
Cornwall
Ottawa

Fergus Falls
Brainerd
Little Falls
Mille Lacs
.381
Cloquet
Ashland
.573
Ironwood
Iron Mountain
Escanaba
Mackinaw City
Tobermory
Georgian Bay
Owen Sound
Orillia
L. Simcoe
Peterborough
Belleville
Kingston
Brockville

MINNESOTA
Alexandria
Pine City
St. Cloud
Rice Lake
.454
Ladysmith
Rhinelander
Menominee
Petoskey
Alpena
Midland .573
Barrie
637.

45°N
15
Willmar
Minneapolis-St. Paul
River Falls
Chippewa Falls
Wausau
Merrill
Stevens Point
Sturgeon Bay
Grayling
Bay City
Saginaw
Port Elgin
Goderich
Kitchener
Waterloo
Hamilton .200
Toronto
St. Catharines
Rochester
Syracuse
NEW YORK

Minnesota
Marshall
New Ulm
Mankato
Faribault
Red Wing
Eau Claire
Marshfield
Appleton
Green Bay
WISCONSIN
Oshkosh
Manitowoc
Sheboygan
MICHIGAN
Cadillac
Muskegon
Ludington
Midland
Flint .385
Sarnia
London
St. Thomas
Fredonia
Buffalo
Niagara Falls
Seneca Lake
Utica
Albany

Worthington
Estherville
Spencer
Albert Lea
Austin
Decorah
.300
Mason City
Madison
Janesville
Beloit
Kenosha
Racine
Milwaukee
Grand Rapids
Lansing
Kalamazoo
Ann Arbor
Jackson
.358
Détroit
Windsor
Lake Erie
Erie
Meadville
.424
Jamestown
775.
Olean
Binghamton
Ithaca
Kingston

Storm Lake
Fort Dodge
Webster City
Waterloo
Dubuque
Freeport
Rockford
Elgin
De Kalb
Rochelle
Chicago
Battle Creek
Toledo
Sandusky
Ashtabula
Cleveland
Youngstown
PENNSYLVANIA
Clearfield
Williamsport
Scranton
Newburgh

Omaha
Council Bluffs
IOWA
Denison
Ames
.290
Newton
Cedar Rapids
Iowa City
Moline
Davenport
Princeton
Morris
Joliet
Gary
South Bend
Fort Wayne
Findlay
Mansfield
Canton
Johnstown
956.
Altoona
.706
Harrisburg
Reading
Trenton

Nebraska City
Bethany
Kirksville
300.
Keokuk
Galesburg
Peoria
236.
Bloomington
Lafayette
Rantoul
Kokomo
Lima
Kenton
Pittsburgh
.424
Wheeling
Greensburg
Lancaster
Philadel

40°N
St. Joseph
Atchison
Chillicothe
Macon
Hannibal
Quincy
Beardstown
Decatur
ILLINOIS
Champaign
Danville
Muncie
Anderson
Springfield
Columbus
Newark
Cambridge
Fairmont
Cumberland
Hagerstown
Wilmington
MARYLAND
NEW JERS
Atlantic City

Leavenworth
367.
Marshall
Columbia
Litchfield
Alton
Jacksonville
Springfield
Terre Haute
307.
Bloomington
INDIANA
Indianapolis
Richmond
Dayton
OHIO
Washington Court House
Chillicothe
Athens
Marietta
Parkersburg
Clarksburg
1222 Bickle Knob
Elkins
Baltimore
Washington DC
Annapolis
Cape May

Kansas City
Topeka
Independence
Sedalia
Jefferson City
St Louis
Vandalia
Effingham
322
Cincinnatti
Hillsboro
412.
Portsmouth
WEST VIRGINIA
Charleston
1476 Spruce Knob
.1234
Arlington
Alexandria
Culpeper
Fredericksburg
Lexington
Park
Salisbury

Ottawa
Emporia
Clinton
Sullivan
Festus
Mt. Vernon
Jasper
Bedford
Louisville
Maysville
Huntington
Morehead
Richwood
Charlottesville
VIRGINIA
Richmond

MISSOURI
Fort Scott
Nevada
Lebanon
Lake Ozark
Rolla
Perryville
540.
West Frankfort
.314
Evansville
Owensboro
Elizabethtown
Berea
Williamson
Pikeville
1247
Beckley
Lynchburg
Petersburg
Williamsburg
28°
Hampton
Newport News

Independence
300.
Bolivar
Springfield
.510
Cape Girardeau
Cairo
Central City
KENTUCKY
Hazard
Bluefield
1743
Roanoke
Martinsville
Danville
Roanoke Rapids
Ahoskie
Elizabeth City

Miami
Bartlesville
Joplin
Aurora
Neosho
Branson
Poplar Bluff
Hardy
Paducah
Bowling Green
Lake Cumberland
Glasgow
Somerset
532
Marion
Wytheville
Mount Rogers
784
Mount Airy
Winston Salem
Greensboro
Durham
Rocky Mount
Cape Hatteras

Tulsa
Tahlequah
Ozark Plateau
Fayetteville
Marshall
Clarksville
Blytheville
Dyersburg
307.
Cumberland
Nashville
Murfreesboro
Kingsport
1026
1743
Mount Rogers
Knoxville
2025
Clingmans Dome
Hickory
Kannapolis
Charlotte
50
Goldsboro
Greenville
New Bern

Muskogee
ARKANSAS
Jonesboro
Jackson
Columbia
TENNESSEE
Lawrenceburg
Fayetteville
.876
Chattanooga
2026
Rockwood
Clingmans Dome
Cleveland
Asheville
Hendersonville
NORTH CAROLINA
Charlotte
Fayetteville
Rockingham
Pamlico Sound

Henryetta
Fort Smith
Poteau
Conway
West Memphis
.100
Memphis
Savannah
Florence
Huntsville
Greenville
Spartanburg
Morehead City

35°N
McAlester
95°W   90°W   85°W   80°W   75°W

n   o   p   q   r   s   t   u   v   w   x   y   z

19   20

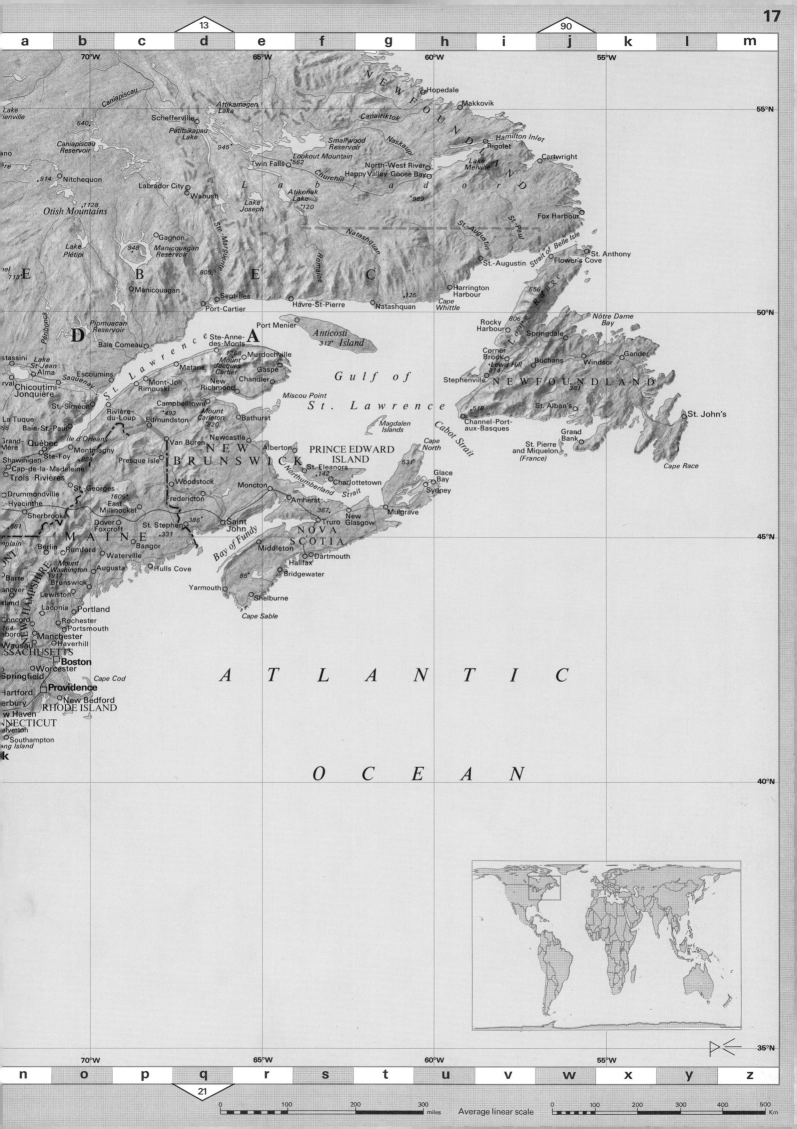

35°N 120°W

Santa Cruz
Santa Barbara 2435
Mojave Barstow
Lancaster Ludlow
CALIFORNIA Lake Havasu City
San Bernardino Palm Springs
Santa Rosa Los Angeles
605
Long Beach Anaheim Santa Ana Blythe
Channel Santa Catalina
Islands Oceanside Escondido
San Nicolas Salton 70 Sea
San Clemente El Cajon Calexico
San Diego Yuma
Tijuana Mexicali San Luis Desert
Rosarito Rio Colorado
La Misión 1829
Ensenada Pinacate 540
Desert 1206
Cerro Pinacate Sonoyta
San Vincente El Chinero Puerto Tajito
Colnett San Felipe Peñasco Tubutama
3055 Agua El Socorro Caborca
de Chale Estación Santa Ana
Trincheras

Kingman
Cottonwood
Mayer Show Low
Prescott 3122
ARIZONA
1732
Phoenix Globe
Mesa
Casa Grande
Gila Safford
Tucson
Sásabe Sierra Douglas
Vista Nogales Agua Prieta
2039 Cananea
Magdalena
Arizpe
Bavispe
Nuevo Casas
Grandes

Flagstaff Holbrook
Albuquerque 1509
Belen Santa Rosa Hereford
Socorro Vaughn Clovis
Magdalena Portales
NEW Roswell Levelland
Sierra UNITED
Blanca Peak Alamogordo
3658 Artesia Hobbs
Silver City Las Cruces MEXICO Carlsbad
Lordsburg Deming El Paso 2667
Ciudad Juárez Guadalupe Peak
Ascensión El Porvenir 1603 Pecos Fort Stockto
Janos Van Horn
Villa Alpine
Ahumada Sanderson

30°N

Rosario
de Arriba
Misión
San Fernando
Guadalupe
Punta Prieta
Rosarito
Sebastián
Vizcaino Bay
Cedros
Vizcaino
Desert 935
Laguna
San Ignacio
Ballenas
Bay

Cape
Lobos
Angel de
la Guarda
Tiburón 1218
Los Angeles
Lower
Sebastián
Gulf
La. Ojo El Arco
de Liebre
Volcán Tres
Vírgenes 1995
Santa Rosalía

Moctezuma
Carbó
Hermosillo
Avispas
Soyapa
Yepachic
Guaymas Guásimas
Torim
Empalme 1914
Ciudad Obregón
Navojoa Alamos
Huatabampo
Las Bocas
San Blas

Buenaventura
San Lorenzo El Sueco 2357
Estación Emory Peak
Babícora El Carrizalillo Ojinaga 2385
Sahuaripa Madera Temósachic El Sauz Aldama El Chilicote Altares
Bachinivas Chihuahua 1430 San Guillermo Llanos de
imbea La Junta Cuauhtémoc Meoqui los Caballos
Nuri Yécora Delicias Mestenos Las
Macuarichic 2591 Saucillo Tanque Entimias
El Revés
Boquilla Ciudad Camargo 2291 La Víbora
Reservoir Jiménez Cuatrociéne
San Francisco Hidalgo del Yermo
del Oro Parral La Campana
Santa Villa Ocampo San F
Barbara Santa de C
María La 2668
Bermejillo Colo
Gómez Palacio Pa
Lerdo Matamo
Torreón

25°N

Rocas Alijos

Cape San Lázaro

San Juanico
Ejido Insurgentes
Quiñones

Loreto
Carmen
Sierra Santa
de la Catalina
Giganta 1162
Los Burros San
Los Carlos José
La Paz Espíritu
B. Santo
Las Cruces
La Paz 1250
El Triunfo
Todos Santos
Cape San Lucas San Lucas

Canipole
Ahome
Los
Mochis Guasave
Navolato
Culiacán
El Dorado
Cosalá
Dimas 2778 El Salto
Mazatlán Villa Unión

Guadalupe Guazaparos
y Calvo
Topia Santiago Rodeo
Papasquiaro Nazas
Pericos
Canatlán
Durango 1689
Guadalupe
Victoria
La Parilla
Mezquital 3078

West Santa
María
M E X
Miguel Camach
Auza Juan Camach
Aldama Río G
La M

Tropic of Cancer

160°W

Haena Kauai
Nihau 1598
Mana Lihue
Kaula Oahu
Pearl City Kaneohe
Waipahu Molokai
Honolulu Halawa
Maunaloa Maui
Wailuku Kahului
Lanai 3055
Kahoolawe
Hawi
Mauna Kea 20°N
Kailua 4208
Hawaii Hilo
Mauna Loa
4170
Naalehu

Hawaiian Islands

These islands lie approximately 4000 kilometres
to the west of here, in the Pacific Ocean.

160°W

20°N

San Benedicto
Revilla Gigedo Islands
Roca Partida Socorro

Tres Marias
Islands
Maria Madre
Maria
Magdalena Maria
Cleofas
Banderas
Bay

Tecuala
Tuxpan Santiago
Ixcuintla
Tepico
Compostela
Iktlán
Etzatlán Ameca Guada
Puerto Cocula Chapala
Vallarta 2740 Lake La Barc
Tomatlán Sayula Sahuayo
Autlán Cd.
Tecolotlán Cd. Jacona
Guzmán Zara Tamaz

Escuinapa 2073
Jerez Za
Acaponeta
Mesa del
Nayar
Aguascalien
2957 Tlaltenang
San
Juchipila Lc
San Fr
Tepatitlán
Guada
1540

20°N

Nev. de Colima
3860
Tenacatita Colima
Barra de Navidad Mazamitla Urua
Apatzinga
Tecomán 2764 In
Re

Clarión

P A C I F I C

O C E A N

15°N

115°W 110°W 105°W

This map shows 1/60 of the earth's surface.

a b c d e f g h i j k l m

16

100°W 95°W 90°W 85°W 35°N

O K L A H O M A

A R K A N S A S

S T A T E S

T E X A S

M I S S I S S I P P I

A L A B A M A

G E O R G I A

L O U I S I A N A

F L O R I D A

Altus .751
Lawton
Ada
McAlester
Little Rock 722
Arkadelphia
Pine Bluff
Clarksdale
Corinth
Florence
246
Huntsville
Decatur
Cullman
Gainesville
Marietta
Atlanta
Wichita Falls
Sherman
Paris
Tupelo
Columbus
Gadsden
College Park
Sulphur Springs
Texarkana
Winona
Columbus
Birmingham
Bessemer
.734
Opelika
Macon
.425
Warner Robins
Abilene
.448
Fort Worth
Irving
Garland
Arlington
Dallas
Marshall
Minden
Monroe
El Dorado 67
Lake Providence
Vicksburg 149
Jackson
Meridian
Selma
Montgomery
Phenix City
Columbus
Sweetwater
.233
Tyler
Longview
Shreveport
.113
Natchitoches
Laurel
Greenville
Andalusia
Albany
Dawson
Tifton
.932
Brownwood
Waco
Temple
Killeen
Nacogdoches
Lufkin
Alexandria
Brookhaven
McComb
Hattiesburg
Dothan
.105
Marianna
Thomasville
Chattahoochee
Valdosta
Kerrville
.567
Austin
Bryan
Huntsville
Jasper
L O U I S I A N A
Mobile
Crestview
Pensacola
Fort Walton Beach
Panama City
Tallahassee
San Angelo
.784
New Braunfels
Houston
Beaumont
Lake Charles
Baton Rouge
Hammond
Biloxi
Gulfport Pascagoula
Cape San Blas
Apalachee Bay
Edwards Plateau
Del Rio
Amistad Reservoir
San Antonio
Pasadena
Baytown
Texas City
Lafayette New Iberia
Kenner New Orleans
Slidell
Houma
30°N
Uvalde
Gonzales
Lake Jackson
Galveston
Mississippi Delta
Pearsall
Victoria
.50
Three Rivers

G u l f   o f

M e x i c o

25°N

C U B A

Laguna Madre
Kingsville
Corpus Christi
Laredo .302
Falcon Reservoir
Nuevo Laredo
Laguna Madre
Monclova
Sabinas Hidalgo 2643
Ciudad Mier
Reynosa
McAllen
Harlingen
Brownsville
Matamoros
Monterrey .2796
China
Pinar del Río
Montemorelos
Isla de Pinos
Rayones
La Carbonera
Linares .1794
Desterrada
Pérez
Arenas
Río Lagartos
Cape Catoche
Arramberri
Jiménez
.4054
Ciudad Victoria
Nuevo
Dzilam de Bravo
Chiquilá
Puerto Juárez
Cancún
Puerto Morelos
Straits of Yucatán
Guanahacabibes Peninsula
Charcas
Jaumave
Llera
Tula
Ciudad Mante
Manuel
Triangulos
Arcas
Progreso
Mérida 8
Motul
Espita
Tizimín
Valladolid
Tulum
Cozumel
Salinas
Cerritos
San Luis Potosí
Ciudad Valles
Ciudad Madero
Tampico
Maxcanú
Calkiní
Ticul
Tekax
Peto .100
Río Verde
Cárdenas
Pánuco
Laguna Tamiahua
Campeche
Bolonchén de Rejón
20°N
San Felipe
San Luis de la Paz
Tamazunchale
Tuxpan
Bay of
Sihochac
Chunhuhub
Ascensión Bay
Guanajuato
Silao
Querétaro
Zacualtipan
Poza Rica
Papantla
Campeche
Champotón
Y u c a t á n
Felipe Carrillo Puerto
Espíritu Santo Bay
Celaya
Salvatierra
Pachuca 2426
Huauchinango
Martínez de la Torre
C a m p e c h e
P e n i n s u l a
310.
Salamanca
Acámbaro
Tula
Tulancingo
Teziutlán
Ciudad del Carmen
Chetumal
Maravatío
Tepeji
Apan
Perote
Jalapa
Laguna de Términos
Mamantel
Gulf
Zinapecuaro
Calpulalpan
Apizaco
.1427
Coscomatepec
Honda
of
Mexico City .2240
Texcoco
Puebla
Citlaltepetl 5700
Veracruz
Alvarado
Tlacotalpan
Frontera
Balancán
Altamira
BELIZE
Honduras
Toluca
Popocatepetl 5452
Atlixco
Orizaba
Córdoba
Tierra Blanca
Ciudad del Carmen
Villahermosa
Belize
Turneffe Islands
Swan Island (Hond.)
Cuernavaca
Taxco
Izúcar de Matamoros
Tehuacán
M. Alemán Reservoir
San Andrés Tuxtla .1879
Coatzacoalcos
Comalcalco
Macuspana
Tenosique
Belmopan
Ciudad Altamirano
Jojutla
Iguala
Acatlán
Tuxtepec
Acayucan
Minatitlán
Morelos
Palenque
Chichón 2224
Flores
Cerro de Chula 2868
Huajuapan de León
Huapanapan
I s t h m u s
Villahermosa
GUATEMALA
Chilapa
Coixtlahuaca
Jesús Carranza
of
.2727
San Cristóbal las Casas
Puerto Cortés
Guanaja
Bay Islands
Chilpancingo
Nochixtlán
Tlaxiaco
Oaxaca .1546
Mitla
Matías Romero
Chiapa de Corzo
Roatán
Utila
Trujillo
Tierra Colorada
Ejutla
Juchitán
Ciudad Ixtepec
Arriaga
Comitán
.1122
Tela
La Ceiba
Acapulco
San Marcos
Pinotepa Nacional
Miahuatlán .739
Salina Cruz
Tonalá
Angostura Reservoir
GUATEMALA
Puerto Barrios
San Pedro Sula
HONDURAS
Puerto Escondido
Mar Muerto
Pijijiapan
Huehuetenango
Ametenango .4220
Quezaltenango .2868
Motagua
Patuca
Puerto Lempira
Puerto Ángel
Gulf of Tehuantepec
Huixtla
Tapachula
Guatemala
15°N

100°W 95°W 90°W 85°W

n o p q r s t u v w x y z

22

0 100 200 300 miles   Average linear scale   0 100 200 300 400 500 Km

20

Oklahoma City
Henryetta
Ada
McAlester
OKLAHOMA
Clarksville
Poteau
Fort Smith
95°W
Newport
West Memphis
Memphis
90°W
Jackson
TENNESSEE
Lawrenceburg
Fayetteville
Cleveland
Chattanooga
85°W
80
Asheville
NORTH
Hendersonville
Rock Hill
Charlot
35°N
Conway
Little Rock
100.
Savannah
Corinth
Florence
879.
Huntsville
Dalton
Greenville
Spartanburg
Rockingh
Paris
Sherman
UNITED STATES
ARKANSAS
722
Arkadelphia
Pine Bluff
Clarksdale
246.
Decatur
Cullman
Gadsden
Marietta
Athens
Anderson
Clinton Camden
Columbia
Lake
SOUTH
CAROLI
Charl

OKLAHOMA
Red River
Texarkana
El Dorado
Greenville
MISSISSIPPI
Winona Columbus
152
Bessemer
Birmingham
734.
College Park
Atlanta
GEORGIA
425.
Macon
Dublin
Statesboro
Augusta
Walterboro
Charl

Fort Worth
Irving Garland
Sulphur Springs
Marshall
Tyler
Minden
Monroe
67
Lake Providence
Vicksburg
149
Jackson
Meridian
Jackson
Montgomery
ALABAMA
Eufaula
Greenville
Opelika
Columbus
Warner Robins
Dawson
Tifton
Thomasville
Altamaha
Jesup
Savannah

Dallas
Arlington
TEXAS
233.
Nacogdoches
Toledo Bend Reservoir
113.
Natchitoches
Alexandria
Brookhaven
Hattiesburg
Laurel
Andalusia
Dothan
Marianna
Chattahoochee
Valdosta
Brunswick
Fernandina Beach
Jacksonville

Waco
Temple
Lufkin
LOUISIANA
McComb
Crestview
Fort Walton Beach
Pensacola
Tallahassee
Live Oak
Perry
Lake City
St. Augustine

Killeen
Huntsville
Jasper
Hammond
Baton Rouge
Slidell
Biloxi
Gulfport
Pascagoula
Mobile
Panama City
Apalachee Bay
Chiefland
Gainesville
Palatka
Daytona B

Austin
Bryan
Beaumont
Lake Charles
Lafayette
New Iberia
New Orleans
Cape San Blas
Lake George
Ocala
Crystal River
Leesburg
Altamonte Springs
Titusville
Cape Canav

30°N
Houston
New Braunfels
Gonzales
Colorado
Baytown
Texas City
Galveston
Houma
Mississippi Delta
Winter Garden
Lakeland
Orlando
Melbo

Victoria
Lake Jackson
Tampa
Largo
Brandon
Avon Park
Three Rivers
50.
St. Petersburg
Bradenton
Sarasota
FLORIDA
Fo Pie

Corpus Christi
Kingsville
Gulf of
Port Charlotte
Lake Okeechobee
Pahoke

Laguna Madre
Cape Coral
Fort Myers
Fort Lauderdale

Mc Allen
Harlingen
Brownsville
Matamoros
Mexico
Naples
Cape Romano
Everglades M

25°N
19
Laguna Madre
Cape Sable
Florida Bay
Key Largo

La Carbonera
Key West

Ciudad Madero
Tampico
Pánuco
Desterrada
Pérez
Havana
Matanzas
Güines
Colón
Sa
G

Laguna de Tamiahua
Arenas
Nuevo
Río Lagartos
Chiquilá
Cape Catoche
Yucatan Channel
Pinar del Rio
Guanahacabibes Peninsula
Isla de Pinos
Cienfuegos
Sc
Trini
G

Potrero del Llano
Tuxpan
Triangulos
Dzilam de Bravo
Progreso
Motul
Tizimin
Puerto Juárez
Cancun

Poza Rica
Papantla
Arcas
Mérida
8
Izamal
Espita
Valladolid
Puerto Morelos

Huachinango
Martínez de la Torre
Maxcanú
Calkiní
Ticul
Tekax
Tulum
Cozumel

20°N
Teziutlán
Tlapacoyan
Jalapa
Bay of
Bolonchén de Rejón
100
Peto
Yucatán
Ascensión Bay
Little Cayman
Cayman Is
(U.K.)
C

Apizaco
Perote
4410.
1427.
Veracruz
Campeche
Champotón
Sihochac
Chunhuhub
Peninsula
Felipe Carrillo Puerto
Espíritu Santo Bay
Georgetown
Grand Cayman

Citlaltépetl (Orizaba) 5700.
Coscomatepec
Córdoba
Orizaba
Puebla
Campeche
Alvarado
Tlacotalpan
310
Chetumal
Gulf of

Tehuacán
Acatlán
Tierra Blanca
San Andrés Tuxtla
1879.
Ciudad del Carmen
Frontera
Laguna de Términos
Mamantel
Altamira
Gulf

Huajuapan de León
Tuxtepec
Coatzacoalcos
Villahermosa
Balancán
BELIZE
Belize
of

Coixtlahuaca
Nochixtlán
Jesús Carranza
Isthmus of
Morelos
Macuspana
Palenque
Tenosique
Belmopan
Turneffe Islands
Honduras

Tlaxiaco
1546.
Oaxaca
Mitla
MEXICO
Chichón 2224.
Flores
GUATEMALA
Ejutla
Matías Romero
Tuxtla Gutiérrez
San Cristóbal de las Casas
2127.
1122.

Miahuatlán
Ciudad Ixtepec
Tehuantepec
Juchitán
Arriaga
Chiapa de Corzo
Comitán
Roatán
Guanaja
Bay Islands
Utila

Pinotepa Nacional
Ixtaltepec
Salina Cruz
Mar Muerto
Tonalá
Angostura Reservoir
Pijijiapan
Lago de Isabal
Puerto Barrios
Puerto Cortés
Tela
La Ceiba
Trujillo
I

Puerto Escondido
Puerto Angel
Gulf of Tehuantepec
Amatenango
Huixtla
220.
San Pedro Sula
HONDURAS
Puerto Lempira

15°N
95°W
Motagua
90°W
85°W
80
Cape Gracias á Dios

This map shows 1/60 of the earth's surface.

a b c d e f g h i j k l m

75°W 70°W 65°W

35°N

Goldsboro
New Bern
Jacksonville
mberton
Wilmington
Myrtle Beach
getown

Bermuda
(U.K.)
Hamilton

A T L A N T I C

30°N

Sargasso Sea

O C E A N

25°N

Grand
Bahama
Island
Great
Abaco
Island

Nicholls
Town
Nassau
Eleuthera
New
Providence
Behring
Point
Andros
Islands
Cat

San Salvador

BAHAMAS
Rum Cay
Great
Exuma
Island
Long
Island

Tropic of Cancer

at Bahama Bank
Crooked
Island
Acklins
Mayaguana
Island

Grand Caicos

Morón
Ciego de Ávila
Turks and Caicos
Islands (U.K.)

Nuevitas
Great Inagua
Island

magüey
Victoria de
las Tunas
Banes
Holguín
Bayamo
Palma
Soriano
Baracoa
Manzanillo
Niquero 2005
Santiago
de Cuba
Guantánamo
Port-de-Paix

DOMINICAN
Cap-Haïtien
Puerto Plata

20°N

Mao
Santiago
REPUBLIC
Gonaïves
La Vega
San Francisco
de Macoris
HAITI
St-Marc
3475
San Juan
Puerto Rico (U.S.A.)
Virgin Islands
JAMAICA
Anse
d'Hainault
Port-au-Prince
La Romana
Bayamón
San Juan
Carolina
Anguilla
Montego
Bay
2680
Jacmel
Les Cayes
Barahona
Santo
Domingo
Mayagüez
1338
Caguas
Ponce
St. Martin
Philipsburg
May Pen
Spanish
Town
Kingston
St. Croix
(U.S.A.)
Codrington
Barbuda
Netherlands
Antilles
ANTIGUA AND
BARBUDA
Basseterre
ST KITTS
NEVIS
St. John's
Antigua
A n t i l l e s
Montserrat
(U.K.)
Plymouth
B E A N S E A
Guadeloupe
(France)
Basse-Terre
Pointe-
à-Pitre
Leeward Islands
DOMINICA
Roseau

15°N

0 100 200 300 miles   Average linear scale   0 100 200 300 400 500 Km

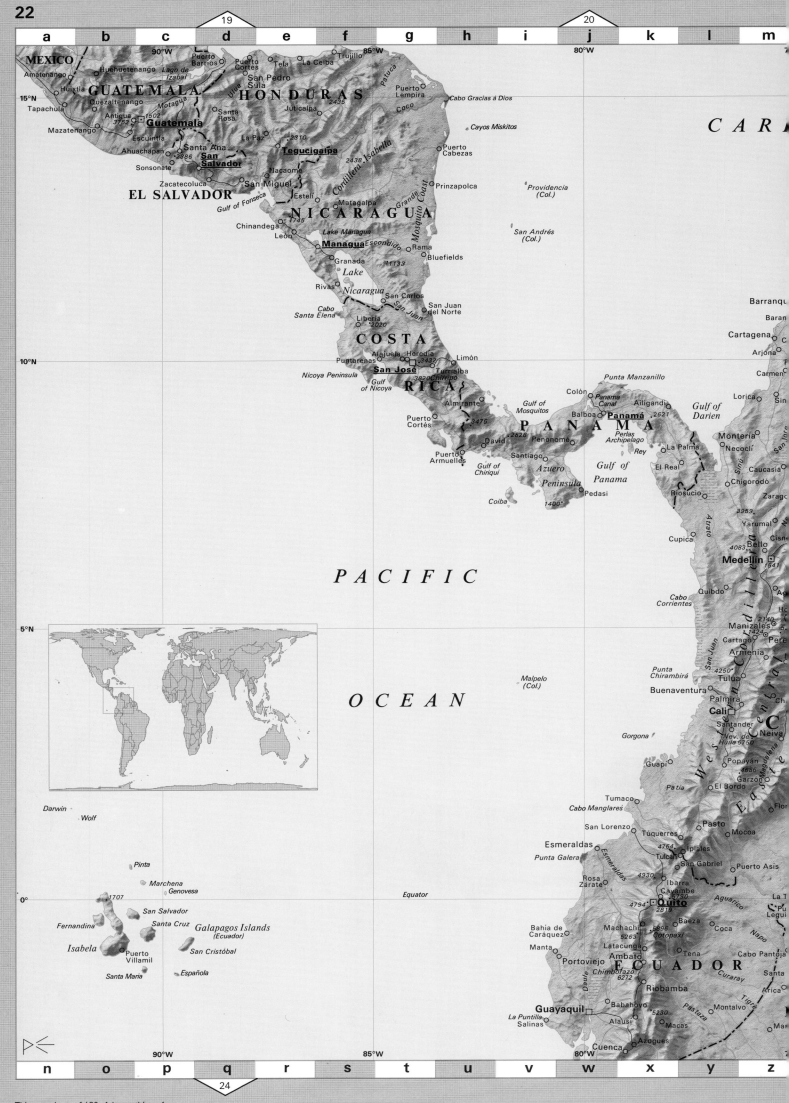

MEXICO

Amatenango
Huixtla
Huehuetenango
GUATEMALA
Quezaltenango
Tapachula
Antigua *3752* *1502*
Guatemala
Mazatenango
Escuintla
Ahuachapan *2386*
Santa Ana
Sonsonate
San Salvador
Zacatecoluca
San Miguel
EL SALVADOR

Puerto Barrios
Puerto Cortés
San Pedro Sula
Tela
La Ceiba
Trujillo

HONDURAS
Lago de Izabal
Motagua
Ulua
Patuca

Juticalpa *2435*
Santa Rosa
La Paz *2310*
Nacaome
Tegucigalpa
Estelí

Puerto Lempira
Cabo Gracias á Dios
Coco

NICARAGUA
Cordillera Isabella *2438*
Chinandega *1745*
León
Lake Managua
Managua
Granada
Lake Nicaragua
Rivas
San Carlos
Cabo Santa Elena
Liberia *2020*

Puerto Cabezas
Prinzapolca
Cayos Miskitos
Providencia (Col.)
San Andrés (Col.)

Matagalpa
Grande
Rama
Bluefields *1133*
Escondido
Mosquito Coast
San Juan
San Juan del Norte

COSTA RICA
Puntarenas
Alajuela Heredia *3432*
San José
Nicoya Peninsula
Gulf of Nicoya *3820* Chirripó
Turrialba

CAR

Barranqu
Baran
Cartagena
Arjona
Carmen
Lorica
Sin

Limón

Almirante
Puerto Cortés *3475*
David *2826*
Puerto Armuelles
Gulf of Chiriqui
Coiba

PANAMA
Punta Manzanillo
Colón
Panama Canal
Balboa Panamá *2621*
Penonomé
Santiago
Azuero Peninsula
Pedasí *1400*
Rey

Ailigandi
Perlas Archipelago
La Palma
El Real
Riosucio

Gulf of Mosquitos
Gulf of Darien
Gulf of Panama

Montería
Necoclí
Caucasia
Chigorodó
Zarag
Cupica *3959*
Yarumal
4083 Bello Cisne
Medellín *1541*

PACIFIC

Cabo Corrientes
Quibdo
Manizales *2140* *1424*
Cartago Pere
Armenia
San Juan
Tulúa *4250*
Punta Chirambirá
Buenaventura
Palmira
Cali
Santander
Nev. de Huila 5750
Neiva

OCEAN

Malpelo (Col.)
Gorgona
Guapi
Popayán *4886*
Garzón
El Bordo
Patía
Tumaco
Cabo Manglares
San Lorenzo
Esmeraldas
Punta Galera
Rosa Zárate
Bahía de Caráquez
Manta
Portoviejo

Darwin
Wolf
Pinta
Marchena
Genovesa
San Salvador *1707*
Santa Cruz
Galapagos Islands (Ecuador)
San Cristóbal
Fernandina
Isabela
Puerto Villamil
Santa Maria
Española

Equator

Túquerres *4764*
Ipiales
Tulcán
San Gabriel
Puerto Asis
Mocoa
Pasto
Mira
4930
Ibarra
Cayambe *5790*
Quito *4794* *2819*
Machachi *5695*
Latacunga
Cotopaxi
Ambato
Baeza
Coca
Tena
Cabo Pantoja
Napo

La T
Pu
Legui
Aguarico

ECUADOR
Chimborazo *6272*
Riobamba
Babahoyo *5230*
Guayaquil
La Puntilla
Salinas
Alausí
Cuenca
Azogues
Macas
Montalvo

Daule
Curaray
Pastaza
Tigre
Arica
Santa
Mar

15°N
10°N
5°N
0°
90°W
85°W
80°W

This map shows 1/60 of the earth's surface.

15°N

DOMINICA Roseau

Martinique-Passage

Fort-de-France Martinique (France)

St.-Lucia-Passage

Castries SAINT LUCIA

St.-Vincent-Passage

SAINT VINCENT AND GRENADINES Kingstown

BARBADOS
Bridgetown

A T L A N T I C

L e s s e r   A n t i l l e s

Saint George's GRENADA

E A N   S E A

Cabo Gallinas

Aruba

Curaçao (Neth.)

Willemstad

Paraguaná Peninsula

Bonaire (Neth.)

Islas Los Roques (Ven.)

Blanquilla (Ven.)

Tobago
Scarborough

TRINIDAD AND TOBAGO

Riohacha

Guajira Peninsula

820

Punto Fijo

Coro

Puerto Cumarebo

Margarita

La Asunción

O C E A N

anta arta

Maicao

San Rafael

Churuguara

Tocuyo

Maiquetia

Cabo Codera

Tortuga

Carúpano

Port of Spain 940

Cristóbal Colón 5800

Maracaibo

La Concepción

Cabimas

7900

Carora

Puerto Cabello

San Felipe

2765

Maracay Caracas

La Victoria

Cumaná

Güiria Gulf of Paria

Trinidad

San Fernando

edupar

Ciudad Ojeda

Valencia

Puerto La Cruz

Barcelona

Caripito

Serpent's Mouth

Machiques

3750

Lake Maracaibo

Barquisimeto

San Juan do los Morros

Piritu

2660

Anaco

Maturin

Cesar

Valera

3652

Acarigua

El Sombrero

Valle de la Pascua

Zaraza

Cantaura

Guanipa

Tigre

Manamo

Tucupita

10°N

pós

Catatumba

Boconó

Guanare

El Baúl

Calabozo

El Tigre

Barrancas

Orinoco Delta

Grande

El Banco

San Carlos del Zulia

Mérida 5007

Barinas

Guárico

Pariaguán

Orinoco

Amacuro Delta

Boca Grande

Ocaña

Casigua

Cordillera de Mérida

Suata

Boca del Pao

Ciudad Guayana 792

San José de Amacuro

Cúcuta

San Cristóbal

El Canton

Bruzual

Mantecal

Apure

San Fernando de Apure

Caicara de Orinoco

Maripa

Ciudad Bolívar

Upata

Serranía de Imataca

Hossororo

ramanga

Pamplona 4100

Arauca

L l a n o s

Capanaparo

Arauca

La Urbana

1863

Las Trincheras

1839

El Callao

La Paragua

Cuyuni

Marlborough

Barrancabermeja

Málaga

Socorro 5493

Cravo Norte

Casanare

Meta

Santa Maria

Puerto Carreño

V E N E Z U E L A

Sierra de Maigualida

Caura

Paragua

Caroní

La Escalera

Mayupa

Angel Falls 2950

1890

El Dorado

Cavanayen

Mazaruni

Suddie

Georgetown

Peters Mine

Bartica

New Amsterdam

Tunja

Sogamoso

La Venturosa

Meta

100

Sabana de Cardona

2285

G u y a n a

2100

Puricama

Gran

2810 Roraima

2040

Pakaraima Mountains

Rockstone

Linden

Tumatumari

Nieuw Nickerie

Totness

26

Zipaquirá

Yopal

Trinidad

Puerto Nuevo

Tomo

Puerto Ayacucho

San Juan

Arabelo

Sabana

Santa Elena de Uairen

1240

GUYANA

Apoera

ogotá

Orocué

Orinoco

2030

Ventuari

El Oso

Meseta del Cerro Jáua

Depósito

Essequibo

Kabalebo Reservoir

SURINAM

Villavicencio

Puerto Lopez

San José de Ocuné

Sucuaro

Vichada

San Fernando de Atabapo

H i g h l a n d s

Uraricoera

Apoteri

Karanambo

Juliana Top 1230

1026

Puerto Limón

Pavon

Santa Rosa

Guaviare

Arrecifal

Orinoco

2579

Serra Parima

Uraricoera

Lethem

Kanuku Mts.

Dadanawa

Isherton

862

Oronoque

OMBIA

Ariari

San José del Guaviare

Guayabero

Inírida

Santa Barbara

2396

La Esmeralda

Serra Parima

Boa Vista

Tacutu

Rupununi

New

Papai

Buenos Aires

Calamar

Morichal

Guainía

Victorino

San José

Boca Mavaca

Serra do Apiaú

Serra Curupira 1047

Caracarai

Biloku

Kamoa Mts. 734

Serra Acarai

Maloca

Miraflores

Mesa de Yambi

Uainambi

San Carlos

El Mango

Serra Tapirapeco

Catrimani

Branco

Cuñaré

San Yanaro

Vista Alegre

3014

Demini

São José do Anauá

Cucui

Pico da Neblina

Araça

Anauá

Puerto Huitoto

Macuje

Apaporis

Mitú

Jibóia

Vaupés

Iuareté

Içana

Negro

Padauiri

Catrimani

ermo

Araracuara

Caquetá

Lérida

Taracuá

Uaupés

Uaupés

Calanaque

Jauapari

100

0°

U

La Chorrera

B R A Z I L

São José

Tapurucuara

Barcelos

Trombetas

mayo

El Encanto

La Pedrera

100

Vila Bittencourt

Cuiuni

Tupanacca

Moura

Nhamunda

Oriximiná

Puerto Miraña

Marcelino

Maraã

Unini

Santa Maria

Faro

San Cristóbal

Arica

Japurá

Airão

Uatumã

Urucará

Santa Clotilde

Santa Clara

Foz do Mamoriá

Fonte Boa

Amazon

Tonantins

Solimões

Santo Antonio

Negro

Parintins

Amazon

0 100 200 300 miles   Average linear scale   0 100 200 300 400 500 Km

22

85°W 80°W 75°W

Tumaco
Patía
El Bordo
Cabo Manglares
Florencia
Buenos
Aires
Mirafle
Calama
San Lorenzo
Túquerres
Pasto
Mocoa
COLOMB
Cuñaré
Esmeraldas
Tulcán
Ipiales
4754
Punta Galera
Puerto Asís
Puerto
Huitoto
Macuje
Rosa
Zárate
4930
Ibarra
San
Gabriel
La Tagua
Araracu
Otavalo
Cayambe
5843
Puerto
Leguizamo
Palermo
0° Equator
La Chorr
Quito
2818
4794
Aguarico
Cotopaxi
Bahía de
Caráquez
Machachi
5896
Baeza
Coca
Napo
Manta
Latacunga
Tena
Cabo Pantoja
ECUADOR
Curaray
Arica
Santa
María
El Encan
Chimborazo
Ambato
6272
San
Cristó
Portoviejo
Ríobamba
Jipijapa
Babahoyo
Pastaza
Marsella
Santa
Clotilde
Guayaquil
5230
Montalvo
La Puntilla
Alausí
Macas
Andoas
Mazán
Salinas
Azogues
Tigre
Iquitos
Puná
Cuenca
Vargas
Guerra
Sargento
Lores
Tamsh
Gulf of
4138
Morona
Guayaquil
Santa
PACIFIC
Machala
Isabel
Corrientes
Zarumilla
Puerto
Pardo
Santa
Tumbes
Santa Isabel
Santiago
Clotilde
Zorritos
Loja
Zamora
Borja
Concordia
Nauta
Santa
Máncora
Cariamanga
3910
Sta. María de Nieva
Bagazán
Cabo Pariñas
Las Lomas
Orellana
Barranca
Marañón
Requena
Elv
Talara
3139
Jeberos
Bretaña
5°S
San Ignacio
Paita
Chulucanas
Mayo
Yurimaguas
Nueva
Santa
Alejandría
Sant
Piura
Huancabamba
3779
Pacaya
Isabel
Piura
4153
Jaén
Bagua
Rioja
Huallaga
Dos de Mayo
Ucayali
Punta Aguja
Bayóvar
Olmos
3840
Moyobamba
Rodrig
517
4193
Chachapoyas
Boa P
Lobos Island
Santa Cruz
Bambamarca
Tarapoto
Orellana
Lambayeque
Ferreñafe
Saposoa
609
Cruzeiro
Chiclayo
Cajamarca
Juanjuí
Contamaná
do Sul
4694
Juruá
Pacasmayo
Bolívar
Tiruntán
4333
Cajabamba
Pucallpa
San Pedro de Lloc
4467
Masisea
Chicama
Otuzco
4947
Tocache
OCEAN
Trujillo
Santiago de
Nuevo
Tauma
Chuco
Tayabamba
Huacrachuco
Virú
Santa
Aguaytía
Puerto Inca
Caraz
Aguaytía
Tingo María
Chimbote
6788
Huascarán
Llata
Puerto
Portillo
Casma
La Unión
Huánuco
Huaraz
Ambo
Bolognesi
Huarmey
4936
10°S
Chiquián
Yerupaja
6634
Cajatambo
5748
Oxapampa
Pativilca
Cerro de Pasco
Atalaya
Huacho
La Merced
Uruñamba
Puesta
Varadero
Huaral
La Oroya
Satipo
Chancay
Jauja
5334
Camisea
Matucana
Huancayo
Puerto
Fitzc
Rico
Callao
Lima
Pampas
Yauyos
Huancavelica
Huanta
Quillabamba
5231
Pumasillo
Huamanrazo
Ayacucho
6246
Urub
San Vicente
de Cañete
Castrovirreyna
Apurímac
Chincha Alta
Chincheros
Huancapi
Chincha Islands
Pisco
Andahuaylas
Abr
5350
Chalhuanca
Ica
Ica
Palpa
Coracora
1725
Nazca
Lampalla
San Juan
5522
Cot
Chala
Caravell
Chuquib
Atico
Ocoña
Camana
Mol

This map shows 1/60 of the earth's surface.

70°W 65°W 60°W 55°W

Uainambi San Carlos El Mango Serra Curupira GUYANA Biloku Kamoa Mts. Serra Acaraí

VENEZUELA

Mitú Jibóia Vista Alegre Cucuí Pico de Neblina 3014 Caracaraí Paru de Oeste

Vaupés Iuareté Içana Demini São José do Anauá Anauá 734

Apaporis Taracuá Uaupés Uaupés 360 Tapurucuara Calanaque Catrimani Branco Jauperi Mapuera Trombetas

0°

Caquetá Lérida São José Negro Tupanacca Nhamundá Oriximiná

La Pedrera Vila Bittencourt Marcelino Barcelos Unini Moura Airão Santa Maria Uatumã Faro Óbidos

Puerto Miraña Japurá Maraã Cuiuni Jaú Santo Antônio Urucará Parintins Santarém Belterra

Santa Clara Foz do Mamoriá Fonte Boa Alvarães Badajós-See Piorini Manacapuru Manaus Itacoatiara Tupinambarama 100

Içá Tontantins Santo Antônio de Içá Tefé Piorini-See Badajós Anamã Nova Olinda do Norte Maués Brasília Legal

São Paulo de Olivença Renascença Amazon (Solimões) Codajás Madeira Mucajá Itaituba

Caballococha Leticia Boca do Mutúm Concórdia Coari Purus Diamantina Borba Maués Laranjal San Luis de Tapajós

5°S

Caxias Benjamin Constant 100 Carauari Urucu Itaboca Arumã Terra Preta Santa Helena

Jutaí Jutaí Juruá Liberdade Jaburu Piranhas Prato do Igapó-Açu Novo Aripuanã Lajinha Jamanxim

Três Bocas Itul Tapauá Alianca Boca do Acará Manicoré Canumã Jacareacanga 200 Posto Curuá

Eirunepé Soledade Santos Dumont Tapauá Aliança Castanhal Sucunduri Sauré Creporizinho

BRAZIL

Canindé Tarauacá Envira Boca do Moaco Pauiní Lábrea Pirapetinga Prainha Nova Barra do São Manuel Manuelzinho

Envira Feijó Manuel Urbano Foz do Pauiní Mamoriá Manjuriã Humaitá 100 Jatuarana Samaumá Recreio Arapari

10°S

Santa Rosa 138 Purus Boca do Acre Boca do Curequeté Pôrto Velho Calama Jiparaná Jacaretinga Gêlo Cachimbo Serra do Cachimbo

Sena Madureira Pôrto Alegre Bom Jardim Jamari Caratianas Tabajara Theodore Roosevelt Aripuanã Serra dos Apiacás

Iaco Rio Branco Macapá Manoa Abunã 404 Jaciparaná Iracema Aarão Aripuanã Serra do Norte Pôrto do Cajueiro

Canamaria Acre Abunã Taquaras Ariquemes Jarú 200 Fontanillas Pouso Alegre Pôrto Atlântico

Xapuri Villa Bella Antuerpia Rondônia Acampamento de Indios Pôrto dos Gauchos Serra dos Chidis

356 Brasileia Puerto Rico Guajará Mirim Serra dos Pacaas Novos Rondônia Pimenta Bueno Serra do Tombador Carmem

Iñapari Cobija Porvenir Madre de Dios Riberalta 800 Presidente Hermes José Bonifácio Vilhena Juruena Uariari Marape Lucas

Las Piedras Iberia Fortaleza Beni Yata Fortaleza Serra dos Costa Marques Santo Antônio Pimenteiras Santa Isabél Ponta da Pedra 702

Manú Puerto Maldonado Puerto Heath Cavinas Lago Rogaguado San Joaquin Mategua Puerto Alegre Campo dos Parecis Diamantino

Quince Mil Astillero Madidi 100 Lago Rogagua Magdalena El Carmen Santa Isabél Parecis Mato Grosso Plateau

Auzangate 6394 Ixiamas Santa Ana Lago de San Luis La Esperanza Puerto Alegre Tapirapua Rosario Oeste

Macusani Reyes Apere San Martin La Noria 1095 Várzea Grande Cuiabá

5852 Carabaya 5443 Sandia Rapulo San Borja Trinidad Perseverancia Mato Grosso 1150 Cáceres Poconé Jaciara

5999 Pelomani Apolo San Ignacio Loreto Llanos de Mojos Salinas Pôrto Esperidião 283

Yauri Ayaviri Azángaro Huancané BOLIVIA Concepción San Matias Descalvados São Lorenço

5641 Puerto Acosta Santa Ana Puerto Marquez Ascensión San Javier San Ignacio San Matias

Juliaca Lake Titicaca 6388 Ancohuma Achacachi Coroico Puerto Villarroel San Pablo Salinas

Puno 5822 Achacachi Chuluman 3577 San Grande Concepción San Cruz Santa Corazón

5496 Juli Mazo Cruz La Paz Viacha Illimani 6402 Todos Santos Puerto Villarroel Rio Grande El Cerro Pôrto Jofre

Arequipa 2304 5213 Guaqui Corocoro Illimani Cochabamba Montero Santa Cruz Laguna Uberaba Itiquira

5781 Moquegua 6542 Sajama Sicasica 5035 Quillacollo 2558 Portachuelo 614 Laguna Concepción San José de Chiquitos Pedro Gomes

Tambo Charaña Umala Desaguadero 3200 Totora El Cerro

Tarata 5988 Yacora Putre Oruro 5383 Uncia Aiquile Comerapa Santa Cruz Robore Llanos de Chiquitos Amolar

Arica 70°W 65°W 60°W 55°W

miles 0 100 200 300 Average linear scale Km 0 100 200 300 400 500

VENEZUELA

Caurá 2100 Mayupa 1890 La Escalera Rockstone New Amsterdam Totness **Paramaribo** Mana
2950 Linden Nieuw Nickerie Groningen Moengo Sinnamary
Cavanayen Tumatumari Paranam St. Laurent
Puricama *Gran* 2040 Apoera Brokopondo Apatou Kourou **Cayenne**
Arabelo *Sabana* Roraima 2810 *Prof. van* Aurora Grand Montsinery Kaw
5°N *Meseta del* Santa Elena *Blommestein* Santi
Cerro Jaúa Paragua de Uairén Maturuca 1240 *Lake* 694 Grand *Cabo Orange*
Catisimiña Depósito S U R I N A M FRENCH Régina St. Georges Oiapoque
Uraricoera *Juliana Top* 1026 Bakrakondre Patience GUIANA Saul
1230 Intelewa Ouaqui Camopi Vila Velha
Lethem Serra Cunani
Kanuku Mts. Oronoque 882 Maloca Kawatop Calçoene
Boa Dadanawa Papaï Velha 680 Tumucumaque 635 Lorenço Amapá
Vista Isherton Pôrto Poet Serra Lombarda *Maracá*
Biloku Meriruma *Cabo Norte*
Kamoa Mts. Serra Acaraí Araguari Aporema
734 Terezinha Ferreira Gomes
Caracaraí Maloca Serra Pôrto Janaucú
São José Malaripó do Navio Grande Macapá *Caviana*
do Anauá 315 Acampamento Pôrto *Mexiana* *Cabo*
Catrimani Jari Santaná Afuá Chaves *Maguari*
Calanaque Paru Barraca Queimada
0° Arere da Boca Souré
Morro Monte 228 Boca do *Marajó*
Barcelos Grande Dourado Jari Anajás Cachoeira
Moura 629 Ramos Almeirim Breves do Arari
Tupanacca Santa 305 Grande de Gurupá Abaetetuba Moju
Maria Oriximiná Mulata Prainha Pôrto Cametá Moçajuba
Airão Nhamunda Óbidos de Moz
Santo Antônio Faro Alenquer Monte Portel Baião
Manaus Urucará Santarém Alegre Pacajá
Manacapuru Parintins Belterra Curua-Uná Victoria Pindobal
Amazon Itacoatiara Pacoval Belo Monte
Anama Ilha Maués Brasília Caíma Altamira
Nova Olinda Legal 229 Tuéré Tucuruí Gurupi
do Norte Mucajá Itaituba Rurópolis Lontra
Codajás Pôrto Jatobal São
Coari Madeira Alegre Jacundá Félix
Diamantina Borba Laranjal Sem-Tripa Marabá São
Itaboca Terra Preta Jatobá Félix de Ara
Tapajós Forte
Jaburu Piranhas Lajinha Santa Paga- Veneza José
Tapauá Manicoré Helena Conta São Sebastião Rodrigues Carajás
Boca do Acara Canumã Jacareacanga Posto Araras BRAZ
Aliança Castanhal Sauré Curuá Cajueiro São Félix Tucumá Xinguara
Pirapetinga Sucunduri Creporizinho do Xingu Babaçu
Lábrea Prainha Nova Barra do Manuelzinho Jojoca Posto Xinguara
Humaitá Jatuarana São Manuel Cocraimore Gorotiré Araguaína
Calama Samaumá Garimpo Redenção
Pôrto Jamari Recreio Araparí Cumaru Conceição
Velho Tabajara Jacaretinga Gêlo Serra do Cachimbo do Araguaia
Jaciparaná Caratianas Aarão Aripuanã Cachimbo Campo Santana do Araguaia
Iracema Plara-Açu Alegre Araguacema
Ariquemes Barreira Miracema
Antuerpia Jarú Pôrto do do Campo do Norte
Rondônia Fontanillas Cajueiro São José Santa Cristalandia
Presidente 242 do Xingu Teresinha Fátima
Hermes Acampamento Pôrto dos Pôrto Gurupi Natividá
Fortaleza Pimenta de Índios Gauchos Posto Alto Diauarum Alegre
Costa Marques Bueno Manissaua Campo de São Félix
José Diauarum Bananal Alvorada
San Bonifácio Pouso Alegre Xingu Pôrto dos Peixe
Joaquim Juruena Marape Carmem Meinacos
Magdalena Mategua Pimenteiras Uariti Lucas Pôrto Artur Garapu Araguaçu
BOLIVIA Puerto Santa Ponta da Pedra Pôrto Porangatu
Alegre Isabel Mato Grosso Alto Pa
El Carmen Plateau 635

This map shows 1/60 of the earth's surface.

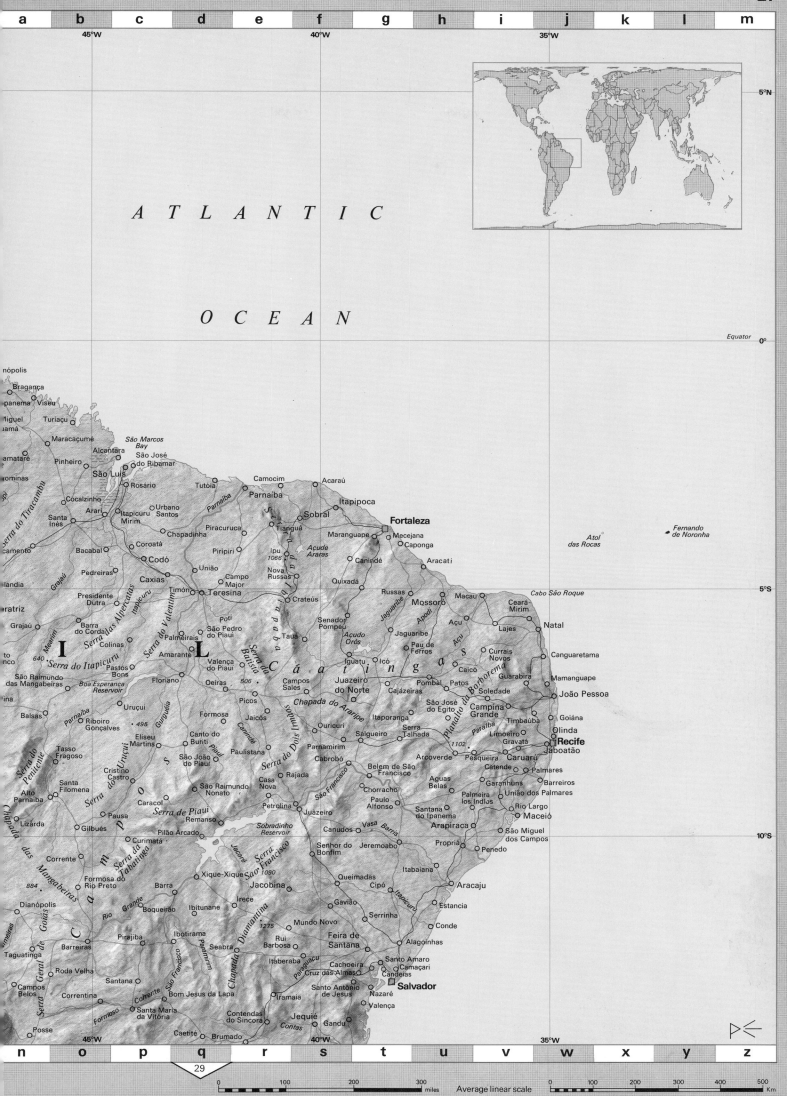

a b c d e f g h i j k l m

PERU

BOLIVIA

PACIFIC OCEAN

PARAGUAY

ARGENTINA

CHILE

URU

Buenos Aires

Montev

Asunción

Santiago

n o p q r s t u v w x y z

This map shows 1/60 of the earth's surface.

80°W   75°W   70°W   65°W

35°S

40°S

45°S

50°S

55°S

Juan Fernández Islands
(Chile)
Alejandro   Robinson
Selkirk   Crusoe

Valparaíso   Tupungato 6800
Santiago   San Martín   San
San Bernardo Tunuyán   Luis   Rio
San Antonio   5830   La Paz   Mercedes   Cuarto
                                              Vicuña   La Carlot
Rancagua   5290   San Rafael   Mackenna
                                              Justo
Santa   5160   Diamante   Buena   Daract   Laboulaye
Cruz   San Fernando   Salado   Esperanza   Huinca
        Curicó 4860   Renancó
                4090   General   Gene
Constitución Maule Talca   Alvear   Unión   Villeg
                4020   Rivada
                      Malargüe 3810   Eduardo   Gene
                                              Victorica Castex   Pico
Talcahuano   Santa   Santa
Concepción   Chillán   Algarroho   Isabel   Rosa
Punta Lavapié   del Águila
                      4115   Barrancas   Bañados
Lebú   Los Ángeles   Chos Malal   3680   del   A
              Bío-Bío Colorado   Atuel Chacharramendi General
Victoria 2969   Cerros   Acha   Ca
              Las Lajas Colorados
Temuco 3124 Curacautín Reservoir   Plaza
              Zapala Neuquén Huincul Neuquén   N
Villarrica   Cutral-Co   Chelforó Río Colora
              3740 Picún   General
              Junín Leufú   Ezequil Ramos Roca Choele
Valdivia   de los   Mexía Reservoir   Limay Choel   Colora
Lago de Ranco Andes San Martín
              de los Andes   T
Osorno   2660 Peso Limay   Sierra   General   Carm
              Lago   Colorada Valcheta Conesa   Pata
Lago Nahuel   Los   San Antonio
Llanquihue Huapi San Carlos Menucos Oeste Viedm
              de Bariloche   San Matías
Puerto   Maquinchao   Gulf
Montt Ancud   Ingeniero   Puerto Punt
              Jacobacci E   Lobos Norte
Chiloe Castro   Gastre   Puerto Vale
              2440   Telsen   Madryn Pen
Cabo Quilán Chaitén Esquel Gangan   Nuevo Punt
Gulf of Guafo   José de   Gulf   Delg
              2260 Tecka San Martín N Trelew Rawson
              2400   Paso de los Indios Florentino
Chonos   Las Plumas   Gran Ameghino
Archipiélago Puerto 2800   Laguna Reservoir
        Cisnes   Chubut Salada
        Magdalena   Chico Camarones
              2860 Facundo Lago Lago
Tortao   Puerto   Musters Colhué Maispina
Peninsula   Aisén Coihaique   Huapi Gulf of
        San Valentín   Sarmiento San Jorge
        4058 Rio Mayo Comodoro
Penas   Lago Gen. Lago Chile Perito Rivadavia Caleta
Gulf   Carrera Buenos Aires Chico Moreno Las Heras Olivia
        3440 Cochrane   Pico   Cabo Tres Puntas
Campaná 3700 San Lorenzo Bajo Caracoles Truncado Jaramillo
                              Deseado Puerto
        Lago   Gobernador Deseado
        O'Higgins Lago   Gregores El Salado
        4375 Cardiel   Puerto
Wellington   Lago Viedma Tres Lagos San Julián
        Murallón 3600   La Chico
        Lago Argentino Santa Cruz Julia Piedrabuena
        2330 El Calafate 2150   Puerto Santa
Hanover   Lago del   Esperanza Cruz
        Toro Yacimiento   Bahía
Nelson Strait Puerto Rio Gallegos Río Gallegos Grande
        Natales Turbio 1285
        1750   Laguna Punta Delgada
Magellan Str.   Blanca Cerro Sombrero
Desolación Punta Arenas Magellan Straits Porvenir Tierra del
        Brunswick   Fuego Río Grande
Santa   Peninsula   Lago Fagnano
Inés   Sarmiento Pen. Cabo San Diego
                          Ushuaia Staten Island
        Hoste
                Cape Horn

PACIFIC

OCEAN

This map shows 1/60 of the earth's surface.

29

60°W
55°W
50°W
45°W

Gualeguay
Mercedes
Duranzo
Treinta-y-
Tres
San Nicolas
URUGUAY
San Pedro
Carmelo
Cardona
Venado
Tuerto
Florida
Pergamino
Zárate
C. del
San Jose
Sacramento
de Mayo
Martinez
Minas
Luján
Canelones
Rocha
oln
Junín
Mercedes
Buenos
Chacabuco
Lanús
Aires
Chivilcoy
Lobos
La Plata
Montevideo
Maldonado
iamonte
Magdalena
35°S
9 de Julio
San Miguel
del Monte
Chascomús
Pehuajó
Saladillo
Samboronbón
Bay
ue
Las Flores
Salado
Dolores
Punta Norte
San Carlos
de Bolívar
mini
Azúl
Rauch
Olavarria
Ayacucho
General Juan Madariaga
Coronel
Tandil
Suárez
s
Coronel
Benito
Pringles
Juárez
Mar del Plata
243
Loberia
ía Blanca
Tres
Arroyos
Miramar
Cnel. Dorrego
unta
Necochea
Alta

Bahía
Blanca

River Plate

A T L A N T I C
40°S

O C E A N
45°S

50°S

Falkland Islands/Islas Malvinas
(U.K.)
West-
Falkland
East
Falkland
Port Stanley

South Georgia Islands
(U.K.)
55°S

60°W
55°W
50°W
45°W

0　100　200　300 miles　　Average linear scale　　0　100　200　300　400　500 Km

a   b   c   d   e   f   g   h   i   j   k   l   m

Greenland
(Denmark)
Scoresby Sound
Scoresbysund

Jan Mayen
(Norway)

70°N

20°W   15°W   10°W   5°W   0°

A   R   C   T

Denmark Strait

Cape Horn
Ísafjörður
Arctic Circle
Fontur
O   C   E

Húna Bay
Akureyri

I C E L A N D
•1765

Breidhi Fjord

65°N
Akranes
1400
Vatnajökull
2119•
Djúpivogur
Faxa Bay
Reykjavík
Keflavik
Reykjanes

Faeroe Islands
(Denmark)

Shetland
Islands
Lerwick

60°N

A T L A N T I C

Orkney
Islands
Cape
Wrath
Pentland Firth
Lewis
Thurso
N O R

Minch
Moray Firth
Inverness
Elgin
Loch
Highlands
Ness
•1309
Aberdeen

90

Hebrides
Skye
S C O T L A N D
Fort William ○•1343
Mull
Perth
Dundee
Stirling
Edinburgh
Islay
Glasgow
Berwick
upon
GREAT BRITAIN
Tweed
Ayr
AND
Newcastle
upon Tyne
North Channel
Londonderry
Carlisle
Sunderland
NORTHERN
IRELAND
NORTHERN IRELAND
Middlesbrough
S E
55°N
Donegal
Belfast
Lough Neagh
Bay
Portadown
Isle of
Sligo
Man ○ Douglas
Dundalk
Blackpool
Leeds
York
Kingston upon Hull
Westport
IRISH
Irish Sea
Athlone
Liverpool
Manchester
OCEAN
Galway
Blackpool
Sheffield
Dublin
Holyhead
Stoke-on-
886
Anglesey
Trent
Nottingham
Roscrea
1085
Derby
Arklow
Norwich
Limerick
Birmingham
Leicester
920
Wexford
WALES
Coventry
Cambridge
REPUBLIC
Aberystwyth
Ipswich
Killarney
Waterford
Fishguard
Oxford
Luton
Cork
Swansea
Thames
Southend-
Cardiff
Reading
London
on-Sea
St. George's Channel
Bristol
Dover
Bristol Channel
Southampton
Bournemouth
Brighton
Oster
Cape Clear
Exeter
Isle of
Calais
Wight
Lille
Plymouth
Valencien
50°N
Land's End
Penzance
English Channel
Abbeville
Cherbourg
Amiens
St.
Le Havre
Rouen
Com
Guernsey
Caen
Channel Islands
Évreux
(U.K.) Jersey
Gulf of St. Malo
Granville
Paris
Brest
St. Brieuc
F R A N
Alençon
Chartres
Rennes
Le Mans
Orléan
Lorient
Loire
Au
Angers
Tours
St. Nazaire
Nantes
0°

20°W   15°W   10°W   5°W

This map shows 1 / 60 of the earth's surface.

32

5°W 0° 5°E 10°E

Southampton
GREAT BRITAIN
Bournemouth
Plymouth Exeter Brighton Dover Calais Gent Brussels BELGIUM Aachen Cologne Bad Hersfeld Erfurt
Land's End Penzance Isle of Wight Strait of Dover Lille Valenciennes Charleroi Liège 689 Bonn Koblenz 774 983 Plauen
50°N English Channel Cherbourg Abbeville Amiens St Quentin Sedan LUXEM- Trier Wiesbaden Frankfurt Bamberg Ge
Channel Guernsey Le Havre Rouen Compiègne Reims BOURG Luxembourg Thionville 816 Saarbrücken Mannheim Würzburg Nuremberg
Islands (U.K.) Jersey Caen Seine Metz Karlsruhe Regens
Gulf of St. Malo Évreux Nancy Strasbourg Stuttgart GERMANY
Brest St. Brieuc Granville Alençon Paris Chartres Troyes Chaumont Mulhouse Freiburg Augsburg Munich
Rennes Le Mans Orléans Auxerre Dijon 1493 Lake Constance Memmingen
ATLANTIC Angers Loire Tours Moulins Chalons-sur- Besançon Basle Zürich Zugspitze 2963
St. Nazaire Nantes Loire Poitiers Aller Saône Berne LIECHTEN- Landeck Innsbr
FRANCE Lausanne STEIN Vaduz 3774
La Roche- Châteauroux Mâcon Lucerne SWITZERLAND Chur
sur-Yon 288 Limoges Clermont- Geneva Lake Brig Bernina Bolzano Dolomites
La Rochelle Angoulême Ferrand Lyon Geneva Rhône Monte Rosa 4026 3554 3342 Co
OCEAN Bordeaux Brive Le Puy 1885 St. Étienne Annecy Mont Blanc 4502 Como Bergamo Lake
Bay of Gironde Aurillac Massif Grenoble 4807 Aosta 4061 Novara Milan Garda Vicenza
Biscay Dordogne Central Valence Pelvoux Alessandria Turin Brescia Verona Padua
45°N Lot Cévennes Rhône 4102 3847 Cuneo Piacenza Parma Po
Landes Agen Garonne Nîmes Digne Maritime Alps Genoa Modena Ferrara Rav
Adour Montpellier Avignon Nice 2120 La Spezia Bologna
Bayonne Pau Toulouse Arles Aix-en- MONACO Gulf of Florence SAN
San Sebastián Tarbes Carcassonne Narbonne Provence Genoa Imperia Pisa MARINO
Santander Bilbao 2604 Gulf of Lion Marseilles Toulon LIGURIAN Livorno Arezz
Gijón Vitoria Pamplona 3404 Perpignan SEA Bastia Elba Siena Viterbo
Corunna Oviedo Cantabrian Mountains Jaca Pico ANDORRA Gerona Costa Corsica 2710
2417 2583 de Aneto 2923 Brava (France) Civitavecchia
Cape Santiago de Logroño Huesca Ajaccio Rome
Finisterre Compostela Ponferrada León 2142 Soria Saragossa Lérida Bonifacio Olbia
Vigo Orense Burgos Ebro Str. of Bonifacio Sassari Nuoro Sardinia
Miño Zamora Duero Calatayud Barcelona (Italy)
Braga Valladolid Tarragona 1834 Oristano TYRRH
Oporto 1382 Salamanca Tortosa Cágliari SEA
Aveiro Douro SPAIN 2430 Segovia Guadalajara Teruel Castellón Balearic Islands Menorca
Guarda Ávila Madrid 2020 Alcudia
40°N Coimbra 2592 Talavera Toledo Tagus La Almarcha Palma Mallorca Cape
Leiria de la Reina Valencia Teulada
PORTUGAL Tagus Cáceres Trujillo Ciudad Real Guadiana Albacete Júcar Gandia Ibiza M E D I T E R
Lisbon Mérida Badajoz Puertollano Segura Cabo de
Setúbal Évora Guadiana La Nao
Sines Beja Aracena Sierra Morena Úbeda Murcia Alicante
Odemira Mértola Córdoba 2036 Lorca Cartagena
Sagres Algarve Lagos Guadalquivir Jaén Baza Aguilas
Cape Faro Huelva Sevilla Écija Granada 3478 Almería
St. Vincent Gulf of Antequera Sierra Nevada Motril Dellys Binzert
Cádiz Jerez de la Costa del Sol Málaga Algiers Tizi Bejaia Skikda Annaba Gulf of Cape Bon
Frontera Ténès Blida Ouzou Constantine 586 Tabarka Tunis Kélibia
Algeciras Gibraltar (U.K.) Khemis Medea Setif Souk Tunisia Teboursouk
Tangier Ceuta (Sp.) Str. of Gibraltar Mostaganem Miliana Bordj Bou- Ahras Lé Kef 1357 Zaghouan Pantell
Tétouan Melilla (Sp.) Oran Cheliff Arreridj Batna Ain Beïda Sousse Pelagie Islan
Asilah Chechaouen Beni Saf Mohammadia Tiaret Metlili Chaamba Khenchela Kairouan (Sicily)
Al Hoceima Sidi-bel- 1983 2326 Tebessa Kasserine El Djem Lampedusa
Ksar el Kebir Aknoul Oujda Abbès Tell Atlas Bou Saada Biskra Fériana Cape Kaboudia
35°N MOROCCO Ouertha Tlemcen 767 Djelfa Gafsa Sfax Kerkenna
Chellala Monts des Ouled Naïl Chott Islands
Marhoum Hauts Plateaux Ouled Djellal Melrhir Tozeur Gabès Gulf of Gabès
Aflou Messaad Chott Kebili Djerba
Méchéria El Bayadh 1977 Saharan Atlas Chott Djerid Médenine Zarzis
Bougtob Laghouat -40 Gabès
Ain Sefra 2236 Brézina Guerara El Meghaier Touggourt 238 Ben Guerdane
ALGERIA El Oued Al Azizi
Ghardaïa Chebka El Oued Gh
du Mzab Bordj Jadu
Ain Oussera Bourguiba 688
Ouargla Remada Nalut
Western Erg 502 Hassi Messaoud 306 Bir Zar
Great Eastern Erg El Goléa Sinawan
5°W 0° 5°E 10°E

36

This map shows 1/60 of the earth's surface.

33

Dresden 15°E Wałbrzych Wrocław 20°E Kielce Lutsk 25°E Rovno Korosten 30°E Kiev Reservoir Nezhin 35°E Sumy

1490 POLAND Zamość L'vov Novograd Volynskiy Kiev Priluki Akhtyrka

CZECHOSLOVAKIA Katowice Krakow Rzeszow Przemyśl Ternopol' Zhitomir Lubny Khar'kov

Olomouc Ostrava Bielsko-Biala Zakopane 725 Žilina Prešov 1346 Uzgorod Khmel'nitskiy SOVIET UNION Poltava Vaiki

Jihlava Brno Zvolen Košice 2043 Ivano-Frankovsk Mukachevo Dniester Vinnitsa Cherkassy Kremenchug Pereshchepino

Znojmo Danube Miskolc Nyíregyháza Satu Mare Chernovtsy Kamenets-Podol'skiy Mogilev Podol'skiy UKRAINE Uman' Znamenka Kirovograd Dneprodzerzhinsk Novomoskovsk

Linz Vienna Bratislava Győr Váč Debrecen Baia Mare Suceava Botoşani Bel'tsy Dnepropetrovsk

2075 AUSTRIA Veszprém Budapest HUNGARY Oradea Pietrosu 2305 Iaşi MOLDAVIA Orgejev Kishinev Tiraspol Pervomaysk Krivoy Rog Nikopol Zaporozh'ye

Leoben Balaton Lake Dej 2103 Bacău Siret Nikolayev Kakhovskoye Reservoir

Graz Nagykanizsa Cluj Napoca Tirgu Mureş Odessa Kherson Novaya Kakhovka Melitopol

Klagenfurt Maribor Pecs Szeged Arad ROMANIA Sibiu Braşov Galati Bolgrad 18. Karkinitskiy Bay Dzhankoy

Ljubljana Varaždin Subotica Timişoara Deva Belgorod Crimea Sea of Azov

Zagreb Osijek Zrenjanin Vršac Negoiu 2548 Mouths of the Danube Simferopol Feodosiya

Rijeka Karlovac Brod Novisad 2509 Turnu-Severin Piteşti Ploieşti Tulcea 45°N Sevastopol Jalda

Pula Krk YUGOSLAVIA Belgrade Smederevo Craiova BUCHAREST Constanţa

Cres Bihać Banja Luka Tuzla Danube Svetozarevo Roşiori BLACK

Pag Zadar Šibenik 2107 Sarajevo Titovo Užice Morava Vidin Danube Ruse SEA

Zenica Jablanica Niš Vraca Pleven Kolarovgrad

Brac Hvar 2387 Leskovac Pirot Tŭrnovo Varna

Korčula Peljesac Ivangrad Priština Balkan 2376 Sliven

Dubrovnik Titograd 2693 Prizren SOFIA BULGARIA Burgas Cape Ince

Campobasso 2793 Shkodër Kumanovo Musala 2925 Plovdiv Stara Zagora Sinop

Foggia Skopje 2747 Blagoevgrad Rhodope Kŭrdzali Edirne Samsun

Benevento Bari ALBANIA Titov Veles 2191 Komotini Luleburgaz Istanbul Ereğli Karabük Kastamonu 2565

Durrës Ohrid Lake Bitola Serra Kavalla Tekirdağ Üsküdar Adapazari Bolu Corum 2068

Salerno Tiranë Prespa Lake Edessa Thessaloniki Thasos Sea of Marmara Izmit Gerede Turhal

Potenza Korça Chalkidike Bandirma Bursa Kizilirmak

Brindisi Vlorë GREECE Imbros Canakkale Bilecik 2543 Eskişehir Ankara Kirikkale Kayseri

Lecce Kozáni 2633 2911 Gulf of Thermai Lemnos Troy Balikesir Kütahya Yozgat 40°N

Taranto Gulf of Taranto Capo Santa Maria di Leuca Corfu Jánina Trikala Lárisa AEGEAN Ayvalik Manisa Akhisar Afyon Anatolia Lake Tuz 2345

Sapri 2248 Corfu Pindus Vólos Northern Sporades Lesbos Izmir 2446 Akşehir TURKEY Kayseri 3976

Corigliano Lamia SEA Chíos Alaşehir Aksaray Karaman

Cosenza Delphi Euboea Aydin Menderes Konya Niğde Kozan

Catanzaro Levkas Agrinion Chalkis Taurus 3488 Ereğli Adana Geyhan

Cephalonia Gulf of Corinth IONIAN Patras Athens Andros Sámos Muğla Antalya Mersin

Lipari Islands 1965 Messina Reggio SEA 2224 Korinth Piraeus Tínos Cyclades Southern Sporades Gulf of Antalya 3086 Alanya Silifke Iskenderun 1870

Etna 3340 Riposto Zante Pyrgos Tripolis Náxos Fethiye Finike Cape Anamur Anamur Antakya

Enna Catania Kalamai Milos Rhodes 1215

Canissetta Agrigento Gela Syracuse Noto Cape Akrítas Cape Maléa Kithira Rhodes Cape Andreas

Ragusa Sea of Crete Kárpathos CYPRUS Latakia

Valletta MEDITERRANEAN Kánea Melambes 2456 Iráklion Nicosia Famagusta 1385

MALTA Crete Cape Arnauti Olympus 1951 Larnaca 35°N

Paphos Limassol Tartus

SEA Tripoli 3097

LEBANON Beirut Zahlé

Damascus

Al Bayda Darnah Sur Qunaitra Golan Heights Dar'a

Al Marj 882 Haifa Irbid

Benghazi Al Jabal al Akhdar Tobruk Hadera 1247

Al Abyar Qaminis 169 Al Adam Al Burdi Nile Delta Baltim ISRAEL Zarqa

Gulf of Sirte Al Adam Sallūm Sīdi Barrāni Mersa Matruh Rosetta Dumyat Tel-Aviv-Jaffa Amman

Beni Walid Buerát el Hsun LIBYA Marmarica Fuka Alexandria EGYPT Damanhūr Al Mansura Port Said Gaza Dead Sea Al Karak

Sirte 15°E 20°E 25°E Damietta Suez Canal Ar'Arish Beer Sheba 35°N 30°E 35°E Jerusalem Amman

37 38

0 100 200 300 miles Average linear scale 0 100 200 300 400 500 Km

PORTUGAL **SPAIN** **MOROCCO** **ALGERIA**

WESTERN SAHARA

MAURITANIA

MALI

ATLANTIC

OCEAN

Canary Islands
(Spain) Tenerife

Madeira (Portugal)

This map shows 1/60 of the earth's surface.

a b c d e f g h i j k l m

35 · 35

MEDITERRANEAN SEA

Sicilian Channel

Egadi
Marsala
Sciacca
Agrigento
Licata
Gela
Ragusa
Noto
Pachino
Corleone
Caltanissetta
Enna
Catania
Syracuse
Sicily
Riposto
Adrano
Etna
Bova Marina
ITALY

Pantelleria (It.)

Linosa
Pelagie Islands (Sicily)
Lampedusa

Gozo
Valletta
MALTA

15°E

35°N
30°N
25°N
20°N

5°E · 10°E · 15°E · 20°E

Algiers
Dellys
Bejaia
Skikda
Annaba
Binzert
Mateur
Tabarka
Beja
Tunis
Cap Bon
Kélibia
Hammam Lif
Zaghouan
Boufarik
Blida
Medea
Tizi Ouzou
Djidjelli
Constantine
Setif
Guelma
Souk-Ahras
Ain Beïda
Le Kef
Teboursouk
Ksar el Boukhari
Bordj-Bou-Arreridj
Metlili Chaamba
Bou Saada
Batna
Tebessa
Khenchela
Kairouan
Sousse
Msaken
Mahdia
El Djem
Cape Kaboudia
Sfax
Kasserine
Fériana
Redeyef
Gafsa
Metlaoui
Kerkenna Islands
Djelfa
Tolga
Biskra
Aflou
Ouled Djellal
Messaad
Monts des Ouled Naïl
Atlas
Laghouat
Tilrhemt
Berriane
Guerara
Dzioua
Djamaa
El Oued
Ghardaia
Temacine
Touggourt
Ain Oussera
El Meghaier
Neffa
Tozeur
Kebili
Gabès
Djerba
Zarzis
Médenine
Ben Guerdane
Zuwarah
Janzur
Tripoli
Tajura
Khoms
Zliten
Misurata
Al Aziziyah
Tarhuna
Al Oued
Guémar
Chott Djerid
TUNISIA
Gulf of Gabès
Remada
Nalut
Jadu
Zintan
Gharian
Beni Walid
Mizda
Bordj Bourguiba
Bir Zar
Sinawan
Tripolitania
Al Qariyat
Ash Shwayrif
Bu Ndjem
Buerát el Hsun
Sirte
Gulf of Sirte
Benghazi
Qaminis
Ajdabiya
Al Aqaylah

Great Eastern Erg
Ouargla
Hassi Messaoud
Hassi Touareg
Hassi Maroket
Hassi Inifel
Ez Zemoul el Akbar
Bordj Messouda
Ghadames
Darj
Hamada el Homra
Tinrhert Hamada
Waddan
Suknah
Hun
Maradah
El Goléa
Hassi bel Guebbour
Ohanet
Hamadat Tingharat
Awaynat Wanin
Zella
Tlisen
Sirte Desert
Harudj el Asued

Bordj Omar Driss
In Amenas
Tiguentourine
Edjeleh
Idhan Awbari
Brak
Idri
Umm el Abid
El Fugha
Irharharene
Amguid
Illizi
Tarat
Ubari
Sabha
Semnu
LIBYA
Jarma
Fezzan
Zuwaylah
Timsah
Terbu
Tmed Bu Haschlscha
Arak Bordj
Tassili-n-Ajjer
Al Awaynat
Murzuq
Ghat
El Barcat
Djanet
Idhan Murzuq
Qatrun
Wau el Kebir
Wau en Namus
Ahaggar
Fort Gardel
Djebel Tahat Telertheba
In Ekker
Ideles
Hirafok
Djebel Serkout
In Afeleh
Anaï
Tajarhí
Ramlat Rabyana
Tropic of Cancer
In Amguel
Abalessa
Tit
Atakor
Silet
Tamanrasset
Amsel
Mangueni Plateau
Tumu
Auzu
Jabal Nuqay
Pic Toussidé
Bardai
Yebbi Bou
Tibesti
Zouar
Sherda
Tarso Ahon
Emi Koussi
Gouro
In Ébeggi
Ténéré du Tafassâsset
Djado Plateau
Madama
Tassili Oua-n-Hoggar
In Azaoua
Djado
Dao Timni
Bouressa
Tin Zaouatene
In Guezzam
Assamakka
Seguedine
Cheffadene
Yeggueba
CHAD
In Azaraf
In Abalene
Talak
Aïr
Iférouane
Timia
Bagzane
Fachi
Erg du Ténéré
Achénoumma
Dirkou
Bilma
Grand Erg de Bilma
Yarda
Borkou
Azouak
Agadez
Aouderas
Dibella
Zoo Baba
Aney
Kichi Kichi
Faya
Gourou

NIGER

ALGERIA

0 100 200 300 miles
0 100 200 300 400 500 Km
Average linear scale

n o p q r s t u v w x y z

41 · 41

38

a b c d e f g h i j k l m

20°E · 25°E · 30°E · 35°E

GREECE

Kithira · Cape Maléa · Rhodes · Finike · TURKEY · Aleppo

Sea of Crete · Gulf of Antalya · Anamur · Idlib · Maskan

Kárpathos · Rhodes · Cape Anamur · Cape Andreas · Antakya · SY · Hama

CYPRUS · Latakia · 1385 · Hama

35°N · Cape Arnauti · Olympus · Famagusta · Tartus · Homs

Nicosia · 1951 · Larnaca · Tall Kalakh · Nabk

Paphos · Limassol · Tripoli · Baalbek · Zahle · 659

MEDITERRANEAN · Beirut · LEBANON · Damascus

SEA · Sur · Qunaitra · Golan Heights · Syria

Gulf of Sidra · Nile Delta · Haifa · Daraa · 1735

Benghazi · Al Mekhily · Tobruk · Al Burdi · Dumyat · Hadera · Irbid · Mafraq

Qaminis · Al Adam · Sidi Barrâni · Rosetta · Baltim · Port Said · Tel-Aviv-Jaffa · Zarqa · Amman

Ajdabiyah · Sallûm · Mersa Matruh · Alexandria · Damanhûr · Al Mansura · Suez Canal · Gaza · JERUSALEM · Amman

Cyrenaica · Marmarica · Fuka · Tanta · Zagazig · Ismâilîya · Ar Arish · Beer Sheba · Al Karak · JORDAN

169 · Libyan Plateau · Al Alamein · Al Hammam · Lower Egypt · Great Bitter Lake · Quseima · Bayir · Al Isawiya

30 · Wadi al Hamim · Fort Qarain · Qattara-Depression · Shubra al Kheima · Cairo · Suez · Nakhl · Elat · Petra · Ma'an

30°N · Al Jaghbub · Giza · Helwân · Sûdr · Sinai · Aqaba · Al Mudauwara

Jaghbub Oasis · 713 · Qara · 123 · Pyramids · Memphis · Ain Sukhna · 850 · 1626 · Nuweiba · Al Bad · Al Mugha

Awjilah · Siwa · Al Faiyûm · Beni Suef · Ras Ghârib · Katherina 2637 · Dahab · Tabuk · Al Bir

Jalu · Siwa Oasis · Baharia Oasis · Beni Mazâr · Gemsa · Ofira · Ash Sharmah · Duba

Jalu Oasis · Bawîti · Al Minyâ · Dairût · Ras Muhammad · Hurghada · 1990

LIBYA · Farafra · Farafra Oasis · Asyût · Abu Tig · Port Safaga · Al Wajh

37 · Akhmîn · Wadi Qena · Arabian Desert

Tazirbu 184 · Sohâg · Qena · Qusair · Wadi al Hamo

Zighan · Qasr · Al Balyana · Qus · Karnak · Marsa Alam · Umm L

25°N · Kufrah Oasis · Dakhla Oasis · Mût · Al Khârja · Isna · Luxor · Thebes · Ras Abu Madd

Rabyanah · Al Jawf · Al Khârja Oasis · Idfu · Upper Egypt · Marsa Alam · Yanb al Ba

Tropic of Cancer · 625 · Bâris · Kom Ombo · Wadi Garara · 1977 · Berenice · Ras Banas

Gilf Kebir Plateau · 1st. Cataract · Aswân · Wadi Hadah · Bir al Hasa

Lake Nasser · Wadi Allaqi · Ras Abu Dara

Abu Simbel · Wadi Iblo · Halaib · Ras Hadarl

1893 · Uweinat · 2nd. Cataract · Wadi Halfa · 2217 · Dungunab · Ras Abu S.

Nile · Wadi Gabgaba · 2218 Erba · Muhamm

Kosha · Nubian Desert · Qol

20°N · Delgo · 2260 Oda · Port S

Kerma · Abu Hamed · Suakin

Ounianga Kebir · Erdi · Dongola · 3rd. Cataract · Umm Mirdi · Amur · Sinkat

CHAD · SUDAN · Al Khandaq · Karima · 4th. Cataract · 5th. Cataract · Berber · Musmar · Tokar

Merowe · Korti · Atbara · Haiya

Mourdi Depression · Baiyuda · Derudeb · Adarama

Fada 545 · Ennedi · al Milk · White Nile · Atbara · Mitatib · 738

Archei · Howar · 6th. Cataract · Shendi · ET

Haouach · Wadi Seidna · 517 · Khartoum North

20°E · 25°E · Omdurman · 30°E · 35°E

n o p q r s t u v w x y z

This map shows 1/60 of the earth's surface.

a b c d e f g h i j k l m

40°E 45°E 50°E 55°E

Raqqah
Al Hasakah J463
ayr az Zawr Sinjar Tall 'Afar Mosul
Suwar Sharqat Arbil Saqqez Qojur Qazvin Amol Ghaem Damghan Mayamey
Zab Baneh Shahr Damavand
Wadi ath Tharthar Kirkuk Sulaimaniyah Bijar Takestan Elburz Mts. 5671 Damavand
Lesser Zab Takestan Karaj Zarand Semnan Torud
al Hayl Tigris Tikrit Tuz Khurmatu 1097 Sanandaj Razan Saveh Garmsar
Abu Kamal Euphrates Anah Jalaula Ravansar Hamadan Qom Daryacheh-ye-Namak 35°N Dasht-e-Kavir
Al Hadithah Ba'qubah Karand Bakhtaran Kangavar 3572 Qarah Su
Wadi Hawran 1322 Malayer Arak Khor Tabas
al at Ar Ramadi Diyala Eslamabad-e-Gharb Borujerd Mahallat 3365 Natanz Ardestan Anarak
hef Baghdad Ilam 2656 3075 Azna Meymeh 3899 Nain Aliabad
Ar Rutbah I R A Q Al Aziziyah Mehran 2041 Khorramabad Daran Najafabad 1590 Isfahan
866 Karbala Al Hillah Dehloran Karkheh Keshvar 4324 Oshtoran 4294 Shahr-e-Kord Ardakan Aliabad
Al Kut Dezful 4548 3197 Yazd Darband
Wadi Tibal An Najaf Ad Diwaniyah Shush Masjed-e-Soleiman Qomsheh Izadkhast 4074 Mehriz Bafq Ravor
raif An Nukhaib 321 Ar Rifa' Al Amarah Karun 4298 Abadeh Abarqu Zarand
Al Jalamid Wadi Ar'ar Ahwaz Ramhormoz 3746 Dehbid 3472 Rafsanjan 3143 Kerman
1070 Ar'ar Ash Shubaiyai An Nasiriyah Hawr al Hammar Ramshir Behbahan Dinar 3965 Saadatabad Baghin 30°N
Abu Qasr As Samawah Euphrates Basra Bandar-e-Khomeini 4432 3218 Daryacheh-ye-Tashk
Sakakah Ad Duwaid As Salman Umm Qasr Khorramshahr Hendijan Nurabad Persepolis Hoseinabad Laleh Zar
Al Jawf As Busaiyah Abadan 1539 Shiraz Daryacheh-ye-Bakhtegan Sirjan 4374 Baft
Rafha Al Faw Bubiyan Bandar-e-Rig Kazerun Neiriz
k Abu Qasr KUWAIT Bandar-e-Rig Borazjan Fasa Aliabad
An Nafud Jahra Kuwait Bushehr Firuzabad 3188 Jahrom Dowlatabad
Jubbah Linah Ansab 299 Ahmadi Ras Halileh Khormuj 1960 Lar 2804 3279
Al Maiyah NEUTRAL ZONE Al Wafra Mina Saud Zeydan Mand Juyom Hajiabad
Ha'il Bir Shari Ad Dibdibah Kangan Qotbabad
1500 Tabah Al Qaisumah Safaniyah ARABIAN Gavbandi Bandar Abbas Minab
Hulaifah Samirah Al Artawiyah Qaryat al 'Ulya Sarar Abu Hadriyah Bastak Dezhgan Qeshm
S A U D I Az Zilfi Al Hasa Al Jubayl Bandar-e-Margam Qeys Bandar-e-Lengeh Str. of Hormuz
Khayber Uqlat al Suqur Buraidah Ash Shumlul Ras Tannurah GULF 2081 Ash Sha'am Musandam Pen.
Buwatah Unaizah Al Majm'ah Dhahran Damman Ras al Khaimah OMAN Dibba
Al Hanakiyah Wadi ar Rimah Ushairah Abqaiq Manama Ar Ruwais Sharjah Shinas
Medina Shaqra Khurais Al Udailiyah BAHRAIN G. of Bahrain QATAR Dubai Fujairah Gulf of Oman Sohar
Al Qurain Khuff Al Hufuf Dukhan Doha Jebel Ali 25°N
Wadi al Jarin Durma Riyadh Karana Umm Sa'id Abu Dhabi Al Ain Al Khaburah
As Sidr Mahd adh Dhahab Ad Dawadimi Sulaimaniyah Salwa Marawah Abu al Abyad Al Khaznah Al Batinah Al Khabura
Ir Hunain Afif Harad As Sila Jabal adh Dhanna UNITED ARAB Habshan Ibri
asturah Muhairiqah Halaban Tarif Sabkhat Matti Bu Hasa EMIRATES 3018
Zalim Al Hillah As Sawadah Taraq An Nashash Bahla
Buwatah Khulais As Suq Jabal Tuwayq Ad Dahna Liwa Oasis
Madrakah A R A B I A Layla 1012 Al Jafurah Umm al Samim
Mecca 1630 Ar Rauda Wadi ad Dawasir Wadi Aswad
Arafat Taif Turabah Al Khamasin Al Uruq al Mutaridah
2386 2386 As Sulaiyil Ar Rub' al Khali O M A N
Al Lith Bani Sar Qal'at Bishah Wadi Tathlith
Al Ulaya Tathlith 20°N
Al Qunfudhah An Nimas Wadi bin Khawtar Wadi Qitbit Sahil al Jazir Sauqira Bay
Kasar 3133 Khay Al Ghaydah Dhofar Sharbithat
Abha Khamis Mushait Hima' Sanaw Thamarit Salalah Mirbat Ras Sharbithat
Ad Darb Zahran Jabal al Qara Kuria Muria Islands
Mersa Teklay Najran Thamud REPUBLIC OF YEMEN Jabal al Qamar Raisut Ras Mirbat
Farasan Is. Sa'dah REPUBLIC OF YEMEN Jabal al Qamar Qamar Bay ARABIAN SEA
siwa Jizan Huth Al Hazm Al Ghaydah
Dahlak Islands Midi Al Hazm Al Jiz Qamar Bay
Hajjah 3360 Wadi al Jawf Haynan Sayun Wadi Masilah Ras Fartak
40°E 45°E 50°E 55°E

n o p q r s t u v w x y z

60

0 100 200 300 miles Average linear scale 0 100 200 300 400 500 Km

15°W   10°W   5°W

Moudjéria
Boûmdeïd   •600
Boutilimit   Tamchaket
Mederdra   Aleg   Montagnes   Oualâta   In Alay   Oudeika
        Mâl   Kiffa   de l'Affolé   Néma   Bamba
Rosso   Bogué   'Ayoûn el Atroûs
    Senegal   MAURITANIA   Kobenni Amourj   Niafounké   Tombouctou
Dagana   Kaédi   Timbedgha   Bassikounou   Goundam
St. Louis   Mbout   Kankossa   Hamoud   Nampala   Lac
        Maghama   Sélibabi   Nioro du Sahel   Nara   Débo   Hombori
Louga   Matam   Birou   Ballé   Sokolo   •1155
    Fourdou   Macina   Mopti   Douentza

15°N
Dakar   Thiès Mbaké   Kidira Kayes   Koniakari Diéma   MALI   Bandiagara   Djibo
Cape Verde   Ferlo   D?   Ségou   Bani   Ouahigouya
Mbour   Kaolack   Bamba Diamou Bafoulabé Didiéni Banamba   San   BURK
    SENEGAL Malème-Hodar   Toukoto Kolokani Koulikoro Bla   Nouna   FA
    Koumpentoum Tambacounda Dialafara   Fana   Dédougou
Karang   Georgetown Dialakoto   Kati Bamako Baguinéda   Koudougou Ouagadou
Banjul GAMBIA Basse   Niokolo Saraya   Mpessoba Koutiala   Yako Toéssé Tenk
Sere Kunda Santa Su Koba Kédougou Satadougou   Ouéléssébougou Koundougou   Po
Brikama Bignona Kolda   Houndé   Léo Zab
Ziguinchor Casamance Farim   •1538   Sikasso   Bobo-Dioulasso Gaoua
    Bissora Gaoual   Fouta Touqué Siguiri   Bougouni •820   •505   Navrongo
GUINEA-BISSAU Bafatá Djalon Labé Dinguiraye GUINEA Garalo Manankoro   Banfora Wa   Yala
Mansôa   •1264 Pita   Kouroussa   Pogo
Bissau Corubal Boké Télimélé Dabola •1028 Kankan   Samatiguila   Bolgatanga
        Kogon Fria •1421 Dalaba •1015   Odienné Ouangolodougou   Bouna Sawla
Bissagos Islands Catió   Konkouré Mamou •1094 Faranah   Ferkéssédougou   Bole
        Fatala Kindia Sanouyah   Bohodoyou Bako Korhogo Kong   Maluwe
Boffa Boké   Morondo   Kanawolo   •430   Koutouba
10°N   Forécariah Kabala Kissidougou Kérouané   Kani   Bamboi
Conakry   Little Scarcies Loma •948   Beyla   Koro   Katiola   Bondoukou Kintampo
    Kambia Makeni Mts.   Macenta Tibé Touba Séguéla   Goumeré •700   GHAN
Freetown SIERRA Koidu   •1656 •1257 •1185 Man Kossou   Bouaké   Techiman
    LEONE   Zorzor Nzérékoré Biankouma Reservoir   Berekum Sunyani
Bo Pendembu   •1752   IVORY COAST Bouaflé Abengourou Kumasi Mampo
Sewa Kenema Loffa Sanniquellie Danané   Yamoussoukro   Konongo Nkawkaw
Sherbro Pujehun Moa   Gbarnga Ganta Guiglo Duékoué Daloa Dimbokro Akoupé Awaso Obuasi
Island   Bomi St. Paul   Touléplou Toumodi   Agboville •554 Dunkwa Kofor
        Mano Hills Bong LIBERIA Tapeta   Gagnoa Lakota   Konoe   Oda
Monrovia River   Tchien Tai Soubré   Agboville   Prestea Ac
        Mani   Cavally   Sassandra Bandama Abidjan Tarkwa Cape
Buchanan   Cess   Juarzon •396   Dabou Grand Grand Bassam Sekondi-
5°N   Grain   Greenville   Niénokoué Tabou   Lahou Bassam   Takoradi
        Coast   Grabo Sassandra   Ivory Coast   Gold Co
        Plibo   San Pédro
        Harper

A T L A N T I C   O C E   E

Equator

15°W   10°W   5°W

This map shows 1/60 of the earth's surface.

a b c d e f g h i j k l m

5°E · 10°E · 15°E

NIGER

•500 · Anou Mellene · Aouderas · Akrereb · Dibella

Tegguidda-n-Tessoum · Agadem · Homodji · Toro Doûm

Ménaka · In Talak · Tillia · •500 · Mazalet · Ouyu Bezze Denga · 280

Ansongo · Tchin-Tabaradene · Termit N · Massif de Termit •710 · Ngourti · Moul

Niger · Tilemsès · Aderbissinat · Task · Idaye · •255 · Rig-Rig · Nokou

•550 · Tillabéri · Tanout · Nguigmi · Kanem · Mao · Am Raya

Téra · Ouallam · Filingué · Illéla · Madaoua · •403 · Zinder · Gouré · Goudoumaria · Bosso · Lake Chad · Mondo · Moussoro

•302 · Matankari · Illela · Tessaoua · Maradi · Mainé-Soroa · Baga · Ngouri

Niamey · Torodi · Dogondoutchi · Burni-Nkonni · Katsina · Dungas · Nguru · Gashua · Geidam · Komadugu · Massaguet · Massakori · Ngoura

Say · Dosso · Sokoto · Argungu · Kaura Namoda · Hadejia · Dapchi · Damakar · Dikwa · 296 Fort-Foureau · **N'Djamena** · Karmé · 442

Kantchari · Koulou · Birnin-Kebbi · Talata Mafara · Anka · Gusau · Kano · Wudil · Hadejia · Potiskum · Damaturu · Maiduguri · 1141 · **CHAD**

Diapaga · Gaya · Kamba · Faskari · Funtua · Feggo · Kari · Buni · Bama · Djermaya · Massenya

-adal-gourma · Zuru · Yelwa · Zaria · Zalanga · Gongola · Gombe · Biu · Mubi · Mokolo · Maroua · Guélengdeng · Bousso

Tanguiéta · •550 · Béroubouay · Kontagora · Birnin Gwari · Kaduna · •1594 Goura · Bara · Wuyo · Bongor · Ham

Natitingou · Bembéréké · Kainji Reservoir · Tegina · Bauchi · Numan · Yola · Garoua · Pala · Kélo · Lai · 10°N

Boukombé · **BENIN** · Wawa · **NIGERIA** · Jos · Kafanchan · 1625 Kagora · Pankshin · Jalingo · Poli · Guidjiba · Moundou

Djougou · Yashikera · Minna · Abuja · 1518 · Zamko · Mbé · Tchollité · Doba

Lama-Kara · Parakou · Kaiama · Jebba · Bida · Akwanga · Wamba · Numan · Toubouro · Baïbokoum · Gore · Koumra

Bassari · Bassila · Igbetti · Baro · Lafia · Ibi · Wukari · Beli · Béka · Ngaoundéré · Bélel · Bocaranga · Bébora

•772 Sokodé · Kilibo · Agoaré · Ilorin · Niger · Benue · Makurdi · Takum · Adamaoua Highlands · Douafayel · Bossangoa

TOGO · Blitta · Savé · Ogbomosho · Oshogbo · Lokoja · Ayangba · Oturkpo · Banyo · Meiganga · Garoua Boulaï · Bozoum

•845 · Savalou · Iwo · Ife · Ado-Ekiti · Kabba · Okene · Ogoja · 1890 · Nkambe · Tibati · Bétaré-Oya · Babaoua · Bouar · **CENTRAL**

Kpessi · Iseyin · Oyo · Ede · Ilesha · Ikerre · Akure · Owo · Ikom · Bamenda · 2335 · Foumban · Yoko · Carnot · Bossembélé · Bombale

Atakpamé · Abomey · Ibadan · Abeokuta · Ondo · Enugu · 3008 · 2740 · Mamfe · Bafoussam · Goyoum · **AFRICAN**

-ndu · Nuatja · Ilaro · Ijebu Ode · Benin City · Onitsha · Dschang · Bafang · **CAMEROON** · Berberati

Kpalimé · Tsévié · **Porto Novo** · Lekki · Sapele · Afikpo · Cross · 2050 · Nkongsamba · Ndjolé · Bertoua · Bania · 5°N

Lomé · Ouidah Cotonou · **Lagos** · Warri · Aba · Bafia · Yabassi · Sanaga · Nanga Eboko · Batouri · **REPUBLIC**

Ughelli · Port Harcourt · Calabar · Buea · Kenzou · Nola

Slave Coast · Brass · Bonny · Mt. Cameroon 4100 · Douala · **Yaoundé** · Abong Mbang · Yokadouma · Bayanga

Malabo · Limbé · Edéa · Eséka · Mbalmayo · Boumba · Ouesso · Bomassa

1890 · Luba · Bioko Island · Nyong · Ebolowa · Sangmélima · Lokomo · Moloundou

2662 · **EQUATORIAL** · Ebebiyin · Bitam · Ntam · Souanké · Sembé · Liouesso

GULF · **GUINEA** · Bata · Niefang · Oyem · 937 · 1200 Tembo · Nkolabona · Mékambo · Pikounda

of · Mbini · 1200 · Mbini · Evinayong · Mitzic · Makokou · **CONGO**

Guinea · Principe · Cocobeach · Kougouleu · Lalara · Likouala · Makoua

SÃO TOMÉ · Nkolabona · Libreville · 980 · Booué · Kellé · 500 · Owando

AND PRINCIPE · São Tomé · Ndjolé · Lastoursville · Ewo · Kouyou

São Tomé 2024 · **GABON** · 875 · Okondja · Boundji · Zaïre

Annobón (Equa.Guinea) · Port-Gentil · Lambaréné · Ogooué · Koulamoutou · Moanda · Okoyo · Mossaka · **ZAÏRE**

Omboué · Mouila · Mimongo · Franceville · Lake Onangue

5°E · 10°E · 15°E

n o p q r s t u v w x y z

0 100 200 300 miles · Average linear scale · 0 100 200 300 400 500 Km

20°E · 25°E · 30°E

Bodêlé

Fada

Archei

Ennedi

Haouach

Koro Toro

Ouagat

Kapka ·1220

Ma ba

Karma

Tiné

Umm Saggat

Sindi

Magrur

Hamrat al Shaikh

Sodiri

Kordofan

Haraza ·1127

Umm Inderaba

Nile

Shendi

6th Cataract

Wadi Seidna

·517

Omdurman

Khartoum North

Khartoum

15°N Salal

Sahel

Biltine

Haddad

Abéché

Adré

al Junayna

Gurgei ·2351

Kebkabiya

El Fasher

Umm Keddada

Umm Saiyala

al Dueim

El Hasaheisa

Wad Med

El Gezira

al Ouaday

Ati

Oum Hadjer

Batha

CHAD

Batha

Zalingei ·3071

Jebel Marra

Menawashei

Dam Gamad

Wad Banda

El Obeid

Kirim ·640

Er Rahad

Tendelti

Bara

Umm Rûwaba

Kosti

Rabak

Sennar

Singa

Blue Nile

Guedi ·1506

Mangalmé

Mongo

Kass

Nyala

Ghubeish

al Nahûd

Abu Zabad

al Udaiya

Dilling

Renk

Ed Damazin

Lake Roseires

1613·

Bitkine

Abou Deïa

Azum

'Idd al Ghanam

Gandi

al Da'ain

al Fûla

Babanusa

al Muglad

Kadugli

Nuba Mountains ·1325

·842

Turum ·1122

Mélfi

Zakouma

Am Timan

Azoum

Rahad al Berdi

Ibra

S U D A N

Talodi

Kurmuk

Erguig

Kendégué

Haraze

Salamat

Birao

Oulou

Dango ·790

Bahr al Arab

Sumaih

·1093

Tungaru

Paloich

Bambesi ·2185

10°N

Chari

S

Kéita ou Doka

Ouandja

Tiroungoulou

Yata

d a

n

Bentiu

Tonga

Malakal

Koumra

Sarh

Aouk

Tété

Toussoro ·1330

Bora

Raga

Aweil

Bahr al Ghazel

Sobat

Nasir

Maro

Ouham

Bangoran

Ndélé

Massif des Bongos

·850

Ouadda

·1050

Sopo

Pongo

Wau

Toni

Rumbek

White Nile

Kongor

Akobo

Dem

Gambela

Kabo

Batangafo

Ouandago

Gribingui

Kaga Bandoro

Mbrès

Bamingui

Kotto

Ndji

Haute Kotto

Busseri

Maridi

Angeleri ·838

Mvolo

Bor

Pibor Post

Kenamu Swamp

Bossangoa

Bouca

Dékoa

Bria

Boungou

Yalinga

Vovodo

Ouara

Tambura

Suê

Ibba

Mundri

Medi

Mongalla

CENTRAL AFRICAN

Sibut

Bambari

Ouaka

Kotto

Mbari

Chinko

Obo

Li Yuba

Juba

Bogangolo

REPUBLIC

Tomi

Dembia

Rafaï

Zémio

Garmabe

Ngangala

·1940

Kapoeta

Lok

5°N

Damara

Bossembélé

Oubangui

Kouango

Alindao

M'bomou

Doruma

Yambio ·1067

Maridi

·1065

Yei

Lalyo

Torit

Kinyeti ·3187

Bangui

Bimbo

Zongo

Gbadolite

Mobaye

Mobayi-Mbongo

Kongbo

Gambo

Bangassou

Matundu

Monga

Bili

Bili

Api

Ango

Ese

Niangara

Dungu

Aba

Faradje

Kajo-Kaji

Nimule

Kaabong ·2381

Loyoro

Mbaïki

Zinga

Lobaye

Boyabo

Libenge

Lua Dekere

Bosobolo

Yakoma

Uele

Bondo

Api

Bambili

Baranga

Rungu

Watsa

Laropi

Arua ·1310

Atiak

Kitgum

Pajule

Moro

CONGO

Enyélé

Gribingui

Kungu

Businga

Gemena

Dua

Abumonzali

Angu

Likati

Titule

Bambesa

Poko

Isiro

Gombari

Aru

Gulu

Anaka

Lira

Soroti

Dongou

Mobeka

Budjala

Mongala

Lisala

Aketi

Tele

Buta

Medje

Nepoko

Wamba

Watsa

Mahagi ·2448

Fataki

Lake Albert

Masindi

Lake Kyoga

Mbale

Impfondo

Makanza

Modjamboli

Ibembo

Bumba

Izimbiri

Dulia

Zambeke

Kole

Ituri

Bomili

Nia Nia

Mambasa

Bunia

Komanda

Hoima

Nakasongola

Kamuli

Kaliro

Iganga

Tororo

U G A N D A

Giri

Z A I R E

Busu-Djanoa

Lopori

Bongandanga

Basoko

Aruwimi

Yambuya

Lindi

Bengamisa

Batama

Bafwabalinga

Hoyo ·1450

Ntoroko

Fort Portal

Kyanjojo

Mubende

Kampala

Jinja

Kaka

Zaïre (Congo)

Basankusu

Waka

Yahuma

Yekana

Isangi

Yangambi

Kisangani

Madula

Boyoma Falls

Opienge

Butembo

Stanley ·5109

Kasese

Lake Edward

·2197

Masaka

Entebbe

Sese Islands

Kisun

Mbandaka

Ruki

Ingende

Busira

Lulonga

Bolomba

Befale

Maringa

Lingomo

Djolu

Samba

Befori

Yatolema

Pene-Tungu

Ubundu

Lubero

Ruwenzori Mountains

Beni

Lake

Victoria

0°

Likouala-aux-Herbes

Oubangui

Kalamba

Bikoro

Lake Tumba

Boende

Watsi

Wema

Ekoli

Opala

Zaïre

Kirundu

·956

Lubutu

·2341

Mfumbiro Mountains

Ishasha River

Kigati

Bushenyi

Mbarara

Kikagati

Bukoba

Lake Victoria

Ukerewe Island

Tarime

Yandja

Bolia

Inongo

Kiri

Lake Mai-Ndombe

Watsi-Kengo

Busanga

Ikela

Yalifafu

Yolombo

Likoto

Monkoto

Punia

Miumba Mountains

Kabunga

Walikale

Masisi

Karisimbi ·4507

Giseni

Lake Kivu

Kayonza

Kigali

RWANDA

Rutshuru

Kabale

Ruhengeri

Kyaka

Bunda

Musoma

Banagi

T A N Z A N I A

Nansio

Ntadembele

20°E

Kavumu

Kabunga

25°E

30°E

This map shows 1/60 of the earth's surface.

a b c d e f g h i j k l m

Derudeb
2589 Mersa Teklay
40°E 45°E 50°E
Mitatib Keren Nakfa Thamud Wadi al Jiz Al Ghaydah
738 Barka Mersa Teklay *Sa'dah Makrah Qamar
Kasala Akordat Asmara 2617 Mitsiwa Jizan Midi Huth al Hazm Haynan Sayun Wadi Masilah Bay Ras
Showak 2374 Dahlak Islands Hajjah *al Mahdad Haynan Sayun Fartak
Adi Quala Adi Keyih Farasan Islands Az Zaydiyah San'a Sirwa al Shihr Sayhut
Humera Aksum Adwa Adigrat Hodeida Bait al Faqih Dhamar al Baida al Rawda Riyan al Mukalla 15°N
Mesfinto Adi Arkay Asimba 3248 Zabad Ibb Manar 3350 al Baida 2185 al Mukalla
Metema Mekele Kwiha Red Hays Ta'izz Lawdar Ahwar
Gonder Ras Dashen 4550 Sea Az Zuqar al Mukha Turbah Lahej Ghadir Aden
Gorgora 2223 Maychew Danakil Ramlu 2130 Aseb 850 Gulf of Aden Abd al Kuri
Bahir Dar Lake Tana Addis Zemen Debre Tabor Kobbo Asb Musa Ali 2063 Bab al Mandab Cape Guardafui
Beleya 3131 Danglia Guna 4135 Weldiya DJIBOUTI Randa 1783 Tadjourah Hodda 1400 Bereda
Beles Bati Kembolcha Tendaho Asayta Arta Djibouti El Gal
Debre Markos Karakore Dese Abuye Meda 4305 Gewane Ali-Sabieh Dikhil Lake Abbe Mait al Mado 1826 Las Koreh Bosaso 2200
ETHIOPIA Dejen Fiche Debre Birhan 1789 Berbera Erigavo Las Davé Ras Hafun
Highlands Amara 3146 3292 Addis Ababa 2408 Awash Asbe Tafari Harer 1856 Babile Jijiga Buramo Hargeisa Burao Arde 1858 Carcar Mountains Wadi Giahel
Nekempt Hagere Hiywot Debre Zeit Nazret Gugu 3060 Ahmar Mountains 2064 Kirit El Dab Bur Anod 1097 Gardo Bender Beila 10°N
Arjo Ghion 3719 Mieso Sheno Fik Las Anod Rabableh Sinugif Garoe Eil
Bedele Welkite Lake Ziway Asela Degeh Bur Warder Baduen El Hamurre
Agaro Jima Lake Abiyata Lake Langano Kaka 4190 Shibeli Hamarro Hadad Galcaio Berdale
Maiguido 2386 Lake Shala Shashemene 2119 Awetu Fafen Kebri Dehar Ghelinsor Mirsale
Bonga Shishinda Awasa Goba Imi Godinlave Dusa Mareb
Mizan Teferi Sodo Dila Wendo Mendebo Mountains Megalo El Kere Gode Shilabo Kelafo Sinadogo Obbia
Maji Arba Minch Lake Abaya Lake Chamo Kibre Mengist Hargele Mustahil SOMALIA
Jinka Gidole 1441 Negele Filtu Lema Shilindi Yet Ferfer Obbia
Key Afer Konso Yabelo Dawa Bokol Mayo Belet Huen El Bur 5°N
Kelem Chew Bahir Lake Chelago Dolo Hoddur Tigieglo Maas
Banya Fort Mega Ramu Mandera Lugh Ganana Calie Corar 566 El Dere
Lake Turkana Moyale 1280 Bulo Burti
North Horr Sololo Baidoba 600 Mahaddei Uen
Chalbi Desert Buna El Wak El Uach Bur Acaba Uanle Uen Giohar Adale INDIAN
Loiyangalani Dinsor Afgoi
Lokichar Marsabit Tarbaj Bardera Mogadishu OCEAN
Nyiru 2752 South Horr Wajir Juba Saco Uen Coriolei Merca
KENYA Baragoi Laisamis Habaswein Dugiuma Shibeli Brava
Kapedo 2375 Mado Gashi
Maralal Kisima Archer's Post Garba Tula Belesc Cogani Afmadu Gelib
Baringo Lodge Nyahururu 2360 Isiolo Meru Liboi Hagadera Giamama Equator 0°
Gilgil Nanyuki Kenya 5200 Saka Garissa Araara
Naivasha 3994 Embu Tana Kisimaio
Narok Kijabe Thika Mwingi Kitui
Nairobi Machakos Mutomo
Magadi Kajiado Mokowe Patta Island
40°E 45°E 50°E

n o p q r s t u v w x y z

45

0 100 200 300 miles | 0 100 200 300 400 500 Km
Average linear scale

a b c d e f g h i j k l m

SÃO TOMÉ AND PRINCIPE
São Tomé
Equator

GABON

CONGO

ZAÏRE

ANGOLA

ATLANTIC

OCEAN

NAMIBIA

BOTSWANA

CABINDA (Angola)

Cocobeach
Mitzic
Mékambo
Lulonga
Waka
Yekana
Isang
Libreville
Kougouleu
Lalara
Pikunda
Bolomba
Lingomo
Djolu
Yatole
Ndjolé
Booué
Makoua
Owando
Ngende
Mbandaka
Ruki
Busira
Samba
Maringa
Befori
Ekol
Port-Gentil
Lambaréné
Okondja
Bonda (Lastoursville)
Ewo
Boundji
Mossaka
Irebu
Kalamba
Boende
Watsi
Wema
Busanga
Ikela
Omboué
Mimongo
Moanda
Franceville
Okoyo
Gamboma
Bouanga
Lake Tumba
Bolia
Kiri
Monkoto
Yalifafu
Yolombo
Mouila
Boumango
Mayoko
Bambama
Nsah
Ngo
Inoni
Yandja
Inongo
Lake Mai-Ndombe
Lomela
Ndendé
Nioki
Kutu
Tchibanga
Mossendjo
Mapati
Bandundu
Lukenie
Dekese
Lodja
Mayumba
Kibangou
Sibiti
Oshwe
Bagata
Kasai
Bena Dibele
Sounda
Madingou
Brazzaville
Kinkala
Masia-Mbio
Cuango
Fatunda
Kapia
Ilebo
Bena-Tshadi
Lu
Loubomo
Boko
Kinshasa
Mayamba
Kenge
Bulungu
Mweka
Kakenge
Lusan
Bas-Kouilou
Luozi
Zaïre
Madimba
Masi-Manimba
Kikwit
Idiofa
Mpata
Luebo
Demba
Dimbelenge
Mbuji-M
Pointe-Noire
Tshela
Seke Banza
Inkisi-Kisantu
Banda
Kilembe
Kananga
Lândana
Lukula
Tsangila Falls
Mbanza-Ngungu
Ngidinga
Kimvula
Popokabaka
Feshi
Gungu
Tshikapa
Kazumba
Kamiji
Gandajika
Mwene
Lup
Cabinda
Boma
Matadi
Kimpese
Muanda
M'Pala
Maquela do Zombo
Kasongo-Lunda
Kahemba
Luachimo
Kaniama
Soyo
M'Banza-Congo
Quimbele
Forte Carumbo
Tombôco
Damba
Verissimo Sarmento
Kapanga
Bembe
Sanza Pombo
Lucapa
Mussera
Uige
Negage
Luremo
Caungula
Camaxilo
N'Zeto
Quitexe
Camabatela
Ambriz
Nambuangongo
Quibaxe
Samba Caju
Cuango
Luanda
Caxito
Lucala
Kalandula
Xá-Muteba
Saurimo
Sándoa
Tshimbalar
Catete
Muxima
N'Dalatando
Malange
Xinge
Muriege
Dondo
Cuanza
Mona-Quimbundo
Calulo
Nova Gaia
Cacolo
Luau
Dilolo
Kasa
Quitapa
Muconda
Matong
Porto Amboim
Quibala
Dala
Gabela
Buçaco
Luena
Cassai
Ikelenge
Mwinil
Sumbe
Waco-Kungo
Mussende
Moxico
Chicala
Cazombo
Andulo
Camacupa
Cuemba
Luena
Lobito
Alto Hama
Bailundo
Lucusse
Lumbala
Benguela
Balombo
Kuito
Cassamba
Luzi
Zambesi
Kabomp
Caala
Luvuei
Catengue
Ganda
Cachingues
Lutembo
Chitembo
Mumbué
Sessa
Lumbala N'Guimbo
Lukulu
Caconda
Menongue
Longa
Negola
Capelongo
Cuchi
Cacula
Gambos
Cuito Cuanavale
Chiume
Mongu
Lubango
Cassinga
Chibia
Cuvelai
Caiundo
Mavinga
Chianje
Mulundo
Rivungo
Senanga
Quiteve
Cubango
Luengué
Chibaranda
Oncócua
Savate
Rito
Luiana
Roçadas
Naulila
Obombo
Oshakati
Ondangwa
Cuangar
Mucusso
Kongola
Capivi Strip
N'Giva
Rundu
Shakamu
Shakawe
Sepoa
Opuwa
Cape Frio
Purros
Etosha Pan
Namutoni
Keibeb
Numkaub

This map shows 1/60 of the earth's surface.

n o p q r s t u v w x y z

a   b   c   d   e   f   g   h   i   j   k   l   m

UGANDA
KENYA
SOMALIA
RWANDA
BURUNDI
TANZANIA
MALAWI
MOZAMBIQUE
ZIMBABWE
A M B I A
E

Kisangani · Madula · Opienge · Beni · 5109 · Fort Portal · Kyanjojo · Kayunga · Kaliro · Iganga · Tororo · Eldoret · Loruk · Archer's Post · Mado Gashi · Afmadu

30°E · Kasese · Mubende · Jinja · Kakamega · Baringo Lodge · Isiolo · Garba Tula · Belesc Cogani

Pene-Tungu · Butembo · Kasindi · Kampala · Entebbe · Kisumu · Kapsabet · Nyahururu · Meru · Hagadera · Liboi

Lindi · Lubero · Lake George 2197 · Bushenyi · Masaka · Kericho · Nakuru · Gilgil · Mt. Kenya 5200 · Embu · Saka · Equator 0°

Kirundu · Lubutu · ·956 · Lake Edward 2341 · Ishasha River · Mbarara · Kisii · ·3100 · Naivasha · Garissa · Kisimaio

Maiko · Masisi · Karisimbi 4507 · Goma · Gisenyi · Kikagati · Bukoba · Lake Victoria · Kilkoris · 2775 · Kijabe · Nairobi 1662 · Machakos · Kolbio

Lubutu · Lowa · Walikale · Kabale · Ruhengeri · Kyaka · Sese Islands · Narok · Thika · Mwingi · Hola

Miitumba Mountains · Rutshuru · Kipuye · Kigali · Gitarama · Kayonza · Ukerewe Islands · Tarime · Meru · Kitui · Mutomo · Mokowe · Patta Island

·1047 · Kabunga · 3044 · Kavumu · Bukavu · RWANDA · Cibitoke · Kayanza · Nansio · Musoma · Mera · Magadi · Kajiado · Mombasa

Ulindi · Kalima · Mwenga · BURUNDI · Bujumbura · Kibondo · 2670 · Mwanza · Geita · Nyakanazi · Ngudu · Shinyanga · Nyiri Desert · Namanga · Kilimanjaro 5895 Meru 4555 Moshi · Same · Manyami · Malindi

Punia · Kingombe · Kitutù · Kalole · ·2073 · Serengeti Plain · Oldeani · ·3188 · Arusha · Oloitokitok · Makuyuni · Mwatate · Kilifi

Pangi · ·1019 · Kasongo · Kasulu · Kigoma · Uvinza · Kahama · Nzega · Ibotogero · Ndareda 3420 · Babati · Katesh · ·2124 · Mkomazi · Kwale

Kasambule · Kampene · Kalima · Kipaka · Lake Kivu · 2373 · Malagarasi · Tabora · Igombe · Mbulu · Masai Steppe · Korogwe · Mombasa

Kibombo · Kwanga · Samba · Tshofa · Lubao · ·1052 · Kalemie · Lake Tanganyika · Mpanda · Sikonge · Manyoni · Singida · Kondoa Irangi · ·2193 · Handeni · Segera · Tanga · Pemba Island · 5°S

Kabalo · Lukuga · Nyunzu · Niemba · Ugalla · Itigi · Manyoni · Gairo · Mvomero · Zanzibar · **INDIAN**

Katompi · Zaire · Sange · Moba · Luvua · Namanyere · Lake Rukwa · Rungwa · Kisigu · Dodoma · Mpwapwa · Msata · Bagamoyo · Chalinze · Zanzibar Island

Kaloko · Manono · Kiambi · Kapona · ·2460 · Sumbawanga · 2418 · Kipembawe · Iringa · ·2287 · Kilosa · Morogoro · Dar-es-Salaam · Kisarawe

Mulongo · Malemba Nkulu · Marungu Mountains · Pweto · Sumbu · Kasanga · Makongolosi · ·2072 Sao Hill · ·2576 · Ifakara · ·2646 · Mikumi · Mbuyuni · Rufiji · Mafia Island

Kikondja · ·1133 · Lake Upemba · Mitwaba · Chiengi · Chunya · Chimala · Mbeya · Uyole · Makambako · Mahenge · Kilindoni

Kamina · Luena · Kabondo Dianda · Mukana · Lake Mweru · Mpulungu · Mbala · Nakonde · Itungi · 2961 Rungwe · Njombe · Luhombero · Nangurukuru · Mohoro · **OCEAN** 46

Busanga · Bunkeya · Kasenga · Nchelenge · Mporokoso · Chambeshi · Tunduma · Karonga · Livingstone Mountains · Lukumburu · 10°S

Luambo · Kasembe · Kawambwa · Kapatu · Kasama · Isoka · Mbesuma · Chitumba · Gumbiro · Songea · Nachingwea · Masasi · Mtwara · Lindi

Kambove · Likasi · Minga · Mansa · Luwingu · Chinsali · Luangwa · 2608 · Livingstonia · Tunduru · Nangomba · Newala · Diaca · Cape Delgado

Lubumbashi · Kipushi · Chembe · Mpika · Chama · Rumphi · Lake Malawi · Chamba · Masuguru · Mueda · Mocimboa da Praia

Kitwe · Mokambo · Kapalala · Mukuku · Chilonga · Chikwa · Mzuzu · Nkhata Bay · Mzimba · Maniamba · Litunde · Marrupa · Nantulo · Macomia

Chillabombwe · Chingola · Ndola 1261 · Chibembe · Lundazi · Jenda · Dwangwa · ·1836 · Lichinga · Malanga · Nungo · Montepuez · Metoro · Pemba

Luanshya · Serenje · Kanona · Chifwefwe · Luangwa · Nkhotakota · Kasungu · Malanga · Messalo · Maúa · Namapa · Nacaroa

Kapiri Mposhi · Petauke · Katete · Chipata · Mchinji · Salima · Massangulo · Cuamba · Lúrio · Ribaué · Nacala

Kabwe · Nyimba · Kachalola · Bene · Chitunde · Lilongwe · Dedza · Mangochi · Mandimba · Mutuali · Namialo · L'umbo · Monapo · 15°S

Landless Corner · Mumbwa · Rufunsa · Fingoè · Songo · Zomba · Balaka · Lake Chilwa · Gurue · ·2419 · ·200 · Nampula · Moçambique

Lusaka 1279 · Zumbo · Cabora Bassa Reservoir · Chiúta · Blantyre · Limbe 3000 · Mulanje · Alto Molócuè · Nametil · Liupo

Namwala · Mazabuka · Zambezi · Kafue · ·560 · Tete · ·2054 · Nsanje · Mocuba · Mucubela · Moma · Angoche

Kalomo · Choma · Kariba Reservoir · Kariba · Mkumbura · Mount Darwin · Changara · Tambara · Sena · Namacurra · Quelimane

Livingstone · Victoria Falls · Binga · Mhangura · Mvurwi · Nyamapanda · Guro · Caia · Mopeia · Chinde

Hwange · Gwai River · Dete · Gokwe · Kadoma · Mutoko · **ZIMBABWE** · Harare 1472 · Chegutu · Rusape · Inyanga · ·1868 · Gorongosa · Inhaminga · ·105 · 40°E

30°E · 35°E

0 · 100 · 200 · 300 miles · Average linear scale · 0 · 100 · 200 · 300 · 400 · 500 Km

25°E · Kaloko · 30°E · Mpanda · 35°E · Bagamoyo · 40°E
Kaniama · Kabongo · Sange · Moba · Kitunda · Kilosa · Chalinze · Dar-es-Salaam
Manono · Kiambi · Kapona · Rungwa · Mbuyuni · Mikumi · 2646 · Morogoro · Kisarawe
·1060 · Mulongo · 2460 · Namanyere · Rungwa · 2287 · Iringa · Kibiti
Pidi · Kikondja · Malemba Nkulu · Kapona · Lake · Sumbawanga · Kipembawe · 2576 · Ifakara · Mafia Island
Kikondja · Marungu Mountains · 2418 · Makongolosi · Chunya · Sao Hill · Mahenge · Kilindoni
ZAÏRE · Mitwaba · Pweto · Sumbu · Kasanga · Chimala · 2072 · Makambako · Mohoro
Kamina · 1139 · Lake Mweru · Kasanga · Mbeya · Uvole · Luhombero · Nangurukuru
Kabondo Dianda · Chiengi · Mpulungu · Mbala · 2959 · Njombe
Mukana · Nchelenge · Mporokoso · Nakonde · Tunduma · Itungi · TANZANIA
Busanga · Kawambwa · Kasama · Isoka · Karonga · Lukumburu · Lindi
10°S · Kasembe · Kapatu · Mbesuma · Chilumba · Gumbiro · Mingoyo · Mtwara
Kambove · Kasenga · Mununga · Luwingu · Chinsali · 2608 · Livingstonia · Nachingwea
Kolwezi · Likasi · Minga · Mansa · 1475 · Rumphi · Songea · Nangomba · Newala · Masasi
Mwinilunga · Chisasa · Solwezi · Lake Bangweulu · Samfya · Chisoso · Chikwa · Mzuzu · Tunduru · Masuguru · Diaca · Mocimboa da
Kipushi · Lubumbashi · Chembe · Mpika · Chama · Nkhata Bay · Chamba · Ruvuma · Mueda
Chililabombwe · Mokambo · Mukuku · Chilonga · Mzimba · Lake Malawi · Macomia
Chingola · Mufulira · Kapalala · Chibembe · Jenda · Maniamba · Nantulo
Kitwe · ·1350 · Ndola · Lundazi · Dwangwa · 1836 · Litunde · Marrupa · Montepuez · Metoro
Luanshya · ·1261 · Kanona · Nkhotakota · Lichinga · Malanga · Nungo · Pemba
ZAMBIA · Chifwefwe · Serenje · Kasungu · Massangulo · Maúa · Namapa
Kapiri Mposhi · Chipata · Mchinji · Salima · Lúrio · Nacaroa · Nacala
Kabwe · Petauke · Katete · Lilongwe · Mandimba · Cuamba · Ribauè · Namialo · Moçamb
Kaoma · Lubungu · Nyimba · Dedza · Mangochi · Mutuali · Monapo
15°S · Mumbwa · Landless Corner · Kachalola · Chitunde · MALAWI · Balaka · Gurué · Nampula
Namwala · Rufunsa · Bene · 2035 · Zomba · Molócuè · Nametil · Liupo
1220 · Lusaka · 1279 · Zumbo · Cabora-Bassa Reservoir · Chiúta · Blantyre · 200 · Angoche
Mazabuka · Zambezi · Songo · Tete · Limbe · 3000 · Errego · 760
Choma · Kariba Reservoir · Mkumbura · 560 · Mulanje · 2054 · Moma
45 · Kalomo · Kariba · 1204 · Karoi · Mount Darwin · Nsanje · Mocuba · Mucubela
Sesheke · Livingstone · Binga · Mhangura · Nyamapanda · Changara · Tambara · Pebane
Katima Mulilo · Victoria Falls · Mvurwi · Bindura · Caia · Quelimane
Kazungula · Hwange · Nembudziya · 1472 · Harare · Mutoko · Guro · Vila de Sena · Namacurra
1108 · Dete · Gwai River · Chegutu · 2592 · Catandica · Mopeia
Pandamatenga · Kenmaur · Kadoma · Inyanga · 1862 · Gorongosa · 105 · Chinde
ZIMBABWE · Kwe Kwe · Rusape · Chimoio · Dondo
Basotho · 1000 · Nkayi · 1447 · Chivhu · Mutare · Beira
Kanyu · Nata · Tsholotsho · Gweru · Chatsworth · Dorowa · Chimanimani · 2436
Tsoe · Mosetse · 1028 · Bulawayo · Masvingo · Nyanyadzi · Nova Golegã · Sofala Bay
Makgadikgadi Pans · 1345 · Zvishavane · Chipinge · Espungabera
Xhumo · 974 · Letlhakane · Plumtree · Zimbabwe · Rupisi · 502 · Bassas da India (France)
20°S · Tlalamabele · Antelope Mine · Gwanda · Chiredzi · Inhassoro
BOTSWANA · Francistown · Mazunga · Rutenga · Macane · Jofane · Bazaruto
Metsiamonong · Serule · 1000 · Bubye · Tswiza · 500 · Massangena · Pambarra
Serowe · Selebi-Phikwe · Tuli · Chicualacuala · 167 · Mabote · Europe Island (France)
Kikao · Shoshong · Palapye · Beitbridge · Machaila · Mapinhane
Soje · Mahalapye · Pontdrift · Messina · Pafuri · 438 · Mapai · Chigubo · Funhalouro
Marken · Louis Trichardt · Shingwedzi · 132 · Massinga
Mosomane · Ellisras · Pietersburg · Tzaneen · Drakensberg · Inhambane
Letlhakeng · Thabazimbi · 2128 · Phalaborwa · Massingir · Panda
Molepolole · Jwaneng · 2085 · Nylstroom · 1856 · Satara · 169 · Quissico
Gaborone · Dwarsberg · Warmbad · Steelpoort · Guijá · Massinga
25°S · Kanye · Lydenburg · Sabie · Skukuza · Manjacaze · Xai-Xai
Lobatse · Rustenburg · Groblersdal · Witrivier · Magude · Macia
Zeerust · 1333 · Pretoria · Nelspruit · 515 · Maputo
Mmabatho · Roodepoort · Witbank · Waterval Boven · Namaacha
SOUTH AFRICA · Middelburg · Komatipoort · Mbabane · Bela Vista
Lichtenburg · Benoni · Carolina · Manzini · Catuane
Johannesburg · Springs · Bethal · SWAZI-LAND
1253 · Germiston · Ermelo · 1440 · Standerton
Delareyville · Potchefstroom · Vereeniging
25°E · Klerksdorp · 30°E · 35°E · 40°E

MOZAMBIQUE

Straits of

This map shows 1/60 of the earth's surface.

a b c d e f g h i j k l m

45°E 50°E 55°E 60°E

10°S

INDIAN OCEAN

Aldabra Island

Moroni
COMOROS

Comoros
Moheli *Anjouan*
Islands

○ Antsiranana

○Dzaoudzi
Mayotte (France)

Ambilobe○

Nosy-Bé
Hell-Ville○

○ Iharaña

Tsaratanana
2876
Mountains

○ Sambava

Antsohihy○

○ Andapa

○ Antalaha

Befandriana Av.○ ○ Ambohitralanana
1218
Maroantsetra○ Mahalevona○

Mahajanga○ Port-Bergé-
Vaovao○
Mandritsara○
Marovoay○ Mampikony○

○ Mananara

1301

Miarinarivo○

Nosy Boraha

1325

Maevatanana○

Andriamena○

M A D A G A S C A R
·1545

Morafenobe○

Vohidiala○
Toamasina○

Antsalova○

Ankazobe○

Tsiroanomandidy○ **Antananarivo**
1381

2643·

Mandoto○

Mahanoro○

Betafo○ Antsirabe○
Tsimafana○

Tsiribihina *2140·* Fandriana○

Morondava○
Mahabo○

Ambositra○

Mandabe○

Mananjary○

Fianarantsoa○
Irondro○

Morombe○

Ambalavao○
Manakara○

2658·

Ankazoabo○
·1348 Ihosy○ Ivohibe○

Manombo○

○ Farafangana

Toliara○ Andranovory○

Betroka○ ○Vangaindrano
1824

Manaoara

○ Betioky

·1957

Ampanihy○
Antanimora○

○Taolañaro
Ambovombe○
Tsihombe○

Juan de Nova

Manambolo

Mahajanga (river labels)

Betsiboka

Mozambique

Mangoky

Tsiriihina

Isalo Mountains

MAURITIUS **Port Louis**

Saint-Denis
3069· *Réunion (France)*

Tropic of Capricorn

15°S

20°S

25°S

n o p q r s t u v w x y z

45°E 50°E 55°E 60°E

0   100   200   300
miles   Average linear scale   0   100   200   300   400   500
Km

a b c d e f g h i j k l m

10°E
15°E
20°E

Moçâmedes
Chibia
Cassinga
Chiume
Mong

Tômbua
(Porto Alexandre)
Chianje
Mulundo
Cuito Cuanavale

Cuvelai
Caiundo

Senan

OTambor
Quiteve
1265
ANGOLA
Savate
1190
Rito
Rivungo

Oncócua
Roçadas
Cubango
Luengué
1160
Chibaranda
Luiana

Iona
N'Giva
Xamavera
Mucusso

Foz do Cunene
Cunene
Naulila
Cuangar
Rundu
Okavango

Ruacana
Obombo
Ondangwa
Shakamku
Shakawe

Orupembe
Oshakati
Ovamboland
Sepopa

Cape Frio
Opuwa
1096
Gumare
Okava
Delta

1784
Etosha
Pan
Namutoni
Keibeb
Numkaub
950

OPurros
1093
Tsumeb
Tsumkwe
Mount Aha
1070
Tsau

Kowares
Okaukuejo

Terrace Bay
Kamanjab
Otavi
2149
Grootfontein
Dekar

869
Goreis
Outjo
Ghanzi

20°S
Khorixas
Otjiwarongo
Okakarara

1932
Kalkfeld
NAMIBIA
Hochfeld
Kalkfontein
BO

Brandberg
2579
Omaruru
2350
Steinhausen
1537
Buitepos
Takatshwaan

Uis Mine
Usakos
Okahandja
Gobabis
Kalaha

Cape Kruis
Anschluss
Windhoek
1654
Witvlei
Kule

Henties Bay
160
Dordabis
Ukwi
1000

Swakopmund
Leonardville
Kang

Walvis Bay
2334
Rehoboth
Derm
Tshane

Tropic of Capricorn
Abbabis
Kalkrand
Aranos

ATLANTIC
Sesriem
Stampriet
Mpaathutlwa
Pan
Makopo

Zaris
Maltahöhe
Marien tal
T

25°S
Naribis
Gochas
1046
Nossob
Tshabong

Asab
Asanib
Twee
Rivier
Koës

Helmeringhausen
1185
Aroab
Twee Rivieren
Molopo
Frylinc

Great Tiràz
1867
Bethanie
Keetmanshoop

Lüderitz
Aus
Narubis
Gr. Karasberge
2202
Gemsbok
1000

Goageb
Kurun
Sishen
1832
Danie

Pomona
Witpütz
1107
Karasburg
Upington

Grünau
Ariamsvlei
903
Keimoes
Postmasb

OCEAN
Orange
1341
Augrabies
Falls
Kakamas
Griekwa

Alexander Bay
Vioolsdrif
Onseepkans
Groblershoop

Port Nolloth
Steinkopf
Pofadder
Kenhardt

30°S
Nababeep
Springbok
Namies
Marydale

Garies
Platbakkies
Van Wyksvlei
Copperton

Loeriesfontein
Brandvlei
Vosburg
Bri

Bitterfontein
Nieuwoudtville
Carnarvon
Loxton

Vanrhynsdorp
Calvinia
Williston

Clanwilliam
Fraserburg
A

Slippers Bay
Citrusdal
Sutherland
Komsberg
1721

Vredenburg
1040
Prince Albert Road
Great Ka

Saldanha
Gr. Winterhoek
2078
Laingsburg
Little Swartberge
2325
Willow

Malmesbury
Wellington
Touws River
Oudtshoorn
Haarle

Cape Town
Strand
Worcester
Little Karoo
George
K

Cape of
Good Hope
Caledon
Swellendam
Mosselbaai

Cape Agulhas
Witsand
Stilbaai

Agulhas

35°S

This map shows 1/60 of the earth's surface.

n o p q r s t u v w x y z

a b c d e f g h i j k l m

45

25°E 30°E 35°E 40°E

Mumbwa Rufunsa Fingoé Chiúta Zomba Gurué Nampula Moçambique
Lusaka *1279 Zumbo Cabora Bassa - Reservoir Songo MALAWI Liupo
*1220 Namwala Lake Zambezi *560 Tete Blantyre Limbe Molócuè Nametil
Kafue Kafue Mazabuka Mkumbura *3000. Errego *200
Mulanje *760 Angoche
Kariba Mhangura Mount Changara Nsanje Mocuba Mucubela Moma
Kariba Karoi Darwin Tambará *2054.
Reservoir Nyamapanda Vila de Sena Namacurra
Kalomo Choma *1204 Mvurwi Guro Mopeia Quelimane
Sesheke Banket Bindura Mutoko Catandica Inhaminga
Katima Livingstone Binga Harare Chegutu *1472 Inyanga *2592 Gorongosa Chinde
Mululo Victoria Falls Gokwe Kadoma Rusape *1862 *105
Kazungula Hwange ZIMBABWE Chimoio Dondo
Kataba Dete Gwai River Kenmaur Kwe Kwe Chivhu Mutare Beira
*1108 Pandamatenga *1447 Dorowa Sofala
Gweru Chatsworth Nyanyadzi Chimanimani Bay
Nata *1000 Tsholotsho Masvingo Chipinge Nova
Tsoe Basotho Bulawayo *1343 Zvishavane Rupisi Golegã 20°S
Plumtree Espungabera
Tshumo Mosetse *1028 Gwanda Mwenezi *502
*974 Letlhakane Tlamabele Antelope Mine Rutenga Chiredzi Macane Save
Francistown *500 Jofane Inhassoro Bassas
Mazunga Massangena da India
Serule Bubye Mabote Pambarra Bazaruto (France)
Kalamare Selebi- Tuli Tswiza *167
Phikwe Beitbridge Chicualacuala Machaila Mapinhane Europe Island
Metsiamonong Serowe *1000 Pontdrif Messina Machaila (France)
Palapye Pafuri *438 Mapai Chigubo
Kikao Kalamare Mahalapye Louis Shingwedzi Funhalouro Massinga
Soje Trichardt *132.
Ilwe Mosomane Ellisras Marken Phalaborwa Massingir Panda Inhambane
Letlhakeng Pietersburg Tzaneen *169
Molepolole *2128. Satara Guijá
Vaalwater Potgietersrus *1856 Manjacaze
Gaborone *2085 Nylstroom Steelpoort Magude Quissico 25°S
Kanye Thabazimbi Warmbad Sabie Skukuza
Lobatse *1479 Dwarsberg Groblersdal Lydenburg Witrivier Macia
Zeerust Nelspruit *515 Xai-Xai
Molopo Rustenburg Pretoria *1333 Middelburg Waterval Komatipoort
Mmabatho Roodepoort Benoni Boven Maputo 46
Lichtenburg Johannesburg Witbank Carolina Mbabane Namaacha
kweng Germiston Ermelo Manzini Bela Vista
Delareyville Potchefstroom *1661. Bethal SWAZI Catuane
Vereeniging Piet Retief LAND Lavumisa
ryburg Klerksdorp *1440 Standerton Pongola
Parys Vaal Frankfort Volksrust *2277 Mkuze
Wolmaransstad Vaal Reservoir Utrecht Lake
vilo Heilbron *1532 St. Lucia
Schweizer- Bloemhof Kroonstad Reitz Vryheid Mtubatuba
Reneke Reservoir Newcastle Ulundi
Christiana Bethlehem Dundee INDIAN
rrenton Bultfontein Winburg Harrismith Eshowe
Barkly West Senekal Ladysmith Richards Bay
Kimberley Ficksburg Estcourt Tugela Greytown
Clocolan *3285 Pietermaritzburg
TH *1426 Maseru *3482 Himeville
Bloemfontein *3096 Durban 30°S
town Luckhoff Mafeteng LESOTHO Ixopo
Fauresmith Wepener *1000
Trompsburg Smithfield Zastron Moyeni Kokstad Umzinto
P.K. le Mount Harding
Roux Colesberg Aliwal North Fletcher Port Shepstone
Reservoir Hanover Burgersdorp Lady Grey Maclear Mount Frere Port Edward
*2052 Barkly East
ddelburg Steynsburg Elliot *1677
ICA Lady Frere Umtata Port St. Johns
Graaff- Queenstown Idutywa Coffee Bay
Reinet Cradock Stutterheim
Graaff- King William's Town
Somerset Fort *500 East London
East Beaufort Grahamstown
Kirkwood Bell
ytlerville Port Alfred
Uitenhage Port Elizabeth
nsdorp Jeffreys Bay OCEAN 35°S

Mozambique Channel

INDIAN

OCEAN

ZAMBIA BOTSWANA SOUTH AFRICA MOZAMBIQUE

n o p q r s t u v w x y z

25°E 30°E 35°E 40°E

0 100 200 300 miles 0 100 200 300 400 500
Average linear scale Km

a b c d e f g h i j k l m

70°E 75°E 80°E 85°E 90°E 95°E 100°E

I C   O C E A N

85°N

S e v e r n a y a   Z e m l y a

Ushakova
Schmidta
Komsomolets
Pioner
Cape Berga
80°N
262 Oktyabr'skoy Revolyutsii 800
Cape Mednyy
Shokal'skogo Str.
Bolshevik

Vize

West Siberian Sea

Isačenko

Nordenshel'da
Russkiy
Cape Oskara

Mys Zelaniya

Troynoy

Arkticheskogo
Instituta

Mikhaylova

Taimyr Arch.
Taimyr
Niz Taimyra
75°N
512

T a i m y r   P e n i n s u l a

171

Pyasina Bay

B y r r a n g a   M o u n t a i n s

Belyy

Šokalsky

Dikson
Makarova
279
Pjasina
223
Tareya
Pura
Verkh. Taimyra
Lake
Taimyr

Drovyanaya
47
Sibirjakov
Oleni
Zyryanka
415
Gol'chikha
Oshmarino
Agapa
Ust'-Avam
Dudypta
Payturma Boganida
Isayevskiy
Lake
Labaz
Novay

Tambey
Taran
Gyda Bay
Yuribey
Gyda
Yakovlevka
Yangoda
Kresty
Volochanka
Kargo
Kheta
Kheta
Pol'kyko

Y a m a l
75
Lake
Neyto
Gyda Peninsula
Tanama
Chernaya
Dolgany
Kochikha
Boyarka
70°N

P e n i n s u l a
Napalkovo
160
Karaul
Khokiley
Ust'-Port
Dudinka
Lake
Pjasina
Lake Lama 1612
P u t o r a n a
Ayan 1403
Malneca

sale
66
Yaptiksale
Antipayuta
Taz Bay
202
Noril'sk
766
1274
M o u n t a i n s
2030 Kamen
Changada

Yarongo
82
Lake
Yarroto
Yamburg
Massoyakha
Potapovo
Ambar
Lake Keta
Lake
Anama
Chirinda

Novyy Port
Yepoko
Nakhodka
Khantayka
Lake
Khantayskoye
Kureyka
Kotui

Yada
Tazovskiy
Taz
Khantayskoye
Reservoir
Kotuikan

Gornyy Kazymsk
Shuga
Nyda
Nyamboyoto
Sidorovoko
Yermakovo
Igarka
65
814
Agata
Lake
Vivi
Koskhun

Polui
Pangody
Pur
Yanov Stan
Karasino
Ust'-Kureyka
Severnaja
Tembenchi

Staryy Nadym
Urengoy
Taz
Krasnosel'kup
Turukhan
Farkovo
Turukhansk
Tutonchany
Vivi
Tembenchi
65°N

112
Nadym
168
Vyngapur
Alvasabdapur
Chasel'ka
Tolke
42
Tolka
22
Kostino
T u n g u s k o y e
Bugarikta
698
Niznaja Tunguska
Tutonchany
Chiskovo
Uchami
Vivi
Tura
619

Kazymskaya
Kazym
Numto
Khalesavoy
Kikiakki
Ratta
Noginskiy
M o u n t a i n s
552
Uchami
Nidym

N
USvatly FS.SR.
Noyabr'sk
Nizhneimbatskoye
Bakhta
970

Nazym
Ljamin
Pokacheva
Matyl'ka
Verkhneimbatskoye
Kuzmov'ka

U   N   I   O   N
Yermakovo
Agan
Kolik'yegan
Yeloguy
Kellog
Bakhta
Poligus
Baykit
Cunja
Korda
Mutoray

Kedrovyy
Pim
Ob'
77
Sabun
Korliki
Yeloguy
Sumarokovo
Podkamennaya Tunguska
Podkamennaya Tunguska

Khanty-Mansiysk
Surgut
Ust'Kolik'yegan
Vach
55
Lar'yak
Osinovo
Velmo1-oye
Vayvida
Ust'Kamo

Irtysh
Nizhnevartovsk
Strezhevoy
Sym
Yartsevo
Polkan 951
Teya
Taimba

Aleksandrovskoye
Vanzhil'kynak
Sym
Novoyerudinskiy
695
Kamo
60°N

99
Kintus
Nazina
Negotka
Tym
Kadzhi
S I B E R I A
Nazimovo
Yarkino
Panovo

Demyanskoye
S
Katyl'ga
B
Vasjugan
Ust'Tym
E
Kargasok
R
Lugovatka
Ust'Ozernoye
Ket
Ust'Pit
Bryanka
Kamanka
Bedopa
Kova

Cherpiya
Demyanka
Onegva Yar
Staritsa
Parabel
Alipxa
Belyy Yar
Vorozheyka
Lesosibirsk
Strelka
Rodina
Angara
Boguchany
636

kalovo
Gerasmikova
Kolpashevo
Baturino
Yeniseysk
Galapino
Chuna
Karamysheva

Tobol'sk
Bystryy
Mogochin
Parbig
Komsomol'sk
211
Altat
Predivinsk
Asansk
Shelayevo
Vydrino

S . S . R .)
Tevriz
142
L'vovka
Bakchar
Moryakovskiy
Zaton
Tegul'det
Birilyussy
Meletsk
698
Aban
530
Nevanka
Bratsk

Tara
Tara
Biaza
258
Tomsk
Asino
Achinsk
Shivera
Kan
Kansk
Chunskiyo
Tayshet

Golyshmanovo
122
Panovo
124
Bol'sherech'ye
166
Pikhtovka
Ob'
Mariinsk
Bogotol
Nazarovo
Pamyat
Krasnoyarsk
818
Borodino
Uyar
100°E

Ishim
Nazyvayevsk
Tyukalinsk
Chumakovo
Pokrovka
Yurga
Anzhero-
Sudzhensk
95°E

n o p q r s t u v w x y z

0 100 200 300 miles   Average linear scale   0 100 200 300 400 500 Km

105°E 110°E 115°E 120°E 125°E 130°E

Byrranga Mountains *Laptev Sea*

75°N

Vezdekhodnaya
Lake Taimyr
Bol. Balakhnya
Novoryonye Korennoye Nordvik
Sagyr Khatanga Novyy Begichev
Novay Lukunskiy Kozhevnikovo Cape Nordvik Dunay
Bychez Popigay Khorgo Stannakh- Turkannakh Sagastyr
Khatanga Star. Kayakhnyy Fomich Suolama Uryung- Uele Khocho Ary Antipinskiy
Kotuykan Popigay Khaya Ust'- Trofimovsk
Saskylakh Olenëk 211 Taymylyr Orto-Aya
536 Anabar •268 Ot-Siyen Pur Sklad Tit-Ary
Popigay Amakinskiy •128 405 Chekurovka •921
Bor-Yuryakh Khasalakh Kyusyur Tiksi
Dzhelinde Kuoyka Govorovo Buor-
70°N Tas-Tum
•98

Central
Ulgumun Siktyakh Kel' Sakhandzha
Mongolo Olenëk Ukukit Sukhana Lena Dzhardzhan •1291
Kirbey Dzhara Kyuekh-Bulung Siligir Molodo Menkere Sut
Tukalan Ylas-Yuryakh Kirbey Olenëk Motorchuna Kystatyam Menkere Sencha Dzhelon
Yessey Arga-Sala Muna Zhigansk •2389
Kotui *Siberian* Olenëk Eyakit- Tyung Khoronnokh Kharalakh Tirekh
Murukta Tërdë Eyik Bakhynay
Vilyuy Mountains Udachnyy Onkuchakh S O V I E T
Ekonda Aykhal Markha Andyngda Amysakh Borolgustakh Tungus- Endybal
65°N Vilyuy Khaya
Uplands Vilyuy Markoka Bagadzha Mastakh Linde Dalgoye
Kochechum •823 Engerdyakh Tyukyan Kyrgyday Lena Batamay
Niznaya Tunguska Yeyka Ygyatta Malykay Ulgumdzha Vilyuy Khampa Kobya
Kananda Kysyl-Yllyk Nyurba Vilyuysk Ebe Tyugene Kangalassay
Amo Yukta Novyy Sheya Verkhnevilyuysk Ilbenge Kiriyestyakh Yakutsk
501 Ust'-Ilimpeya Ankacho Chernyshevskiy Mirnyy Khordogoy Khochot
Chuyengo Ilimpeya Simenga Almaznyy R U S S I A N Kerekyano Pokrovsk
Taimura Tunor Bugorkan Viljujskoje Tas- Suntar Olëng- Sala Tenke Tongulakh Nel
Čunja Ayan Reservoir Yuryakh Sinyaya Kytyl-
Strelka- Yerbogachen Dzhunkun Chamcha Ergedzhey Atakh- Yet-Kyuyel Zhura Kachikattsy
Čunja Ulakhan Botuobuya Yuryakh Lena Khoro
51 Sosna Dulga-Kyuyel Lensk Nyuya Olekminsk Sangyyakhtakh Taloye
Vanavara Kulinda Yerema Nyuya Khamra Cherendey Uritskoye Tegyultë-
Khomokashevo Khabalakh Bol. Patom Patom Tuolba Tërde
60°N Ust'-Chayka Tokko
Chemdal'sk Tolon Andreyevskiy Berezovskaya Kudu- Amga Ugoyan Verkhnyaya
Kamanga Ayan Ika Nepa Vitim Chuya 1639 *Patomskoye Plateau* Khopurruo Kyuyel Amga
Panovo Bur Kureyskaya Polovinka Chara Dikimdya Tommot
Kata Volokon Cherkashina Vorontsovka Chara Olëkma Yenyuka Aldan Ust'-
Angara Ichera Kropotkin Torgo Usmun •1612 Timpton
Ust'Ilimsk Lena 1771 Suon- Ugun Chagda
Vorob'yeva Vitimskiy Severomuysk Tokko Sit Bol. Gynym
Garmenka Romanova Kirensk Bodaybo Berezovka Khatymy
Ilimsk Riga Ul'Kan Yermaki Gorno- Vitim Sinyuga Lake Khani Neryungri Berkakit
Bratsk Chuya Chuyskiy *North* Karalon Oron Nichatka Chara Taluma 1870
Vidim Suvorka Ust'-Kut Chaya *Baykal* Udokan Ust'Nyukzha Lopcha *Stanovoy Mount*
Bratskoye Orlinga Kazachinskoye Injaptuk *Plateau* Ust'- 2467 Nagornyy Sutam
Reservoir Yukhta 2579 Uoyan Tonnel'nyy Muya Kalar Larba Tynda Chapa
55°N Nižneangarsk *Vitim* Bambuyka Sredniy Vetekhtina Ugagli Zeyski
Atalanka Žigalovo Sugdža Baykal'skoje Baunt Kadali Kalar 1592 Gulya Belen'kaya
763 *Baykal'skiy* Oron *Plateau* Kalakan Tupik Bam Solov'yevsk Ogoron
Ust'-Kada *Mountains* Mogojto Bagdarin Ust'-Karenga Koltovkinda Amazar Urusha Skovorodino Zeya
Balagansk Sosnovka 2573 Jeleminskij Zel'onoje Mogoča Luoguhe Dzhalinda Magdagachi
Zima Zalari 2069 Bugunda Ozero Chulugli 1911 Silka •557 Petropavlovka
Čeremchovo 774 Bol. Onguren Barguzin Ust'-Džilinda Meča Mosëgda 1249 Gulian Ershiyizhan
Usolje Manzurka Romanovka Bukačača Yimuhe Walagan Oktyabrskiy
Sibirskoje Ust'-Ordynskij Maksimicha Isinga Telemba Cernyšev Ust'- Qiqian Mangui Ushumun
Angarsk Chajm 2049 1322 Karsk Novorossiyka
Šelichov *Lake Baykal* Uda Cernyšev Versino- Sretensk Nerchinskiy Kurleja Bys
3266 Irkutsk Tataurovo Chorinsk Chita Darasunskij Zavod Mordaga Linhai Shimanovsk
Kyren Kamensk Silka Ingoda Baley Karymskoje *Borshchovochnyy* Jinhe Huma Svobodnyy
Sl'ud'anka Listv'anka Ulan-Ude Chilok Darasun Klin C H I N A Shisanzhan Novokiyev
Tanchoj Petrovsk *Yablonovyy Mountains* Ulety Olov'annaja Priargunsk Argun •827 Belogorsk
2304 Zabajkal'skij Tanga Il'a Gol Yuoqi Kalaqi Oroqen Amur
Gusinoozersk Chilok Jamarovka 1248 Argun Tulihe Zizhiqi
Džida Selenga 120°E
Zakamensk Džida
105°E 110°E 115°E 120°E 125°E 130°E

51

This map shows 1/60 of the earth's surface.

94

135°E 140°E 145°E 150°E 155°E 160°E

New Siberian Islands

75°N

Bel'kovskiy · Kotel'nyy
Kotel'nyy
320
Ambardakh
Stolbovoy
Mal. Lyakhovskiy
Fedorovskiy
Bol. Lyakhovskiy
Kigilyakh
Chay-Povarnaya
420
Laptev Strait

Bennetta

Bol'shoye
Zimov'ye
Novaya Sibir'

East Siberian Sea

Cape
Buorkhaya
zhamm
Kuogastakh
Kular
eriske
Oyun-Yurege
Kumsa
Bytantay
Ali-Bagata
hoyansk
Tokuma
lom

Uyëdey
Kazach'ye
Yana
Ust'-Kuyga
Saydy
Orto-Kyuyel'
Batagay

Kharstan
Star.Dom
Balagannakh
Tumat
Tenkeli

Boru

Khroma

Kokuora
Ukta
Byyangnyr

Chikhacheva
Kiseleva
Tabor
Kolesovo
Indigirka Chokurdakh
Alekseyevo

Ulovo

70°N

Kolymskiy
Plain

914
Kondakovo
Khara-Tala
Ilimniir
Kyrbana

Balagannakh
Mys
Cherskiy
Volochsk

U N I O N

1919
Tuostakh
1726
Ust'-
Charky
1926

Tirekhtyakh
Oyun-
Kyuyel'
Chibagalakh
Suordakh
Khobolchan

Uyandi 1221
Deputatskiy

Uyandina

Bertes
Tyugyuren

Mayor-Krest

Syagannakh
Druzhina
Shestakova
Urdakh

Khongsey
Pastakh
Srednekolymsk

Ozhogino
Tenalr

Malaya
Oysurdakh

Chernyy
Mys
Zhirkova

Omolon

Arctic Circle

Zatish'ye
721

Shcherbakovo

65°N

Kusagan-
Olokh
Khara-
Tas
35

Nel'gese
Astakh
Cheulik
Adycha
1627

Alyaskitovyy

Chibagalakh
2703
Tyubelyakh
Udanna
Mama

3147

Kycham-
Kyuyel'

Erozionnyy

Yugo-Tala
Zyryanka

Sededema

Rassokha

Bulun

Berezovka

Oroyek
Korkodon

Korkodon

Suglan
Tompo
1714

Ust'-Nera
Marshal'skiy
Tirgelin
Nera
2341

Artyk
2558

Razdolnoye

im Chapayeva
2038

Kolyma
1347

Ust'-Sugoy

Abkit

Munugudzhak
Omolon
1550

Aldan
Khara-Aldan
Dyalinnya
Dal'stroy
Kysyl-
Suluo

Oymyakon
Tomtor
Sordongnokh

Khuzdzhakh
Arkagala

Khongo

Seymchan

1830

Omsukchan
Galimyy

Gizhiga

Khandyga
Sayylyk
2933

Byuchennyakh
Adygalakh
Burkhala

Debin
Orotukan

Nayakhan

S. F. S. R.
Okhotskiy-
Perevoz
Kennya

Gvardeyets
Khatyngnakh

Pik Aborigen
2586
Strelka

Viliga-
Kushka

El'dikan
Zolotoy
Allakh-Yun'
Ancha
Kencha

Kolyma

Vetrennyy
im Gastello

Myakit
Atka

Tumany

Ust'-Maya
Ayaya

Burgakhchan

2350
Arka

Neter

Inya
1585

Kandychan

Ugulan

Cape
Taygonos

10

Ust'-Mil'
Ulukuut
Sordongnokh
Maya

Yudoma-
Krestovskaya
Urak

Bulun
Star.
Kheydzhan
Shilkan

Kuntuk
Talon
Balagannoye

Arman
Magadan
Malkachan

Gulf of
Shelekhova

60°N

chi
Aim
Ingili
Omnya

Kurun Uryak
Kaval'kan
Alachakh
Chigul'bach
Nel'kan

Amka
Ul'ya

Okhotsk
Inya

Motykleyka

Nyurchan
1549
Sivuch

Yame
Yamsk
Sredniy

Cape
Tolstoy

Lesnaya

Palana

Ust'-Tigil'
Tigil'

Khakhar
Topko
1906
Batomga
Kemkara

Khanyangda
Enkan

Cape
Alevina

Cape
Yelizavety

2531

Utkholok

Kekuk
Esso

Maymakan
Ayan

Nemuy
1500

Chasovnya-
Uchurskaya

Dzhugdzhur Mountains

Sea of
Okhotsk

Ust'-Belogolovoye

Ust'-Sopochnoye

Oblukovino
Tvayan
Icha
3621

Atlasovo
Ichinskaya
Sopka
4750

Mil'kovo

Kronok

55°N

Uda
Udskoye
Burandzha
Shevli
Baladek
ihek
Ekimchan
2295
vinka

Chumikan

Shantar

Tugur
Usal'gin
Litke

Nyvrovo
602

Okha
Bol.
Vlas'evo
Nikolayevsk-
na-Amure

Paromay

Kirovskiy
Pymta

Sredinnyy Mountains
1870

Malka

Pushchino
Zhupanovskiy

Nalychevo

Maya

Sofiysk
Yashkino
Guga
Gaktsynka
Lake
Chukehagirskoye
1462

Tyr
Mariinskoye
Sofiysk
De Kastruskoye

Bogorodskoye
Boatasyn

Sakhalin

Nysh

Paratunka

Oktyabr'skiy
Bol'sheretsk

Petropavlovsk-
Kamchatskiy

Ust' Niman
Bolodzhak
Urgal
2010
Mogdy

Duki
Kondon
Boktor
Gornyy
Komsomol'sk-
na-Amure

Amur

Novoilinovka
Siziman

Aleksandrovsko-
Sakhalinskiy
1609
Tymovskoye

Paramušir

135°E 140°E 145°E 150°E 155°E 160°E

n o p q r s t u v w x y z

59

0 100 200 300 miles
Average linear scale
0 100 200 300 400 500 Km

a b c d e f g h i j k l m

Ostashkov
Torzhok
Nelidovo
Rzev
Staritsa
Klin
Dubna
Dmitrov
Zagorsk
Jaroslavl'
Ivanovo
Kovrov
Kineshma
Krasnyye-Baki
Uren
Yaransu
Yoshkar Ola
Kilmez
Izevsk
Votkinsk
Malmyz
Agryz
Sarap
Nefte

Volokolamsk
Moscow
Mytišči
Balashikha
Noginsk
Vladimir
Dzerzhinsky
Nizhniy
Novgorod
(Gor'kiy)
Volga
Cheboksary
Kazan'
Mamadysh
Naberezhnyje
Celny

Gagarin
Vyaz'ma
Smolensk
Odintsovo
Mozhaysk
Orechovo-Zujevo
Elektrostal
Murom
Arzamas
RUSSIAN
S.F.S.R.
Al'met'yevsk
Oktyabr'sk
Davlek

Obninsk
Podolsk
Kolomna
Temnikov
Sergach
Kanash
Chistopol
Tetyushi
Kuybyshevskoje
Reservoir
Yelkhovka
Aksakovo

Serpuchovo
Rjazan
Nazarovka
Zubova-
Polyana
Saransk
Inza
Alatyr
Ul'yanovsk
Togliatti
Severnoye
Bugul'ma

Kaluga
Chekalio
Tula
Novomoskovsk
Skopin
Shatsk
Morshansk
Kamenka
Penza
Baryš
Kuznetsk
Syzran
Chapayevsk
Samara
Krotovka
Buguruslan
Sharly

Belev
Plavsk
Troyekurovo
Michurinsk
Tambov
Mordovo
Kirsanov
Rtishchevo
Vyzakova
Vol'sk
Balakovo
Maryevka
Buzuluk
Sorochinsk
Oren

Orel
Zmiyevka
Yelets
Lipetsk
Gryazi
Tugolukovo
Atkarsk
Kalininsk
Balashov
Saratov
Engel's
Pushkino
Dergachi
Ural'sk
Aksay
Sol

Kursk
Gorshechnoye
Livny
Voronezh
Borisoglebsk
Rogachevka
Jryupinsk
Rudnya
Rovnoye
Novo
Uzensk
Chapayevo
Mergenevo
Antonovo

Obšči Syrt

SOV

Khar'kov
UKRAINE
Belgorod
Alekseyevka
Valuyki
Kantemirovka
Veshenskaya
Mikhaylovka
Log
Kamyshin
Nikolayevsk
Kaysatskoye
Furmanovo
Mastekskay

Poltava
Sumy
Akhtyrka
Izyum
Millerovo
Kalach-
na-Donu
Volgograd
Elton
67
Lake
Aralsor
Inderborskiy
Kulagino

Kremenchug
Pereshchepino
Kramatorsk
Lugansk
Kamensk-
Shakhinskiy
Morozovsk
Primorsk
Krasnoslobodsk
Kapustin-Yar
Makat
Sarychik
Iskine

Dneprodzerzhinsk
Novomoskovsk
Pavlograd
Stakhanov
Yenakievo
Novoshakhtinsk
Tsimlyanskoye
Reservoir
Solodniki
Chernyy
Yar
Mikhaylova
Caspian Depression

Dnepropetrovsk
Gorlovka
Makeyevka
Donetsk
Shakhty
Volgodonsk
Novocherkassk
Kotel'nikovo
Dubovskoye
Kharabalio
Zhagaly
Gur'yev

Krivoy Rog
Zaporozh'ye
Chaplino
Taganrog
Rostov
Bataysk
Sal'sk
Lake
Manych
Gudilo
Elista
Utta
Krasnyy-Yar
Astrakhan
Canyushikino

Nikopol
Melitopol'
Berdyansk
Yeysk
Sosyko
Tikhoretsk
Divnoye
Yashkul'
Zelenga
Karaton
Oporny

Kherson
Novaya
Kakhovka
Sea of
Azov
Primorsko-
Akhtarsk
Kropotkin
Kugulta
Ulan-Khol
Mumra
Zhagaly

Simferopol'
Feodosiya
Kerch'
Kavkaz
Kuban'
Krasnodar
Armavir
Stavropol'
Velichayevskoye
Kultay

Sevastopol'
Jalda
Crimea
Novorossiysk
Maykop
Čerkessk
Pjatigorsk
Kislovodsk
Kuma
Kochubey
Kulaly

Tuapse
Soči
Elbrus
Nal'čik
Prochladnyj
Terek
Kiz'lar
Fort-Sevčenko
Šetpe

Suchumi
Caucasus
Grozny
Vladikavkaz
Machačkala
Ševčenko

BLACK
SEA
Poti
Kutaisi
Kazabegi
Derbent
Kyzyk
Fetisovo

Cape Ince
Sinop
GEORGIAN
S.S.R.
Tbilisi
Rustavi
Kuba
Kara-
Bogaz-
Gol

Pontine
Kastamonu
Karabük
Samsun
Batumi
Hopa
Marneuli
Mingecaurskoje
Reservoir
Bekdaš

Gerede
Çorum
Trabzon
Giresun
Gümüşhane
Ardahan
Leninakan
Kazach
Gandsya
Sumgait

Mountains
Turhal
Erzurum
Kars
Kirovakan
Jevlach
AZERBAYDZHAN
S.S.R.
Baku
Žioj

Ankara
Kırıkkale
Yozgat
Sivas
Erzincan
Askale
ARMENIA
S.S.R.
Yerevan
Agdam
Krasnovodsk

Kayseri
Divriği
Kara Dag
Patnos
Ararat
Nachičevan
Araks
Saljany
Čeleken

Aksaray
Niğde
Malatya
Ar'Dağ
Bingöl
Lake
Van
Maku
Khoy
Ahar
Ožalilabad
Astara
Ogurčinskij

Lake
Tuz
Gurun
Elazig
Murat
Nehri
Tatvan
Van
Marand
Ardebil

Konya
Ereğli
Maras
Kozan
Diyarbakir
Kurtalan
Hakkâri
Droumieh
Maragheh
Mianeh
Bandar Anzeli
Rasht

Anamur
Karaman
Adana
Mersin
Siverek
Urfa
Kızıltepe
Nusaybin
Khoy
Zanjan
Ramsar

Cape Anamur
Silifke
Antakya
Aleppo
Al Hasakah
Tigris
Mahabad
Qazvin
Amol

CYPRUS
MEDITERRANEAN
SEA
Cape
Andreas
Latakia
Idlib
Asi
SYRIA
Maskana
Raqqah
Suwar
IRAQ
Sinjar
Tall
'Afar
Mosul
Arbil
Sulaimaniyah
Bijar
Baneh
Saqqez
Tehrān

35°E
40°E
45°E
50°E

n o p q r s t u v w x y z

This map shows 1/60 of the earth's surface.

a b c d e f g h i j k l m

Kungur Pervoural'sk 60°E **Sverdlovsk** Talitsa 65°E Tevriz Irtysh 75°E .142

Krasnoufimsk Bogdanovich Yalutorovsk .122 Tara Tara Biaza

Ufa Nyazepetrovsk Degtyarsk Sysert' Kamensk-Ural'skiy Shadrinsk Ishim Panovo Tyukalinsk Bol'sherech'ye .124

Asha Min'yar Suleya Zlatoust Kasli Kurgan Makushino Nazyyayevsk Lyubinskiy Kalachinsk Barabinsk 55°N

Chernikovsk Ust'-Kata **Chelyabinsk** Shumikha Petukhovo Petropavlovsk Isil'kul **Omsk** Chistoozernoye Lake Chany

Ufa Plast Chudinovo Ust'-Uyskoye Presnovka Petrovka Krasnoarmeysk Kyzltu Cherlak Kupino

Krasnousol'skiy Beloretsk Verkhneural'sk Troitsk Kurtamysh Dem'yanovka Mar'yevka Volodarskoye Kokchetav .887 Lake Ul'kenkaroy Zhelezinka Karasuk

Sterlitamak Kaga **Magnitogorsk** Komsomolets Borovskoye Uritskiy Peski Aydabul' Makinsk Stepnyak Aksu Bestobe Lake Azhbulat Kachiry

Kumertau Baymak .447 Bredy Varna Kustanay Stavropolka Ruzayevka Kokchetav Shuga

Troitskoye Krasnoyarskiy Dznetygara Dzhambul Naurzum Yesil Dzhaksy Atbasar Zhaltyr Alekseyevka Tortkuduk Yermak **Pavlodar** Jamyševo

Saraktash Akkarga Derzhavinsk .391 Novoishimskiy Tselinograd Ekibastuz Maykain

Orsk Terensay Dombarovskiy Tolybays Aksuat Arkalyk Sabyndy Novodolinka Karashoky Ajryk

Mednogorsk Kabyrga S t e p p e Lake Tengiz Nura Kurgal'dzhino Aktau .621 50°N

Martuk Khrom-Tau Turgay Shenber Sonaly .633 Temirtau Ul'yanovskoye Karaganda

E T U N I O N Saga Brali Ulutau Zahksykan Abay Saran Dar'inskiy **K a z a k h** Korobovskiy Kiikkaškan Kajnar

.316 Temir Emba Irgiz Kyzyluy Nikol'skiy Kyzyl-Dzhar Atasu Uspenskiy Nuru Myylybulak Karagayly Dagandely

Karaulkeldy Shakhty Togyz Baykonyr Dzhezkazgan Ayshirak Agadyr **U p l a n d s**

Zharkamys **K A Z A K H** Chelkar Aral'sk Beleutty .59 Kiik Mointy Zhamshi

Chushakyl' .343 Akespe S S R Lake Arys **Betpak-Dala Steppe** Karazhingil Balkhash Sajak

Sokyrbulak Kulanoy Bugun Kazalinsk Leninsk Dzhusaly Bet-Pak-Dala Kashkanteniz **Lake Balkhash** Tomar Karabas

Aral Sea Vozrozhdeniya Barsa-Kel'mes Uzynkair Erimbet **Kyzyl-Orda** Syrdarja Kamkaly Mynaral Kuyygan Burylbaytal Uštobe .603 45°N

Šatlyk Muinak Urga Lake Sudočje Zhanay Chilli Yany-Kurgan .2176 Aksumbe Algatart Furmanovka Khantau Čemolgan Aktogaj Saryozek Karatal

Kazakdarya .146 Kentau Uyuk Čemolgan Kaskalen **Alma Ata** .4376

Kungrad Chimbay .335 Turkestan Tatty Kapčagajskoje Reservoir Čilik

Lake Sarykamyškoje Bol'ševik Chodzeili .473 Mynbulak Uchkuduk Kara Tau Džambul Lugovoi Frunze Čemolgan **K I R G I Z I Y A**

Kun'a-Urgenč Tašauz **K y z y l K u m** Zarafshan Arys' .592 Cimkent .3817 Kara-Balta Rubačje Lake Pževal'sk Issyk-Kul'

Urgenč Turtkul' Cardara Cirčik Toktogul Res. Toktogul Čajek Ottuk **S S R**

.81 Lebap **U Z B E K I S T A N** Cardarinskoje Reservoir **Tashkent** Namangan Taš-Kumyr Naryn Taragay Karasaj

T U R K M E N I Y A Gorel'de **S. S. R.** Jangijul' Angren Andižan Kok-Jangak Oš Lake Catyrk'ol .4925 Sari Bulak Pik Dankowa .5982 Čatyrtaš Akqi Toxkan

Darvaza Gizhduvan Navoi Gulistan Kokand Margilan Fergana Gul'ča .4641 Sugun Sanchakou

S.S.R. Buchara Kagan Džizak Leninabad Bekabad Ura J'ube Darvaut-Kurgan Irkeštam 40°N

Kabakly Kattakurgan .5509 Lenina .7134 Kashgar

K a r a K u m Alat Mubarek Ajni Džirgatal Lake Kərakul Bulunkol Kungur Shache

Jerbent .224 Samarkand **T A D Z H I K I S T A N** .4643 Novabad Mt.Communism .7495 Arkbajtal .7719 **C H I N A**

Kizyl-Arvat **Čardžou** Šachrisabz Karši **S. S. R.** Višarv Murgab Mamazair Yecheng

Bachardok Repetek Denau **Dušanbe** Kul'ab .6093 Chorog Kungur .7190 Hasalbag Muji

Ašchabad Tezejet Mary Bajram Ali Nička Keriči .222 Kurgan-T'ube Dusti Faidzabad **P a m i r** .7690 Arkbajtal **P A K I S T A N**

.2243 Tedžen .293 Termez Dušanbe Zebak Tirich Mir Mastuj Yasin .6525 Misgar Mazar

Bojnurd Quchan Dušak Sarakhs Andkhoy Aqcha Khulm Kunduz Taliqan Baghlan Chitrál .5715 .7367 Rakaposhi .7788 Gilgit .7228 .6611

Sabzevar Neishabur Mashhad Murgab Sheberghan Mazar-i-Sharif **A F G H A N I S T A N** Drosh **Karakoram Range**

Bala Murghab Qaisar Maimana Sar-i-Pul Aibak Doab-i Mikhe Zarin Doshi Kunar **Hindu Kush** Chilas Indus .75°E

miles 100 200 300 Average linear scale 0 100 200 300 400 500 Km

n o p q r s t u v w x y z

SOVIET

RUSSIA

KAZAKHSTAN S.S.R.

KIRGIZIYA S.S.R.

MONGO

CHINA

Onegva Yar · Staritsa · Kolpaševo · Belyj Yar · Yeniseysk · Vorozheyka · Lesosibirsk · Strelka · Galanino · Rodina · Angara · Boguchan · Oktjabr'sk · Vy

Vasyuganье · L'vovka · parabel · parbig · Mogočin · Baturino · Komsomol'sk · Čulym · Meletsk · 211 · Altat · Predivinsk · Asansk · Shelayevo · 698 · Aban · Kansk · Neva

142 · Tara · Biaza · Bakčar · Asino · Tegul'det · Birilyussy · Shivera · 698

Pokrovka · Čumakovo · Pikhtovka · 258 · Moryakovskiy Zaton · Tomsk · Mariinsk · Bogotol · Achinsk · Pamyat · Krasnojarsk · Uyar · Borodino · Zamzo

Chistoozernoye · Kupino · Lake Chany · Ordynskoye · Ob' · Yurga · Anzhero-Sudzhensk · Nazarovo · 818 · Krasnoyarskoye Reservoir · Bujedžul · Sum · Gutara · Ta

55°N · Novosibirsk · Cherepanovo · Kemerovo · Tsentral'nyy · Sira · Sorsk · Bellyk · 1778 · Art'omosk · Pik Grandioznyj 2922 · Pokrov

Barabinsk · Karasuk · Kamen-na-Obi · Suzun · T'agun · Kiselʻovsk · Novokuzneck · 2178 · Černogorsk · Minusinsk · Burgon · Kazyr

Lake Azhbulat · Kachiry · Khabary · Len'ki · Tal'menka · Prokopjevsk · MežDuречensk · Abakan · Sušenskoje · Uda Alygdžer

Pavlodar · Blagovščenka · Pavlovsk · Barnaul · Mundybaš · Tastagol · Taštyp · Sajanogorsk · Savan Mountains · 2456 · Bujba · Sevi · Toora-Chem · Bol Yenisey

Yermak · Jamyševo · Kulunda · Rodino · Alejsk · Bijsk · Biła · Turočak · Abakan Mts. · 2930 · Idzim · 2682 · 2684

Kulundinskaya · Šcerbakty · Dolon · Rubcovsk · Gorn'ak · Caryšskoje · Lake Teleckoje · Čel'uš · Ak-Dovurak · 2972 · Uvs Nuur · Samagaltaj · 2668

Steppe · Molgary · Bel'agaš · Semonaicha · Tuekta · 2820 · Inja · Kuraj · Kyzyl-Chaja · Orog Nuur · Uvs Nuur · Saryg-Sop · Kyzyl-Chem

Ajryk · Semipalatinsk · Ušt'-Kamengorsk · Katun · Kuraj · Koš-Agač · 4029 · Turgen · Malčin · Sagonar · Naryn

50°N · 606 · 2776 · Argut · 4506 · Čagaan Nuur · Chovd Gol · Baruun Turuun · 2928 · Bajan-Uul · Cagaan-Uul

Kiikkaškan · Kajnar · Čarsk · Serebr'ansk · Georgiievka · 1608 · Bol'šenarymskoje · Korti Linchang · Čagaan Gol · Uigij · Ulgij · Chirgis Nuur · Ojgon Nuur

Bestamak · Karaul · Žarma · Kokpekty · 2645 · Lake Markakol · Altaj · Tolbo Nuur · Erdene Büren · Char Nuur · Telmen Nuur

KAZAKHSTAN · Madenijet · Ajaguz · Kurčum · Buran · Ertix He · Burqin · 3743 · Kobdo · Char Us Nuur · Döröö Nuur · Jaruu · Aldar · Uliastaj

S.S.R. · Sajak · Aktogaj · Tarbagataj · Belaja Škola · Zajsan · Lake Zajsan · Beitun · Manchan · 4362 · Mönch Chajrchan · Ovoot · 3578 · 3905 · Bujant

Taskesken · Urdžar · 2992 · Tacheng · Muz Tau 3816 · Ulungur Hu · Fuyun · Sarbulak · Dzereg · Cagaan-Olom

Karabas · Lepsy · Zarsuat · Lake Sasykkol · Utubulak · Jili Hu · Ulungur · Mönch · Tamc · Delger · Altaj

55 · Matai · 756 · Lake Alakol' · Toli · Urho · Ulungur Gol · Türgen · Bugat · Beger

603 · Sarkand · Ebinur Hu · 2923 · Karamay · Manas Hu · Junggar Pendi · Bulgan · 3479 · Dzachuj

Uštobe · 4442 · Wenquan · Bole · Tachakou · Ertai · Gov'Chonin · 3802 · Bajan-Ondor

45°N · Taldy-Kurgan · Sayram Hu · Jinhe · Jiangjumiao · Santanghu · Altaj

Aktogaj · Saryozek · Panfilov · Ining · Nilka · Usu · Shihezi · Qitai · Barkol Hu · Nom

Kapčagaj · Kapčagajskoye Reservoir · Cilik · Qapqal · 5500 · Manas · Changji · Bogda Feng 5445 · Barkol Kazak · Yiwu

Čemolgan · Alma Ata · Cundža · Tekes · Xinyuan · Narat · Urumchi · 3951 · Qijiaojing · Liaodun · Yandun · 4925 Karlik Shan

Kaskalen · 4876 · Zhaosu · 3638 · Houxia · Qiquanhu · Hami · Mergol · G

Kegen · Narynkol · Tekes · Baiyanghe · Turpan 154 · Liushuquan

Rubačje · Ananjevo · Prževal'sk · 4553 · Bulguntay · Ewirgol · Shanshan · Mingshui

Ottuk · Lake Issyk-Kul' · Pik Pobedy 7439 · Kéyi · Yengisar · Qarqi · Yangi Huizu Zizhixian · 1524 · Weiya · Xingxingxia · Gongpoquan

KIRGIZIYA S.S.R. · Naryn Taragaj · Kuqa · Dalaoba · Korla · Bosten Hu · Yuli · Daquan · Hongliuyuan · Jiangjuntai

Karasaj · Pik Dankowa 5982 · Yakrik · Xinhe · Kongi · Tarim · 1238 · Bei Shan · 1762 · Jiangquanzi

Čatyrtas · Toxkan · Aksu · Tarim · Tarim Liuchang · Zhangjiaquan · Anxi · Qiaowan

4929 · Sari Bulak · Akqi · Awat · Aral · Kongi · Lop Nur · Šule · Kumkuduk · Dunhuang · Dongbatu · Choushu

40°N · Sanchakou · Bachu Liuchang · Yarkant · Tarim · Yengisu · Shazaoyuan · H · Changma · Jiayug

Sugun · Yopurga · Markit · Tarim Basin · 1066 · Ikanbujmal · 1699 · C · Aksay · Qilian Shan 5547 · Jiuqua

Hasalbag · Yecheng · Koxlax · 1082 · Luobuzhuang · Dongluk · Miran · Obo Liang · 5798 · Huahaizi · Tsi

Muji · Shache · Tongguzbasti · Takla Makan · Aktaz · Qarqan · Waxxari · Altun Shan · Xorkol · Niubiziliang · 2774 · Lenghu · 5827

Zanggui · Zawa · 1570 · East · Qiemo · Hadilik · 5910 · Youshashan · Tsaidam Basin · Iqe · Har Hu

Yutian · Qira · Minfeng · Turkestan · Andirlangar · Tura · 6140 · Ayakkum Hu · Gas Hu · Mangnai · Shaliangzi · Da Qaidam · 5030

Mazar Yarkant · Hotan · Bostan · 6748 Aqqikkol Hu · Nur Turu · Dabsan Hu · Qarhan · Holt Taria · Delingha

Kangxiwar · Tekiliktag 6466 · Pulu · Aktag · Muztag 7723 · 7720 · Boluntai · De Juh · Golmud · Nan Hülsan Hu · Nomhon

7228 · 80°E · Karakax · Kunlun · Karasay · S · h · a · 85°E · 90°E · 95°E · 5026 · Xian

This map shows 1/60 of the earth's surface.

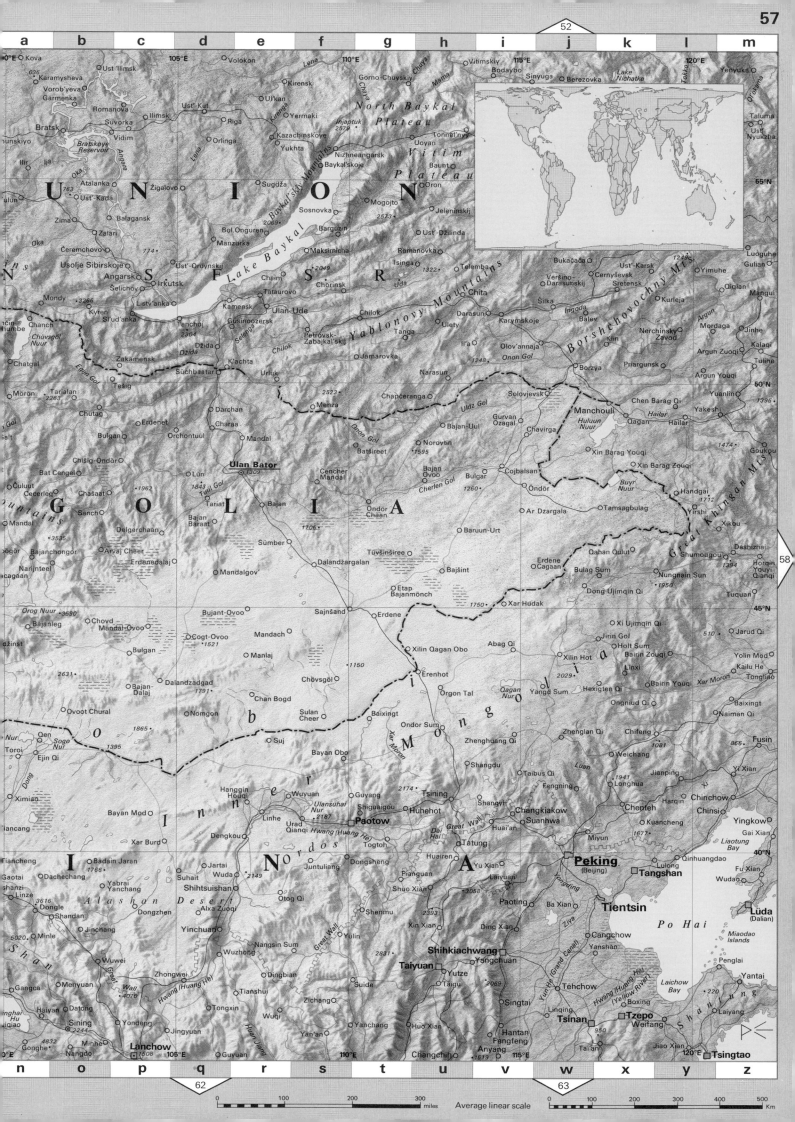

SOVIET UNION

120°E

125°E

130°E

135°E

Ingoda
Baley
Klin
Nerchinsky Zavod
Borzya
Priargunsk
Argun Zuoqi
Argun Youqi
Nchen Barag Qi
Manchouli
Hulun-Nur
Hailar
Qagan
Xin Barág Youqi
Xin Barag Zuoqi
Buyr-Nur
Tamsagbulag

MONGOLIA

Gobi

Inner

Dong Ujimqin Qi
Qagan Qulut
Bulag Sum
Nungnain Sum

C H I N A

Jirin Gol
Holt Sum
Xi Ujimqin Qi
Xilin Hot
Linxi
Hexigten Qi
Bairin Youqi
Ongniud Qi
Zhenglan Qi
Chifeng
Weichang
Jianping
Longhua
Chengteh
Fengning
Miyun
Great Wall

Shimanovsk
Svobodnyy
Uval
Zeya
Novokiyevskiy
Ust'Niman
Urgal
Chegdomyn
Duki
Bolodzhak
Kondon
Komsomol'sk-na-Amure
Amursk
Bolon

R U S S I A N   S.F.S.R.

Belogorsk
Blagoveshchensk
Zavitinsk
Bureya
Arkhara
Talandzha
Izvestkovyy
Mogdy
Birobidzhan

S O V I E T   U N

Linhai
Huma
Shisanzhan
Heihe
Raychikhinsk
Xunke
Bikin
Amur
Fuyuan
Khabarovsk
Kruglikovo
Khor

Dayangshu
Huolongmen
Sunwu
Wuyiling
Wuying
Yichun
Hokang
Jiamusi
Schwangyashan
Dongfanghong
Luchegorsk
Svetlovodnaya
Yasnaya
Sinn
Velikaya

Manchuria

Harbin

KOREA

NORTH
KOREA

Pyongyang

SOUTH
KOREA

Seoul

Yellow
Sea

SEA OF

JAPAN

East China
Sea

This map shows 1/60 of the earth's surface.

a b c d e f g h i j k l m

140°E 145°E 150°E 155°E

Kamchatka

Sofiysk
Mariinskoye

Novoilinovka
De Kastruskoye

Amur
Nysh

Aleksandrovsk-
Sakhalinskiy
1609
Siziman
Tymovskoye

Paramušir

urskoye
•*1628*

N
Koto

Sakhalin

U.S.S.R.
1324

50°N

Gavan
Poronaysk

Onekotan

Makarov

Adzhima

OKHOTSK

Samarga

Kholmsk
Yuzhno-Sakhalinsk

Simušir

Svetlaya
Korsakov

Gulf of Tartary

laksimovka

La Pérouse Strait

Urup

Wakkanai

Kuril Islands

•*1129*

45°N

Iturup

Asahikawa
Kitami

•*2290*
Kunašir

Asahi-dake

Otaru
Hokkaidō
Nemuro

□ **Sapporo**

2052
Obihiro
Kushiro

Muroran

Uchiura
Bay
Erimo

PACIFIC

Hakodate

Tsugaru Channel
Ōma

Aomori

1625

40°N

Akita
Marioka

1914

Sakata
Kesen

Ishinomaki

Yamagata
Sendai

Niigata
Fukushima

•*2105*

Kashiwazaki
Kōriyama

1917
Iwaki

OCEAN

Honshū

Nagano
Utsunomiya

JAPAN

Maebashi
Mito

Matsumoto

Hachioji

iirane-san
Tōkyō
Chōshi

192
Kawasaki
Chiba

3176
Yokohama

ama

Yokosuka

35°N

Shizuoka

amatsu

140°E 145°E 150°E 155°E

n o p q r s t u v w x y z

SEA OF

SOVIET UNION

Mayamey
Quchan
Sabzevar
Neishabur
Mashhad
Sarakhs
·3147
60°E
Murgab
Andkhoy
Aqcha
Mazar-i-Sharif
Khulm
Kunduz
Faidzabad
Qala Panja
Taliqan
Zebok
·7890 Mastuj
Tirich Mir
·7575

35°N
Bardeskan
Kashmar
Torbat-e-Heidariye
Torbat-e-Jam
·3415
Kuska
Takhta Bazar
Bala Murghab
Qaisar
Maimana
Sari-i-Pul
Sheberghan
Aibak
Baghlan
Doshi
Doab-i Mikhe Zarin
Charikar
Chitral
Drosh
·5751

Dasht-e-Kavir
2578·
Bidokht
Ferdows
Tabas
Ghorian
Quala-i Nau
Jawand
Herat
Hari Rud
·3592
Chaghcharan
Daulat Yar
·3704 Qarah Tarai
Kuh-e-Baba
Bamian
Behsud
Kota-i Ashro
·1799
Kabul
Asadabad
Khyber Pass
Kabul
Sorabai
Jalalabad
Peshawar
Mardan
Besham Qila
Muzaffar
Abbotabad
Islamabad

Aliabad
Deihuk
Khusf
Birjand
Sarbisheh
Yazdan
·2561
Tayebad
Farsi
Shindand
Sangan·
·3925
·3850 Khurd
·4182 Qaisar
Gardez
Ghazni
Matun
Rawalpindi
Gujarkham
Chakwa

Darband
Naiband
·2992
·2729
Nehbandan
2488·
·716
Zabol
Lasho Joayin
Farahrod
Farah
·2560
Dilaram
Nauzad
Girishk
Uruzgan
Tarin Kot
Shahjui
Zarghunshar
Kalabagh
Bannu
Lakki
Mianwali
Sargodha
Gujra

Bafq
Zarand
Kerman
Siraj
·2438
·3143
Ravor
Namakzar-e Shadad
·2062
Zaranj
Mirabad
Helmand
Rudbar
Safar
·1371
Registan
·1314
·1746
Chaman
Qila Saifullah
Zargun ·3578
Quetta
Mach
Loralai
·3273
Sakir ·3092
Port Sandeman
Sulaiman Range
·3374
Dera Ismail Khan
Kingri
Leiah
Dera Ghazi Khan
Multan
Jhang Maghiana
Faisalabad
Okara
Sa

I R A N
Dasht-e Lut
30°N
Rafsanjan
Baghin
Hoseinabad
Sirjan
Baft
Laleh Zar ·4374
Tahrud
Darzin
Bam
Shurgaz
Nosratabad
Zahedan
Ribat
·1643
·2462
·2208
Chagai Hills
Chagai
Nushki
Sibi
Kahan
Dera Bugti
·1262
Rajanpur
Uch
Bahawalpur
Rahimyar-Khan
Ganga
Sutlej
Chenab

Aliabad
Hajiabad
Qotbabad
Dowlatabad
·3379
Kahnuj
·1564
Sabzevaran
·2548
·3503 Bazman
Khash
Mirjaveh
·2333 Sultan
Taftan ·3941
Nok Kundi
Dalbandin
Ras Koh ·3005
Raskoh
Kharan
Besima
Surab
Khuzdar
·2101
Kalat
Jacobabad
Shikarpur
Larkana
Sukkur
Khairpur
Tanot
Sri Mohangarh
Shahgarh
Jaisalmer
Bap
Pokaran
Bika

Bandar Abbas
Jaghin
Minab
Qeshm
Remeshk
·1950
Bampur
Bampur
Iranshahr
Saravan
Kuhak
Panjgur
Jebri
·2283 Patandar
Wad
Kirthar Range
Moro
Sehwan
Sanghar
Myajlar
Phalsund
Balotra
Pali
B a l u c h i s t a n
Central Makran Range
Makran Range

Qeshm
Straits of Hormuz
·2100
Al Sha'am
Ras Musandam
Nikshahr
·2710
Sarbaz
Pishin
Turbat
Hoshab
·1454
Awaran
Bela
Hab
Kotri
Mirpur Khas
Gurha
Barmer
Thar
Desert
Arayalli Range
Sirohi ·1722
Guru Sikhar

OMAN
Ras al Khaimah
Dibba
Sharjah
Dubai
Fujairah
Jask
Bahu Kalat
Chabahar
Dasht
Kikki
Pasni
Ormara
Hab Chauki
Hyderabad
Thatta
Badin
Jati
Virawah
Tharad
Udai

Al Ain
Shinas
Sohar
As Suwaiq
Ras Kuh Lab
Jiwani
Ras Nuh
Karachi
25°N
Rann of Kutch
Lakhpat
Radhanpur
Palanpur
Him

Al Khaburah
As Sib
Muscat
Quraiyat
Gulf of Oman
Indus Delta
Bhuj
Rampur
New Kandla
Mahesana
Ahmedabad

Ibri
Sumail
Sur
Ras al Hadd
Tropic of Cancer
Mandvi
Gulf of Kutch
Jamnagar
Morvi
Dhandhuka
Nac
Vac

Nazwa
Izki
Adam
Al Kami
Al Hajar al Sharqi
A R A B I A N
Dwarka
Rajkot
Kathiawar
Khambhat
Bharuch
Nar

OMAN
Umm as Samim
Ramlat al Wahiba
Al Ashkhirah
Porbandar
Junagadh
Bhavnagar
Surat
Navs

S E A
Diu
Veraval
Gulf of Cambay
(Gulf of Khambhat)
Valsad
Daman

Masirah
Jawhar
Thane
We

20°N
Duqm
Bombay

Ras Madrakah
P

Sharbithat
Ras Sharbithat
Sahil al Jazir
Janjira

Kuria Muria Islands
Koy
Reserv

Chiplun

Ratnagiri

This map shows 1/60 of the earth's surface.

a b c d e f g h i j k l m

75°E 80°E 85°E 90°E

Misgar Mazar Moyu Qira Minfeng Karasay Bostan Altun Shan Aqqikkol Hu Boluntay
Yarkant He Karakax He Kangxiwar Yutian Pulu Aktag Muztag 7723 7720
kaposhi K2 8611 Dahongliutan Pixa 6250 Kerya He Hoh Xil Shan Qumar Heyan
Ronda 7821 Skardu Kizyl Jilga Tielongtan Muztagkax He 7102 Kunlun Margai Caka Xijir Ulan Hu 35°N
Kargil Pamzal Leh 6920 Dogai Coring 7500 Luanhaizi
JAMMU AND KASHMIR Saser 7672 Pangong Tso Wujang 6800 Como Moron Us He Tongtianheyan
Srinagar Chushul 6400 Banvalot 6549 Tangula Shan Wenquan 6104
Anantnag Zangla Chumar CHINA Nyainrong
Kishtwar 4413 Zaskar Rabang Lugu Kangro Parding Amdo Nagqu
Jammu Chamba Shiquanhe Qagcaka Yanhuqu Gérzè Zhaxi Co Lhazhong Do'gyaling Dongqiao
Dharmsala Ge'gyai Xungba Yagra Ngangla Ringco Nyima Siling Co Baingoin Nu Jiang
Amritsar Hoshiarpur Garyarsa 7216 Tibet Urru Co Namco
Jallundur Ludhiana Simla Kalpa Moincêr Tangra Yumco Ombu Gyaring Co Xainza Namco
Chandigarh Nifang 7189 Barga La'nga Co Mapam Yumco Lunggar Gogên Zhari Namco Tomra Nam Co Damxung
Ambala Nanda Devi 7816 Burang 7728 Samsang Kangmar 7088 Yangbajain
Dehra Dun Karnaprayag 7040 Simikot Paryang Saga Raka Zangbo Yarlung Zangbo Jiang Qungtag 30°N
Saharanpur Almora 7043 Zhongba Ngamring Lhaze Zigazê Maizhokunggar Lhasa
Muzaffarnagar Dandeldhura Mustang Saga Tingri Kangmar Nyêmo Gonggar Nêdong
Meerut Dailekh Dhaulagiri 8078 Annapurna 8091 Gyirong 6482 Dinggyê Lhozhag Yamzho Yumco Comai Lhünzê
Delhi Hapur Moradabad Pokhara Xixabangma Feng Nyalam Gala Kangto 7060 Qona
New Delhi Ghaziabad Rampur Bareilly Butwal Katmandu Bhaktapur Everest 8848 Makalu Kanchenjunga 8586 Darjeeling Timphu Tongsa Dzong Dirang
Aligarh Budaun Shahjahanpur Sitapur Nepalganj Birganj Bhojpur BHUTAN 4738 Tashigang
Alwar Etah Farrukhabad Balrampur Sun Kosi Sirha Shiliguri Tezpur
Jaipur Mathura Agra Kannauj Lucknow Faizabad Gorakhpur Bettiah Motihari Biratnagar Jalpaiguri Koch Bihar Nowgong
Gangapur Etawah Sultanpur Azamgarh Muzaffarpur Darbhanga Purnia Rangpur Dhuburi Goalpara Gauhati 62
Ajmer Gwalior Orai Fatehpur Ghaghara Ghazipur Patna Raniganj Dinajpur Tura 1412 Shillong 1961
Tonk Jhansi Banda Allahabad Varanasi Arrah Bihar Monghyr Ghugri Bhagalpur Ingraj Bazar Bogra Sylhet 25°N
Kota Shivpuri Chhatarpur Panna Mirzapur Sasaram Gaya Kodarma Dumka Jamalpur Mymensingh Maulvi Bazar Karimganj
ilwara Baran Lalitpur Maihar Rewa Son Garwa Hazaribagh Dhanbad Berhampore Siuri Pabna BANGLADESH Agartala Aizawl
Rajgarh Damon Rihand Reservoir Sonhat Ambikapur Ranchi Puruliya Barddhaman Navadwip Faridpur Dacca Comilla
Narsinghgarh Sagar Jabalpur Shahdol Jashpurnagar Jamshedpur Bankura Khulna Jessore Chandpur Barkal
Ujjain Bhopal Narsimhapur Mandla Sundargarh Chaibasa Calcutta Khatagpur Barisal Chittagong
Indore Hoshangabad 1350 Bilaspur Rourkela Baripada Maghna Cox's Bazar
Mhow Harda Seoni Balaghat Hirakud Reservoir Sarangarh Deogarh 1165 Balasore Ganges Delta BURMA
Khargon Khandwa Betul Raipur Sambalpur Bhadrakh Kyauktaw
Nagpur Bhandara Raj Nandgaon Balangir Talcher Cuttack Palmyras Point Sittwe
Amravati Wardha Garhchiroli Phulabani Bhanjanager Bhubaneswar Mahanadi
Akola Yavatmal Kanker Bhawanipatna 20°N
Buldana Chandrapur Makri Chatrapur Bay of Bengal
Jalna Adilabad Sirpur Indravati Jagdalpur Berhampur
Parbhani Nanded Jagtial Sironcha 1240 Jaypur Parvatipuram 1501
Ahmadnagar Beed Nizamabad Chintalnar Venkataapuram Srikakulam
Latur Karimnagar Warangal Vizianagaram Eastern Ghats
Sholapur Bidar Bhadrathalam Vishakhapatnam
Sangli Gulbarga Hyderabad Khammam Tuni 75°E 80°E 85°E 90°E
Bijapur Mahbubnagar Nalgonda Eluru Kakinada Rajahmundry
Gunter Vijayawada

n o p q r s t u v w x y z

0 100 200 300 miles Average linear scale 0 100 200 300 400 500 Km

Taiyuan
Yangchuan
115°E
Tehchow
120°E
Penglai
Yantai
Cape Chengshan
125°E
Ongjin
Kangnŭng
170
Inch'ŏn
Seoul
Wŏnju
Yutze
Taigu
Singtai
·2069
Linqing
Boxing
·220
Laiyang
Shantung
Ch'ŏngju
Huo Xian
Changchih
Fengfeng
Hantan
Tsinan
Tzepo
Weifang
Jiao Xian
SOUTH
Taejŏn
Andong
ang
1619
Hohpi
Anyang
950
Tai'an
Yellow
Kunsan
Chŏnju
Taegu
Houma
·2322
Jiaozuo
Sinsiang
Heze
Yanzhou
Tsingtao
KOREA
·1918
Masan
Hwang (Huang He)
Tsining
Liangcheng
Sea
Kwangju
Chinju
35°N
cheng
Sanmenhsia
Chengchow
Kaifeng
Shangkiu
Lienyunkang
MoKp'o
Yŏsu
bao
Loyang
·1440
Qi Xian
Suchow
Binhai
Pingtingshan
Hsuchang
Zhecheng
Huaibei
366
Huaiyin
Cheju
Shangnan
Nanzhao
Luohe
Shangshui
Suhsien
Hongze
Quelpart Island
(Cheju)
Zhenping
Nanyang
Tanghe
Great
Fuyang
Pengpu
Lake
Hungtze
Lake
Kaoyu
·1612
Huai He
1140
Xinyang
Luoshan
Hwainan
Yangchow
Taichow
EAST CHINA
Siangfan
Sui Xian
Huangchuan
N
Chu Xian
Nanking
Changshu
Nantung
Han Shui
A
Hefei
Macheng
Lujiang
Chang Jiang
Wuhu
Nanchang
Wuhi
SEA
Ichang
Yidu
Plain
·1860
Anking
Xuancheng
Lake
Tai
Suchow
Shanghai
Mianyang
Wuhan
Hwangshih
Yangtze
Tonkling
·1187
Kashing
Shasi
Tongshan
·1841
Hangchow
30°N
Li Xian
Kiukiang
Xingzi
Tunxi
Shaohing
Ningpo
Guoju
Zhoushan
Islands
Changteh
Lake
Tungting
1596
Xiushui
Kingtehchen
Xin'anjiang
Kinhwa
Linhai
Jiang
Yueyang
Nanchang
Shangjao
Quzhou
Xian
Yiyang
Gao'an
Cuixi
2158
Pucheng
Yunhe
Wenchow
Changsha
Xinyu
Fuzhou
Anhua
Siangtan
Chuchow
Gongxi
Shaowu
Zhenghe
Fuding
Liahyuan
Pingsiang
Nanfeng
1290
xi
Shaoyang
Gan Jiang
Ningde
Shaowu
·7871
Pingle
Hengyang
Ji'an
Wuyi
Nanping
Sanming
1494
Quanzhou
Leiyang
·1199
Ruijin
Min Jiang
Minqing
Foochow
ilin
Ningyuan
Chen Xian
Kanchow
Yong'an
Nanxiong
Putian
Lian Xian
·1902
Shaokwan
Longyan
Chilung
Taoyuan
Hainan
Yingde
Huaiji
Qiuling
·1560
Changchow
Mei Xian
Hsinchu
Taipei
Ilan
ongnan
·1282
Longchuan
Zhangpu
Amoy
(Xiamen)
Taiwan Strait
3884
Xueweng
Taichung
Changhua
Hualien
Miyako
Wuchow
Canton (Guangzhou)
Zhao'an
Jieyang
Chiai
3997
TAIWAN
Tropic of Cancer
Luoding
Foshan
Huizhou
Lufeng
Swatow
Chaoyang
Tainan
Si (Xi Jiang)
Shun-te
1704
Kongmoon
(Jiangmen)
Kowloon
Victoria
Kaohsiung
Pingtung
Mowming
Yangjiang
Chuhoi
Macao
(Port.)
HONG KONG
(U.K.)
Fangshan
Hengchun
PACIFIC
hanchiang
Bashi
Channel
OCEAN
Luzon
Strait
Batan Islands
20°N
Hainan
Wanning
Babuyan Islands
Strait
aikow
Cape Bojeador
Cape Engaño
Laoag
Aparri
NA
Luzon
Vigan
Bangued
Tuguegarao
Ilagan
PHILIPPINES
Pulog
2934
115°E
120°E
125°E

Ryūkyū Islands
Okinawa
Naha
(Japan)
Iriomote

0 100 200 300 miles
Average linear scale
0 100 200 300 400 500 Km

a b c d e f g h i j k l m

61

Jawhar
Aurangabad
75°E
Jalna
Chandrapur
80°E
Makri
Berhampur
85°E
Puri

Penganga
Adilabad
Sirpur
Indravati
Jagdalpur
Jaypur
Parvatipuram
1591

Thane
Ahmadnagar
Parbhani
Nanded
Godavari
Sironcha
1240
Chintalnar

Bombay
Pune
Dhond
Beed
Latur
Nizamabad
Karimnagar
Venkatapuram
Ghats
1680
Srikakulam
Vizianagaram

1646
Janjira
Bhor
Barsi
Bidar
Manjra
Jagtial
Warangal
Bhadrachalam
Tuni
Vishakhapatnam

Chiplun
Satara
Pandharpur
Sholapur
Gulbarga
Hyderabad
Khammam
Godavari
Rajahmundry

Koyna Res.
Sangareddy
INDIA
Nalgonda
Kakinada
Eluru

Ratnagiri
Sangli
Bijapur
Mahbubnagar
BAY

Kolhapur
Raichur
Nagarjuna Res.
Guntur
Vijayawada

Belgaum
Krishna
Lingsugur
Kurnool
Krishna
Markapur
Tenali
Machilipatnam

Goa
Ramdurg
Gadag
Adoni
Ongole
BE

Panaji
Dharwar
Hospet
Bellary
Banganapalle
Tungabhadra
Gooty
Kavali

Karwar
Tungabhadra Res.
1100
15°N
Savanur
Kotturu
Anantapur
Nellore

Davangere
Chitradurga
Cuddapah
Penner
Gudur

Sagar
Penukonda
Kadiri
1151

Linganamakki Res.
Bhadravati
Tirupati

ARABIAN
Coondapoor
Bhadra Res.
1923
Chik Ballapur
Vayalpad
Chittoor

Chikmagalur
Tumkur
Kolar
Vellore
Madras

Hassan
Bangalore
Kanchipuram

Mangalore
Mandya
Krishnagiri
Polur

SEA
Madikeri
1745
Mysore
Dharmapuri
Pondicherry

Cannanore
Ootacamund (Udagamandalam)
Salem
1627
Cuddalore

Amindivi Islands
Doda Betta
2636
Erode
Perambalur
Mayuram

Calicut (Kozhikode)
Coimbatore
Tiruchchirappalli
Cauvery
Thanjavur

Lakshadweep (India)
Palghat
Pudukkottai
Coromandel Coast

Trichur
Ernakulam
Anai Mudi
2695
Dindigul

Cannanore Islands
10°N
Cochin
Madurai
Jaffna
Mullaittivu

Malabar Coast
2019
Virudunagar
Rameswaram
Adam's Br.
Mannar
Trincomalee

Nine Degree Channel
Alleppey
Ramanathapuram
Gulf of Mannar
Anuradhapura

Quilon
Tenkasi
Tuticorin

Minicoy
Trivandrum
1664
Tirunelveli
Puttalam
Dambulla
Batticaloa

Eight Degree Channel
Nagercoil
Cape Comorin
Kurunegala
SRI LANKA

Kandy
Pidurutalagala
2518
Badulla
Pottuvil

Colombo
2243
Hambantota

MALDIVES

Galle
Dondra Head

5°N

Male

INDIA

Equator

0°

75°E
80°E
85°E

n o p q r s t u v w x y z

This map shows 1/60 of the earth's surface.

a b c d e f g h i j k l m

62

90°E 95°E 100°E

Ramree
Thayetmyo
Pyinmana
Loikaw
Muang Chiang Rai *1854*
Phayao
Luang Prabang
Ban Ban
Mekong
Sayaboury
Vang Vieng
Xieng Khouang
2820 Bia

Cheduba
Prome
Toungoo
Saluween
Inthanon •2590
Chiang Mai
Nan
Phrae
Lampang
Pak Sane

L A O S

Myanaung
Irrawaddy
Sittang
1056
Vientiane
Kham Keut

B U R M A
Henzada
Phitsanulok
Soul Dao 2102
Wang Saphung
Nong Khai
Thakhek

Pegu
Kyaikto
Thingangyun
Insein
Kanbe
Rangoon
Basseein
Mae Sot
Tak
Miang 2316
Chum Phae
Khon Kaen
Udon Thani
Sakon Nakhon
Mekong

Gulf of Martaban
Thaton
Moulmein
Phetchabun
Chaiyaphum
Maha Sarakham
Roi Et
Kalasin
Yasothon

Pyapon
Tenasserim
Ye
Nakhon Sawan
T H A I L A N D
Nakhon Ratchasima
Ubon Ratchathani

Mouths of the Irrawaddy
Preparis
Sing Buri
Lop Buri
Si Sa Ket
15°N

O F
Suphan Buri
Chao Phraya
Khiaw 1282
Buriram
Surin

Cocos Islands (Burma)
Tavoy
Kanchanaburi
Nakhon Pathom
Prachin Buri *849*
Samrong

A L
North Andaman
Andaman Islands (India)
Ban Pong
Bangkok (Krung Thep)
Sisophon
Angkor

Middle Andaman
Mergui Archipelago
Kadan
Thon Buri
Phetchaburi
Chon Buri
Tonle Sap

South Andaman
Mergui
Siracha
Battambang
K A M P U C H E A

Little Andaman
Andaman
Hua Hin
Klaeng *1633*
Pursat
Kompong Chhnang

Letsok-Aw
Rayong
Chantaburi
1813

Lanbi
1251
Prachuap Khiri Khan
Laem Ngop
Chang
Hat Lek
Phnom Penh

Chumphon
Gulf of Thailand
Kut

Ranong
Isthmus of Kra
Phu Quoc
Kompong Som
10°N

Ten Degree Channel
St. Matthew's
S e a
Phangan
66

Car Nicobar
Samui
Cape Mau

Nicobar Islands (India)
Ban Takua Pa
Surat Thani
Ban Na San
Nakhon Si Thammarat

Katchall
Thap Put
Khao Luang 1835

Little Nicobar
Krabi
Trang
Malay

Great Nicobar
Phuket
Phatthalung
Thale Luang
Songkhla

Hat Yai
Pattani
Sai Buri
Narathiwat

Terutao
Satun
Yala
Sungai Ko-lok
Kota Baharu

Langkawi
Alor Setar
Kelantan

Sungai Petani
Banda Aceh
Sigli
Lhokseumawe
Pinang (George Town)
Butterworth
2171 Chamah
Kuala Terengganu

Bireuen
Pinang
Perak

Calang
Lhoksukon
Idi
Taiping
Sungai Siput Utara
Dungun
5°N

•2855 Geureudong
Peureulak
Ipoh
M A L A Y A
Kuala Lipis
Tapis 1512

Langsa
Kampar *2131*
Raub
Kuantan

Meulaboh
Pangkalanbrandan
Tanjungpura
Kuala Kubu Baharu
Bentong

Leuser 3404
Medan
Kutacane
Tebingtinggi
M A L A Y S I A (WESTERN)

Tapaktuan
Sumatra
Tanjungbalai
Kuala Kubu Baharu
Kuala Lumpur
Kelang
Seremban
Tioman

Kabanjahe
Pematangsiantar
Lake Toba
Petaling Jaya

O C E A N
Singkilbaru
2300 Sibabuhabu
Tarutung
Rantauprapat
Malacca
Muar
Segamat
Blumut 1010
Keluang

Simeulue
Tuangku
Sibolga
Baumun
Dumai
Duri
Rupat
Strait of Malacca
Kulai
Johor Baharu

Nias
Padangsidimpuan
Panyabungan
Balaipungut
SINGAPORE
Riau Islands

Hutanopan
Pakanbaru
Kampar
Lingga Islands

Pini
Ophir 2912•
Lubuksikaping
Lingga

I N D O N E S I A
Payakumbuh
Rengat
Singkep

Tanahbala
Bukittinggi
Padangpanjang
Indragiri
0°

n o p q r s t u v w x y z

90°E 95°E 100°E

68

0 100 200 300 miles
Average linear scale
0 100 200 300 400 500 Km

a b c d e f g h i j k l m

62

BURMA

THAILAND

LAOS

VIETNAM

KAMPUCHEA

MALAYA

MALAYSIA
(WESTERN)

Prome
Toungoo
Myanaung
Pyu
Henzada
Pegu
Kyaikto
Insein Thingangyun
Rangoon
Thaton
Kanbe
Pyapon
Gulf of Martaban
Moulmein
Ye
Tavoy
Irrawaddy
Sittang
Salween
Tenasserim

1854
1056
Inthanon 2590
Phayao
Chiang Mai
Lampang
Phrae
Nan
Sayaboury
Vang Vieng
Bia 2820
Xieng Khouang
Quynh Luu
Gulf of Tongking
Dongfang
1879
Yaxian
Hainan

100°E
105°E
110°E

Pak Sane
Vientiane
Nong Khai
Wang Saphung
Udon Thani
Sakon Nakhon
Savannakhet
Khemarat
Thakhek
Kham Keut
Napé 2285
Rao Go
Ha Tinh
Vinh
Dong Hoi
Sepone
Hue
Da Nang

Tak
Mae Sot
Phitsanulok
Miang 2316
Chum Phae
Phetchabun
Khon Kaen
Kalasin
Maha Sarakham
Roi Et
Yasothon
Soai Dao 2102

15°N

Nakhon Sawan
Sing Buri
Suphan Buri
Lop Buri
Chaiyaphum
Nakhon Ratchasima
Buriram
Surin
Si Sa Ket
Ubon Ratchathani
Warin Chamrap
Det Udom
Pakse
Phiafay
Attopeu
Atouat 2500
2009
Kontum
1570 An Tuc
Pleiku
Qui Nhon

Kanchanaburi
Nakhon Pathom
Ban Pong
Thon Buri
Bangkok
Khiaw 1282
Prachin Buri 849
Samrong
Sisophon
Angkor
Battambang
Khong
Stung Treng
Ban Pu Kroy
Ban Me Thuot
Mdrak

Phetchaburi
Chon Buri
Siracha
Klaeng
Rayong
Chantaburi
1633
Laem Ngop
Pursat
Tonle Sap
1813
Kompong Chhnang
Kompong Cham
Kratie
1544
Da Lat
Nha Trang
Cam Ranh

Hua Hin
Mergui Archipelago
Kadan
Mergui

Tavoy

1251
Khiri Khan Prachuap
Chang
Kut
Hat Lek
Phnom Penh
Kompong Som
Bao Loc
1532
Di Linh
Phu Chong
Bien Hoa

Andaman

Letsok-Aw
Lanbi
755
Chumphon
Gulf of Thailand
Phu Quoc
Long Xuyen
Chau Phu
My Tho
Saigon (Ho Chi Minh City)
Vung Tau
Rach Gia
Can-Tho
Mekong Delta

10°N

St Matthew's
Ranong
Isthmus of Kra
Phangan
Samui
Khanh Hung
Nam Can
Cape Mau

65

Sea

Ban Takua Pa
Surat Thani
Ban Na San
Nakhon Si Thammarat
Spratly Islands

Thap Put
Luang 1835
Krabi
Phuket

Phatthalung
Thale Luang
Songkhla
Trang
Hat Yai
Pattani
Sai Buri
Yala
Narathiwat

SOUTH

Terutao
Satun
Langkawi
Alor Setar
Sungai Ko-lok
Kota Baharu
Kuala Terengganu

Sungai Petani
Pinang (George Town)
Butterworth
Pinang
Kelantan
2171
Chamah
Dungun
North Natuna

5°N

Banda Aceh
Sigli
Lhokseumawe
Bireuen
Lhoksukon
Idi
Geureudong 2855
Peureulak
Langsa
Taiping
Kampar
Sungai Siput Utara
Ipoh
2131
Kuala Lipis
Raub
Tapis 1512
Kuantan
Natuna
Natuna Islands (Indonesia)

Calang
Meulaboh
Leuser 3404
Pangkalanbrandan
Tanjungpura
Kutacane
Kuala Kubu Baharu
Bentong
Kelang
Petaling Jaya
Kuala Lumpur
South Natuna Islands

Tapaktuan
Kabanjahe
Medan
Tebingtinggi
Pematangsiantar
Tanjungbalai
Seremban
Segamat
Tioman
Anambas Islands (Indonesia)
Cape Datu
Binatang
Sarikei

Simeulue
Lake Toba
Sumatra
Sihabuhabu 2300
Rantauprapat
Tarutung
Sibolga
Malacca
Muar
Keluang
Blumut 1010
Malacca Strait
Johor
Kulai
Datuk Bay
Kuching

Nias
Padangsidimpuan
Panyabungan
Dumai
Rupat
Johor Baharu
SINGAPORE
Tambelan Islands
Pinang
Sambas
Pamangkat
Singkawang
Lupar
Band-Sri A

Tuangku
Singkilbaru
Hutanopan
Balaipungut
Duri
Riau Islands

INDIAN

Equator 0°
Pini
2912
Lubuksikaping
Pakanbaru
Kampar
Lingga Islands
Pinang
Ngabang
Sanggau
Pontianak
Sin

OCEAN

Tanahbala
Bukittinggi
Payakumbuh
Padangpanjang
Rengat
Indragiri
Singkep
Bengkolan Bay
Kapuas
Nanga Sokan

Siberut
Padang
Solok
Siberut
Indragiri
Berhala Strait
Cape Jabung
Maya

100°E
105°E
110°E

n o p q r s t u v w x y z

68

This map shows 1/60 of the earth's surface.

a b c d e f g h i j k l m

115°E 120°E 125°E

Babuyan Islands

Cape Bojeador
Laoag
Aparri *Cape Engaño*

Banguéd
Vigan
Tuguegarao

Luzon
Ilagan

Pulog
2934
Bayombong

Lingayen Gulf
Baguio

Lingayen
Dagupan
San Ildefenso Peninsula

San Jose
San Carlos
Masinloc
Tarlac
Cabanatuan

Iba
Angeles
San Fernando

15°N

Olongapo
Caloocan
Polillo Islands

Manila
Quezon

Pasig
Lamon Bay

Manila Bay
Laguna de Bay

San Pablo
Lipa
Lucena
Lopez
Daet

Lubang
Batangas
Naga
Virac

Calapan
Boac
Catanduanes

Halcon 2582
Marinduque
Mayon 2462

Mindoro
Baco 2363
Burias
Legazpi

San Jose
Sibuyan
Bulan
Sorsogon

Calamian Group
Tablas
Masbate
Laoang

P H I L I P P I N E S
Catarman
Calbayog

Zhongye Islands
Nangtud 2117
Roxas
Biliran
Catbalogan

Panay
Masbate
Tacloban

Samar

San Jose de Buenavista
Iloilo
Silay
Cadiz
Bogo
Ormoc

Palawan
Bago
Bacolod
San Carlos
Cebu
Abuyog

Guimaras
2465
Toledo
Mandaue
Leyte

Cleopatra Needle 1602
Binalbagan
Cebu
Maasin
Dinagat

Honda Bay
Puerto Princesa
Bais
Siargao

10°N

Negros
Tagbilaran
Bohol
Surigao

Bayawan
Dumaguete
Camiguin
Butuan

Mantalingajan 2085
Siquijor
Gingoog

Dapitan
Dipolog
Dapitan
Cagayan de Oro
O C E A N

Bugsuk
Oroquieta
Iligan
Malaybalay
Bislig

Balabac
Ozamiz
Tangub
Marawi

Sulu Sea
Pagadian

Malayan
Balabac Strait
Davao

Banggi
Tagum

Cagayan Sulu
Cotabato
Apo 2954

Jambongan
Zamboanga
Digos
Davao Gulf

Sea
Basilan
Koronadal
Mindanao

Kota Kinabalu
Kinabalu 4175
Labuk Bay
Basilan

Sandakan
Jolo
General Santos

Beaufort
SABAH
Sulu Archipelago
Sarangani Islands

Brunei Bay
Tawitawi

5°N

ndar Seri Begawan
Lahad Datu
Tawitawi Group
Kawio Islands

Kuala Belait
BRUNEI
Darvel Bay

Miri
Mulu 2371
Tawau

Celébes Sea
Talaud Islands

AYSIA (EASTERN)
Sebuku Bay

(Sulawesi Sea)

RAWAK
Tarakan

Sangihe

2550
Sangihe Islands

Kayan
Morotai

Guguang 2467
Tanjungredeb

Liangpran 2240
Menyapa 2000
Rapak
Manado
2202
Tobelo

rneo
Tondano
Akelamo

limantan)
Celébes (Sulawesi)
Jailolo

Buol
Paleleh
Ternate
Halmahera

Muarabadak
Dongkalang
2913
Moutong
Tilamuta
Kotamobagu
Weda

N
Mapaga
Kuandang
Gorontalo
Weda Bay

Samarinda
E
S
I
A
0°

Donggala
Palu
Togian Is.
Malik
Molucca
Labuha

Uebonti
2400
Teku
Gulf of Tomini
Sea
Bacan
Gebe

115°E 120°E 125°E

n o p q r s t u v w x y z

69

95°E 100°E 105°E 110°E

S O U T H

Phatthalung
*Thale
Luang*
Trang
Songkhla
THAILAND
Hat Yai
Terutao
Satun
Pattani
Sai Buri
Langkawi
Alor
Setar
Yala
Narathiwat
Sungai
Ko-lok
Kota Baharu
Sungai
Petani
Banda Aceh
Sigli
Butterworth
Pinang
(George Town)
Pinang
Kuala Terengganu
Lhokseumawe
Lhoksukon
Sumatra
*2171
Chamah*
Bireuen
Idi
5°N
*2855
Geureudong*
Peureulak
Taiping
Sungai Siput Utara
Dungun
North Natuna
Calang
Langsa
Ipoh
MALAYA
2137
Kuala Lipis
*Natuna
(Bunguran)*
Meulaboh
Pangkalanbrandan
Kampar
Raub
*Tapis
1512*
Tanjungpura
*Leuser
3404*
Kuala Kubu
Baharu
Kuantan
*Natuna Islands
(Indonesia)*
□ **Medan**
Kutacane
Bentong
South Natuna
Tapaktuan
Tebingtinggi
**Kuala
Lumpur**
**MALAYSIA
(WESTERN)**
Cape Datu
Datuk Bay
Kabanjahe
Pematangsiantar
Kelang
Petaling Jaya
Tioman
*Anambas
Islands
(Indonesia)*
Kuchi
Simeulue
Lake Toba
Tanjungbalai
Seremban
Sambas
Ba
Sri *
Singkilbaru
*Sihabuhabu
2300*
Rantauprapat
Malacca
Muar
*Blumut
1010*
Pamangkat
Singkawang
Tuangku
Tarutung
Sibolga
Dumai
Rupat
Keluang
Johor
Johor Baharu
Pinang
Ngabang
Sang
Nias
Padangsidimpuan
Panyabungan
Duri
Balaipungut
Kulai
□ **SINGAPORE**
Pontianak
Hutanopan
Pakanbaru
Riau Islands
Tambelan Islands
Bengkolan Bay
Equator
Pini
Lubuksikaping
Ophir
2912
Kampar
Lingga Islands
Maya
Bukittingi
Payakumbuh
Rengat
Singkep
Nanga
Tanahbala
Padangpanjang
Indragiri
Berhala Strait
Karimata
Ketapang
Solok
Sumatra
Cape Jabung
Padang
Muarabungo
Hari
Jambi
Karimata Strait
Siberut
*Kerinci
3805*
Bukit Barisan Mountains
Muntok
Pangkalpinang
Bangka
Sipora
Sungaipenuh
Tanjungpandan
Belitung
North Pagai
Sarolangun
Palembang
Sungaigerung
Gaspar Strait
65
*South
Pagai*
Lubuklinggau
Perabumulih
Bengkulu
Lahat
*Dempo
3159*
I
N
D
Bintuhan
Kotabumi
*Pesagi
2231*
Enggano
Tanjungkarang
Telukbetung
(Bandarlampung)
Sunda Strait
Merak
Jakarta
J
5°S
Krakatau
Cirebon
*Cape
Cangkuang*
Bogor
Pekalongan
Sukabumi
Tegal
*Slamet
3418*
Semar
Bandung
J
Tasik Malaya
Purwokerto
Magelang
Sur
Cilacap
Yogya

I N D I A N

O C E A N

95°E 100°E 105°E 110°E

*Christmas Island
(Australia)*

This map shows 1/60 of the earth's surface.

a b c d e f g h i j k l m

115°E   120°E   125°E

Balabac Strait

Sulu Sea

PHILIPPINES

Pagadian

I N A   *N*   *A*

Banggi

Cagayan Sulu

Zamboanga   *Moro Gulf*   Cotabato   Davao   Tagum

Jambongan

Basilan   *Basilan*   Apo 2954   *Davao Gulf*   *Mindanao*

Digos

Malayan Sea

Pangutaran Group

Koronadal

Jolo

General Santos

Kota Kinabalu   Kinabalu 4175   *Labuk Bay*   SABAH

Sandakan

Sulu Archipelago

Sarangani

Beaufort

Lahad Datu

Tawitawi

5°N

Brunei Bay

Darvel Bay

Tawitawi Group

Bandar Seri Begawan

Kawio

Kuala Belait   **BRUNEI**

Talaud Islands

Miri   Baram   Mulu 2371

Tawau

Celebes Sea

Sangihe

Morotai

MALAYSIA (EASTERN)

Sebuku Bay

(Sulawesi Sea)

Sangihe Islands

Tobelo

Sesayap

Tarakan

SARAWAK

Akelamo

Bintulu

2550

Jailolo   Saolat 1508

Rajang

Guguang 2467

Tanjungredeb

Manado   Klabat 2022   Tondano

Ternate   **Halmahera**

Kayan

Kuandang

Weda

Kapuas

Liangpran 2240   Menyapa 2000

Rapak

Dondo Bay   Buol   Paleleh   2217

Kotamobagu

M o l u c c a   *Weda Bay*

Ja Pinoh

Mahakam

Ogoamas 2913

Moutong   Tilamuta   Gorontalo

S e a

0°

B o r n e o

Dongkalang

Bacan Islands

(Kalimantan)

Samarinda   Muarabadak

Mapaga

Gulf of Tomini

Togian Islands

Labuha

Raya 2278

Balikpapan

Donggala

Malik   Teku

Obi

Tumbangsamba

Barito

Buntok   Sarempaka 1380

Palu

2400

Peleng

M o l u c c a s

Uebonti   Batui

Ceram Sea

Palangkaraya   Tanjung

Besar 1892

Lumu   *Celebes (Sulawesi)*

Poso

Taliabu   *Mangole*

70

Sampit   Kandangan

Muratus Mountains

Gandadiwata 3074   Masamba   Wotu

Gulf of Tolo

Banggai Islands

Sula Islands   M

Lambuun

Palopo

Namlea   *Buru*   *Ceram*

Kotabaru

Rantekombala 3455

Gulf of Bone

Mekongga 2799

Strait of Manipa

Banjarmasin

Majene

Kendari

Ambon

D   Batakan   *N*   *Cape Selatan*

Laut

Parepare

Kolaka

Kolono

E   *S*   *I*   *A*

Makassar Strait

Watampone

Jatisiri

Raha   *Muna*

Butung

5°S

Ujung Pandang   Sinjai

2871

Kabaena

Baubau

Tukangbesi Islands

Banda Sea

Bawean

Masalembo

a   *S*   *e*   *a*

Salajar

Madura

Kangean

Tanahjampea   *Kalao*

Barat Daya Islands

angkalan   **Surabaya**

Madura Strait

Bali Sea   *Flores Sea*

L e s s e r   S u n d a   I s l a n d s

Wetar

Probolinggo   Banyuwangi

Semeru 3676

Leti Islands

Malang   Jember   2276   *Bali*

3725

Sumbawa Besar   Raba

Alor

Dili

Denpasar   *Lombok*   Mataram

Ruteng   2400

Maumere   *Solor Islands*

Atambua   2960   *Timor*

Sumbawa

Flores   Ende

Besikama

Waikabubak   Waingapu

Sawu Sea

10°S

Sumba

Kupang

Sawu   *Roti*

Timor Sea

115°E   120°E   125°E

n o p q r s t u v w x y z

0 100 200 300 miles   Average linear scale   0 100 200 300 400 500 Km

130°E   135°E   140°E   14

° *Yap Islands*

Faraulep Atoll

° *Ngulu Atoll*

° *Sorol Atoll*

F e d e r a t e d

Palau
Islands ° *Babel Thuap*
° *Koror*

Woleai Atoll°
Ifalik Atoll

° *Eauripik Atoll*

Palau
(U.S.A.-U.N.)

C a r o l i n e

° *Sonsorol*

5°N

° *Pulo Anna*

° *Merir*

P A C I F

° *Tobi*

° *Helen Reef*

Morotai

° *Mapia Islands*

O C E A

° *Akelamo*
Halmahera

° *Ayu Islands*

Waigeo

0°

69

Dampier Strait

Biak

° *Kwoko*
3000

° *Manokwari*

° *Sorong*

° *Peg Ariak*
2939

Yapen

Misool

C e n d e r a w a s i h

990°

° *Sarmi*

C

Steenkool

Van Rees Mountains

° *Jayapura*

C e r a m
3019°

Bula°

Babo°

Ceram Sea

Fakfak°

INDONESIA

Gulf of
Cenderawasih

Mamberamo

° *Vanimo*

IRIAN

° *Aitape*

Ambon°

° *Tobo*

Bomberai

Kaimana°

Maoke

Jaya
5028

Lumi°

° *Dreikikir*

° *Wewak*

Sepik

Kokonau°

JAYA

M o u n t a i n

Wamena°

N e w

Ramu

Kai
Islands

Mandala
4702

5°S

B a n d a   S e a

G u i n e a

Telefomin°

Bismarck

Aru
Islands

Tanahmerah°

Kopiago°

° *Wabag*

Strickland

° *Mount*
Hagen

Mendi°

Kubor°
4359

Damar°

Tanimbar
Islands

Mappi°

Digul

Lake
Murray

2895

N E W

Babar°

Dolak
Island

Fly

° *Kikori*

Sermata°

° *Selaru*

Cape Vals°

Merauke°

Gulf
Pap

Daru°

A R A F U R A   S E A

Torres Strait

10°S

Badu° ° *Moa*

130°E   135°E   140°E

Prince of Wales
Island ° *Cape York*

73

This map shows 1/60 of the earth's surface.

a b c d e f g h i j k l m

150°E   155°E   160°E

Namenuito Atoll

Fayu   *Murillo Atoll*

est Fayu   *Pikelot*   Hall Islands

Lamotrek Atoll   *Minto Atoll*

S t a t e s   o f   M   i   c   r   o   n   e   s   i   a

(U.S.A.-U.N.)   Truk Islands   *Oroluk Atoll*

Elato Atoll   *Satawal*

                                                        Ponape   *Mokil Atoll*

                          Losap Atoll   *Senjavin Group*

                                                                    Pingelap Atoll

s l a n d s   *Namolok*

                                                          Ngatik Atoll

                              Satawan Atoll   *Mortlock Islands*

                                                                        Kosrae

5°N

I   C

N

                                    Kapingamarangi Atoll

                                                                    Equator   0°

Admiralty Islands

B i s m a r c k   A r c h i p e l a g o   ○ *Kavieng*

B i s m a r c k   S e a   *New Ireland*

                                          Rabaul ○

P A P U A   *Sinewit 2438*

adang   5°S

                                                                Balbi 2743

                Walinga   *New Britain*   *Bougainville*   ○ *Kieta*
Bangeta 4107   *Kandrian* ○   (Papua New Guinea)

○ *Lae*   *Nukiki* ○   *Choiseul*   SOLOMON
                                                        Alu   *Fauro*   ISLANDS

G U I N E A   *Mono*   *Santa Isabel*

rema   ○ *Morobe*   *Vella Lavella*

                                                                  New Georgia   ○ *Buala*
            Popondetta   *Solomon Sea*   *New Georgia Islands*   *Vangunu*

Victoria 4013   *Trobriand or Kiriwina Island*   *Malaita*

                  Woodlark   *Honiara*
Port Moresby *Sogeri*   D'Entrecasteaux Islands   *Popomanaseu 2331*
            Kwikila   *Guadalcanal*

                    ○ *Alotau*   *San Cristóbal*

n o p q r s t u v w x y z

150°E   155°E   160°E

0   100   200   300 miles   Average linear scale   0   100   200   300   400   500 Km

Map labels

Java
Bali
Lombok
Denpasar
Mataram
Sumbawa
Besar
1400
Sumbawa
3726
Raba
Ruteng *2400*
Ende
Flores
Maumere
Solor
Alor
Dili
Atambua *2960*
2421
Timor
Besikama

I N D O N E S I A *Sawu*

Waikabubak
Waingapu
Sea
Sumba *1175*

Sawu
Kupang
Roti

Tim
S

Cartier

Cape
Bougainville
Lond
Kalu

Bonaparte Archipelago
Theda

I N D I A N

Kuri Bay
Kimbe
Pla

Collier
Bay
Mount Hann
776
Panter
Downs
Karu

Cape
Lévêque
Lombardina
Beverley
Springs
Mount House
Tableland

Oobagooma
Mount Ora
927
936
Glenroy

O C E A N

Beagle
Bay
Dampier
Land
Derby
Kimberley
Downs
Mt.
Broome

Coulomb
Point
Camballin

Broome
Roebuck
Plains
Fitzroy
Fitzroy
Crossing

Dampier
Downs
Myroodah
Mount
Huxley
522
Margar
River

Lagrange
247
Nerrima
Christmas
Creek
Bohem
Downs

Frazier Downs

Anna Plains

Eighty Mile Beach
Wallal Downs

15°S

20°S

Port
Hedland
Goldsworthy
Great Sandy Desert
G
Mount *41*
Elliott

Barrow
Island
Dampier
Roebourne
Shay Gap

Cooya
Pooya
Whim
Creek
Kangan
Yarrie
Warrawagine

North West Cape
Exmouth
Yarraloola
Yule
Marble
Bar
Bamboo
Creek
Percival Lakes

Onslow
Pannawonica
Millstream
Mount Florance
W E S T E R N

Mount
Minnie
Wittenoom
Nullagine
Lake
Dora
Lake
Auld

Learmonth
Yanrey
Hamersley
Tom Price
Mount Tom
Price
1073
Fortescue
Talawana
Lake
Blanche
Tabletop
427

Uaroo
Wyloo
Range
1251
A

Winning
Mount
Palgrave
1104
Ashburton
Downs
Paraburdoo
Mount
Meharry
Mount
Newman
1053

Lake
Disappointment

U

S

Ullawarra
Newman
Gibson Desert

Lyndon
Ashburton
Turee
Creek

Minnie Creek
Bulloo Downs

Cape
Cuvier
Lake
McLeod
Mount
Augustus
1105
Augustus
Mount
Vernon
A U S T R A L I

Lyons
Waldburg Range
Kumarina

Carnarvon
Gascoyne
Junction
Gascoyne
Milgun
Three
Rivers
Mount
Essendon *906*
Carnarvon
Range
Glenayle

Cape
Inscription
Shark Bay
Dairy
Creek
Mount
Seabrook
Peak Hill
Neds Creek
738
Granite Peak

Denham
552
Lake
Nabberu
Carnegie

Useless Loop
Byro
732 *Mount Hale*
Karalundi
Wiluna
Yelma
Warburton *6*
M
Ta

Hamelin Pool
Curbur
Mileura
Lake
Carnegie

Tamala
Murchison
Kalli
Meekatharra
Wonganoo

Wannoo
530
Tuckanarra
Gidgee

Kalbarri
Yallalong
Big
Bell
Cue
Booylgoo
Springs
Agnew
Gre
594

Billabalon
Murgoo
Sandstone

Tropic of Capricorn

25°S

110°E   115°E   120°E   125°E

This map shows 1/60 of the earth's surface.

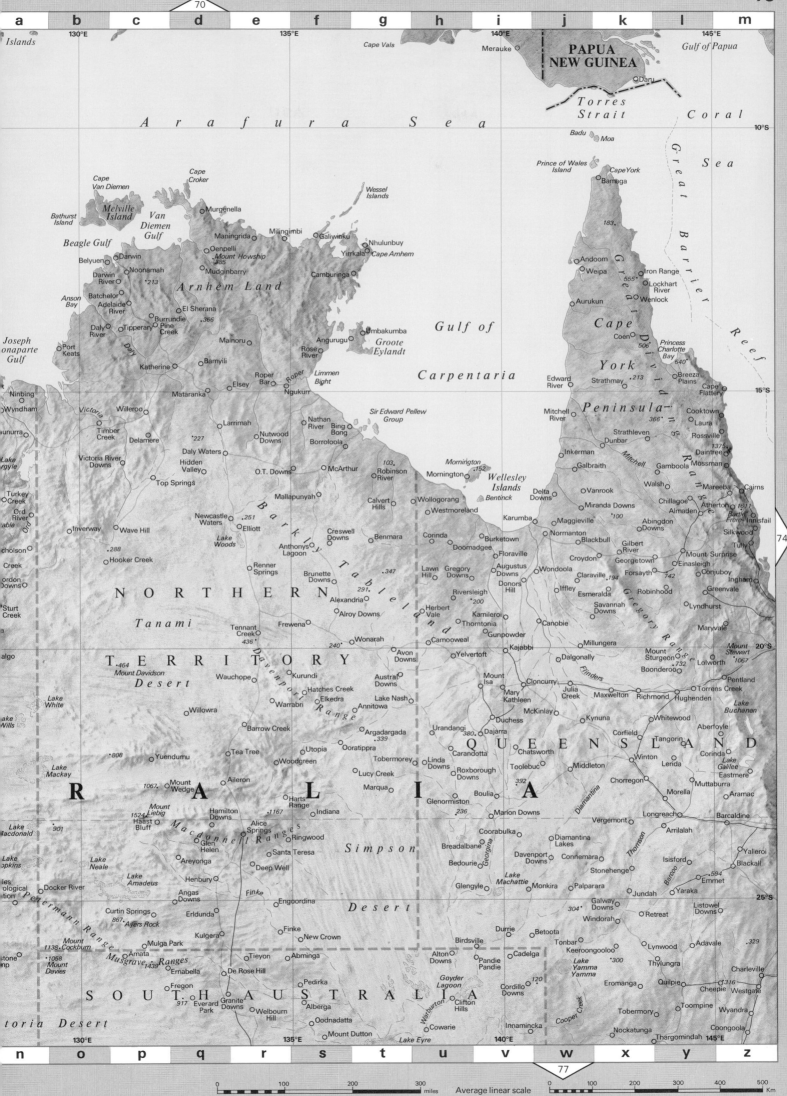

a b c d e f g h i j k l m

130°E   135°E   140°E   145°E

Islands

Cape Vals   Merauke

PAPUA NEW GUINEA

Daru   *Gulf of Papua*

A r a f u r a   S e a

Torres Strait   *Coral*   10°S

Badu   Moa   *S e a*

Cape Van Diemen   Cape Croker

Bathurst Island   Melville Island   Murgenella

Van Diemen Gulf   Prince of Wales Island   Cape York
Bamaga

Beagle Gulf   Maningrida   Milingimbi   Galiwinku

Belyuen   Darwin   Oenpelli   Yirrkala   Cape Arnhem   Nhulunbuy   Andoom   Weipa   Iron Range

Noonamah   Mudginbarry   Mount Howship *385*   183   555   Lockhart River

Darwin River   *213*   Camburinga   Wenlock

Anson Bay   Batchelor   El Sherana   Aurukun

Adelaide River   *366*   *Arnhem Land*   *Gulf of*   *Cape*

Joseph Bonaparte Gulf   Daly River   Burrundie   Pine Creek   Umbakumba   Coen   506   Princess Charlotte Bay

Port Keats   Tipperary   Mainoru   Angurugu   Groote Eylandt   *Carpentaria*   *York*   640

Katherine   Bamyili   Rose River   Edward River   Strathmay   *213*   Breeza Plains

Roper Bar   *Limmen Bight*   *Peninsula*   Cape Flattery   15°S

Ninbing   Wyndham   Willeroo   Elsey   Ngukurr   Roper   Mitchell River   366   Cooktown

Victoria   Timber Creek   Larrimah   Nathan River   Bing Bong   Strathleven   Laura

Lake Argyle   Delamere   *227*   Nutwood Downs   Borroloola   *Sir Edward Pellew Group*   Dunbar   Inkerman   1375   Rossville   Daintree

Turkey Creek   Victoria River Downs   Daly Waters   Hidden Valley   103   *Mornington* 152   Galbraith   Mossman

Ord River   Top Springs   O.T. Downs   McArthur   Robinson River   Mornington   *Wellesley Islands*   Delta Downs   Vanrook   Walsh   Gamboola   Mareeba

Mallapunyah   Calvert Hills   Wollogorang   *Bentinck*   Karumba   Miranda Downs   Chillagoe   Almaden   Atherton   161   Cairns

cholson   Inverway   Wave Hill   Newcastle Waters   *251*   Elliott   Westmoreland   Maggieville   Abingdon Downs   Bartle Frere   Innisfail

Sturt Creek   *288*   Hooker Creek   *Lake Woods*   Anthonys Lagoon   Creswell Downs   Benmara   Corinda   Burketown   Normanton   Blackbull   Gilbert River   Georgetown   Einasleigh   Silkwood

Renner Springs   Doomadgee   Floraville   Croydon   Wondoola   Forsayth   742   Conjuboy   Tully

NORTHERN   Brunette Downs   *347*   Lawn Hill   Gregory Downs   Augustus Downs   Claraville   194   Mount Surprise   Ingham

291   Alexandria   Riversleigh   200   Donors Hill   Iffley   Esmeralda   Savannah Downs   Robinhood   Greenvale

Tanami   Alroy Downs   Herbert Vale   Kamileroi   Thorntonia   Canobie   Lyndhurst

Tennant Creek   Frewena   Wonarah   436   Gunpowder   Maryvale

240   Avon Downs   Camooweal   Millungera   Mount Stewart   20°S

TERRITORY   *464*   Yelvertoft   Kajabbi   Dalgonally   Mount Sturgeon   732   Lolworth   1067

Mount Davidson   Wauchope   Kurundi   *Austral Downs*   Mount Isa   Cloncurry   Julia Creek   Maxwelton   Richmond   Hughenden   Torrens Creek   Pentland

Desert   Hatches Creek   Elkedra   Lake Nash   Mary Kathleen   McKinlay   *Lake Buchanan*

Lake White   Warrabri   Annitowa   Duchess   Kynuna   Whitewood

Willowra   Barrow Creek   Argadargada   339   Urandangi   380   Dajarra   Corfield   Tangorin   Aberfoyle   *Lake Galilee*

Lake Mackay   Yuendumu   Tea Tree   Utopia   Ooratippra   Tobermorey   Linda Downs   Roxborough Downs   Toolebuc   Middleton   Winton   Lerida   Eastmere

Woodgreen   Lucy Creek   Carandotta   Chatsworth   Corinda   Muttaburra

808   Aileron   Harts Range   Marqua   Boulia   392   Chorregon   Morella   Aramac

R   1067   Mount Wedge   Hamilton Downs   1167   Indiana   Glenormiston   236   Marion Downs   Vergemont   Longreach   Barcaldine

Mount Liebig 1524   *A*   Haast Bluff   Alice Springs   Ringwood   *Simpson*   Coorabulka   Diamantina Lakes   Arrilalah

Lake Macdonald   901   *Macdonnell Ranges*   Glen Helen   Santa Teresa   Breadalbane   Davenport Downs   Connemara   Isisford   Yalleroi

Lake Neale   Areyonga   Deep Well   Bedourie   *Georgina*   Stonehenge   Blackall

Lake Amadeus   Henbury   Glengyle   *Lake Machattie*   Monkira   Palparara   594   Emmet

Docker River   Angas Downs   Finke   Engoordina   *Desert*   Galway Downs   Jundah   Yaraka   Listowel Downs   25°S

Petermann Range   Curtin Springs   Erldunda   304   Retreat   Windorah

867   Ayers Rock   Kulgera   Finke   New Crown   Durrie   Betoota   Tonbar   Lynwood   Adavale   329

1138 Mount Cockburn   Mulga Park   Tieyon   Abminga   Birdsville   Keeroongooloo   *Lake Yamma Yamma*   300   Thylungra   Charleville

1058 Mount Davies   Amata   *Musgrave* 1439 *Ranges*   De Rose Hill   Alton Downs   Cadelga   Eromanga   Quilpie   316   Westgate

Ernabella   Pandie Pandie   Cordillo Downs   120   Cheepie

Fregon   917   Everard Park   Granite Downs   Pedirka   *Goyder Lagoon*   Clifton Hills   Toompine   Wyandra

SOUTH   AUSTRALIA   Welbourn Hill   Alberga   *Warburton*   Innamincka   Tobermory   Nockatunga   Coongoola

toria Desert   Oodnadatta   Mount Dutton   Cowarie   Lake Eyre   *Cooper Creek*   Thargomindah

130°E   135°E   140°E   145°E

n o p q r s t u v w x y z

0   100   200   300 miles   Average linear scale   0   100   200   300   400   500 Km

71

145°E   150°E   155°E   160°E

PAPUA
NEW GUINEA

Owen
Mount
Suckling
Stanley
Range
1925   3676

Port
Moresby

D'Entrecasteaux
Islands

M

Honiara
Guadalcanal
2331

Kwikila

Baniara

Normanby

10°S

Robinson
River

Alotau

SOLOMON
ISLANDS

Cape
York

Louisiade Archipelago

e

SOLOMON
l
SEA

Ren
Isla

183

a

P   **A**

Iron
Range

Lockhart
River

Wenlock

Cape

Coen
506

Princess
Charlotte
640

York

Breeza
Plains

Cape
Flattery

Cooktown

15°S

Peninsula

366

Laura

Strathleven

Rossville

Willis Islands

C   **O**   **R**   **A**   **L**

Mitchell

Daintree
1375

Gamboola

Mossman

Walsh

Cairns
Mareeba

Chillagoe

Atherton
Bartle
Frere
1611

Innisfail

Almaden

Silkwood
Tully

Abingdon
Downs

Gilbert
River

Georgetown

Forsayth
742

Einasleigh

Ingham

Esmeralda

Greenvale

Robinhood

Lyndhurst

Gregory

Townsville

Burdekin

Ayr
Mount Elliot
1234

Bowen

S   **E**   **A**

Chesterfield
Islands
(France)

73

Mount
Sturgeon

Lolworth
Mount
Stewart
1076

Charters
Towers

Proserpine

Collinsville

Mount
Dalrymple
1259

20°S

732

Torrens
Creek

Pentland

Richmond

Hughenden

Range

Finch
Hatton

Mackay
Sarina

Sutter

Mount
Coolon

Whitewood

Aberfoyle

Lake
Buchanan

Nebo

Tangorin

Mount
Douglas

Carmila

Winton

Lake
Galilee

Chorregon

Eastmere

Muttaburra

Blair
Athol

Peak
Downs

St. Lawrence

Marlborough

Morella

Aramac

Clermont

Fitzroy

Longreach

Barcaldine

Alpha

Capella

Emerald

Yeppoon

Cato

Arrilalah

Bogantungan

Duaringa

Rockhampton

Mount Morgan

Q U E E N S L A N D

Yalleroi

Springsure

Gladstone

O

Isisford

Barcoo

Blackall

Baralaba

Banana

Wowan

Biloela

Miriam Vale

Stonehenge
594

Emmet

Tambo

Rolleston

Theodore

Monto

Bundaberg

Yaraka

Consuelo Peak
1219

Hervey
Bay

25°S

806

Childers

Fraser
Island

Retreat

Listowel
Downs

A U S T R A L I A

Taroom

Mundubbera

Maryborough

Windorah

Lynwood

Adavale

Augathella
329

Injune

Wandoan

Murgon

Gympie

Thylungra

Charleville

Morven

Mitchell

Miles

Kingaroy

Nambour

Maroochydore

Eromanga

Quilpie

Cheepie

Westgate

Roma

Chinchilla

Yarraman

Moreton
Island

1101

Esk

Caboolture

Tobermory

Bulloo

Wyandra

Albany
Downs

Surat

Dalby

Toowoomba

Gatton

Brisbane

Ipswich

Thargomindah

Coongoola

Glenmorgan

Moonie

Clifton

Gold Coast

Cunnamulla

Bollon

Westmar

Warwick

Murwillumbah

Bulloo
Downs

Paroo

Eulo

St. George

Nindigully

Inglewood

Talwood

Stanthorpe

Dirranbandi

Goondiwindi

Hebel

Thallon

Lismore

Casino

145°E   150°E   155°E   160°E

78

This map shows 1/60 of the earth's surface.

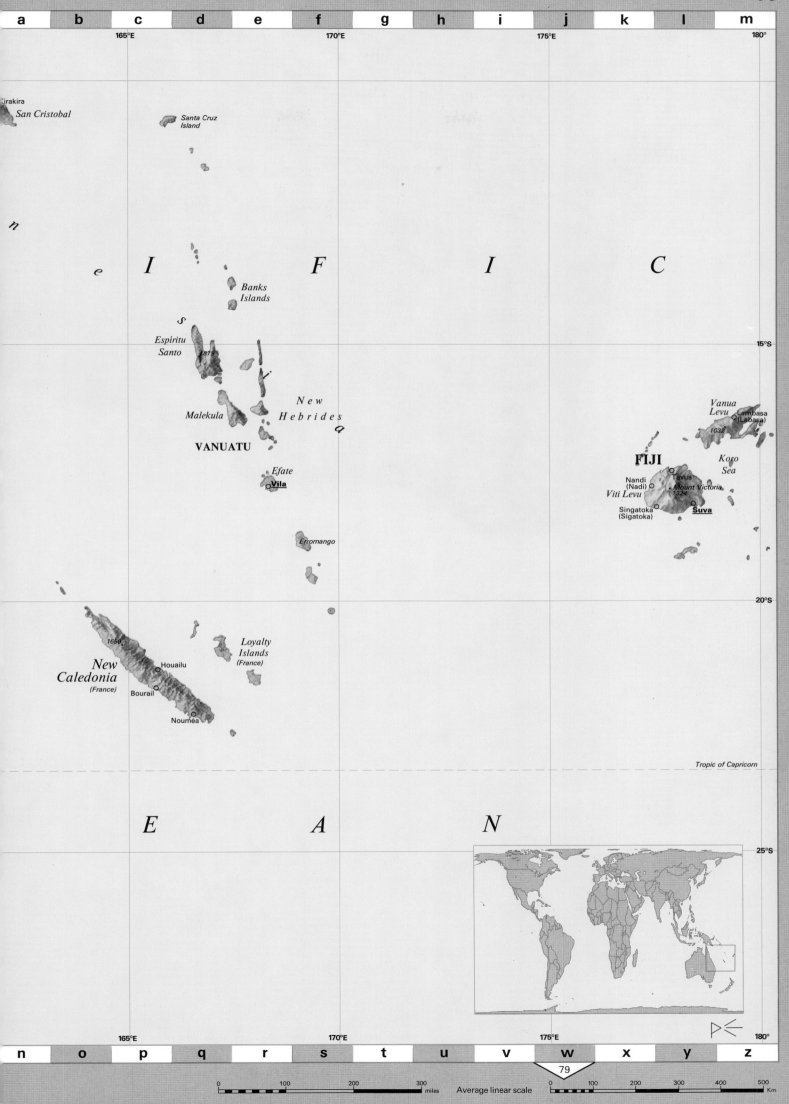

165°E　170°E　175°E　180°

Kirakira
San Cristobal

*Santa Cruz
Island*

n

e　*I*　*F*　*I*　*C*

s

*Banks
Islands*

*Espíritu
Santo*
1879

Malekula

*New
Hebrides*

VANUATU

Efate
Vila

Erromango

*Vanua
Levu*　Lambasa
(Labasa)
1032

FIJI
*Koro
Sea*

Nandi
(Nadi)　Tavua
Mount Victoria
1324
Viti Levu
Singatoka
(Sigatoka)　**Suva**

15°S

20°S

*New
Caledonia*
(France)
1650
Houailu
Bourail
Nouméa

*Loyalty
Islands*
(France)

Tropic of Capricorn

E　*A*　*N*

25°S

165°E　170°E　175°E　180°

0　100　200　300　miles　　Average linear scale　　0　100　200　300　400　500　Km

115°E

120°E

125°E

Docker River

Carnarvon

Kumarina

Mount
Essendon
906

Carnarvon Range

Gibson Desert

Giles
Meteorological
Station

25°S

Cape Inscription

*Shark
Bay*

Gascoyne
Junction

Dairy
Creek

Gascoyne

Milgun

Three Rivers

Glenayle

738

Lake
Nabberu

Granite
Peak

Carnegie

M
Coc
1138

Denham

Lyons

Waldburg Range

Mount
Seabrook

.582

Peak Hill

Neds
Creek

Byro

Karalundi

Wiluna

Yelma

Mount
Talbot
623

Blackstone
Camp

Mou
Davi
105

Useless Loop

Hamelin
Pool

Tamala

Mileura

Mount Hale
.732

Kalli

Wonganoo

W E S T E R N

Curbur

Murchison

Byro

Big Bell

661

Tuckanarra

Gidgee

Lake
Carnegie

Wannoo

Yallalong

.530

Cue

Booylgoo Springs

A U S T R A L I A

Virginia Range

Lake Yeo

466

Kalbarri

Billabalon

Murgoo

Lake
Austin

Sandstone

Agnew

Great Victor

Victoria
Range

Geraldton

Greenough

Northampton

Mullewa

552.

Mount Magnet

Salt Lakes

Leonora

Lake
Carey

Lake
Rason

.259

Houtman
Abrolhos

Wallabi Group

Easter Group

Pelsart Group

Geelvink Channel

Mingenew

Paynes
Find

Lake Barlee

Lake
Raeside

30°S

Green Head

Eneabba

Coorow

Pithara

Lake Moore

.447

Menzies

393

Nullarbor Plain

Cervantes Island

Moora

686.

Deakin

Cape Leschenault

Gingin

Lake Deborah

Kalgoorlie
Coolgardie

Ponton Creek

Rawlinna

Loongana

Swan

Southern Cross

Eucla

Perth

Northam

.381

Kellerberrin

Parker Range

Lake Cowan

Fraser Range

Hampton Tableland

Fremantle

Avon

Norseman

.19
Eyre

Wilso

Mandurah

Johnston
Lakes

Scorpion Bay

Peel Bay

Narrogin

Balladonia

Twilight Cove

Waroona

Peak Charles
658

Cape Culver

Bunbury

Collie

Wagin

Russell Range
585

Great Austr

Busselton

Katanning

.411

Ravensthorpe

Esperance

Israelite Bay

Karridale

Manjimup

Jerramungup

West Group

Sandy Bay

Blackwood

Stirling Range

Bluff Knoll
.1109

Hood Cape

Recherche-Archipelago

Twin Rocks

Flinders Bay

Frankland

Cape Knob

Termination Island

Cape D'Entrecasteaux

Albany

Channel Cape

35°S

Cape Nuyts

*West
Cape Howe*

Bald Cape

40°S

I N D I A N

45°S

115°E

120°E

125°E

This map shows 1/60 of the earth's surface.

73

Lake
Amadeus

Henbury

Angas
Downs

Erldunda

135°E

Engoordina

Finke

NORTHERN TERRITORY

Stonehenge

Emmet

145°E

Blackall

•725

25°S

Glengyle

Lake
Machattie

Monkira

Palparara

Galway
Downs

Jundah

Yaraka

Listowel
Downs

Tambo

Ayers Rock
867

Mulga
Park

Ernabella

Kulgera

Tieyon

Abminga

New
Crown

Simpson Desert

304

Windorah

Retreat

QUEENSLAND

•914

Durrie

Betoota

Birdsville

Tanbar

Keeroongooloo

Adavale

Charleville

Moven

Mitchell

Fregon

Everard
Park

917•

Granite
Downs

Pedirka

Alberga

Alton
Downs

Pandie
Pandie

Cadelga

Lake
Yamma
Yamma

300

Thylungra

Quilpie

316

Westgate

Maranoa

Welbourn Hill

Oodnadatta

Clifton
Hills

Goyder's
Lagoon

•120

Cordillo
Downs

Eromanga

Toompine

Wyandra

•251

SOUTH

Mount
Dutton

Cowarie

Cooper

Gidgelpa

142•

Innamincka

Sturt

Bulloo

Coongoola

St. George

Bollon

•181

11•

Nockatunga

Thargomindah

Cunnamulla

Dirranbandi

Lake Eyre

–16

Cooper

Desert

Paroo

Hebel

Thollon

Coober
Pedy

•205

Warrego

AUSTRAL

GIA

•216

Lake
Maurice

Marree

•427

Milparinka

Wanaaring

Bourke

Brewarrina

30°S

Walgett

sert

AUSTRALIA

Ooldea

Tarcoola

Kingoonya

1186

951
91•

Lake
Torrens

Woomera

Leigh Creek

Lake
Frome

1189

White Cliffs
221•

Wilcannia

Cobar

•419

Crowl

NEW

Nyngan

•1372

Coonamble

Yalata

Head of
Bight

Penong

•168

Ceduna

Lake Everard

Lake
Gairdner

Island
Lagoon

Wilpena

Passmore

Eurilla

Barrier Ra.

Mount Robe
474

Broken Hill

SOUTH

Dubbo

Narromine

n Bight

Fowler's
Bay

Nuyts Arch.
Streaky
Bay

Streaky Bay

Gawler Ranges

•472

307

Iron Knob

Quorn

Port Augusta

Cockburn

Benda Ra.

Ivanhoe

WALES

Condobolin

Parkes

Anxious Bay

250

Eyre
Peninsula

Wudinna

Cowell

Whyalla

Port Pirie

Peterborough

Darling

West
Wyalong

•732

Investigator Group

Pearson Island

Burra

•934

Morgan

Renmark

Murray

Wentworth

Hay

Murrumbidgee

Griffith

Leeton

Narrandera

Cootamundra

Cocoparra Range

Whidby Point

Port Lincoln

Sir Joseph
Banks Group

Thistle I.

Kadina

Wallaroo

Spencer Gulf

Yorke Peninsula

St. Vincent Gulf

Gawler

Adelaide

Murray

Mildura

Balranald

Ouyen

101

Billabong

Deniliquin

Junee

35°S

78

Cape Spencer

Investigator Strait

Kangaroo
Island

Victor
Harbor

Encounter
Bay

Murray Bridge

Pinnaroo

Lake Alexandra

Swan Hill

Corowa

Albury

Wagga
Wagga

AUST.
CAPITAL
TERRITORY

Lodden

Murray

Shepparton

Wangaratta

Hume
Res.

Lake
Eucumbene

Mt.
Kosciusko
2228

The Coorong

Lacepede Bay

Naracoorte

Glenelg

Nhill

Horsham

Lake
Hindmarsh

Donald

VICTORIA

Bendigo

Seymour

Buller
1804

1922

1742

Great Dividing Range

Mitchell

Snowy

Omeo

1320

Millicent

•220

Glenelg

Emu

Maryborough

Ararat

•1011

Ballarat

Healesville

Orbost

Mount Gambier

Hamilton

Melbourne

Geelong

Port
Philip
Bay

Moe

Traralgon

Sale

Ninety Mile Beach

Discovery Bay

Warrnambool

Portland

Wonthaggi

Port Albert

Cape Otway

Apollo
Bay

Waratah
Bay

Wilson's Promontory

Kent Group

Flinders I.

Currie

King Island

Bass Strait

Furneaux
Group

40°S

C　E　A　N

Hunter Island

Three Hummock
Island

Smithton

Arthur

Burnie

Herrick

Banks Strait

Sandy Cape

Devonport

1573

St. Marys

TASMANIA

Mt. Ossa
1617

Launceston

Coles
Bay

Queenstown

Strahan

Macquarie Harbour

1444

Derwent

Oatlands

Swansea

Point Hibbs

Frankland Ra.

New Norfolk
•1327

Hobart

Port Arthur

Elliot Bay

Gordon

Storm Bay

Port Davey

Maatsuyker
Islands

South East Cape

45°S

135°E

140°E

145°E

0　100　200　300　miles
Average linear scale
0　100　200　300　400　500　Km

a b c d e f g h i j k l m

145°E   150°E   155°E   160°E

Böllol
Adavale
316·
Charleville
Quilpie
Cheepie
Toompine
Coongoola
Wyandra
Augathella
914·
Morven
Mitchell
Westgate
251·
Surat
Glenmorgan
Bollon
St. George
Dirranbandi
Thallon
Hebel
Mungindi
Eulo
Cunnamulla
Wanaaring
Bourke
Brewarrina
Walgett

Taroom
Wandoan
Roma
Miles
Moonie
Toowoomba
Talwood
Goondiwindi
Gwydir
Moree
Inverell

Mundubbera
Gayndah
Murgon
Kingaroy
Dalby
Yarraman
Esk
Clifton
Warwick
Inglewood
Stanthorpe
Tenterfield
Glen
Innes

Maryborough
Gympie
Nambour
Caboolture
Moreton
Island
Brisbane
Gold Coast
Murwillumbah
1239·
Casino
Lismore
Grafton

Middleton Reef
Elisabeth Reef

P A

QUEENSLAND

A U S T R A L I A

NEW SOUTH WALES

30°S
Wanaaring
Darling
Cobar
Nyngan
Coonamble
Coonabarabran
1372·
1494·
Narrabri
Gunnedah
Tamworth
Armidale
Round
1608·
Kempsey
Port Macquarie
Barrington
Tops
1585·
Taree
Lord Howe
Island
(N.S.W.)

Crowl
Narromine
Dubbo
Wellington
Coolah
Muswellbrook
Coricudgy
1274·
Ivanhoe
Condobolin
Parkes
Forbes
Orange
Bathurst
Lithgow
Gosford
Newcastle
West Wyalong
Katoomba
1298·
Sydney
Griffith
732·
Cowra
Wollongong
Leeton
Cootamundra
Junee
Goulburn
Nowra
Narrandera
Hay
Murrumbidgee
Lachlan
Macquarie
Great Dividing Range
Coonabarabran

O

35°S
Deniliquin
Murray
Billabong
Wagga
Wagga
1913·
Canberra
Queanbeyan
AUST. CAPITAL
TERRITORY
Corowa
Albury
Hume
Reservoir
Lake
Eucumbene
Cooma
Mt. Kosciusko
2228·
Snowy
1320·
Shepparton
Wangaratta
Buller
1804·
Omeo
Snowy Mts.
Orbost
Cape Howe
Bendigo
Seymour
Healesville
VICTORIA
Mitchell
Bairnsdale
Melbourne
Geelong
Port Phillip
Bay
Moe
Sale
Traralgon
Ninety Mile Beach
Wonthaggi
Port Albert
Waratah Bay
Wilsons Promontory

77

40°S
Kent Group
Bass Strait
King Island
Furneaux
Group
Flinders Island
Hunter
Island
Three Hummock
Island
Banks Strait
Smithton
Burnie
Herrick
Arthur
Devonport
Ossa
1617·
Launceston
1573·
St. Marys
Queenstown
Coles Bay
Strahan
Oaklands
Swansea
Macquarie
Harbour
1444·
New
Norfolk
Hobart
Gordon
Frankland Range
Derwent
Storm Bay
Port Arthur
Elliot Bay
Port Davey
Maatsuyker
Islands
South East
Cape

TASMANIA

T A S M A N

45°S

145°E   150°E   155°E   160°E

n o p q r s t u v w x y z

This map shows 1/60 of the earth's surface.

165°E   170°E   175°E   180°E

30°S

P A C I F I C

Norfolk
Island
(Australia)

Macauley
Island
Kermadec Islands Curtis
(N.Z.)   Island

O C E A N

35°S

Three Kings
Island

North Cape

Ninety Mile Beach
Kaitaia   Bay of Islands

774

Whangarei

Dargaville

Great Barrier
Island

Hauraki
Gulf

Auckland

Bay of Plenty

Te Araroa
East Cape

NORTH ISLAND

Hamilton

Waikato

Tauranga

Tokoroa   Rotorua   Whakatane
1478

Taupo

Taumarunui   Lake Taupo   Wairoa   Gisborne

New Plymouth   Ngauruhoe
Egmont   Wanganui   12291   Hawke Bay
2518   Ruapehu   Napier
Hawera   2797   Hastings

NEW ZEALAND

Wanganui

Palmerston
North

40°S

T A S   Paraparaumu
Collingwood   Tasman   Ruahine Range
Bay   Masterton
Karamea   Nelson   Picton
Bight   Richmond Range   Blenheim Lower Hutt
Westport   **Wellington**
Travers   Cook Strait Cape Palliser
2337

Greymouth   Kaikoura
Hokitika   Arthurs
Pass
SOUTH ISLAND   Waipara
Southern Alps
Arrowsmith   Canterbury Plains
Cook   2796   Christchurch
3764 Lake   Banks
Haast   Pukaki   Ashburton   Peninsula
Twizel   Canterbury
Aspiring Waitaki Timaru   Bight
Milford Sound 3027
Lake   Oamaru
Wakatipu 2035
Te Anau Queenstown
Jane Peak
Alexandra
West Cape   Lumsden
Clutha

Gore   Dunedin
Invercargill
Foveaux Strait
Stewart
Island
Southwest Cape

Bounty
Islands
(N.Z.)

Snares
Islands

45°S

165°E   170°E   175°E   180°E

0   100   200   300   miles   Average linear scale   0   100   200   300   400   500   Km

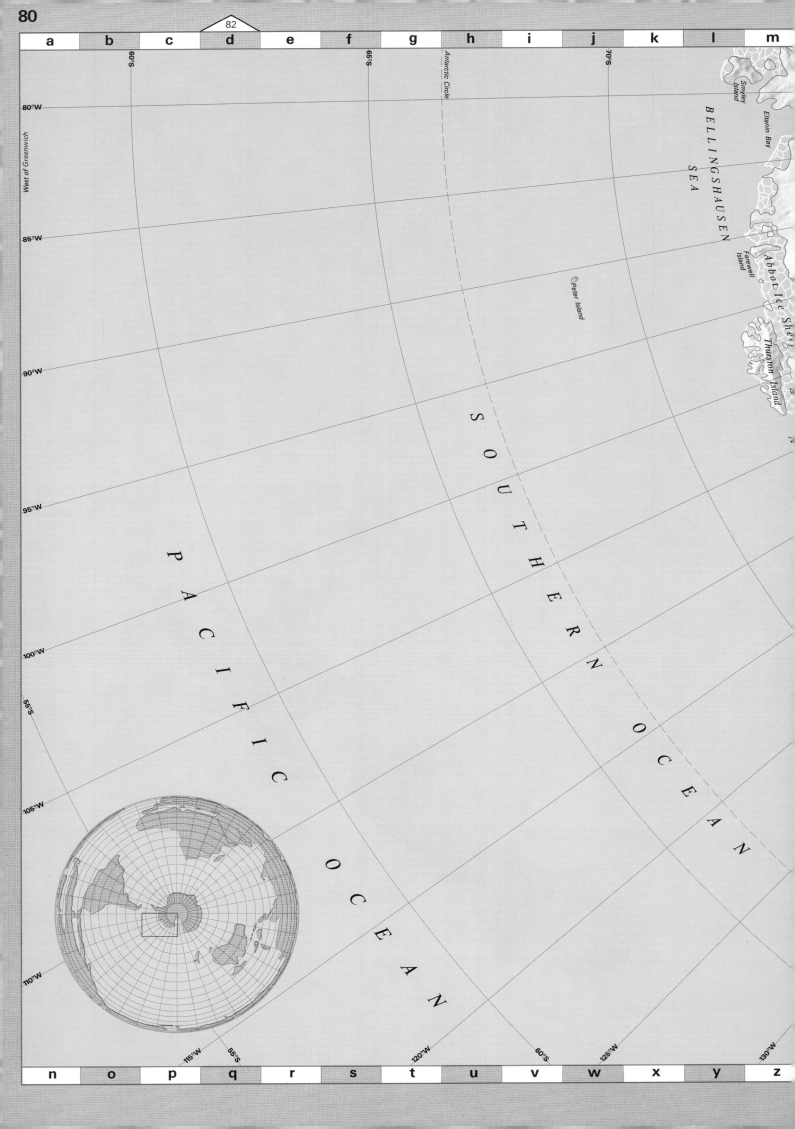

West of Greenwich

60°S

65°S

Antarctic Circle

70°S

80°W

85°W

90°W

95°W

100°W

105°W

110°W

115°W

55°S

120°W

60°S

125°W

130°W

65°S

*Smyley
Island*

Eltanin Bay

*BELLINGSHAUSEN
SEA*

Abbot Ice Shelf

*Farewell
Island*

Thurston Island

○*Peter Island*

S O U T H E R N   O C E A N

P A C I F I C   O C E A N

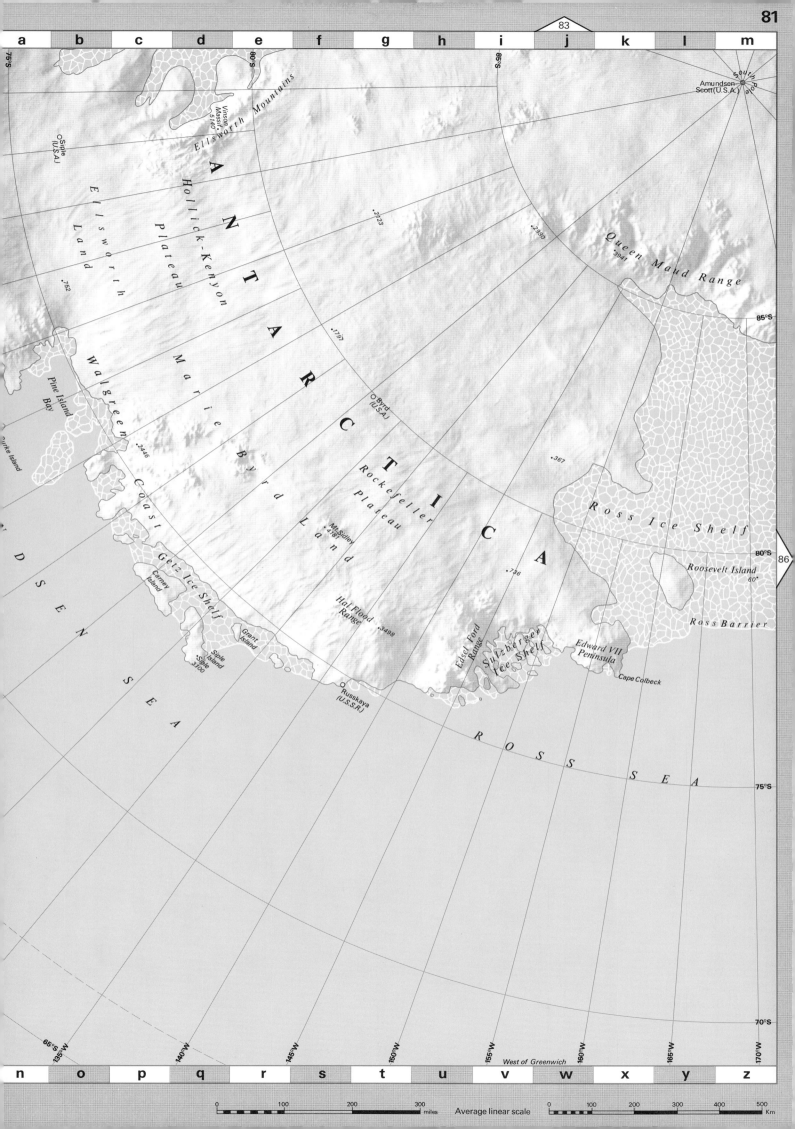

a b c d e f g h i j k l m

75°S
80°S
85°S

Amundsen
Scott (U.S.A.)
South Pole

○ Siple
(U.S.A.)

Vinson
Massif
5140

Ellsworth Mountains

Ellsworth

Land

Hollick-Kenyon
Plateau

.752

A N T A R

Queen Maud Range
.3941

.2123

.2390

85°S

.1797

C T I C A

○ Byrd
(U.S.A.)

Pine Island
Bay

urke Island

Walgreen

Coast

.2446

Marie Byrd Land

Rockefeller
Plateau

.367

Ross Ice Shelf

Getz Ice Shelf

Carney
Island

Grant
Island

Siple
Island
3100

Mt.Sidley
2781

Hal Flood
Range .3498

.736

Roosevelt Island
60 •

80°S

Ross Barrier

A M U N D S E N   S E A

Russkaya
(U.S.S.R.)

Edsel Ford
Range

Sulzberger
Ice Shelf

Edward VII
Peninsula

Cape Colbeck

R O S S   S E A

75°S

70°S

65°S
145°W
140°W
145°W
150°W
155°W
West of Greenwich
160°W
165°W
170°W

n o p q r s t u v w x y z

0   100   200   300   miles   Average linear scale   0   100   200   300   400   500 Km

a b c d e f g h i j k l m

45°W   55°S   40°W   60°S   35°W   30°W

50°W

Scotia Sea

ATLANTIC OCEAN

Coronation Island
Laurie Island
Signy (U.K.)
Orcadas (Argentina)
South Orkney Islands (U.K.)

South Scotia Ridge

55°W   55°S

Powell Basin

WEDDE

Clarence Island

Elephant Island

60°W

Joinville Island

King George Island
Arctowski (Poland)
Comandante Ferraz (Brazil)
Bellingshausen (U.S.S.R.)
Jubany (Argentina)
Esperanza (Argentina)
Petrel (Argentina)
James Ross Island
Marambio (Argentina)

Arturo Prat (Chile)
1298

Trinity Peninsula

Gen. Bernardo O'Higgins (Chile)

Livingston Island

65°W

South Shetland Islands (U.K.)

Primavera (Argentina)

Jason Peninsula

Larsen Ice Shelf

Hearst Island

Anvers Island
Palmer (U.S.A.)
Faraday (U.K.)

Antarctic

Graham Land

Cape Robinson
Cape Agassiz

Peninsula

70°W

Biscoe Island

2328

4190

Rothera (U.K.)

Palmer La

PACIFIC

2396
General San Martín (Argentina)

Batterbee Range

Adelaide Island

Douglas Range

Fossil Bluff (U.K.)

George

OCEAN

Alexander Island

VI

75°W

West of Greenwich

Wilkins Sound

Beethoven Peninsula

Sound

Charcot Island

Latady Island

Ronne Entrance

Spaatz Island

80°W   60°S   65°S   70°S

Smyley Island

n o p q r s t u v w x y z

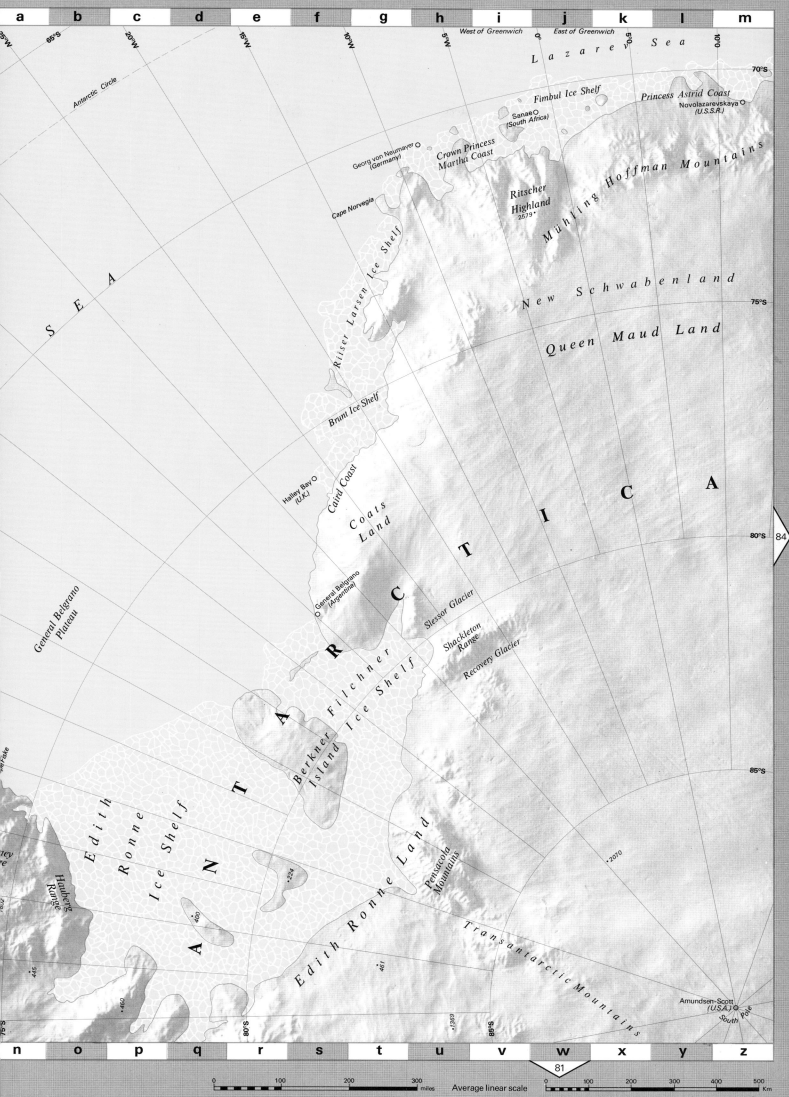

65°S

25°W

Antarctic Circle

65°S

20°W

15°W

10°W

5°W

West of Greenwich   East of Greenwich

0°

5°E

10°E

70°S

L a z a r e v   S e a

Fimbul Ice Shelf

Princess Astrid Coast

Sanae o
(South Africa)

Novolazarevskaya o
(U.S.S.R.)

Crown Princess
Martha Coast

Georg von Neumayer o
(Germany)

M ü h l i n g   H o f f m a n   M o u n t a i n s

Ritscher
Highland
2579·

Cape Norvegia

New   Schwabenland

Riiser Larsen Ice Shelf

75°S

Queen   Maud   Land

S   E   A

Brunt Ice Shelf

S   E   A

Halley Bay o
(U.K.)

Caird Coast

A

Coats
Land

T

I

C

General Belgrano
Plateau

General Belgrano o
(Argentina)

Slessor Glacier

80°S

84

C

Shackleton
Range

Recovery Glacier

R

Filchner

Berkner

T

85°S

Island Ice Shelf

nd Fiske

Edith

Ronne

A

N

Ice Shelf

·224

Pensacola
Mountains

Edith Ronne Land

·2070

Hauberg
Range

iney

·400

·460

T r a n s a n t a r c t i c   M o u n t a i n s

·445

·460

·461

·1369

Amundsen-Scott o
(U.S.A.)
South Pole

75°S

80°S

85°S

81

0   100   200   300
miles   Average linear scale

0   100   200   300   400   500
Km

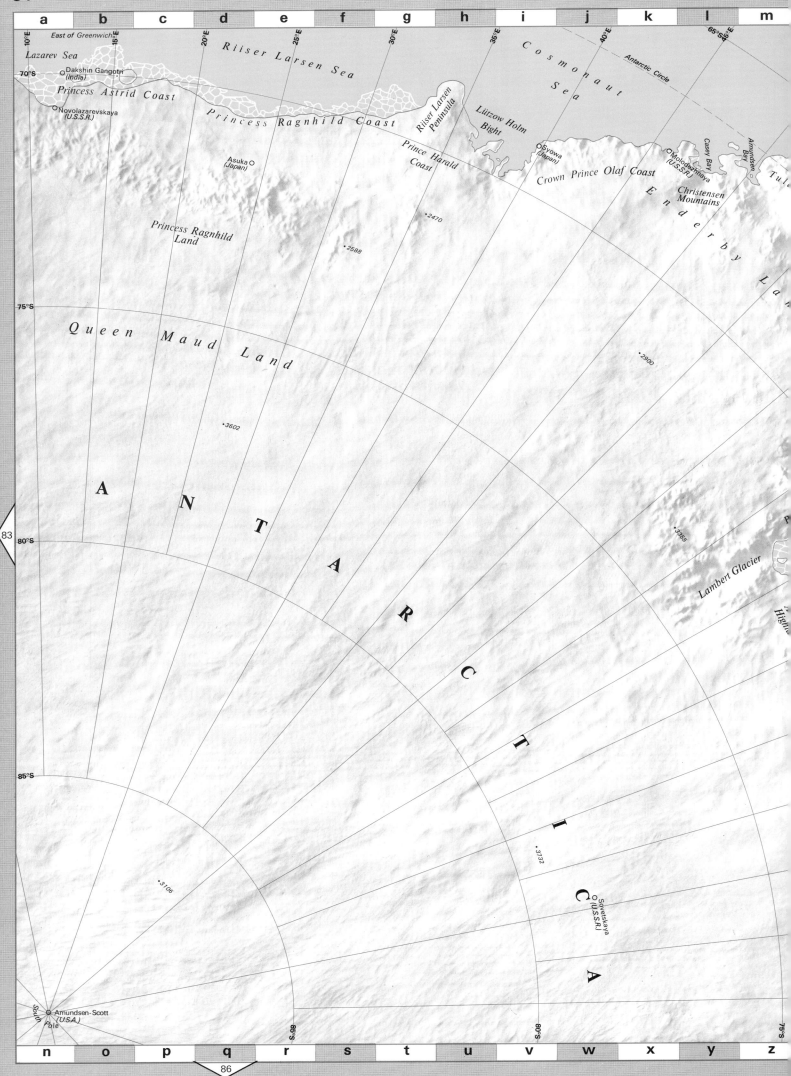

East of Greenwich

Lazarev Sea

Riiser Larsen Sea

C o s m o n a u t

Antarctic Circle

Dakshin Gangotri
(India)

70°S

Princess Astrid Coast

Princess Ragnhild Coast

S e a

Novolazarevskaya
(U.S.S.R.)

Riiser Larsen
Peninsula

Lützow Holm
Bight

Asuka
(Japan)

Prince Harald
Coast

Crown Prince Olaf Coast

Syowa
(Japan)

Molodezhnaya
(U.S.S.R.)

Casey Bay

Amundsen
Bay

Tule

*Princess Ragnhild
Land*

Christensen
Mountains

•2470

E n d e r b y   L a

•2588

•2900

75°S

Q u e e n   M a u d   L a n d

•3602

A

N

•3865

80°S

83

Lambert Glacier

T

Highla

A

•3106

R

•3732

C

85°S

T

Sovetskaya
(U.S.S.R.)

I

C

South
Pole

Amundsen-Scott
(U.S.A.)

A

85°S

80°S

75°S

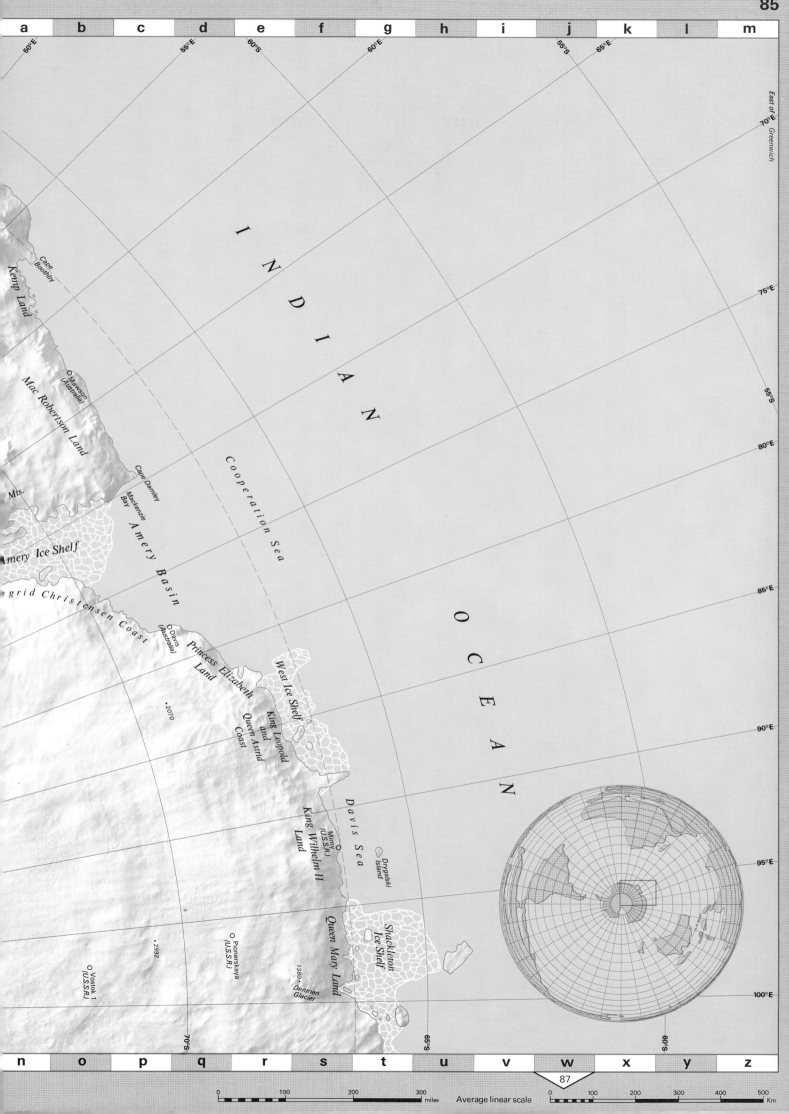

a b c d e f g h i j k l m

50°E 55°E 60°S 60°E 55°S 65°E East of Greenwich

70°E

75°E

80°E

85°S

Kemp Land

Cape Boothby

Mawson (Australia)

Mac Robertson Land

I N D I A N

Cape Darnley

Mackenzie Bay

Mts.

Amery Ice Shelf

C o o p e r a t i o n   S e a

A m e r y   B a s i n

55°S

80°E

grid Christensen Coast

Princess Elizabeth Land

Davis (Australia)

O C E A N

85°E

West Ice Shelf

King Leopold and Queen Astrid Coast

•2070

90°E

D a v i s   S e a

King Wilhelm II Land

Mirny (U.S.S.R.)

Drygalski Island

95°E

•2992

Pionerskaya (U.S.S.R.)

Queen Mary Land

Shackleton Ice Shelf

Vostok 1 (U.S.S.R.)

1380• Denman Glacier

100°E

70°S 65°S 60°S

n o p q r s t u v w x y z

0   100   200   300 miles   Average linear scale   0   100   200   300   400   500 Km

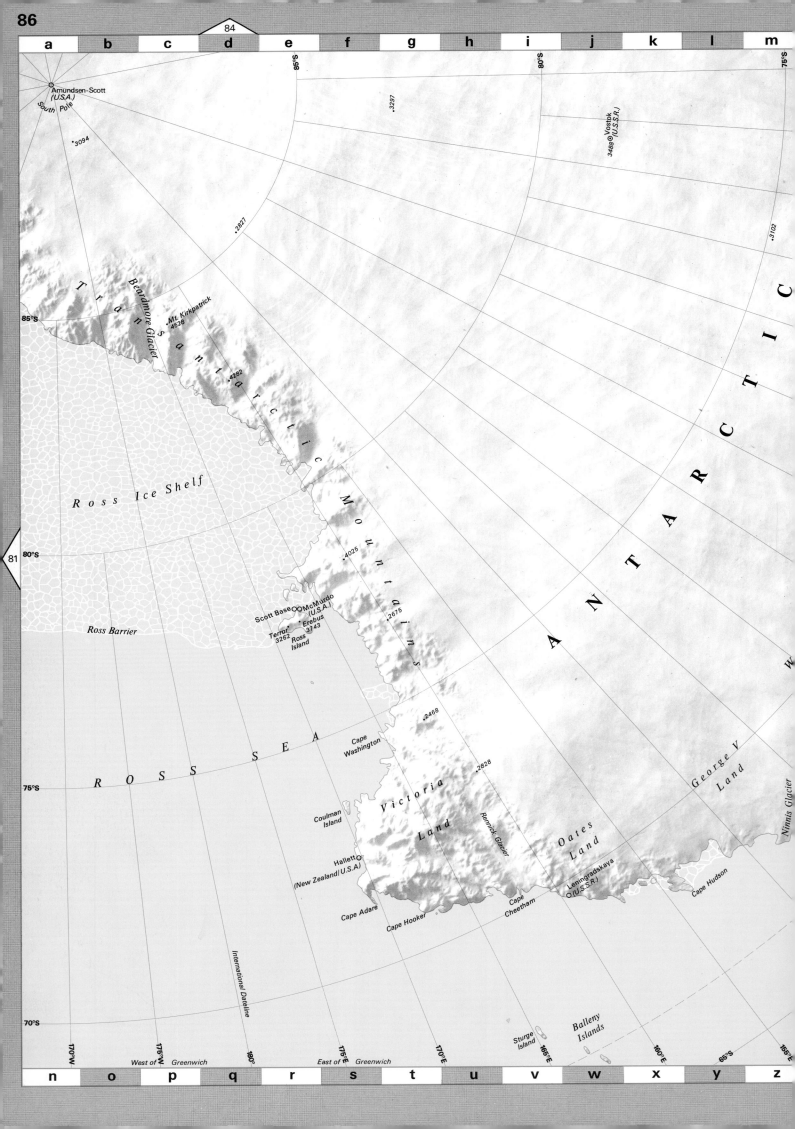

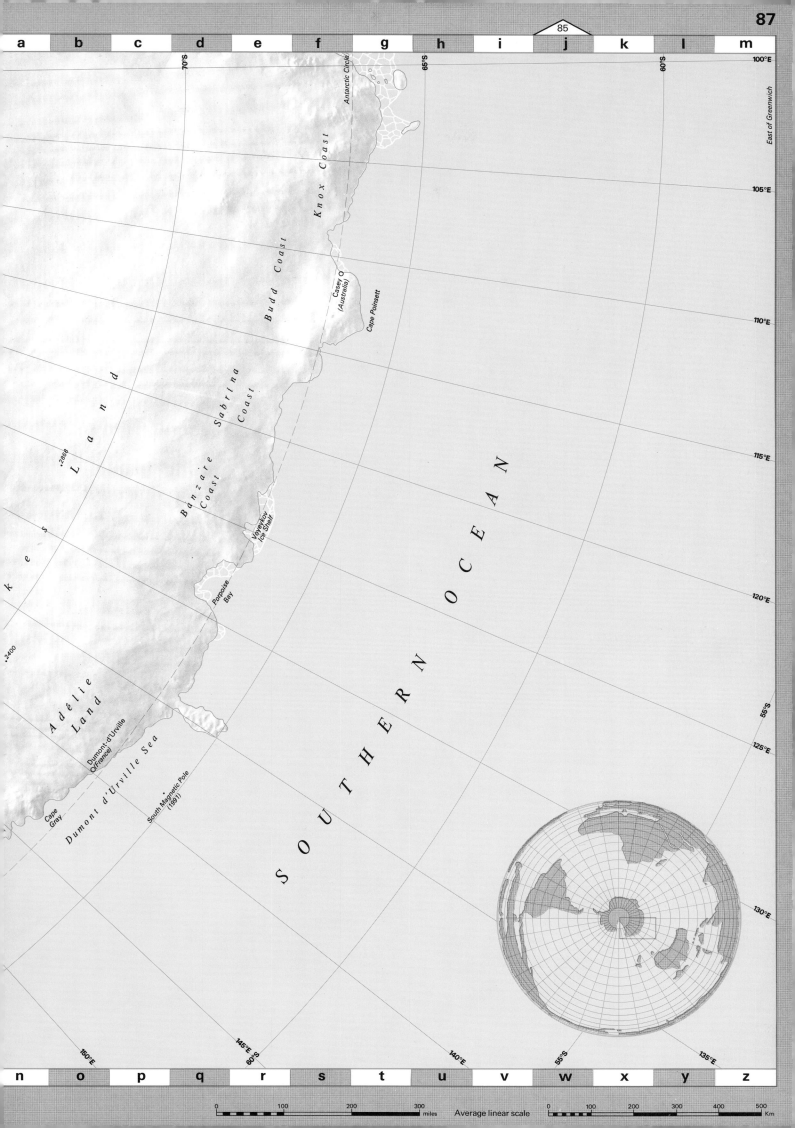

a b c d e f g h i j k l m

n o p q r s t u v w x y z

Antarctic Circle

Knox Coast

Budd Coast

Sabrina Coast

Banzare Coast

Casey
(Australia)

Cape Poinsett

Voyeykov
Ice Shelf

Porpoise
Bay

Wilkes Land

Adélie Land

Dumont-d'Urville
(France)

Dumont d'Urville Sea

Cape
Gray

South Magnetic Pole
(1991)

SOUTHERN OCEAN

East of Greenwich

·2868

·2400

70°S
65°S
60°S
55°S
60°S
55°S

100°E
105°E
110°E
115°E
120°E
125°E
130°E
135°E
140°E
145°E
150°E

0 100 200 300 miles   Average linear scale   0 100 200 300 400 500 Km

90

88

a b c d e f g h i j k l m

80°W

60°N

Bay

Hudson

Onukjuak

Akulivik

Mansel
Island

Ivujivik

Nottingham
Island

Salisbury
Island

•305

Cape
Dorset

Foxe
Channel

65°N

Foxe
Peninsula

Foxe

Arctic Circle

C A N A D A

Foxe
Basin

Prince
Charles
Island

TERRITORIES

N O R T H W E S T

Jens Munk
Island

Rowley
Island

Foley

518•

Rowley

B a f f i n

Eclipse
Sound

Pond Inlet

Bylot
Island•2134

Buchan Gulf

Bay

Povungnituk

QUEBEC

Ungava Peninsula

•540

Salluit

•661

Kangiqsujuaq

Hudson
Strait

Nabukjuak

411
•305

Big
Island

Baffin

Barnes
Ice Cap

•250

1554•

I s l a n d

•Clyde

75°W

L a b r a d o r

aux Feuilles

Koksoak

Kuujjuaq

70°W

•390

Kangiqsualujjuaq

Cape Hopes
Advance

Ungava
Bay

Akpatok
Island

1621•

Ramah

Fraser

NEWFOUNDLAND

•Nutak

•1076

Nain

65°W

Lake
Harbour

Meta
Incognita
Peninsula

Frobisher Bay
(Iqaluit)

R e g i o n

Frobisher
Bay

Hall
Peninsula

•1148

Resolution
Island

Harper
Island

Port
Burwell

Cape
Chidley

Amadjuak
Lake

Kingait

Kouldjuak

Netilling
Lake

Nunatak

Penny
Ice Cap

2597•

Cumberland
Peninsula

Pangnirtung

Cumberland
Sound

Hoare
Bay

Exeter
Sound

Henry Kater
Pen.

Home
Bay

•Kivitoo

Broughton
Island

•2134

Cape Dyer

D a v i s

L a b r a d o r   S e a

60°W

A T L A N T I C

O C E A N

13

55°N

55°W

50°W

45°W

50°N

55°N

40°W

S t r a i t

Sisimiut

Maniitsoq

*Nuuk
(Godthåb)*

•2137

Søndre Strømfjord

Søndrestrømfjord

•2440

•3510

Disko Bay

Qeqertarsuaq
(Godhavn)

Qeqertarsuaq

Uummannaq

Karrats Fj.

Svartenh

Nuussuaq Halvø

G r e e

(K a l o

•4760

Paamiut

Ivittuut

•3660

Qaqortoq

Narsarsuaq

•2740

Nanortalik

King Frederick VI Coast

G

Ikersaassuaq

Danells Fj.

Bernstorff's Isfjord

Cape Moslting

Gyldenløves Fj.

K. Løvenørn

Uummannarsuaq
(Cape Farewell)

Dannebrog Island

Cape Dan

Ammassalik

Kronprins Frederiks

•2986

•Mt. Forel
3360•

King Ch

King Chr

n o p q r s t u v w x y z

35°W

60°N

30°W

a   b   c   d   e   f   g   h   i   j   k   l   m

•1887

North Lincoln Land

Devon Island

75°N

Smith Bay

•2073

Greely Fjord

80°N

Agassiz Ice Cap

Axel Heiberg Island

United States Range •2743

Cape Discovery

Ingelfield Land

Hayes Halvø

Hval Sound (Thule)

Dundas Qaanaaq •796

Cape York

Kane Basin

Prudhoe Land

Washington Land

Alert

Lincoln Sea

ARCTIC

Melville Bay

Cape Séddon

Nares Strait

Hall Land

Nyeboe Land

OCEAN

85°N

Holm I.

Steenstrup Glacier

Knud Rasmussens Land

•945

Nansen Land

•1920

Frederick E. Hyde Fjord

Peary Land •1310

Melville Land •1070

Independence Fjord

Wandels Sea

85°N

King Frederick VIII Land

Danmark Fjord

Crown Prince Christian Land

•760

Nordostrundingen

Ingolf Fjord

n Nunaat)

(Denmark)

•1100 Lambert Land

80°N

92

Dronning Louise Land

Île de France

Spitzbergen 1454

Germania Land •550

Skær Fjord

West Spitzbergen

Greenland

Dove Bay

Prince Karls Foreland

King

Store Koldewey

Sea

Isa Fjord

Christian X Land

•1832

Shannon

Andrées Land

Ardencaple Fjord

Hudson Land

1604•

Clavering I.

Wollaston Foreland

1900•

Kaiser Franz Josephs Fjord

Hold with Hope Pen.

Scoresby Land

Geographical Society I.

Traill I.

King Oscars Fjord •1740

Renland

Liverpool Land

Milne Land

Jameson Land

Gunnbjørn Fjeld

Scoresby Sound

Kangerlussuaq

Ittoqqortoormiit

Cape Brewster

75°N

Cape Dalton

Jan Mayen (Norway)

Denmark Strait

Isafjördur

Cape Horn

•961

Breidhi Fjord

ICELAND

Húna Bay

70°N

65°N

20°W

15°W

10°W

5°W

0°

5°E

10°E

n   o   p   q   r   s   t   u   v   w   x   y   z

0   100   200   300 miles   Average linear scale   0   100   200   300   400   500 Km

100°E
70°N
65°N
60°N

Noyaya
Khatanga
Kheta
P.P'kyko
Kheta
Lake Labaz
Kargo
Volochanka
Kochikha
Tukalan
Yessey
Changada
Murukta
Chirinda
Central
Kocechum
Kotui
Taimura
Tura
Nidym
Mutoray
Vanavara
Mutoray
Kova
Okova
636
Pyasina
Dudypta
Payturma
Ust'Avam
Dolgany
Lake Anama
Putorana Mountains
Avam 1403
Kamen 2037
Lake
Lake Vivi
Vivi
Vivi
Siberian
Chiskovo
970
Baykit
Korda
Taimba
Yarkino
Bedopa
Boguchany
Angara
Cuna
Rura
Agapa
Yangoda
Chernaya
Dudinka
Noril'sk
Potapovo
Khantayka
1274
Lake Keta
Amabar
Agata
Lake Khantayskoye Reservoir
Severnaja
814
66
Bugarikta
Nizhnaja Tunguska
Tutonchany
Uchami
Uchami
552
Uplands
Podkamennaya Tunguska
Osinovo
Tunguska
Yenisey Mountains
Kamenka
Rodina
Strelka
Galanino
Altat
Yenisey Bay
Zyryanka
Golchikha
Kakovlevka
Karaul
Ust'Port
Yenisey
65
Igarka
Karasino
Ust'Kureyka
Turukhansk
Yenisey
Noginskiy
619
Nizhneimbatskoye
Verkhneimbatskoye
Bakhta
Bakhta
Sumarokovo
Yartsevo
Yenisey
Nazimovo
Novoyerudinsky
Bryanka
Yorozhevka
Lesosibirsk
251
Meletsk
Rura
Osharino
Tanama
Khalkey
Bol. Kheta
202
Messoyakha
160
Turukhan
Farkovo
Turukhan
22
Taz
Ratta
Matyl'ka
Yeloguy
Kellog
Kellog
Yeloguy
Sym R.
Sym
Lugovatka
Ust'Ozernoye
Ket
90°E
Strelka
Yenisey Bay
Gyda Peninsula
Gyda Bay
Yurbey
Antipayuta
Nakhodka
Tazovskiy
Taz
Yanov Stan
Sidorovoto
Chaselka
Krasnosel'kup
Tolka
Kikiakki
42
Koriiki
Sabun
Yeloguy
Yenisey
Alipka
Belyy Yar
Baturino
Komsomol'sk
258
Tomsk
Taran
Napalkovo
Taz Bay
Yambung
Yepoko
Pur
Urengoy
Awasedapur
Nyrambovskoy
Khalesavoy
55
Larvak
Vanzhik'kynak
Ostrym
O Kadzhii
Kenytea
Staritsa
Mogoshin
Kolpashevo
Bakhtar
Prikhtovka
50
Yamal
Lake Neyto
Yaptiksale
Lake Yarrote
Nyda
Yada
Pangody
Nadym
Nadym
Nojabr'sk
Kolik'yegan
Ust'Vach
Strezhevoy
Nizine
Napoko
Vasyugan
Kargosok
Parabel
Bakchar
166
Peninsula
66
Mareisale
Narongo
Novyy Port
Shuga
62
Slenvy
Pim
Agan
Nizhnevartovsk
Aleksandrovskoye
Ugut
Ghegva Yar
Lvovka
Biaza
Chumakovo
80°E
Baidarata Bay
Ust'Kara
Shenuch'ye
Gornvy Kazhinsk
Khalmer-Yu
121a
Kolym
Nume
Pokachevo
Yermakovo
55
77
Obyrvy
124
Gerasimikova
Biaza
Tatarsk
Lake Chany
75°E
Khoy
Yangarey
Vorkuta
Yo
Kashgert
Fedunki
Polui
172
Ljamin
Nazym
Ob'
Irtysh
Demyanka
Byal'khovodskiy
Zaton
Tara
Pokrovka
Kaluazhinsk
Chistozernoye
Russian
S.F.S.R.
Soviet
Union
(U.S.S.R.)
Okorovyar
Omta
Abez
1499
Pay-Yer
Symya
Berezovo
North Sosva
Mulgort
Khangokurt
Khanty-Mansiysk
Irtysh
Konda
Demyanskoye
Tara
Omsk
Cherlak
Ulyankarov
70°E
Trosho
Matarikhra
Usa
Pechora
Narodnaja 1894
Saranpaul
Nyaksimvol
Sovetskiy
Komsomol'skiy
Pioneerskiy
78
100
Tavda
Tavda
Tyumen
Kurtamysh
Makinsk
887
Izhma
Olzhma
184
Kadzherom
Kynta 1617
Northern
Ural
Mountains
1108
Tapsui
Suyevatpaul
Polunochnoye
Sos'va
Tura
Turinsk
Talitsa
Bogdanovich
Shadrinsk
Kurgan
Dem Yenovka
Staropolka
Ruzaevka
Ridge
Shomvukvar
Vym'
Zhelenodorozhnyy
Ukhta
Olev Vozh
Ust'Kulom
324
Tratsko-Pechorsk
Porog
303
Kur'ya
Kolva
Cherdyn
Denezhkin 1493
Krasnotur'insk
Verkhny Tura
Nizhny Tagil
321
Artemovsky
Verkhnyaya
Lobva
Tura
Tyumen
Turinsk
55°N
Kurtamysh
65°E
Aydabul
Abasar
Dzhaksy
50°E
55°E
60°N
60°E

0 100 200 300 miles   Average linear scale   0 100 200 300 400 500 Km

Chukchi

Sea

Mys
Shmidta
Krasnoarmeyskiy
Retkucha
Pevek
Ilirney
Northern Anyuskiy Mountains
Southern Anyuskiy Mountains
· 1641
Oscrovnoy
Mal. Anyuy
Cherskiy
Ambarchik
Mal.
Baranikha

Kolymskiy Mountains

Bol. Anyuy
Zatish'ye
Bulun
Korkodon
Korkodon
Yugo-Ta

Gorelova
Volochsk
Zhirkova
Srednekolymsk
Berezovka
Sedezema
Pastakh

Kolymskiy

Mys
Konzaboy
Mys
Chernyy
Oysurdakh
Khongseyo
Malaya
Shestakova

Lake
Nerpich'ye
Chukochye
Balagannakh
Kyrbana
Khara-
Tala
Urdakh

Plain

Ulovo
Ilimnir
Tenali
Ozhogino
· 974
Kondatovo

Bryangnyi
Lake
Ozhogino

Indigirka
Kolesovo
Chokurdakh
Alekseyevo
Ukta

East Siberian

Tabor
Kiselova
Kiseleva

Chikhacheva
Khroma
Boru
Tenk

Sea

Kokuora
Kharstan
Star Dom
Balagankakh

Laptev Str.
Bol.
Lyakhovskiy
Chay-Povarnaya
Kigilyakh
Star Dom

New Siberian Islands

Novaya
Sibir'
Bol'shoe
Zimov'ye

Fedorovskiy
Mal.
Lyakhovskiy
Stolbovoy

Bennetta

ARCTIC

Kotel'nyy
Ambardakh
·320

Antipinskiy
Yu

Kotel'ny
Berkovskiy

Laptev Sea

Trov
Dunn

O C E A N

North Pole

Vezdekhodnaya
Byrranga Mountains

Mal. Taimyr'
·313

Komsomolets
Cape
Peschanyy
Oktyabr'skoy
Revolyutsii
Cape
Berga
Shokal'skogo Str.
Bol'shevik

Vilkicki Str.
·800

Cape
Oskara
Niz Taimyra

96

PRINCIPAL SOURCES OF INFORMATION
REPRESENTED ON THE THEMATIC MAPS

Börsenverein des deutschen Buchhandels (ed.): Buch und Buchhandel in Zahlen. Frankfurt 1987.

British Geological Survey, Natural Environment Research Council: World Mineral Statistics 1979-1983. London 1985.

Dathe, Heinrich and Paul Schöps (eds.): Pelztieratlas. Jena 1986.

Deutsche Gesellschaft für Luft- und Raumfahrt: Astronautische Start-Verzeichnisse und Raumflugkörper-Statistiken 1957-1987.

Diercke Länderlexikon. Braunschweig 1983.

Durrell, Lee: State of the Ark. London 1986.

Encyclopedia Britannica. 15th ed. 32 vls. 1985.

Encyclopedia Britannica Book of the Year 1986. 1987. 1988.

Food and Agricultural Organization of the United Nations (FAO), Rome: FAO Production Yearbook 1985. 1986. FAO Food Balance Sheets 1975-1977. 1979-1981. FAO Yearbook of Fishery Statistics 1983. FAO Trade Yearbook 1986.

Fischer Weltalmanach 1986. 1987. 1988.

Haack. Atlas zur Zeitgeschichte. Gotha 1985.

Herre, Wolf and Manfred Röhrs: Haustiere-zoologisch gesehen. Stuttgart 1973.

The International Institute of Strategic Studies (ILSS): The Military Balance 1986-1987. London 1986.

International Labour Organization (ILO), Geneva: Yearbook of Labour Statistics 1978. 1979. 1980. 1981. 1982. 1983. 1984. 1985. 1986. 1987. Income Distribution and Economic Development. An Analytical Survey. Geneva 1984. Sixth African Regional Conference. Application of the Declaration of Principles and Programme of Action of the World Employment Conference. Geneva 1983.

International Road Transport Union: World Transport Data. Geneva 1985.

International Telecommunication Union: Table of International Telex Relations and Traffic. Geneva 1987.

Inter-Parliamentary Union (IPU): Women in Parliament 1988.

Participation of Women in Political Life and in Decision-Making Processes. Geneva 1988. Distribution of Seats Between Men and Women in National Assemblies. Geneva 1987.

Jain, Shail: Size Distribution of Income. Compilation of Data. World Bank Staff Working Paper No. 190. Nov. 1974. Washington 1975.

Kidron, Michael and Ronald Segal: The State of the World Atlas. London 1981. The New State of the World Atlas (revised ed.). London 1987.

Krüger, Hanfried, Werner Löser et al (eds.): Ökumene Lexicon. Frankfurt 1983.

Kurian, George Thomas: The New Book of World Rankings. New York 1984.

Länder der Erde. Berlin 1985.

Meyers Enzyklopädie der Erde (8 vls.). Mannheim 1982.

Moroney, John R.: Income Inequality. Trends and International Comparisons. Toronto 1979.

Myers, Norman (ed.): GAIA — Der Öko-Atlas unserer Erde. Frankfurt 1985.

Nohlen, Dieter and Franz Nuscheler (eds.): Handbuch der Dritten Welt. 8 vls. Hamburg 1981-1983.

Peters, Arno: Synchronoptische Weltgeschichte. 2 vls. München 1980.

Saeger, Joni and Ann Olson: Der Frauenatlas. Frankfurt 1986.

Serryn, Pierre: Le Monde d'aujourd'hui. Atlas économique, social, politique, stratégique. Paris 1981.

South: South Diary 1987. 1988.

Statistisches Bundesamt, Wiesbaden: Statistik des Auslandes. Vierteljahreshefte zur Auslandsstatistik. 1985-1987. Statistik des Auslandes. Länderberichte.

Stockholm International Peace Research Institute (SIPRI): SIPRI Yearbook 1987. World Armaments and Disarmament. New York 1987.

Taylor, Charles Lewis and David A. Jodice: World Handbook of Political and Social Indicators. New Haven, London 1983.

Tietze, Wolf (ed.): Westermann Lexikon der Geographie. Braunschweig 1968.

UNESCO: Statistical Yearbook 1974. 1975. 1976. 1977. 1978. 1979. 1980. 1981. 1982. 1983. 1984. 1985. 1986. 1987.

UNICEF: The State of the World's Children 1987.

The United Nations (UN): UN Statistical Yearbook 1983/84. UN Demographic Yearbook 1972. 1979. 1984. 1985. 1986. National Accounts Statistics. Compendium of Income Distribution Statistics. New York 1985. UN Energy Statistics Yearbook 1984. UN Yearbook of International Trade Statistics 1982. 1983. 1984. 1986. Selected Indicators of the Situation of Women 1985. UN Industrial Statistics Yearbook 1983. 1984. World Conference of the United Nations Decade for Women: Equality, Development and Peace. Copenhagen 1980. Activities for the Advancement of Women: Equality, Development and Peace. Report of Jean Fernand-Laurent. 1983.

University of Stellenbosch, Department of Development Administration and the Institute for Cartographic Analysis: The Third World in Maps. 1985.

World Almanac & Book of Facts 1985. 1986. 1987.

The World Bank: The World Bank Atlas 1987. World Development Report 1980. 1981. 1982. 1983. 1984. 1985. 1986. 1987. World Labour Report 1984. World Tables 1984. World Atlas of the Child 1979. Social Indicators of Development 1987. World Economic and Social Indicators. Document of the World Bank. 1980.

World Energy Conference 1978: World Energy Resources 1985–2020. Renewable Energy Resources. The Full Reports to the Conservation Commissions of the World Energy Conference. 1978.

The World in Figures. Editorial information compiled by The Economist. London 1987.

World Health Organization (WHO), Geneva: World Health Statistics. Annual.

Völker der Erde. Bern 1982.

Voous, K.H.: Atlas of European Birds. New York 1960.

NATURE, MAN AND SOCIETY
IN 246 THEMATIC MAPS

Each map represents a single theme. As a result, it is possible to dispense with symbols and to allow the information to be expressed entirely in terms of colour. Dark colours stand for high values, light colours stand for low ones. This makes it easy to take in and remember the essential data shown on each map—an important feature, since up to 16 maps can be dedicated to a particular subject.

The maps should be considered in relation to each other. The interweaving and mutual interaction of all spheres of life, the intricacies of nature and culture, of economics, nations and society, mean that each of the 46 topics can be fully understood only when placed in the context of the other 45 double-page spreads.

These 246 thematic maps represent over 40,000 individual pieces of factual data. The main sources of this stupendous wealth of information are the published materials of the United Nations and other international bodies of comparable standing. Where such official figures are not available, estimates have been drawn up in consultation with the leading experts in the various fields concerned.

Since the first edition East and West Germany and North and South Yemen have been unified. Rather than produce an average for the united countries the data will remain unchanged until accurate statistics have been produced.

No interpretation or evaluation of information has been undertaken, in order not to detract from the aim of this Atlas—to enable the user to form an objective and unprejudiced personal picture of the world.

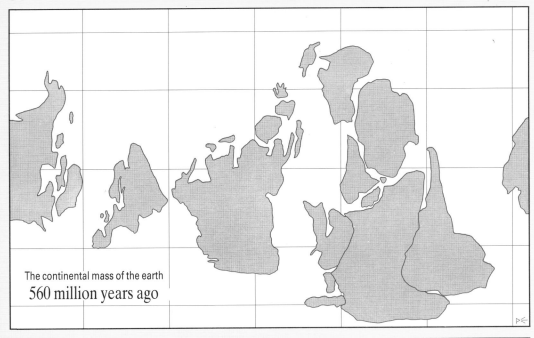

The continental mass of the earth
560 million years ago

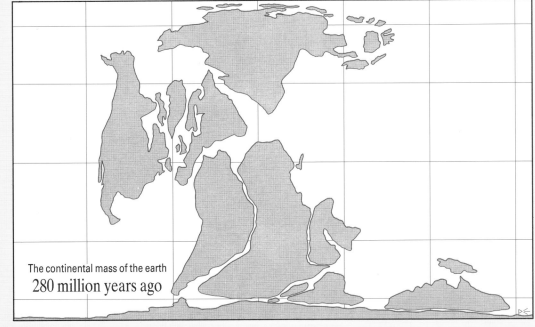

The continental mass of the earth
280 million years ago

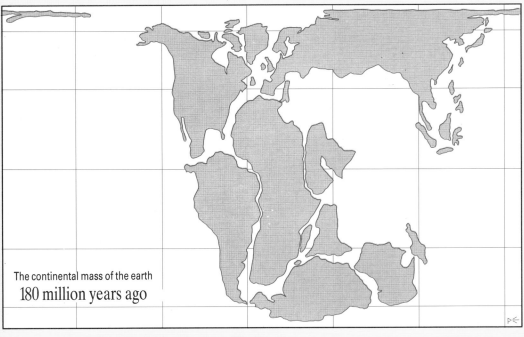

The continental mass of the earth
180 million years ago

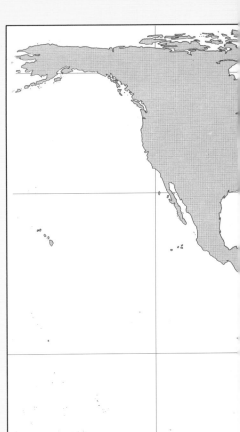

The continental mass of the earth

TODAY

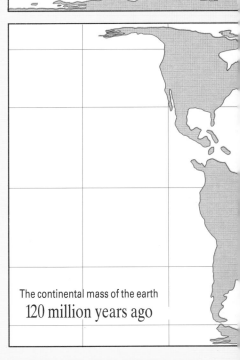

The continental mass of the earth
120 million years ago

THE CON

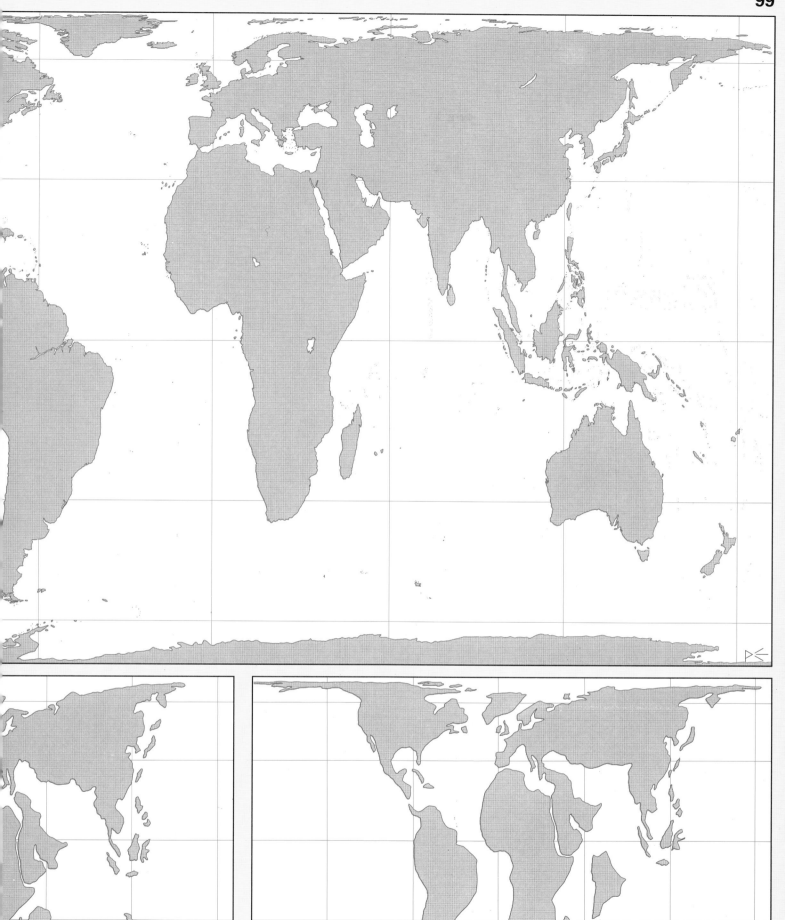

The continental mass of the earth
60 million years ago

TINENTS

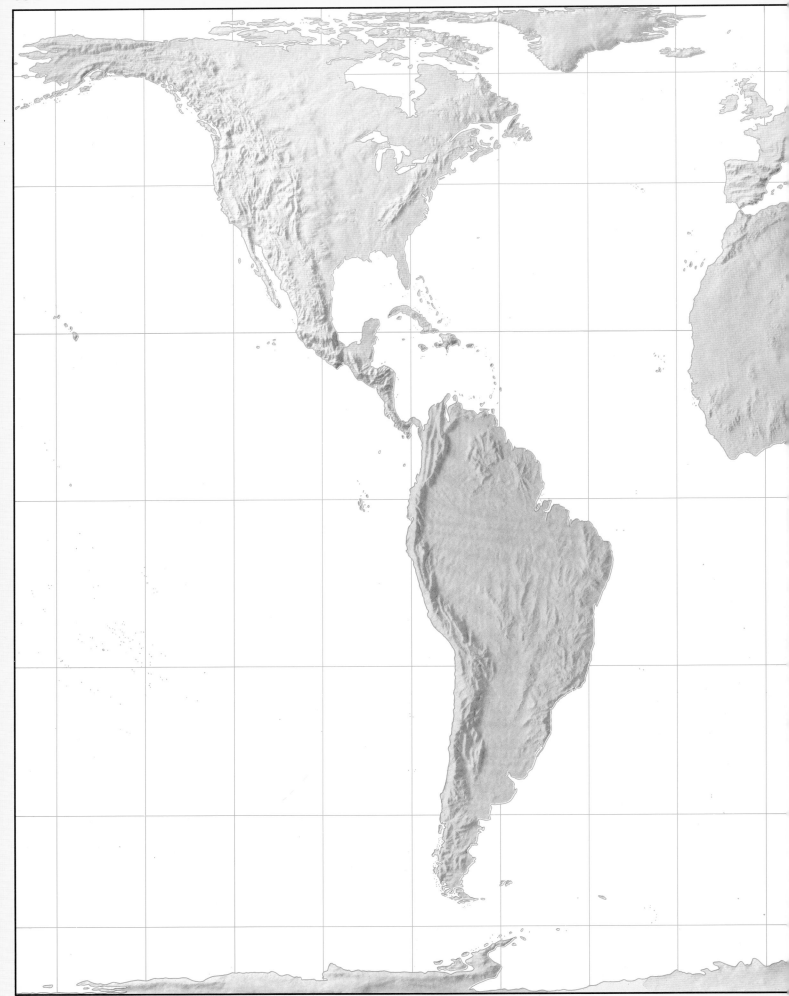

MOUN

AINS

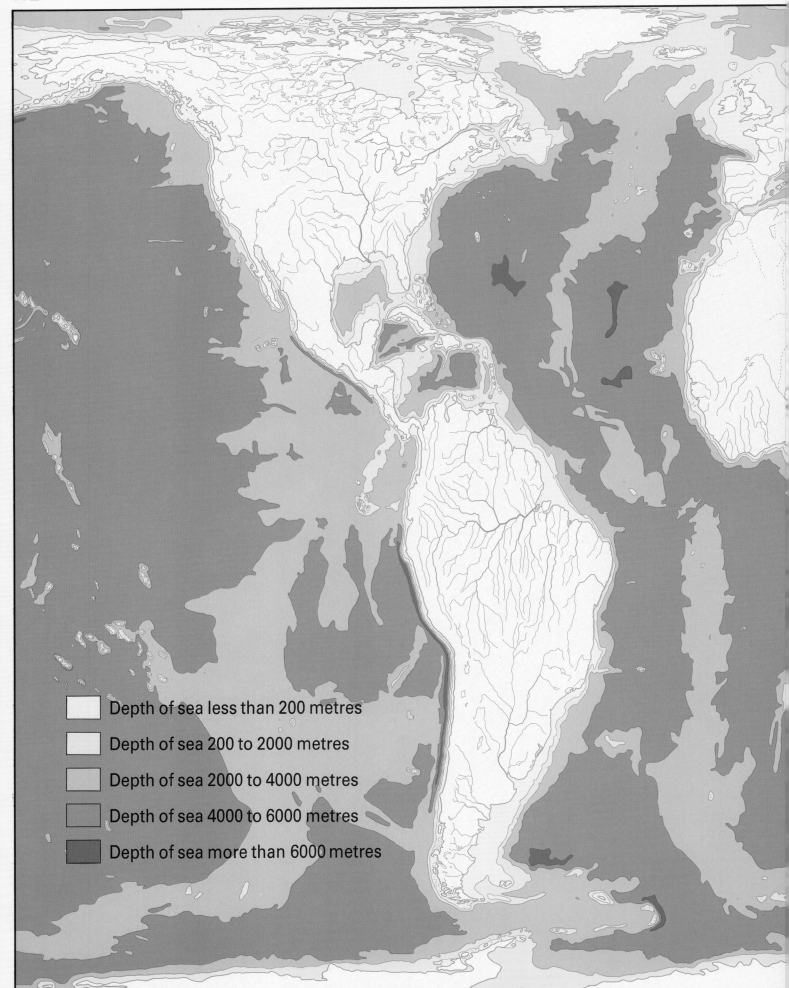

Depth of sea less than 200 metres

Depth of sea 200 to 2000 metres

Depth of sea 2000 to 4000 metres

Depth of sea 4000 to 6000 metres

Depth of sea more than 6000 metres

RIVERS A

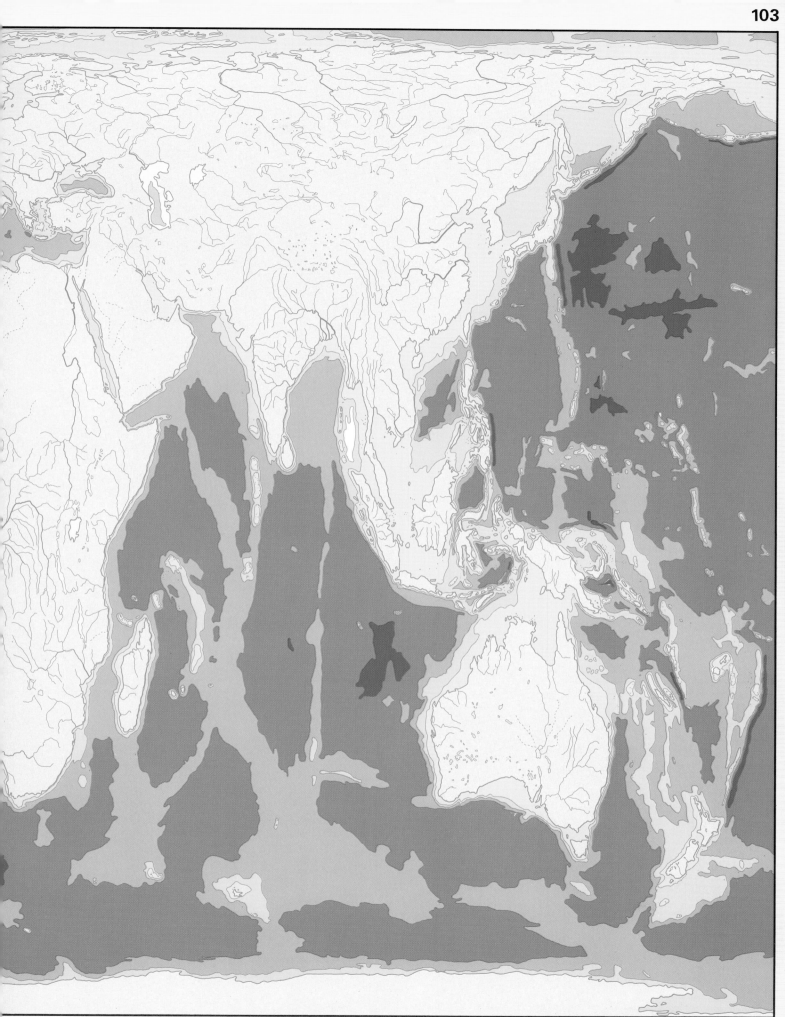

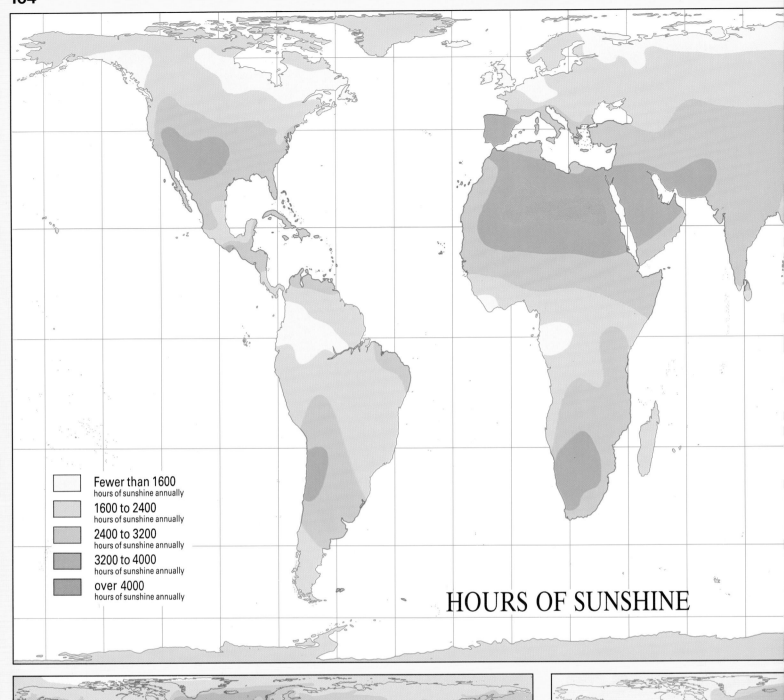

Fewer than 1600
hours of sunshine annually

1600 to 2400
hours of sunshine annually

2400 to 3200
hours of sunshine annually

3200 to 4000
hours of sunshine annually

over 4000
hours of sunshine annually

HOURS OF SUNSHINE

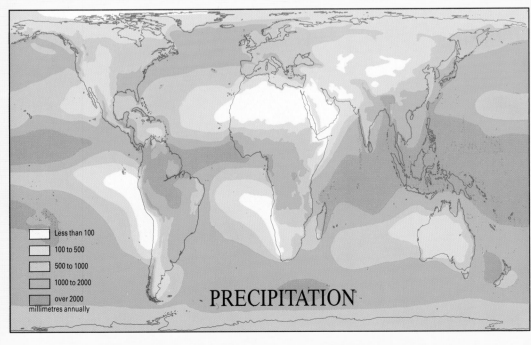

Less than 100
100 to 500
500 to 1000
1000 to 2000
over 2000
millimetres annually

PRECIPITATION

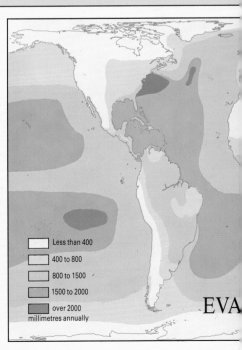

Less than 400
400 to 800
800 to 1500
1500 to 2000
over 2000
millimetres annually

EVA

SUN ANI

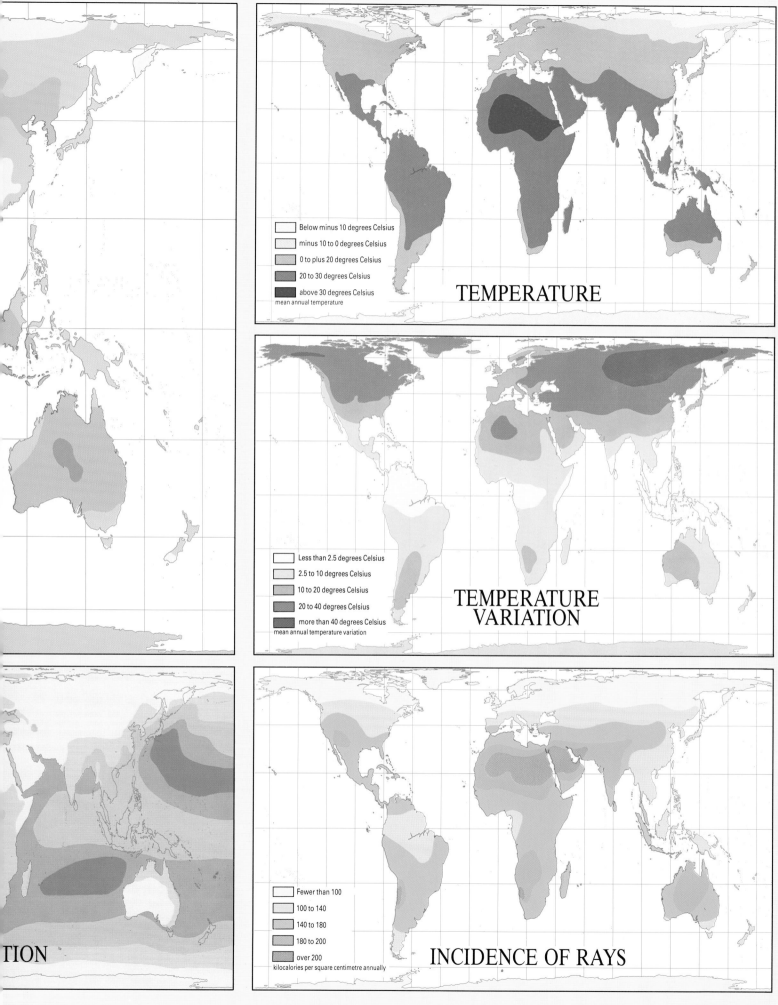

TEMPERATURE

Below minus 10 degrees Celsius
minus 10 to 0 degrees Celsius
0 to plus 20 degrees Celsius
20 to 30 degrees Celsius
above 30 degrees Celsius
mean annual temperature

TEMPERATURE VARIATION

Less than 2.5 degrees Celsius
2.5 to 10 degrees Celsius
10 to 20 degrees Celsius
20 to 40 degrees Celsius
more than 40 degrees Celsius
mean annual temperature variation

INCIDENCE OF RAYS

Fewer than 100
100 to 140
140 to 180
180 to 200
over 200
kilocalories per square centimetre annually

TION

CLIMATE

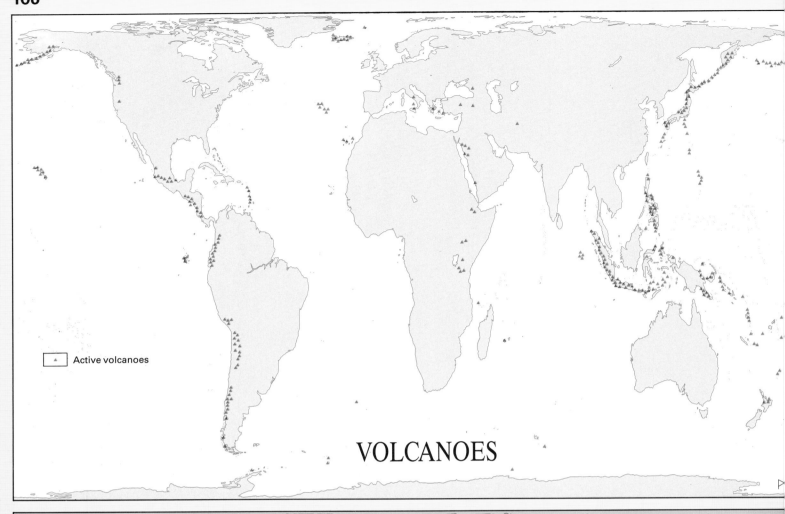

VOLCANOES

Active volcanoes

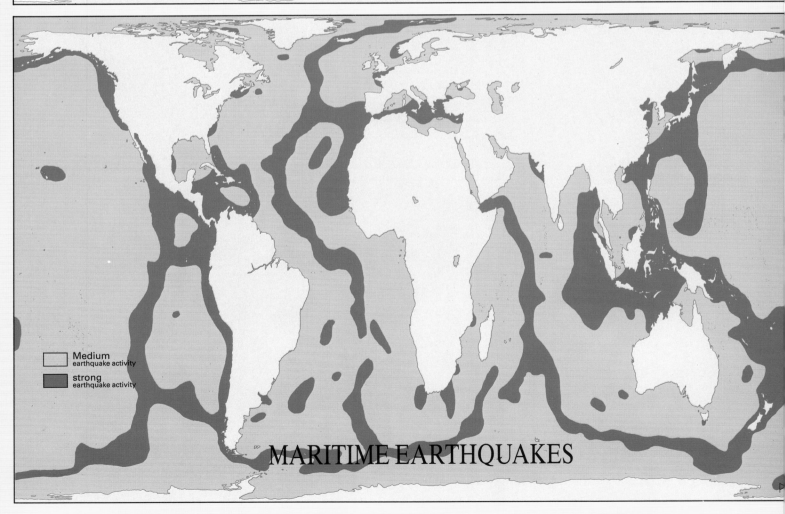

Medium
earthquake activity

strong
earthquake activity

MARITIME EARTHQUAKES

NATURAL

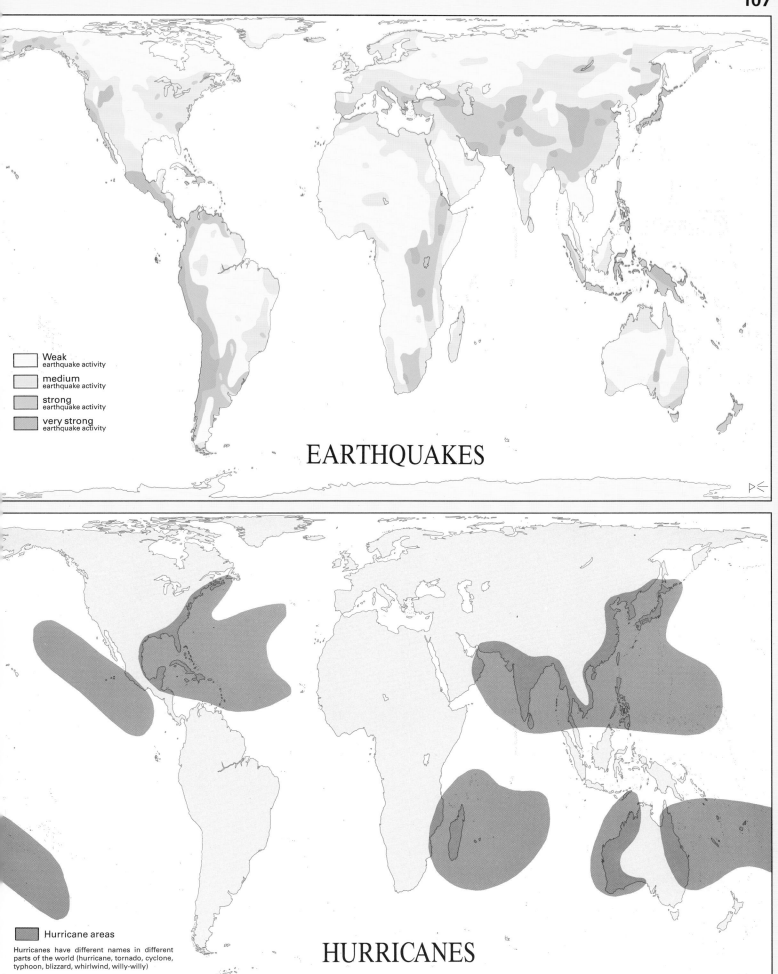

Weak
earthquake activity

medium
earthquake activity

strong
earthquake activity

very strong
earthquake activity

EARTHQUAKES

Hurricane areas

Hurricanes have different names in different
parts of the world (hurricane, tornado, cyclone,
typhoon, blizzard, whirlwind, willy-willy)

HURRICANES

DANGERS

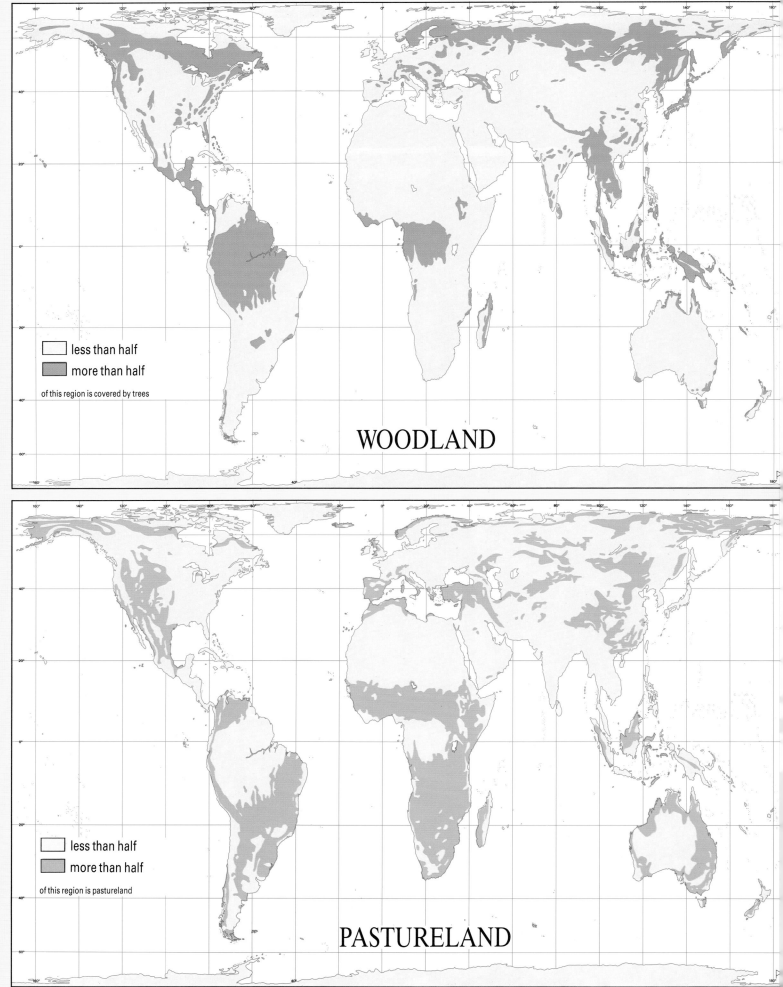

less than half

more than half

of this region is covered by trees

WOODLAND

less than half

more than half

of this region is pastureland

PASTURELAND

VEGET

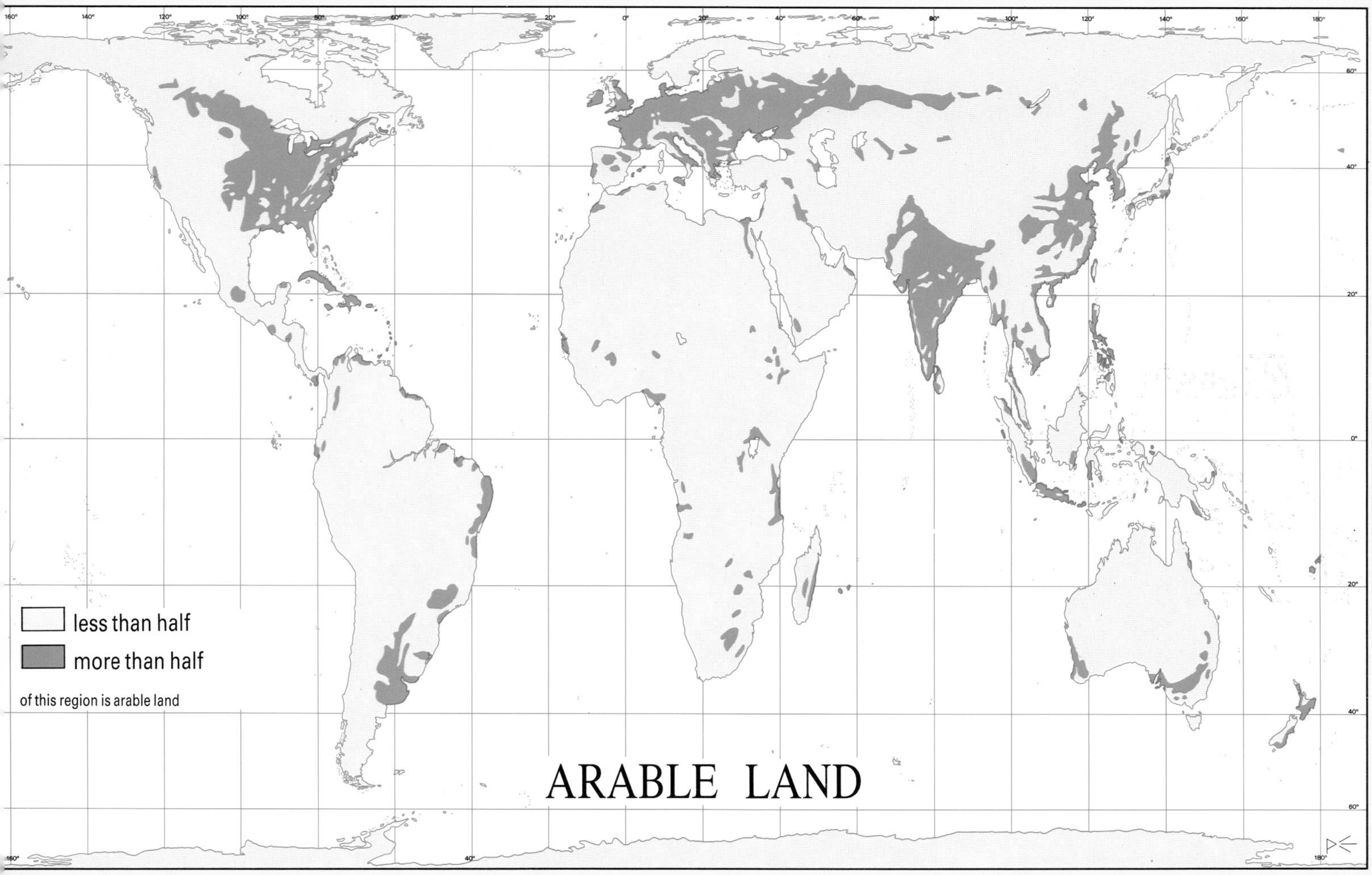

ARABLE LAND

less than half

more than half

of this region is arable land

BARREN LAND

less than half

more than half

of this region is wasteland or desert

ATION

S O V I E T   U N I O N

(U. S. S. R.)

FINLAND

POLAND

ECH
HUNGARY
GOSLAVIA
ALB.
BULGARIA
ROMANIA
GREECE

TURKEY

CYPRUS
LEBANON
SYRIA
ISRAEL
JORDAN
IRAQ
KUWAIT
IRAN

AFGHANISTAN

PAKISTAN

PEOPLES' REPUBLIC
OF MONGOLIA

C H I N A

NORTH KOREA

SOUTH
KOREA

JAPAN

BYA

EGYPT

SAUDI

ARABIA

BAHRAIN QATAR
UNITED
ARAB
EMIRATES

OMAN

NEPAL
BHUTAN

BANGLADESH

I N D I A

BURMA

LAOS

TAIWAN

HAD

SUDAN

REP
OF
YEMEN
DJIBOUTI

THAILAND

KAMPUCHEA

VIETNAM

PHILIPPINES

CENTRAL
AFRICAN
REPUBLIC

ETHIOPIA

S O M A L I A

SRI LANKA

MALDIVES

BRUNEI

M A L A Y S I A

SINGAPORE

ZAIRE

UGANDA

KENYA

RWANDA

BURUNDI

TANZANIA

SEYCHELLES

I N D O N E S I A

PAPUA
NEW GUINEA

SOLOMON

ISLANDS

KIRIBATI

COMOROS

GOLA

MALAWI

ZAMBIA

MOZAMBIQUE

MIBIA

ZIMBABWE

BOTSWANA

MADAGASCAR

MAURITIUS

WESTERN SAMOA

VANUATU

FIJI

TONGA

A U S T R A L I A

SWAZILAND

SOUTH

LESOTHO

AFRICA

NEW ZEALAND

c   t   i   c   a

Fewer than 1 inhabitant
per square kilometre

1 to 10 inhabitants
per square kilometre

10 to 100 inhabitants
per square kilometre

100 to 1000 inhabitants
per square kilometre

more than 1000 inhabitants
per square kilometre. The symbols mean
· 500,000 to 1 million inhabitants
● 1 million to 10 million inhabitants
■ more than 10 million inhabitants

PEOPLE A

ND CITIES

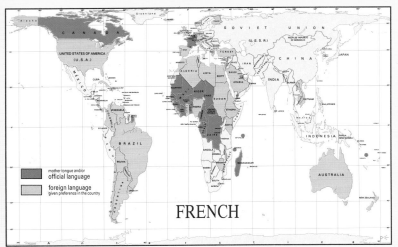

FRENCH

mother tongue and/or
official language

foreign language
given preference in the country

SPANISH

mother tongue and/or
official language

foreign language
given preference in the country

GERMAN

mother tongue and/or
official language

foreign language
given preference in the country

RUSSIAN

mother tongue and/or
official language

foreign language
given preference in the country

MALAY

mother tongue and/or
official language

PROPORTION OF THE WORLD'S POPULATION SPE
ONE OF THESE MAJOR LANGUAGES AS THE MOT

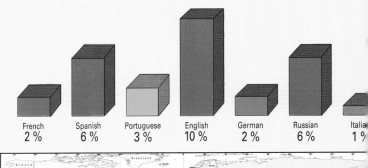

French	Spanish	Portuguese	English	German	Russian	Italia
2 %	6 %	3 %	10 %	2 %	6 %	1 %

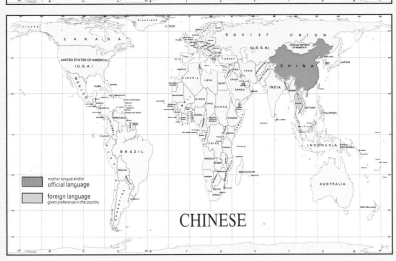

CHINESE

mother tongue and/or
official language

foreign language
given preference in the country

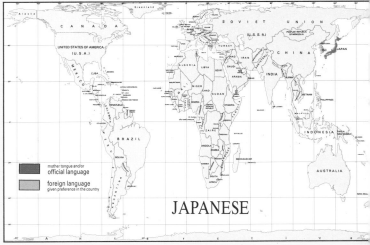

JAPANESE

mother tongue and/or
official language

foreign language
given preference in the country

LANG

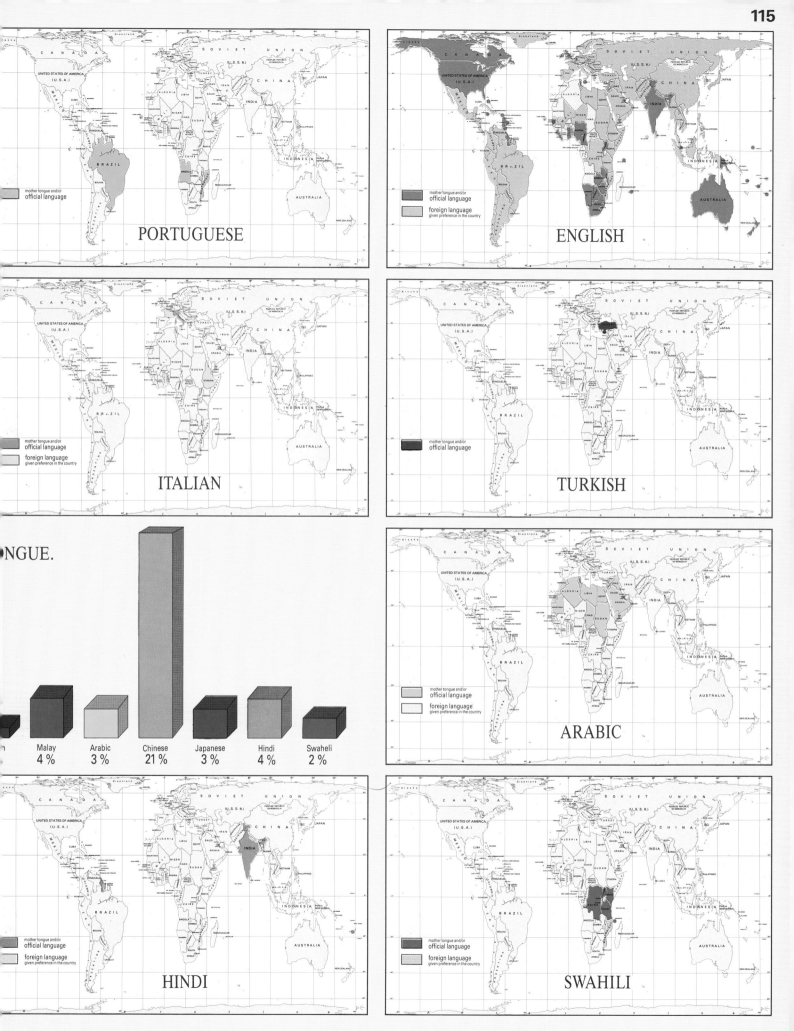

PORTUGUESE

mother tongue and/or
official language

ENGLISH

mother tongue and/or
official language

foreign language
given preference in the country

ITALIAN

mother tongue and/or
official language

foreign language
given preference in the country

TURKISH

mother tongue and/or
official language

ARABIC

mother tongue and/or
official language

foreign language
given preference in the country

·ONGUE.

| Malay 4 % | Arabic 3 % | Chinese 21 % | Japanese 3 % | Hindi 4 % | Swaheli 2 % |

HINDI

mother tongue and/or
official language

foreign language
given preference in the country

SWAHILI

mother tongue and/or
official language

foreign language
given preference in the country

AGES

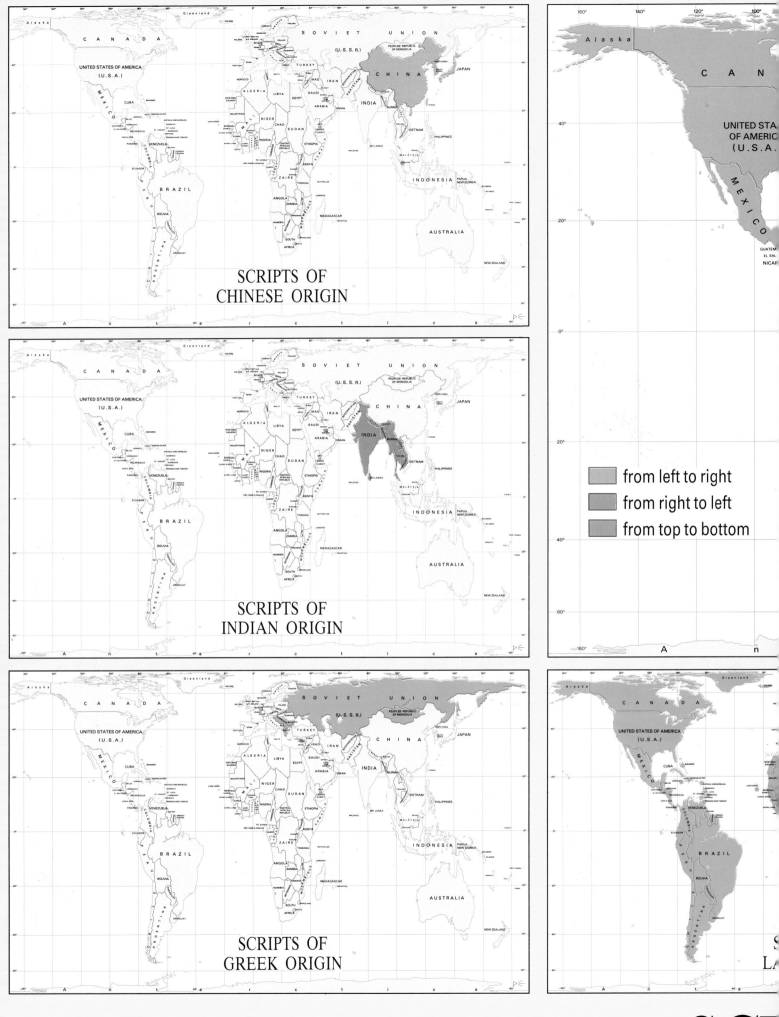

SCRIPTS OF
CHINESE ORIGIN

SCRIPTS OF
INDIAN ORIGIN

SCRIPTS OF
GREEK ORIGIN

from left to right
from right to left
from top to bottom

SC

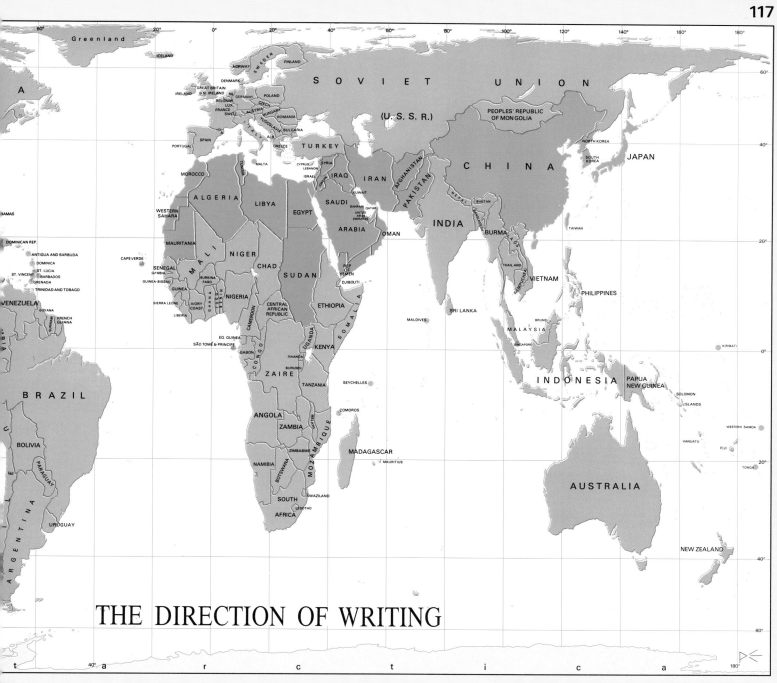

THE DIRECTION OF WRITING

...OF
...IGIN

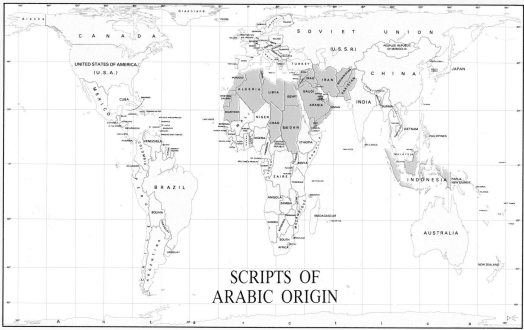

SCRIPTS OF ARABIC ORIGIN

PTS

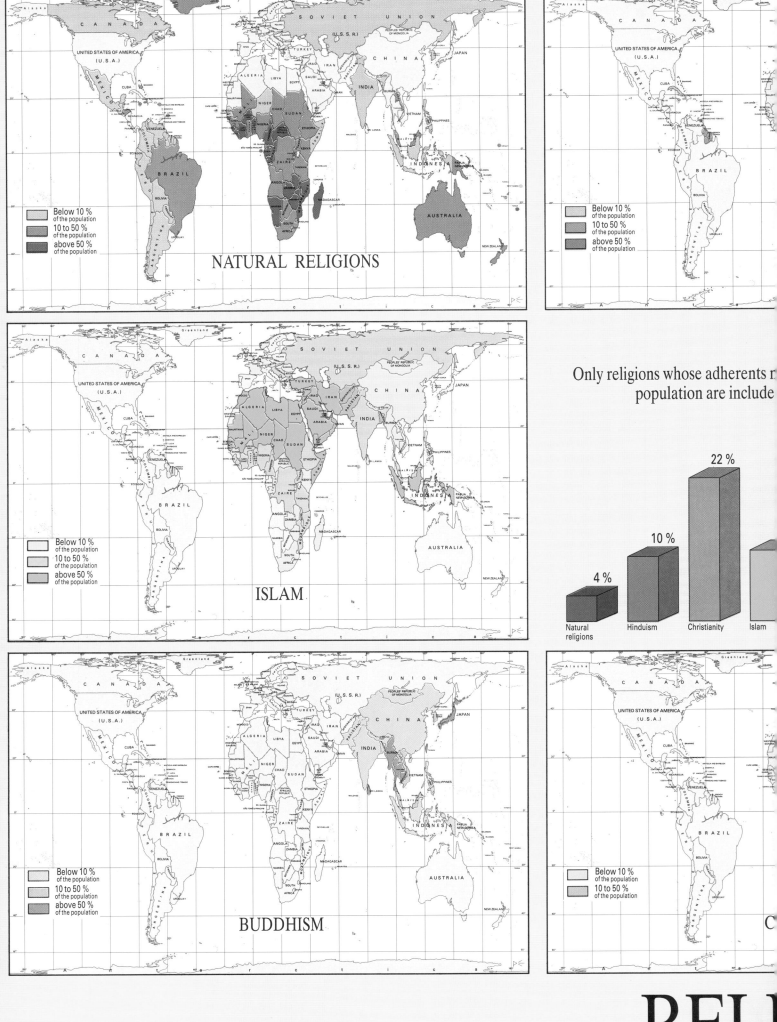

NATURAL RELIGIONS

Below 10 %
of the population
10 to 50 %
of the population
above 50 %
of the population

ISLAM

Below 10 %
of the population
10 to 50 %
of the population
above 50 %
of the population

BUDDHISM

Below 10 %
of the population
10 to 50 %
of the population
above 50 %
of the population

Below 10 %
of the population
10 to 50 %
of the population
above 50 %
of the population

Only religions whose adherents r
population are include

4 %
Natural
religions

10 %
Hinduism

22 %
Christianity

Islam

Below 10 %
of the population
10 to 50 %
of the population

RELI

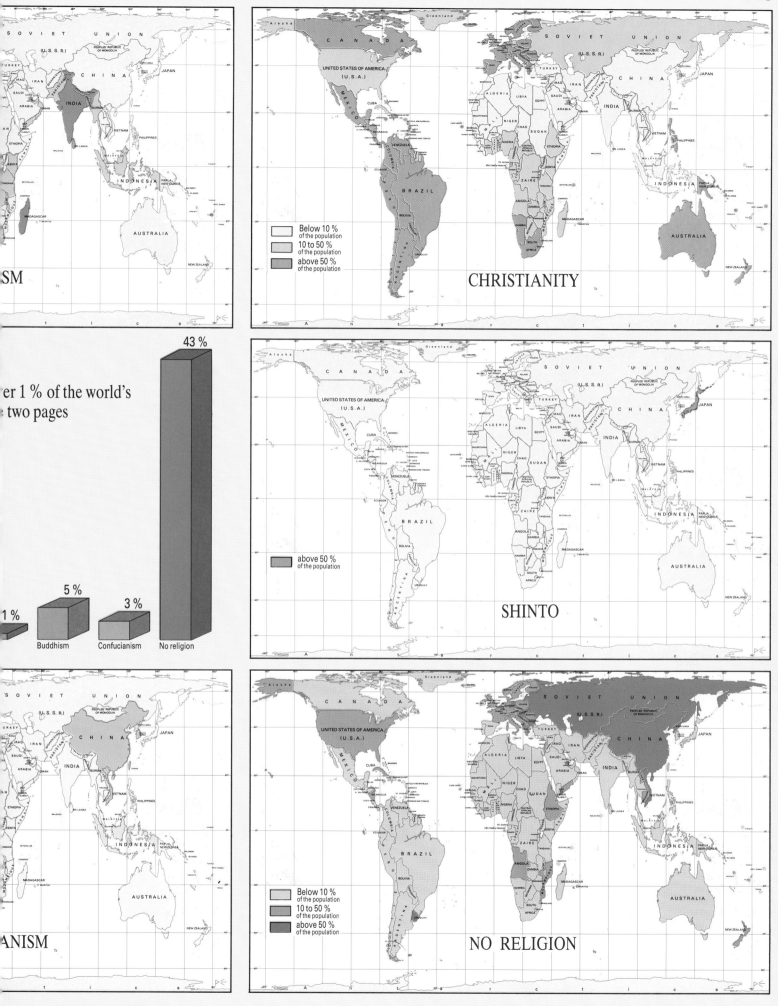

SM

er 1 % of the world's
two pages

43 %

5 %
Buddhism

3 %
Confucianism

No religion

1 %

CHRISTIANITY

Below 10 %
of the population

10 to 50 %
of the population

above 50 %
of the population

SHINTO

above 50 %
of the population

NO RELIGION

Below 10 %
of the population

10 to 50 %
of the population

above 50 %
of the population

ANISM

IONS

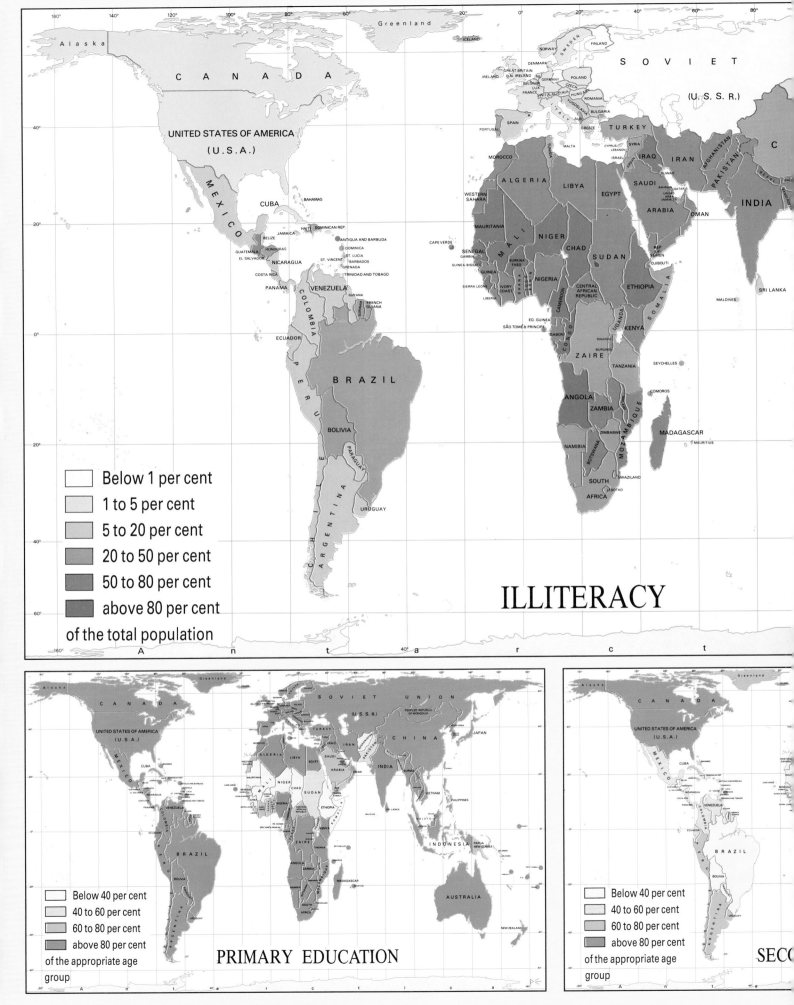

Below 1 per cent
1 to 5 per cent
5 to 20 per cent
20 to 50 per cent
50 to 80 per cent
above 80 per cent
of the total population

ILLITERACY

Below 40 per cent
40 to 60 per cent
60 to 80 per cent
above 80 per cent
of the appropriate age
group

PRIMARY EDUCATION

Below 40 per cent
40 to 60 per cent
60 to 80 per cent
above 80 per cent
of the appropriate age
group

SECO

EDUC

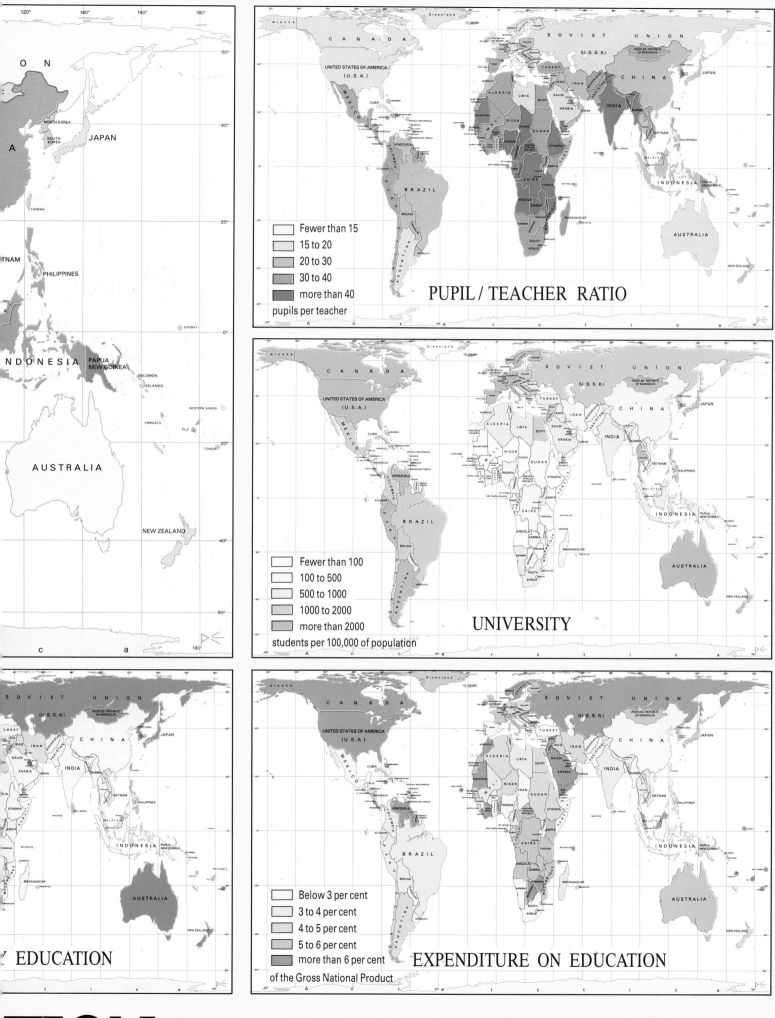

PUPIL / TEACHER RATIO

- Fewer than 15
- 15 to 20
- 20 to 30
- 30 to 40
- more than 40

pupils per teacher

UNIVERSITY

- Fewer than 100
- 100 to 500
- 500 to 1000
- 1000 to 2000
- more than 2000

students per 100,000 of population

EDUCATION

EXPENDITURE ON EDUCATION

- Below 3 per cent
- 3 to 4 per cent
- 4 to 5 per cent
- 5 to 6 per cent
- more than 6 per cent

of the Gross National Product

TION

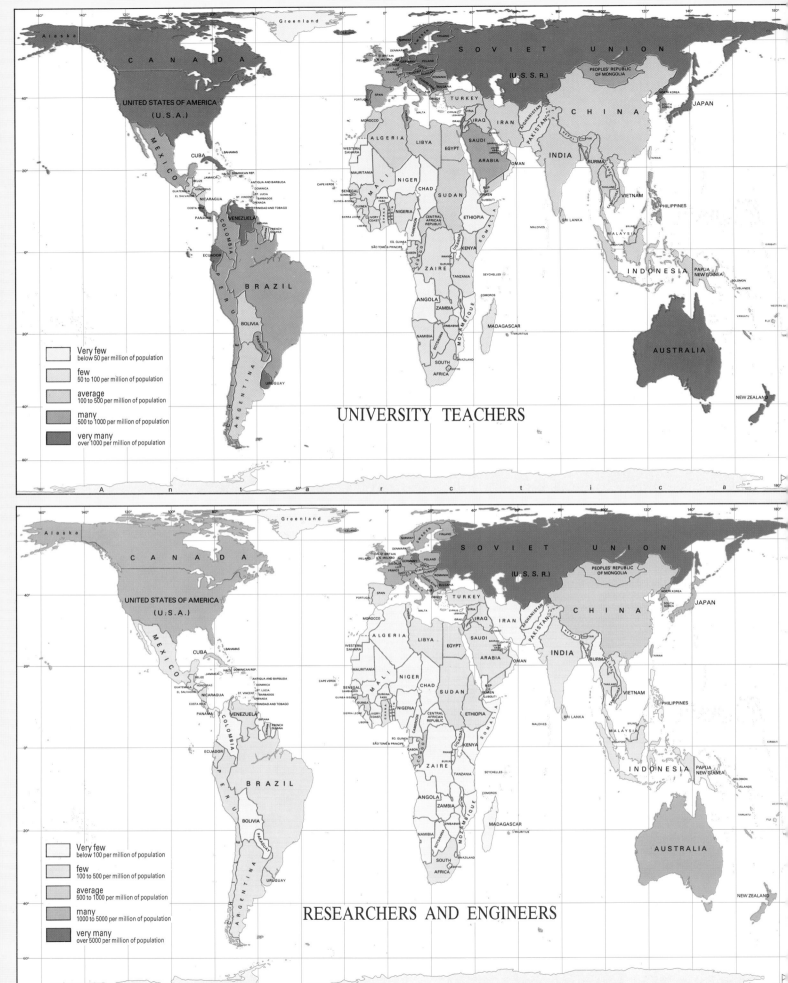

UNIVERSITY TEACHERS

	Very few below 50 per million of population
	few 50 to 100 per million of population
	average 100 to 500 per million of population
	many 500 to 1000 per million of population
	very many over 1000 per million of population

RESEARCHERS AND ENGINEERS

	Very few below 100 per million of population
	few 100 to 500 per million of population
	average 500 to 1000 per million of population
	many 1000 to 5000 per million of population
	very many over 5000 per million of population

THE SO

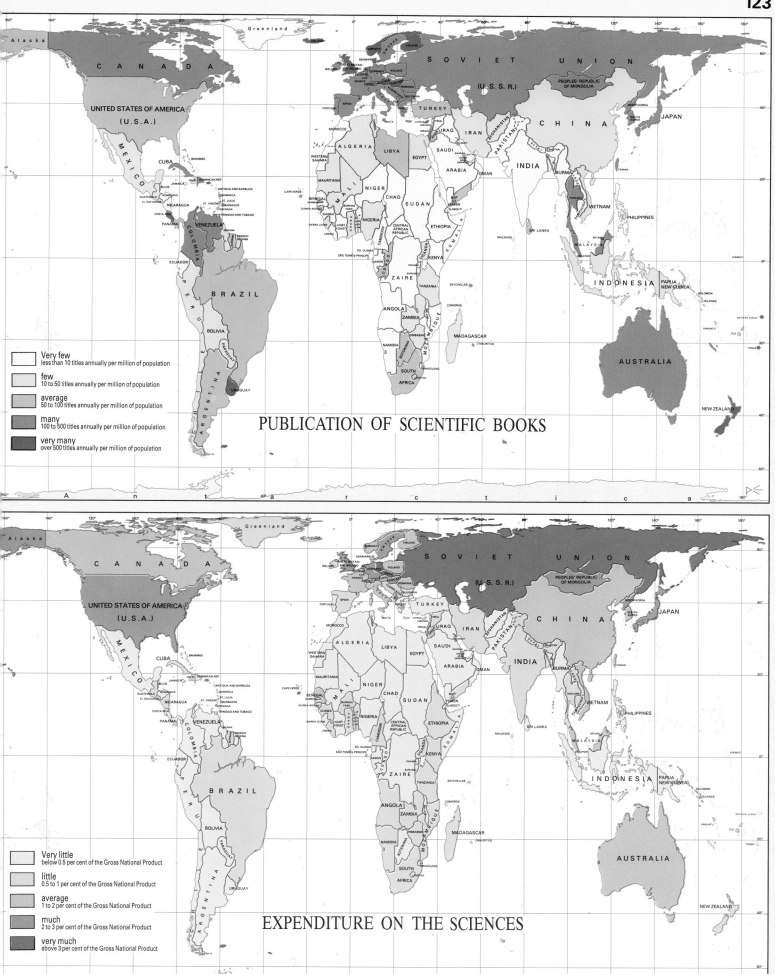

PUBLICATION OF SCIENTIFIC BOOKS

Very few
less than 10 titles annually per million of population

few
10 to 50 titles annually per million of population

average
50 to 100 titles annually per million of population

many
100 to 500 titles annually per million of population

very many
over 500 titles annually per million of population

EXPENDITURE ON THE SCIENCES

Very little
below 0.5 per cent of the Gross National Product

little
0.5 to 1 per cent of the Gross National Product

average
1 to 2 per cent of the Gross National Product

much
2 to 3 per cent of the Gross National Product

very much
above 3 per cent of the Gross National Product

ENCES

124

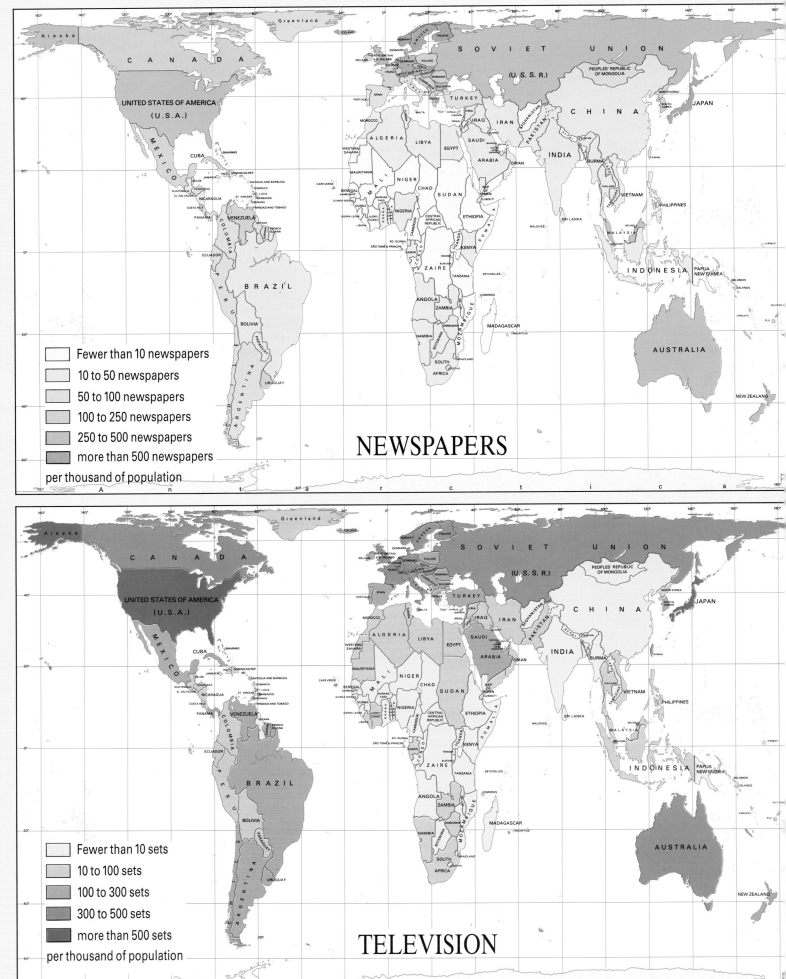

NEWSPAPERS

Fewer than 10 newspapers
10 to 50 newspapers
50 to 100 newspapers
100 to 250 newspapers
250 to 500 newspapers
more than 500 newspapers
per thousand of population

TELEVISION

Fewer than 10 sets
10 to 100 sets
100 to 300 sets
300 to 500 sets
more than 500 sets
per thousand of population

INFOR

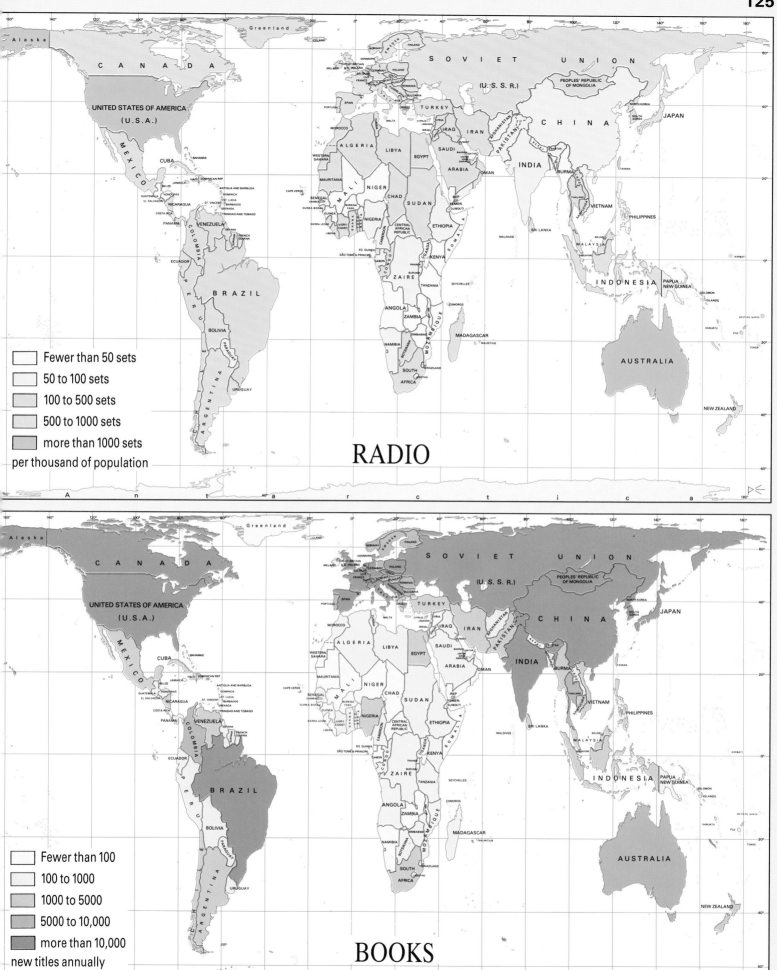

RADIO

Fewer than 50 sets
50 to 100 sets
100 to 500 sets
500 to 1000 sets
more than 1000 sets
per thousand of population

BOOKS

Fewer than 100
100 to 1000
1000 to 5000
5000 to 10,000
more than 10,000
new titles annually

ATION

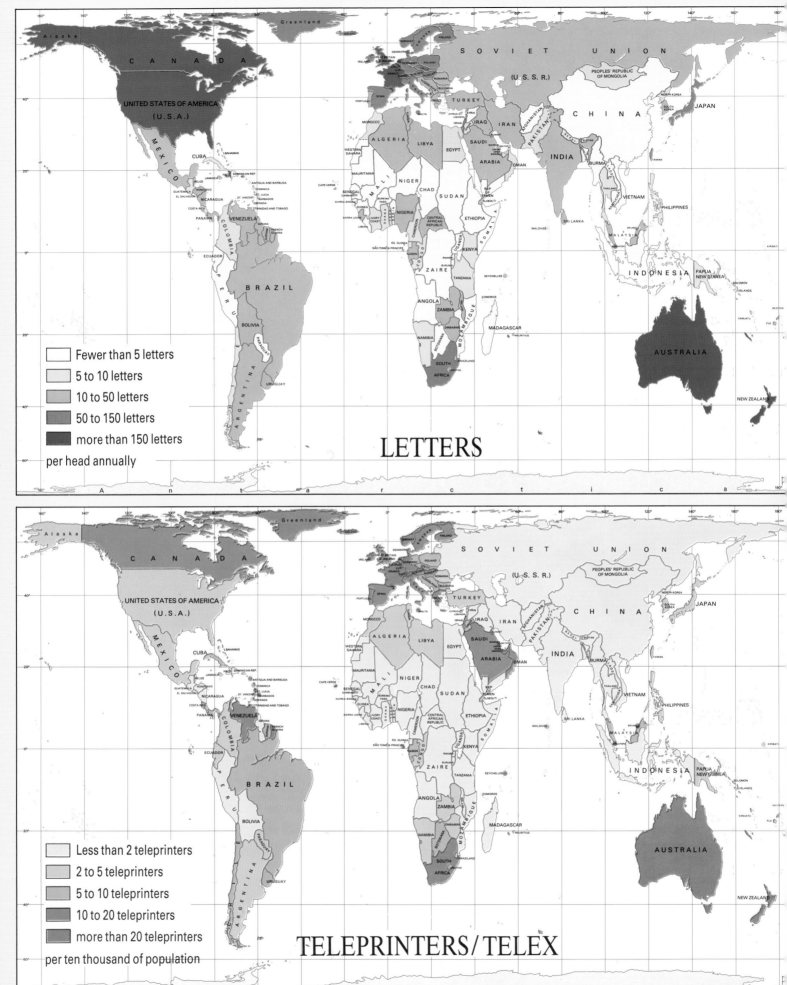

LETTERS

Fewer than 5 letters
5 to 10 letters
10 to 50 letters
50 to 150 letters
more than 150 letters
per head annually

TELEPRINTERS / TELEX

Less than 2 teleprinters
2 to 5 teleprinters
5 to 10 teleprinters
10 to 20 teleprinters
more than 20 teleprinters
per ten thousand of population

COMMU

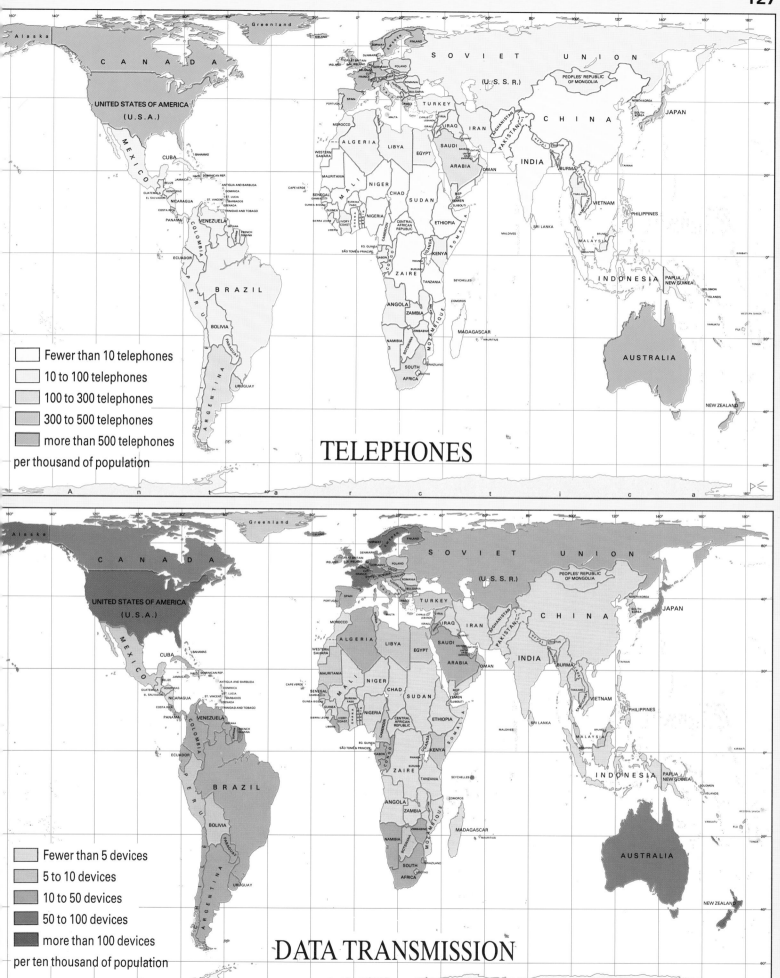

TELEPHONES

Fewer than 10 telephones
10 to 100 telephones
100 to 300 telephones
300 to 500 telephones
more than 500 telephones
per thousand of population

DATA TRANSMISSION

Fewer than 5 devices
5 to 10 devices
10 to 50 devices
50 to 100 devices
more than 100 devices
per ten thousand of population

CATIONS

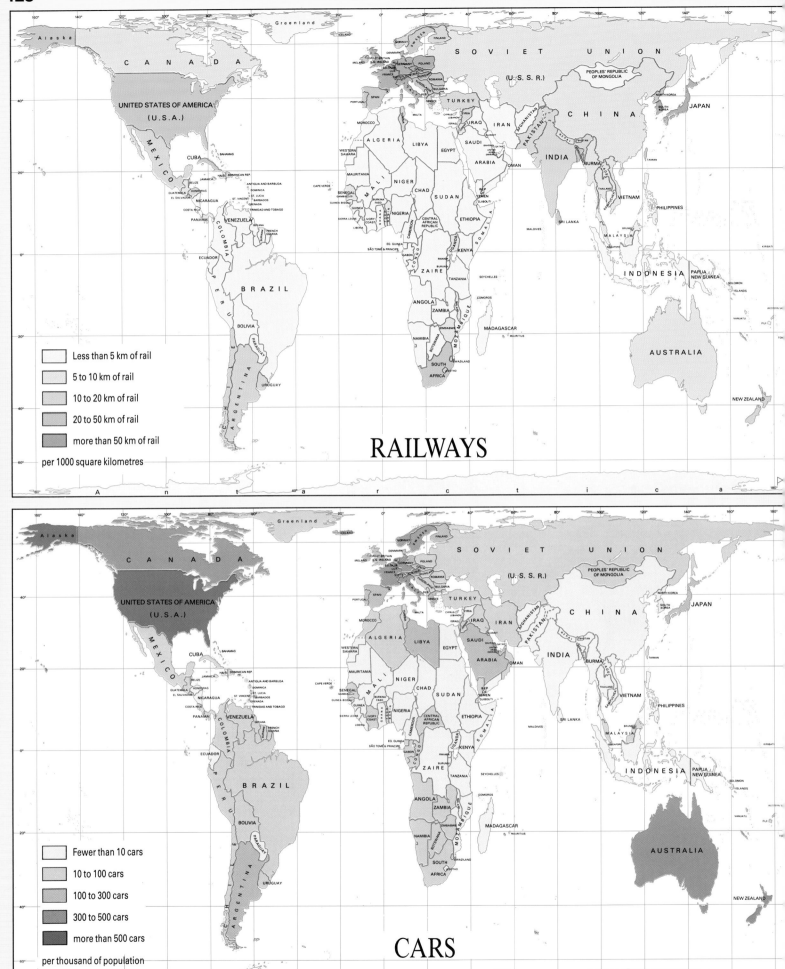

RAILWAYS

Less than 5 km of rail
5 to 10 km of rail
10 to 20 km of rail
20 to 50 km of rail
more than 50 km of rail

per 1000 square kilometres

CARS

Fewer than 10 cars
10 to 100 cars
100 to 300 cars
300 to 500 cars
more than 500 cars

per thousand of population

TRAFFIC

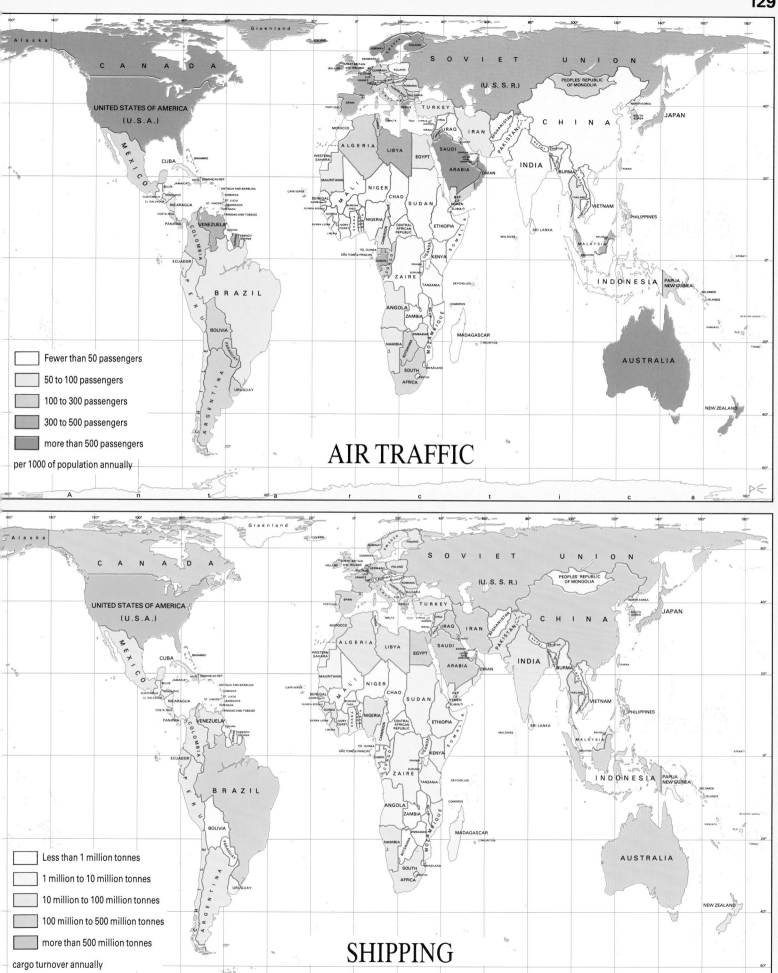

AIR TRAFFIC

Fewer than 50 passengers

50 to 100 passengers

100 to 300 passengers

300 to 500 passengers

more than 500 passengers

per 1000 of population annually

SHIPPING

Less than 1 million tonnes

1 million to 10 million tonnes

10 million to 100 million tonnes

100 million to 500 million tonnes

more than 500 million tonnes

cargo turnover annually

DENSITY

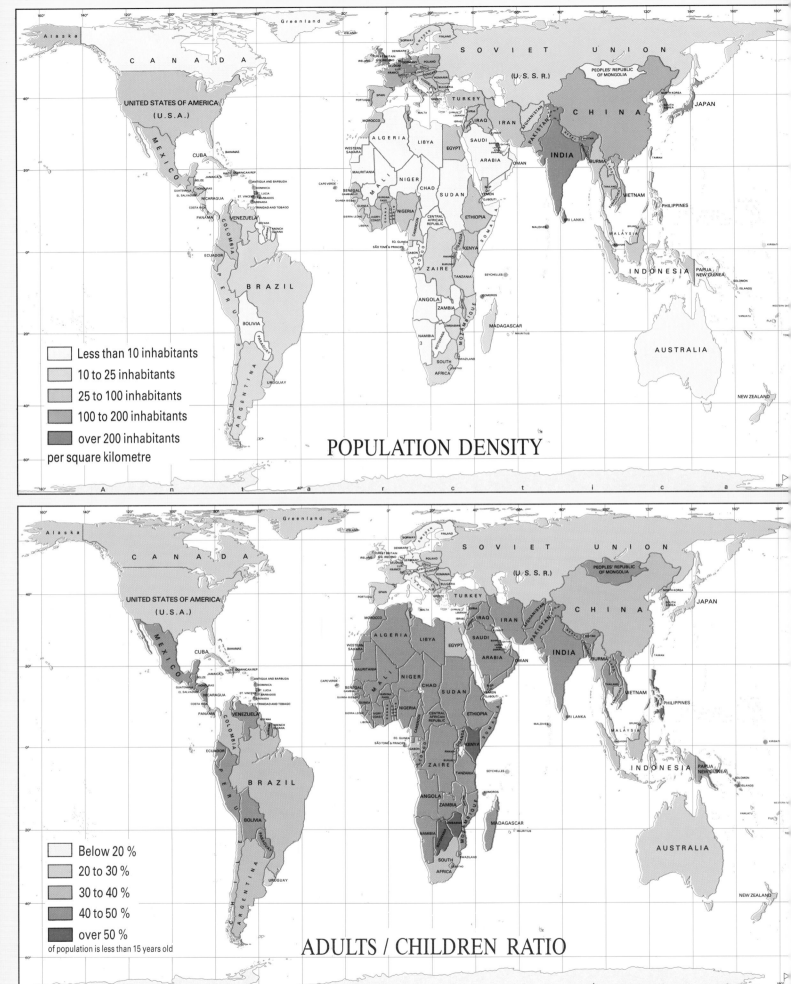

POPULATION DENSITY

Less than 10 inhabitants
10 to 25 inhabitants
25 to 100 inhabitants
100 to 200 inhabitants
over 200 inhabitants
per square kilometre

ADULTS / CHILDREN RATIO

Below 20 %
20 to 30 %
30 to 40 %
40 to 50 %
over 50 %
of population is less than 15 years old

POPULATION

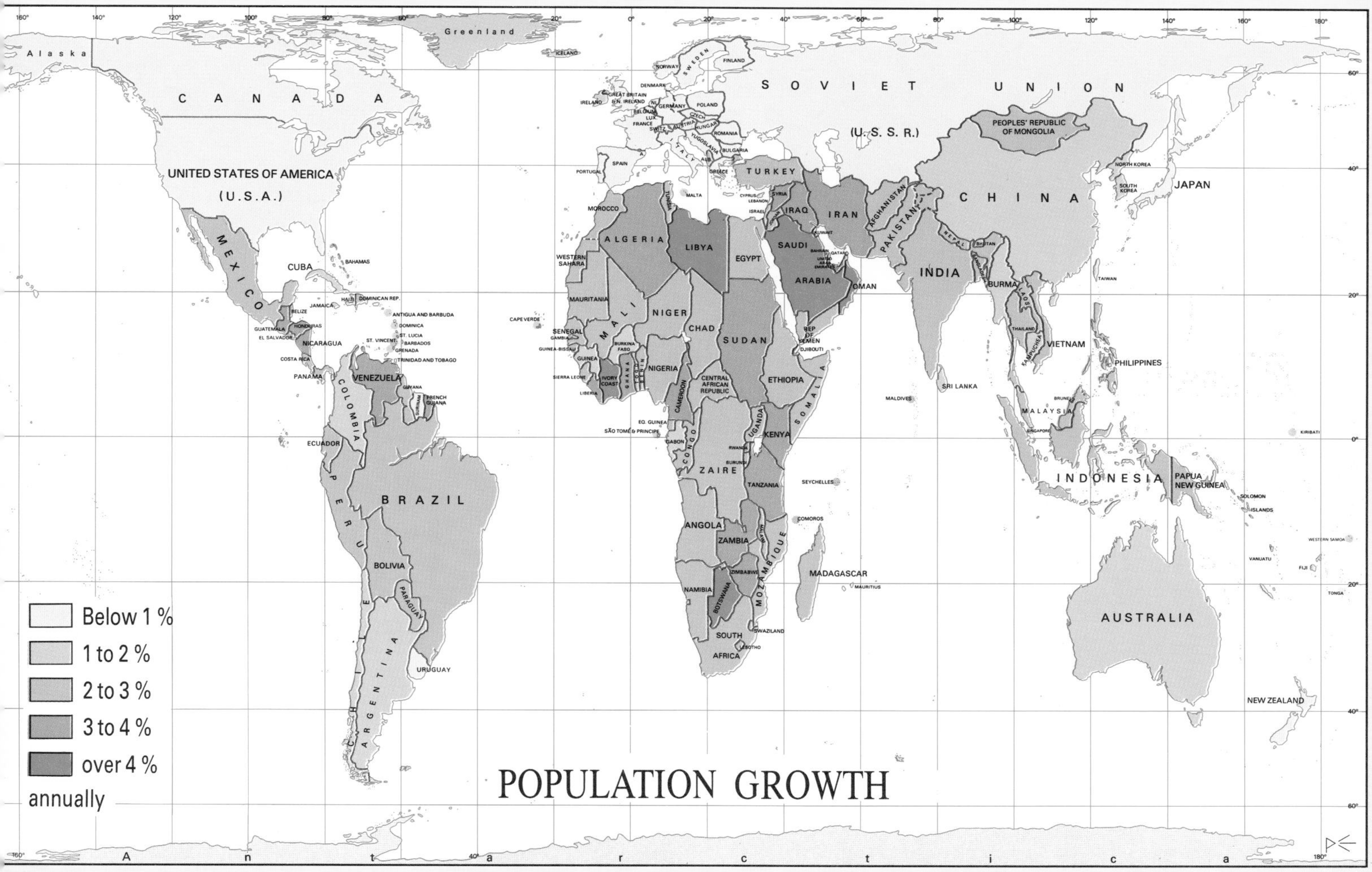

Greenland
Alaska
CANADA
UNITED STATES OF AMERICA (U.S.A.)
MEXICO
CUBA
BAHAMAS
HAITI
DOMINICAN REP.
JAMAICA
BELIZE
GUATEMALA
HONDURAS
EL SALVADOR
NICARAGUA
COSTA RICA
PANAMA
ANTIGUA AND BARBUDA
DOMINICA
ST. LUCIA
ST. VINCENT
BARBADOS
GRENADA
TRINIDAD AND TOBAGO
VENEZUELA
GUYANA
SURINAM
FRENCH GUIANA
COLOMBIA
ECUADOR
PERU
BRAZIL
BOLIVIA
PARAGUAY
CHILE
ARGENTINA
URUGUAY
ICELAND
NORWAY
SWEDEN
FINLAND
DENMARK
GREAT BRITAIN
IRELAND
N. IRELAND
GERMANY
POLAND
BELGIUM
LUX
FRANCE
SWITZ
AUSTRIA
HUNGARY
CZECH
ROMANIA
YUGOSLAVIA
BULGARIA
ALB
ITALY
GREECE
PORTUGAL
SPAIN
MALTA
SOVIET UNION
(U.S.S.R.)
PEOPLES' REPUBLIC OF MONGOLIA
TURKEY
CYPRUS
SYRIA
LEBANON
ISRAEL
IRAQ
IRAN
KUWAIT
SAUDI ARABIA
BAHRAIN
QATAR
UNITED ARAB EMIRATES
OMAN
REP OF YEMEN
AFGHANISTAN
PAKISTAN
NEPAL
BHUTAN
INDIA
BANGLADESH
SRI LANKA
MALDIVES
CHINA
NORTH KOREA
SOUTH KOREA
JAPAN
TAIWAN
BURMA
LAOS
THAILAND
KAMPUCHEA
VIETNAM
PHILIPPINES
MALAYSIA
BRUNEI
SINGAPORE
INDONESIA
PAPUA NEW GUINEA
SOLOMON ISLANDS
KIRIBATI
WESTERN SAMOA
VANUATU
FIJI
TONGA
AUSTRALIA
NEW ZEALAND
MOROCCO
ALGERIA
TUNISIA
LIBYA
EGYPT
WESTERN SAHARA
MAURITANIA
MALI
NIGER
CHAD
SUDAN
CAPE VERDE
SENEGAL
GAMBIA
GUINEA-BISSAU
GUINEA
SIERRA LEONE
LIBERIA
IVORY COAST
GHANA
BURKINA FASO
NIGERIA
CAMEROON
CENTRAL AFRICAN REPUBLIC
ETHIOPIA
DJIBOUTI
SOMALIA
EQ. GUINEA
SÃO TOMÉ & PRINCIPE
GABON
CONGO
ZAIRE
UGANDA
KENYA
RWANDA
BURUNDI
TANZANIA
SEYCHELLES
COMOROS
ANGOLA
ZAMBIA
MALAWI
MOZAMBIQUE
ZIMBABWE
NAMIBIA
BOTSWANA
MADAGASCAR
MAURITIUS
SOUTH AFRICA
SWAZILAND
LESOTHO
Antarctica
Below 1 %
1 to 2 %
2 to 3 %
3 to 4 %
over 4 %
annually
POPULATION GROWTH

Greenland
Alaska
CANADA
UNITED STATES OF AMERICA (U.S.A.)
MEXICO
CUBA
VENEZUELA
COLOMBIA
ECUADOR
PERU
BRAZIL
BOLIVIA
PARAGUAY
CHILE
ARGENTINA
URUGUAY
SOVIET UNION
(U.S.S.R.)
PEOPLES' REPUBLIC OF MONGOLIA
TURKEY
IRAQ
IRAN
SAUDI ARABIA
OMAN
AFGHANISTAN
PAKISTAN
INDIA
CHINA
JAPAN
BURMA
VIETNAM
PHILIPPINES
MALAYSIA
INDONESIA
PAPUA NEW GUINEA
AUSTRALIA
NEW ZEALAND
MOROCCO
ALGERIA
LIBYA
EGYPT
MALI
NIGER
CHAD
SUDAN
NIGERIA
ETHIOPIA
KENYA
ZAIRE
TANZANIA
ANGOLA
ZAMBIA
MOZAMBIQUE
NAMIBIA
BOTSWANA
MADAGASCAR
SOUTH AFRICA
Antarctica
More women
more men
MEN / WOMEN RATIO

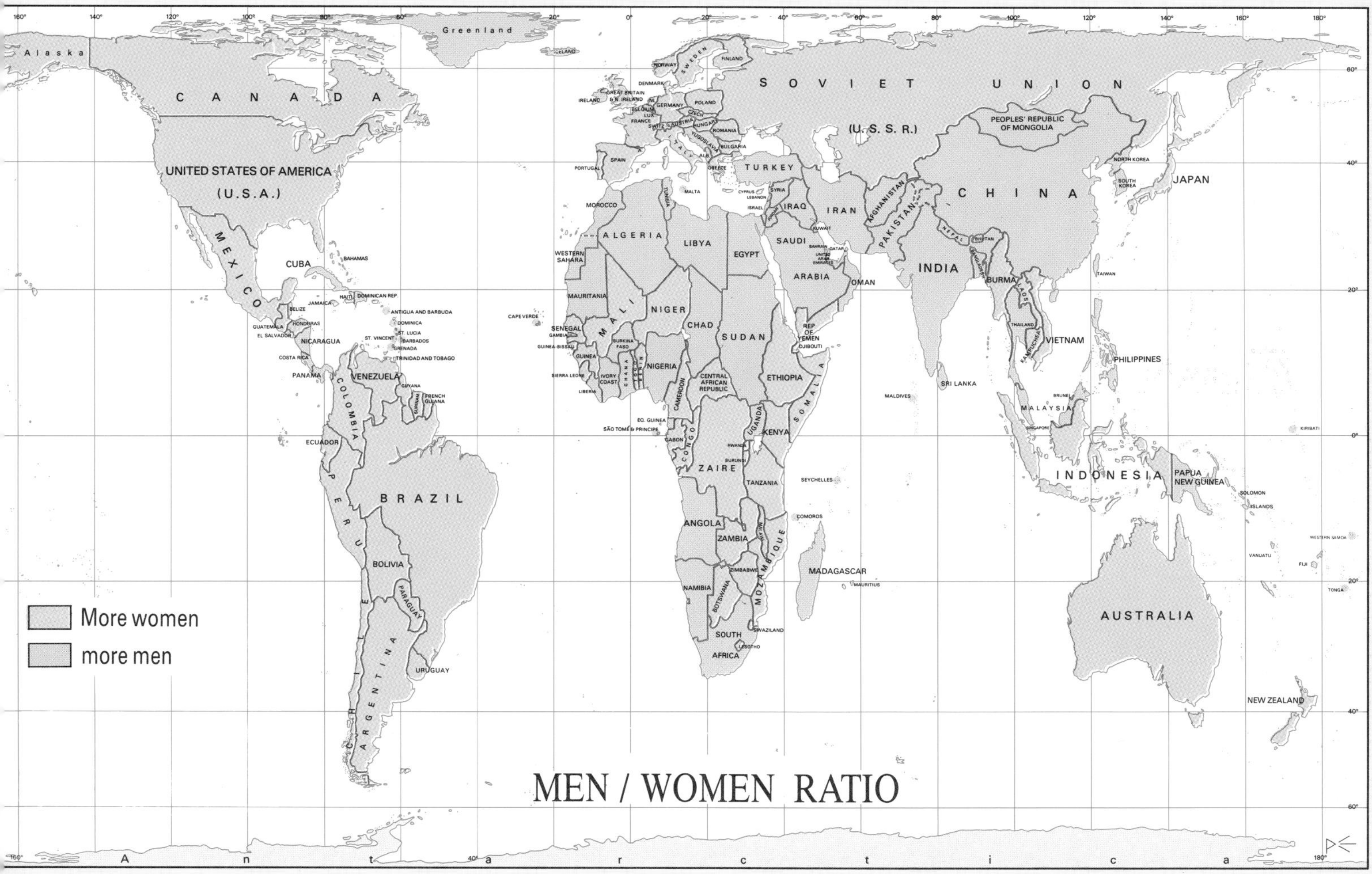

STRUCTURE

Less than 45 years

45 to 55 years

56 to 65 years

66 to 75 years

above 75 years

LIFE EXP

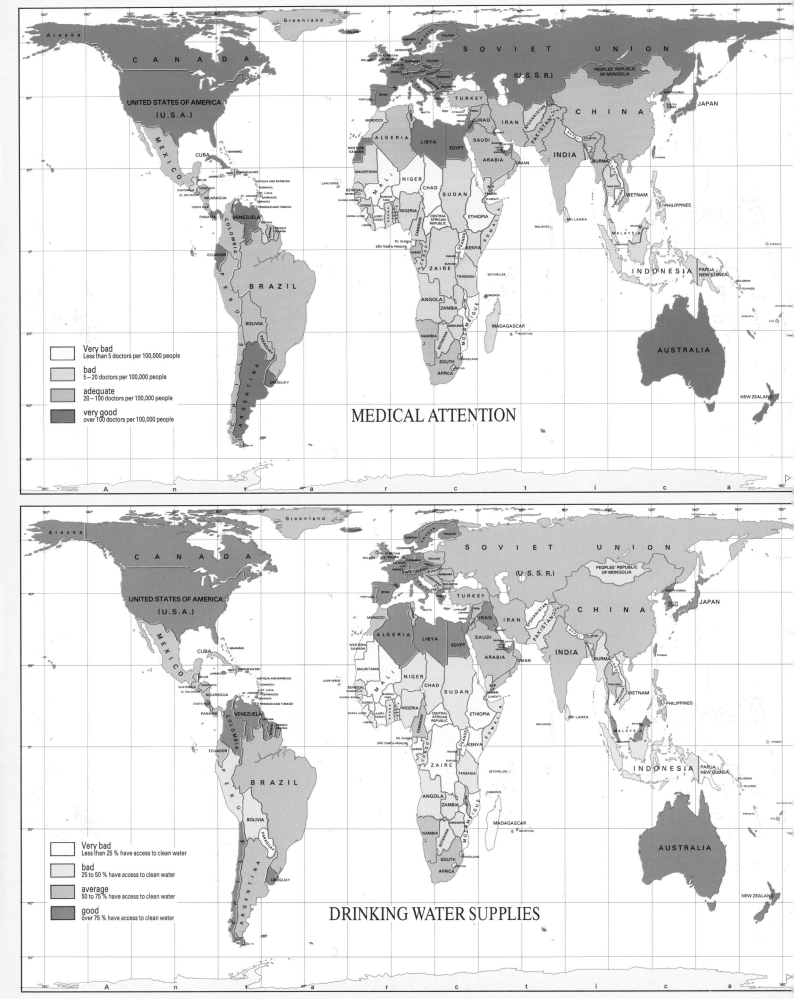

MEDICAL ATTENTION

Very bad
Less than 5 doctors per 100,000 people

bad
5 – 20 doctors per 100,000 people

adequate
20 – 100 doctors per 100,000 people

very good
over 100 doctors per 100,000 people

DRINKING WATER SUPPLIES

Very bad
Less than 25 % have access to clean water

bad
25 to 50 % have access to clean water

average
50 to 75 % have access to clean water

good
over 75 % have access to clean water

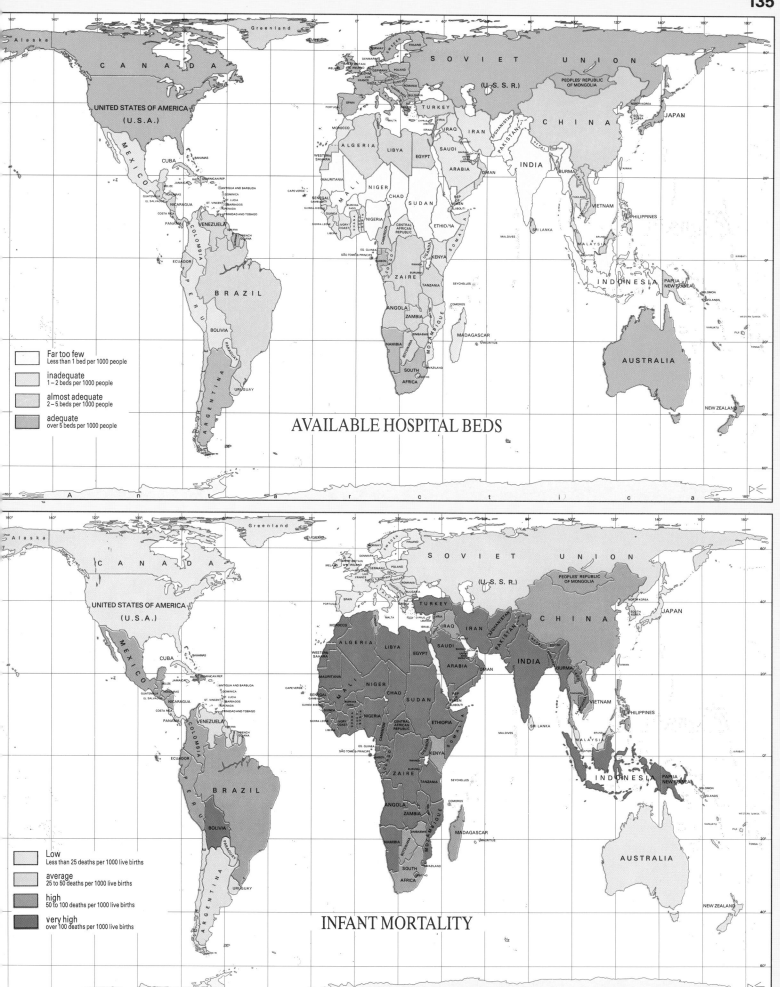

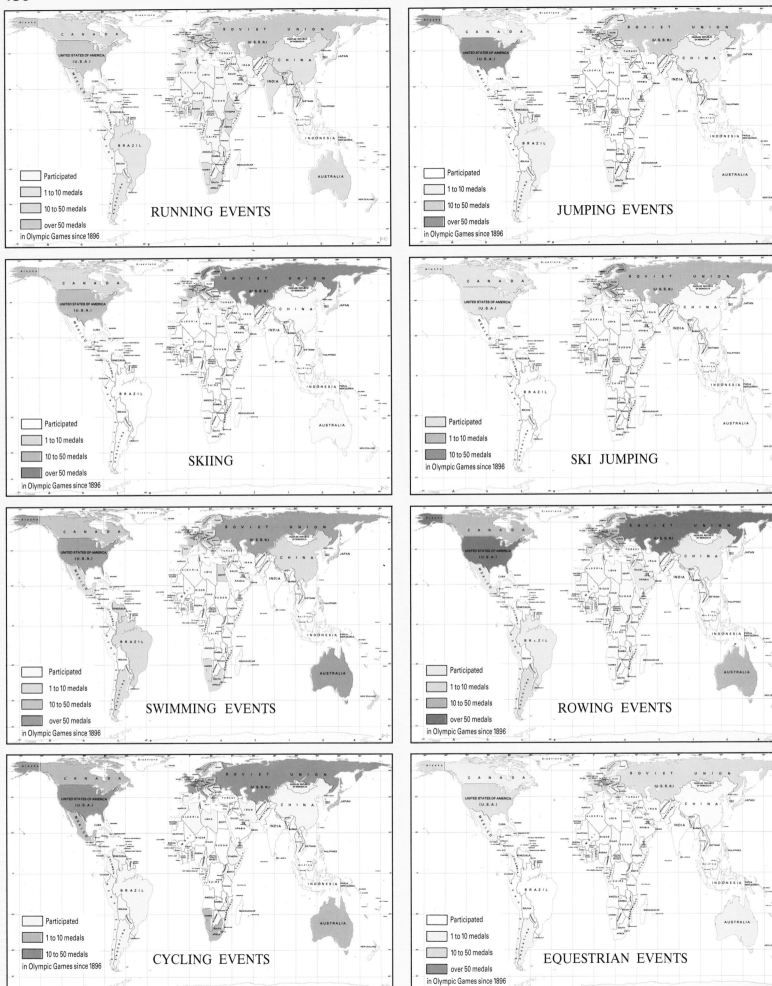

RUNNING EVENTS

Participated
1 to 10 medals
10 to 50 medals
over 50 medals
in Olympic Games since 1896

JUMPING EVENTS

Participated
1 to 10 medals
10 to 50 medals
over 50 medals
in Olympic Games since 1896

SKIING

Participated
1 to 10 medals
10 to 50 medals
over 50 medals
in Olympic Games since 1896

SKI JUMPING

Participated
1 to 10 medals
10 to 50 medals
in Olympic Games since 1896

SWIMMING EVENTS

Participated
1 to 10 medals
10 to 50 medals
over 50 medals
in Olympic Games since 1896

ROWING EVENTS

Participated
1 to 10 medals
10 to 50 medals
over 50 medals
in Olympic Games since 1896

CYCLING EVENTS

Participated
1 to 10 medals
10 to 50 medals
in Olympic Games since 1896

EQUESTRIAN EVENTS

Participated
1 to 10 medals
10 to 50 medals
over 50 medals
in Olympic Games since 1896

SP

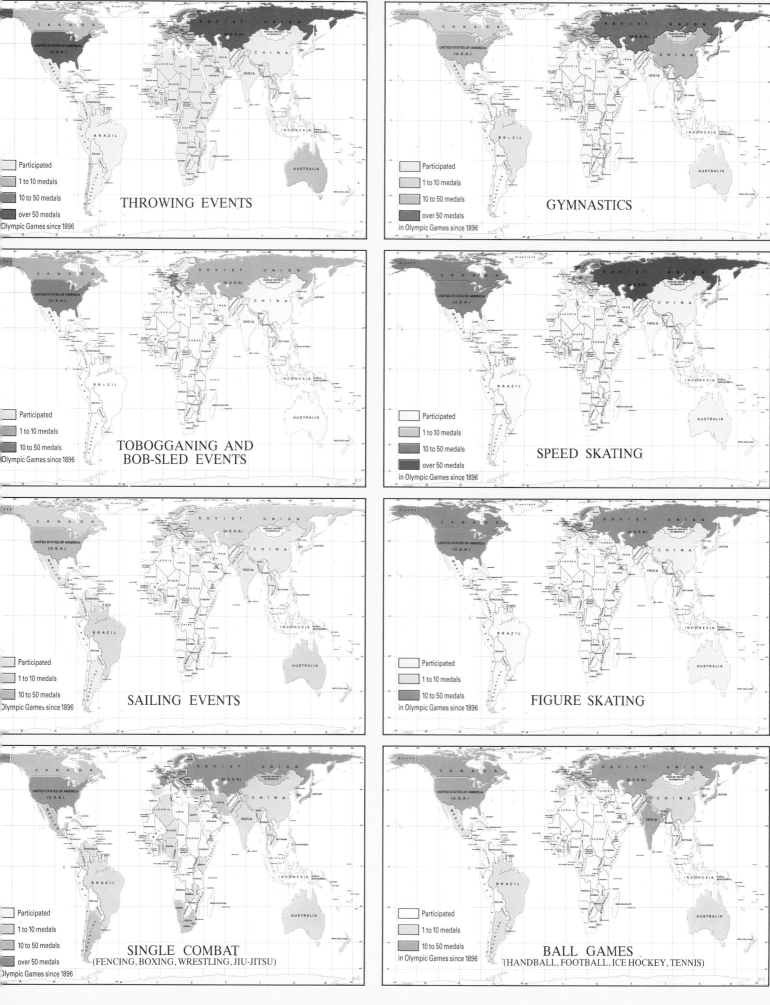

THROWING EVENTS

Participated
1 to 10 medals
10 to 50 medals
over 50 medals
Olympic Games since 1896

GYMNASTICS

Participated
1 to 10 medals
10 to 50 medals
over 50 medals
in Olympic Games since 1896

TOBOGGANING AND
BOB-SLED EVENTS

Participated
1 to 10 medals
10 to 50 medals
Olympic Games since 1896

SPEED SKATING

Participated
1 to 10 medals
10 to 50 medals
over 50 medals
in Olympic Games since 1896

SAILING EVENTS

Participated
1 to 10 medals
10 to 50 medals
Olympic Games since 1896

FIGURE SKATING

Participated
1 to 10 medals
10 to 50 medals
in Olympic Games since 1896

SINGLE COMBAT
(FENCING, BOXING, WRESTLING, JIU-JITSU)

Participated
1 to 10 medals
10 to 50 medals
over 50 medals
Olympic Games since 1896

BALL GAMES
(HANDBALL, FOOTBALL, ICE HOCKEY, TENNIS)

Participated
1 to 10 medals
10 to 50 medals
in Olympic Games since 1896

RT

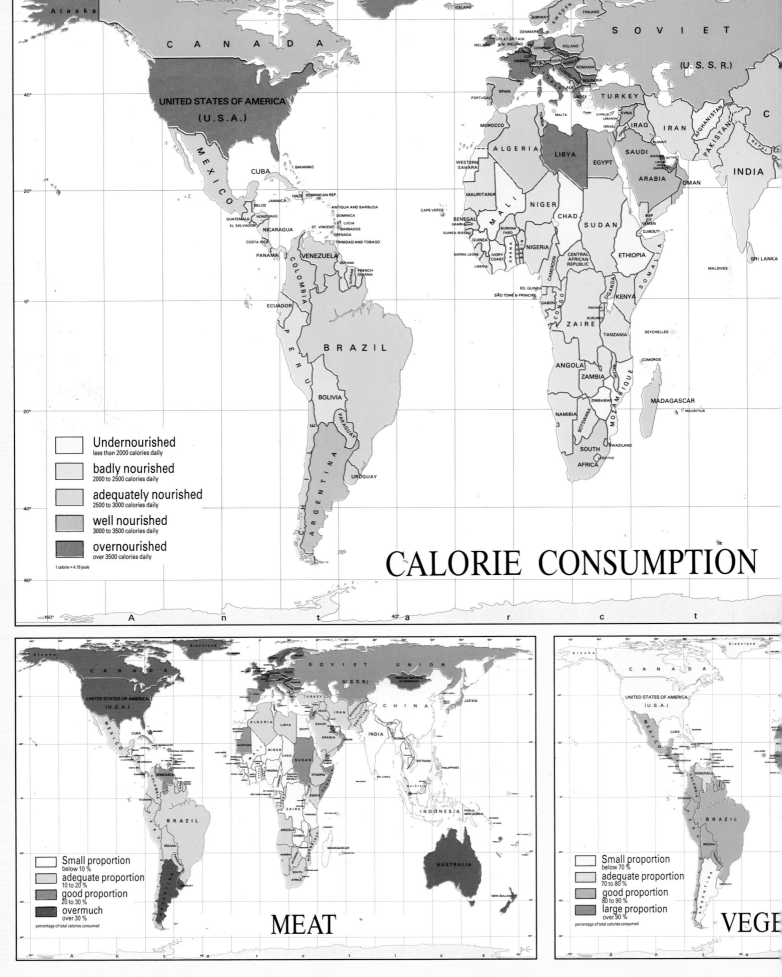

CALORIE CONSUMPTION

Undernourished
less than 2000 calories daily

badly nourished
2000 to 2500 calories daily

adequately nourished
2500 to 3000 calories daily

well nourished
3000 to 3500 calories daily

overnourished
over 3500 calories daily

1 calorie = 4.19 joule

MEAT

Small proportion
below 10 %

adequate proportion
10 to 20 %

good proportion
20 to 30 %

overmuch
over 30 %

percentage of total calories consumed

VEGE

Small proportion
below 70 %

adequate proportion
70 to 80 %

good proportion
80 to 90 %

large proportion
over 90 %

percentage of total calories consumed

NUT

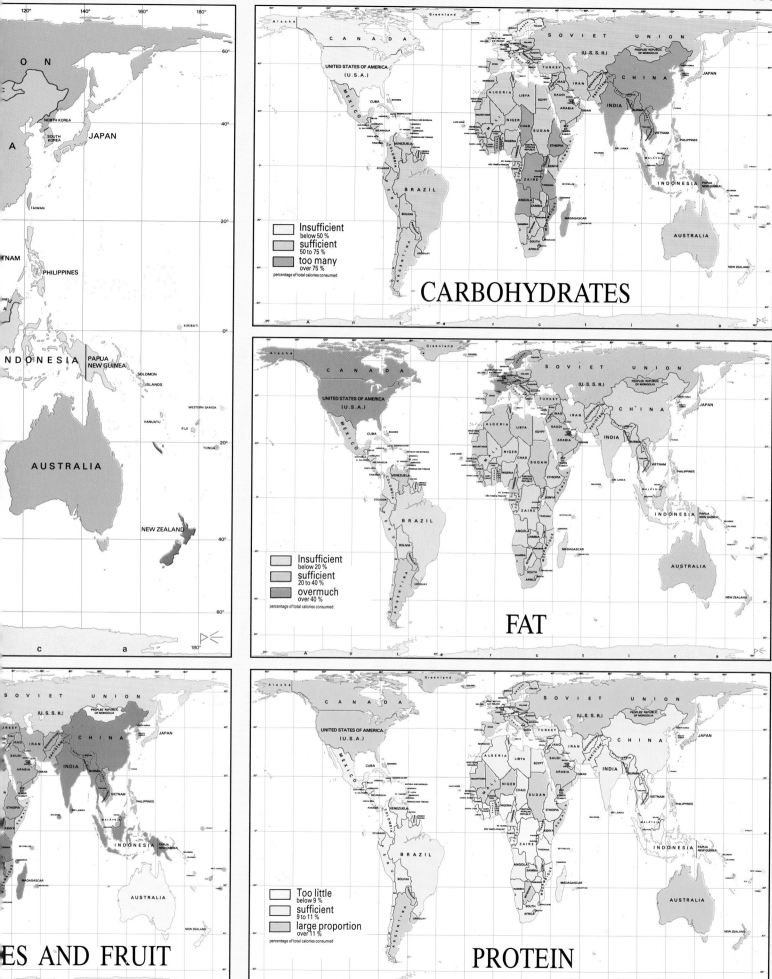

CARBOHYDRATES

Insufficient
below 50 %

sufficient
50 to 75 %

too many
over 75 %

percentage of total calories consumed

FAT

Insufficient
below 20 %

sufficient
20 to 40 %

overmuch
over 40 %

percentage of total calories consumed

ES AND FRUIT

PROTEIN

Too little
below 9 %

sufficient
9 to 11 %

large proportion
over 11 %

percentage of total calories consumed

TION

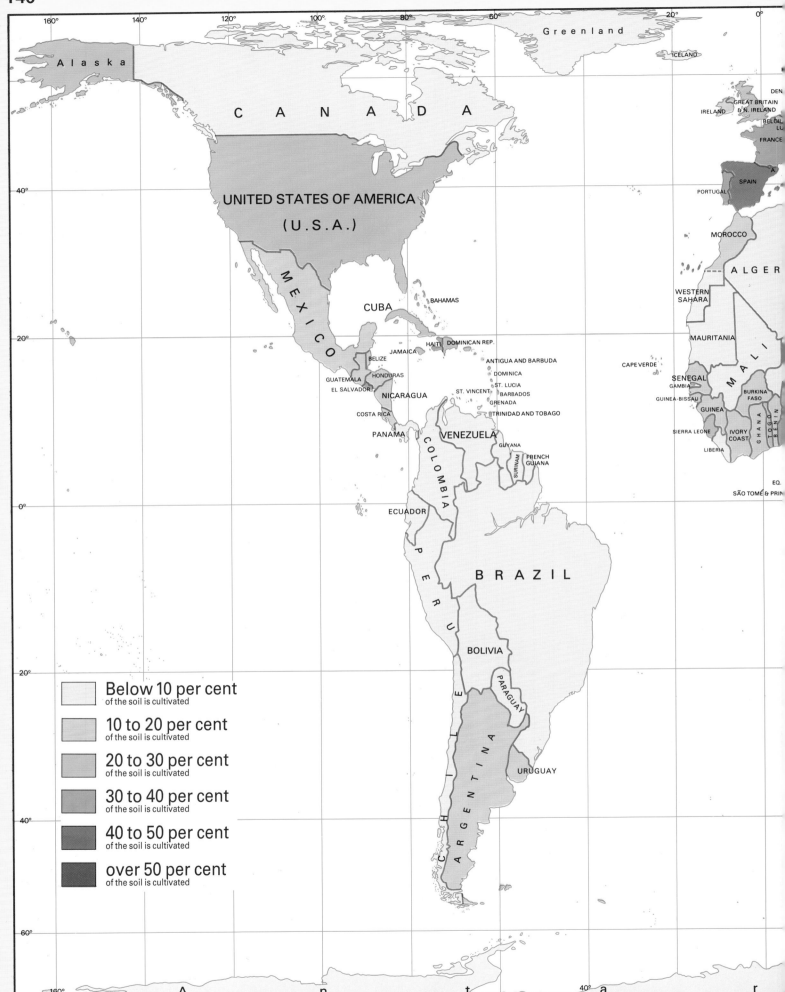

Greenland

ICELAND

Alaska

C A N A D A

DEN
GREAT BRITAIN
& N. IRELAND
IRELAND
BELGIU
LU
FRANCE
A
SPAIN
PORTUGAL

UNITED STATES OF AMERICA

(U.S.A.)

MOROCCO

M E X I C O

ALGER

WESTERN
SAHARA

CUBA

BAHAMAS

MAURITANIA

CAPE VERDE

HAITI DOMINICAN REP.

MALI

JAMAICA

BELIZE

ANTIGUA AND BARBUDA

SENEGAL
GAMBIA
GUINEA-BISSAU

BURKINA
FASO

GUATEMALA
HONDURAS
EL SALVADOR

DOMINICA
ST. LUCIA
ST. VINCENT
BARBADOS
GRENADA

GUINEA

GHANA
TOGO
BENIN

NICARAGUA

IVORY
COAST

SIERRA LEONE

COSTA RICA

TRINIDAD AND TOBAGO

LIBERIA

PANAMA

VENEZUELA

GUYANA

EQ.
SÃO TOMÉ & PRIN

COLOMBIA

SURINAM
FRENCH
GUIANA

ECUADOR

P
E
R
U

B R A Z I L

BOLIVIA

C
H
I
L
E

PARAGUAY

A
R
G
E
N
T
I
N
A

URUGUAY

Below 10 per cent
of the soil is cultivated

10 to 20 per cent
of the soil is cultivated

20 to 30 per cent
of the soil is cultivated

30 to 40 per cent
of the soil is cultivated

40 to 50 per cent
of the soil is cultivated

over 50 per cent
of the soil is cultivated

A   n   t   a   r

SOIL CU

IVATION

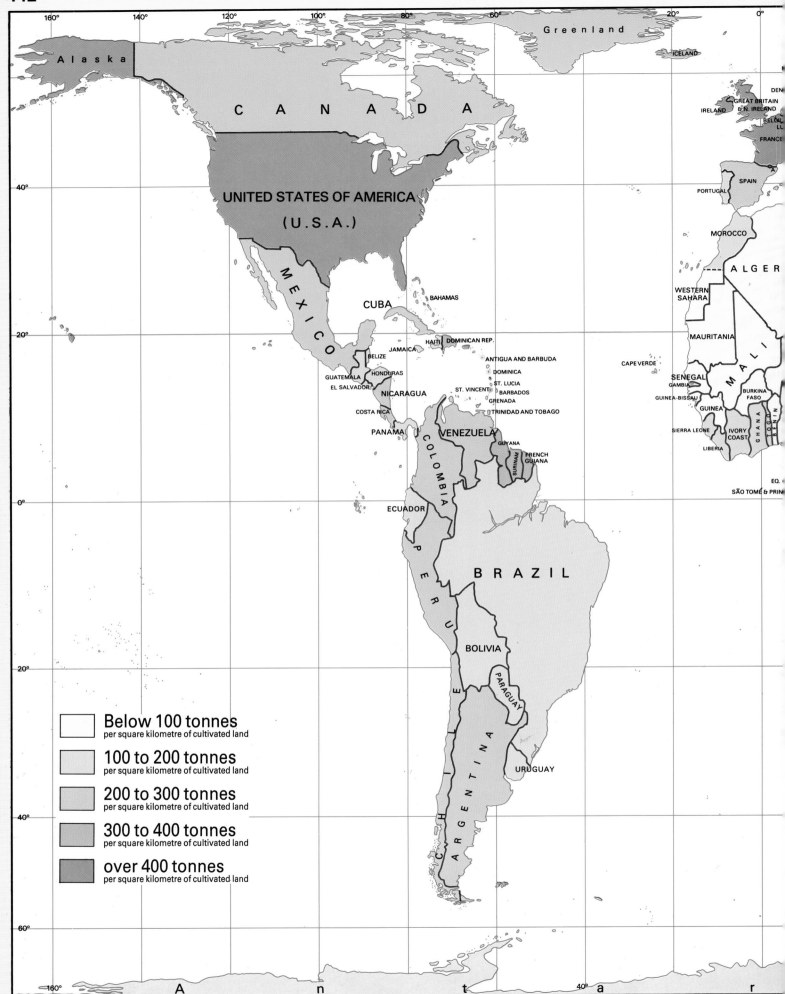

Below 100 tonnes
per square kilometre of cultivated land

100 to 200 tonnes
per square kilometre of cultivated land

200 to 300 tonnes
per square kilometre of cultivated land

300 to 400 tonnes
per square kilometre of cultivated land

over 400 tonnes
per square kilometre of cultivated land

CROP

144

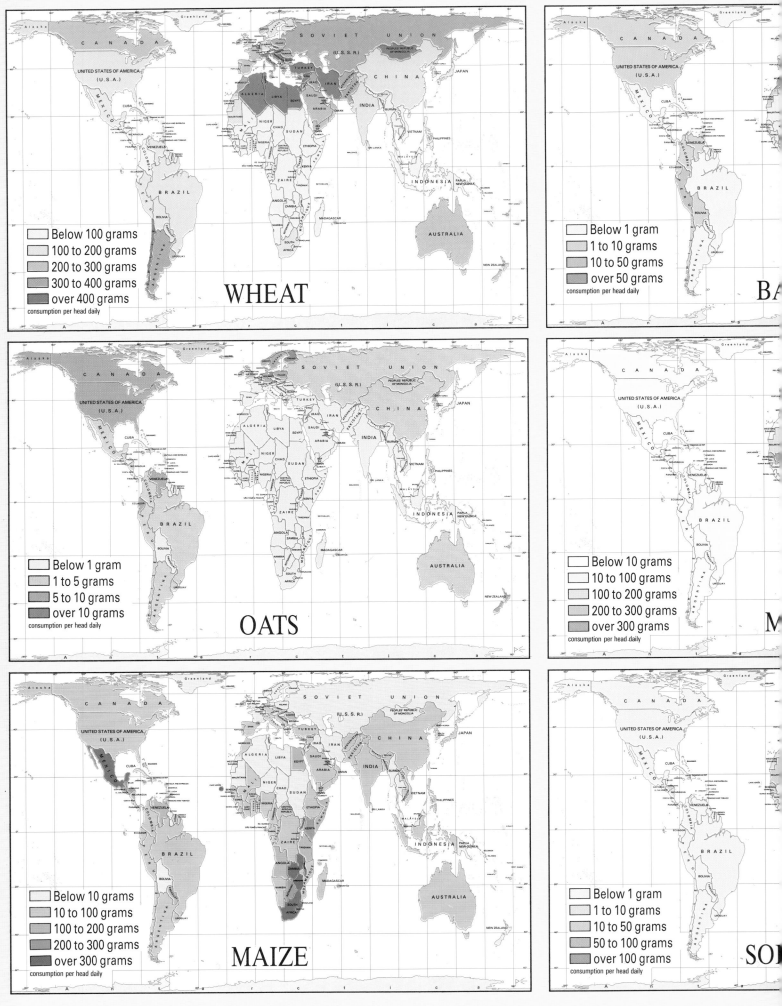

WHEAT

Below 100 grams
100 to 200 grams
200 to 300 grams
300 to 400 grams
over 400 grams
consumption per head daily

BA

Below 1 gram
1 to 10 grams
10 to 50 grams
over 50 grams
consumption per head daily

OATS

Below 1 gram
1 to 5 grams
5 to 10 grams
over 10 grams
consumption per head daily

M

Below 10 grams
10 to 100 grams
100 to 200 grams
200 to 300 grams
over 300 grams
consumption per head daily

MAIZE

Below 10 grams
10 to 100 grams
100 to 200 grams
200 to 300 grams
over 300 grams
consumption per head daily

SO

Below 1 gram
1 to 10 grams
10 to 50 grams
50 to 100 grams
over 100 grams
consumption per head daily

STAPLE FO

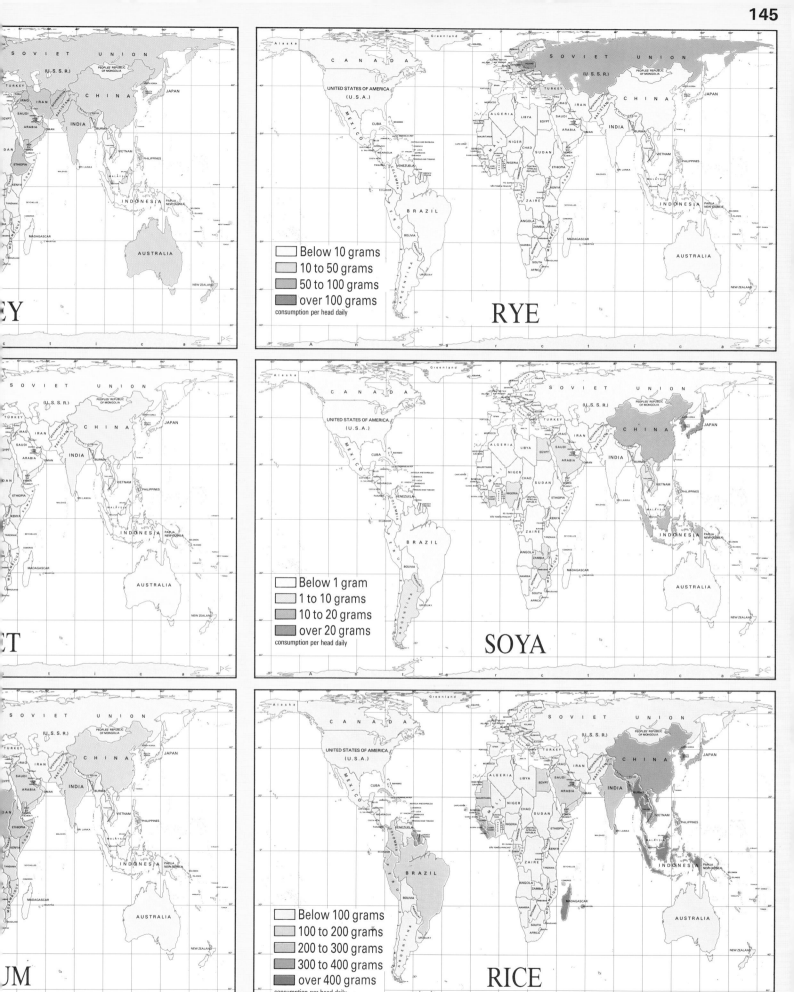

RYE

Below 10 grams
10 to 50 grams
50 to 100 grams
over 100 grams
consumption per head daily

SOYA

Below 1 gram
1 to 10 grams
10 to 20 grams
over 20 grams
consumption per head daily

RICE

Below 100 grams
100 to 200 grams
200 to 300 grams
300 to 400 grams
over 400 grams
consumption per head daily

ODSTUFFS

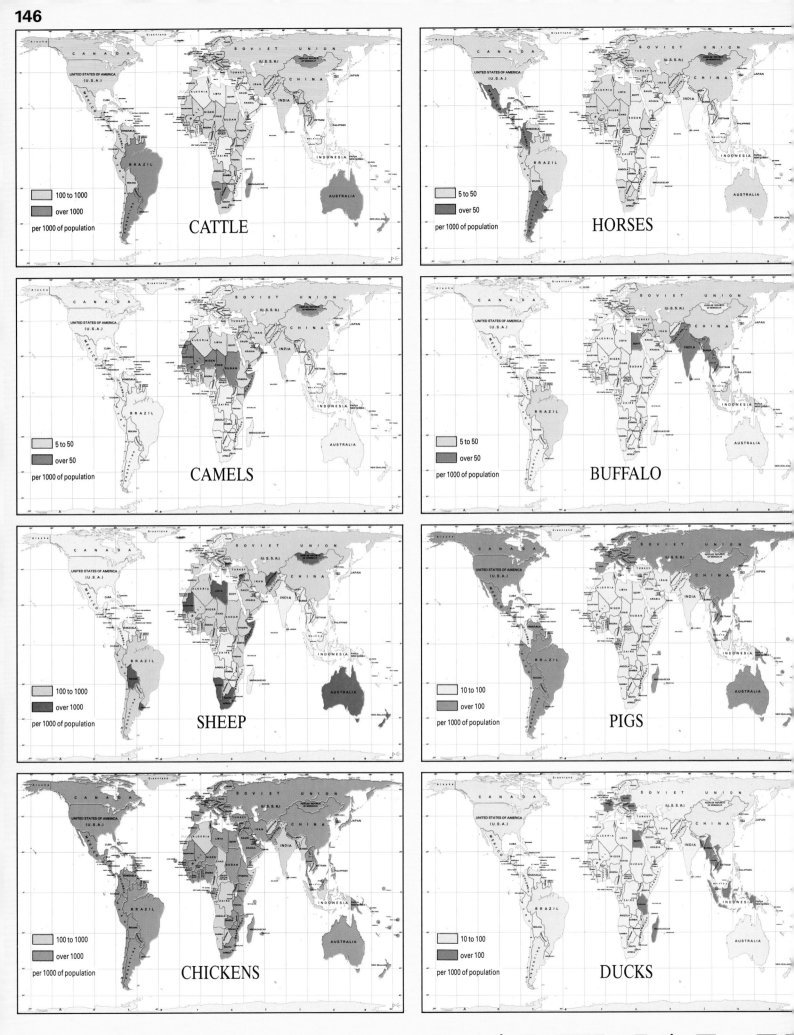

CATTLE
- 100 to 1000
- over 1000
per 1000 of population

HORSES
- 5 to 50
- over 50
per 1000 of population

CAMELS
- 5 to 50
- over 50
per 1000 of population

BUFFALO
- 5 to 50
- over 50
per 1000 of population

SHEEP
- 100 to 1000
- over 1000
per 1000 of population

PIGS
- 10 to 100
- over 100
per 1000 of population

CHICKENS
- 100 to 1000
- over 1000
per 1000 of population

DUCKS
- 10 to 100
- over 100
per 1000 of population

ANIMAL H

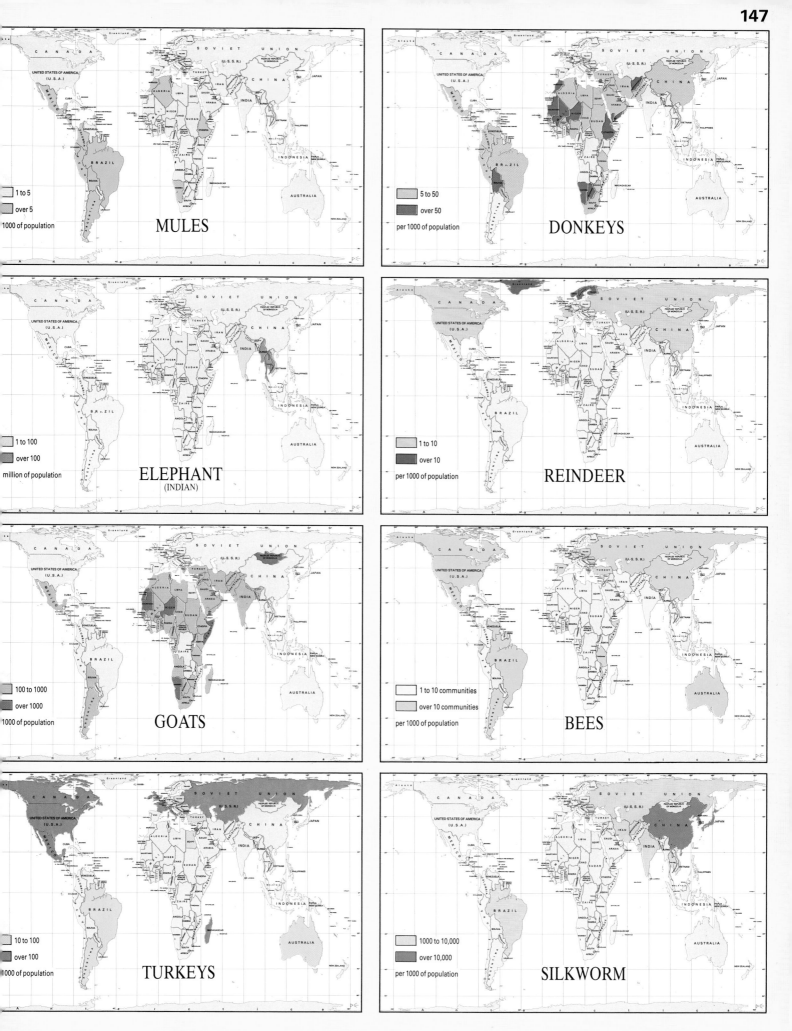

MULES

1 to 5
over 5

1000 of population

DONKEYS

5 to 50
over 50

per 1000 of population

ELEPHANT
(INDIAN)

1 to 100
over 100

million of population

REINDEER

1 to 10
over 10

per 1000 of population

GOATS

100 to 1000
over 1000

1000 of population

BEES

1 to 10 communities
over 10 communities

per 1000 of population

TURKEYS

10 to 100
over 100

1000 of population

SILKWORM

1000 to 10,000
over 10,000

per 1000 of population

SBANDRY

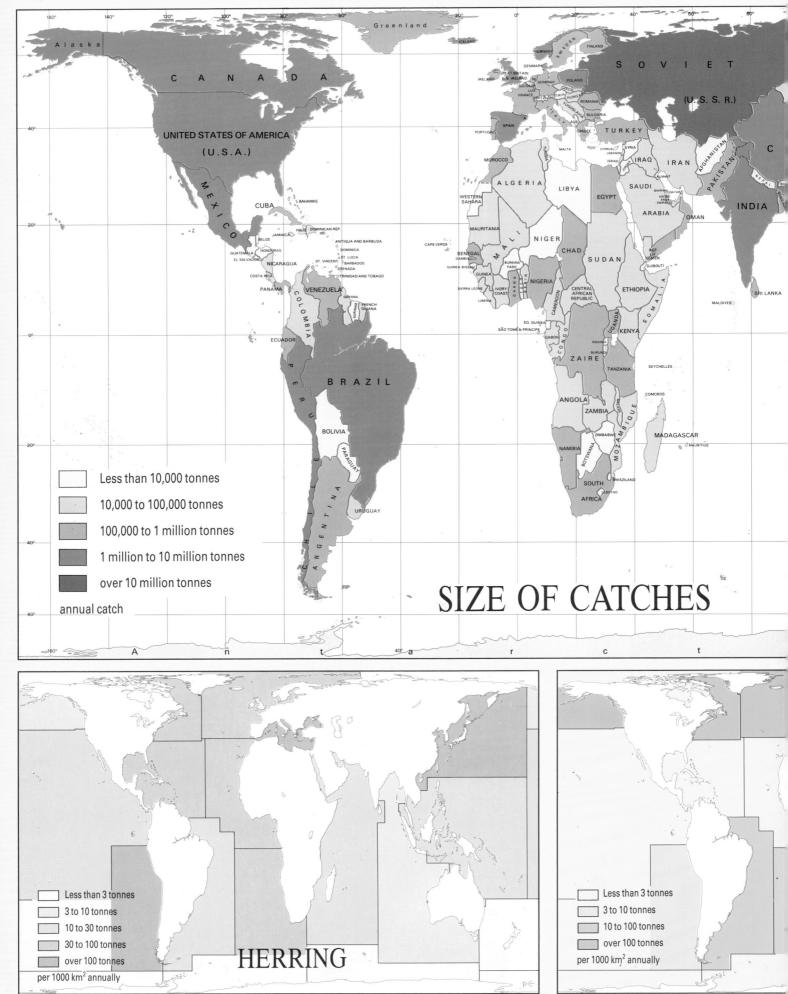

SIZE OF CATCHES

Less than 10,000 tonnes

10,000 to 100,000 tonnes

100,000 to 1 million tonnes

1 million to 10 million tonnes

over 10 million tonnes

annual catch

Less than 3 tonnes

3 to 10 tonnes

10 to 30 tonnes

30 to 100 tonnes

over 100 tonnes

per 1000 km² annually

HERRING

Less than 3 tonnes

3 to 10 tonnes

10 to 100 tonnes

over 100 tonnes

per 1000 km² annually

FIS

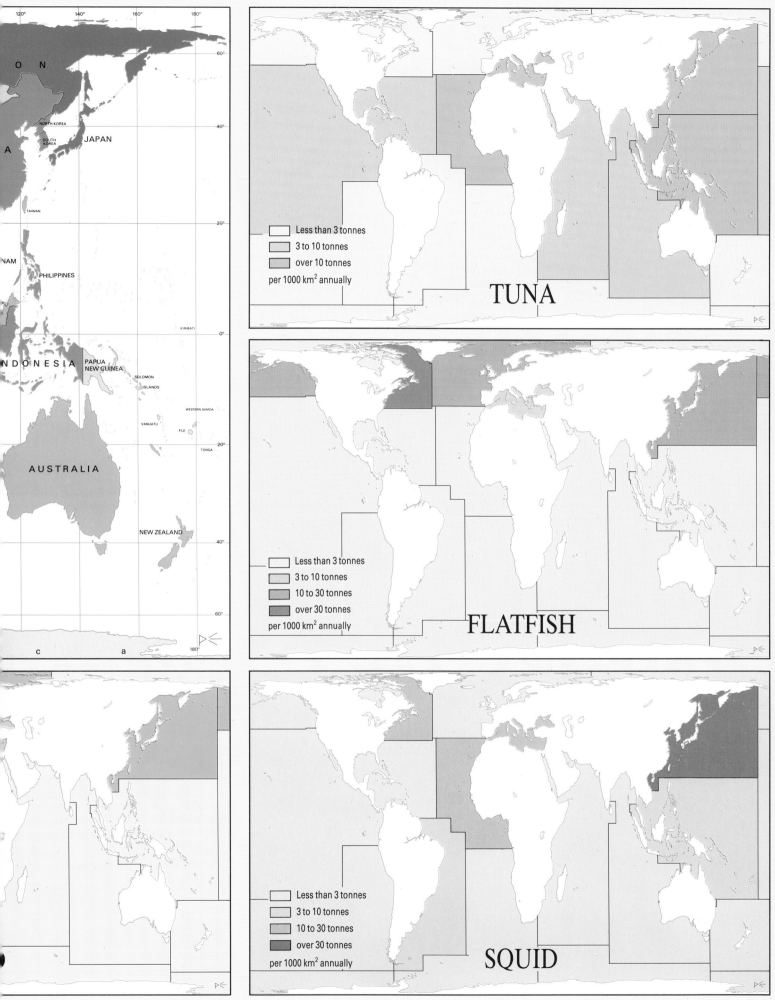

Less than 3 tonnes
3 to 10 tonnes
over 10 tonnes
per 1000 km² annually

TUNA

Less than 3 tonnes
3 to 10 tonnes
10 to 30 tonnes
over 30 tonnes
per 1000 km² annually

FLATFISH

Less than 3 tonnes
3 to 10 tonnes
10 to 30 tonnes
over 30 tonnes
per 1000 km² annually

SQUID

NORTH KOREA
SOUTH KOREA
JAPAN
TAIWAN
PHILIPPINES
KIRIBATI
INDONESIA
PAPUA NEW GUINEA
SOLOMON ISLANDS
WESTERN SAMOA
VANUATU
FIJI
TONGA
AUSTRALIA
NEW ZEALAND

NG

150

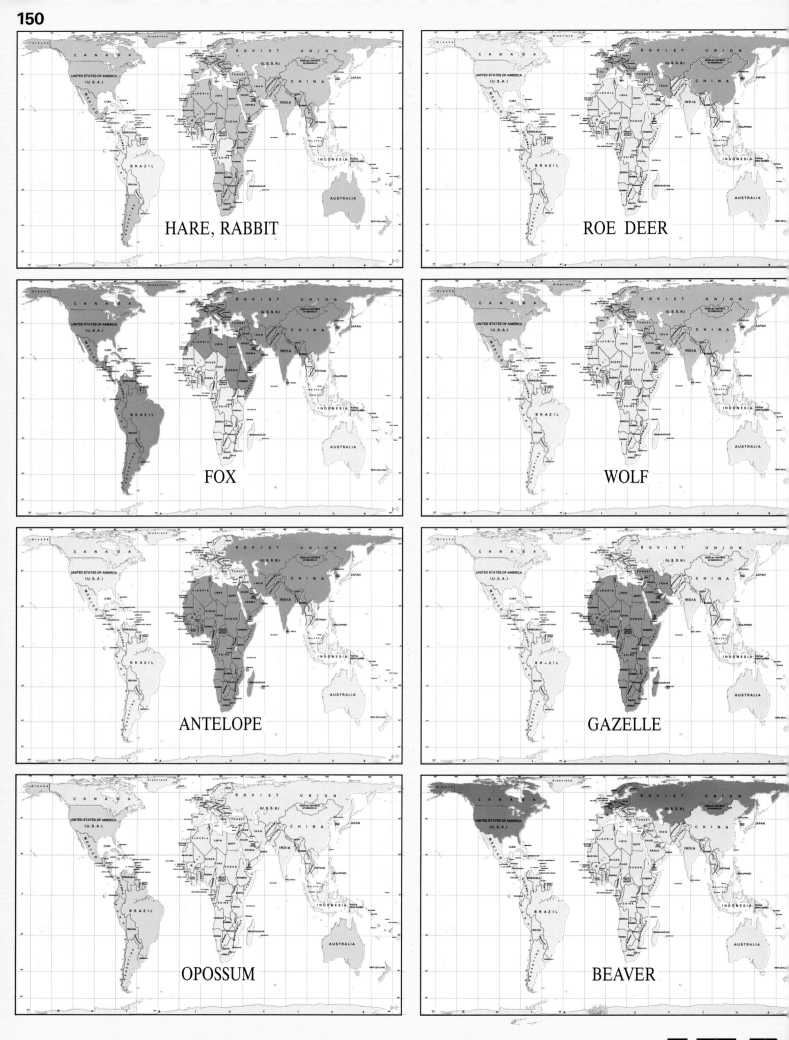

HARE, RABBIT

ROE DEER

FOX

WOLF

ANTELOPE

GAZELLE

OPOSSUM

BEAVER

HUM

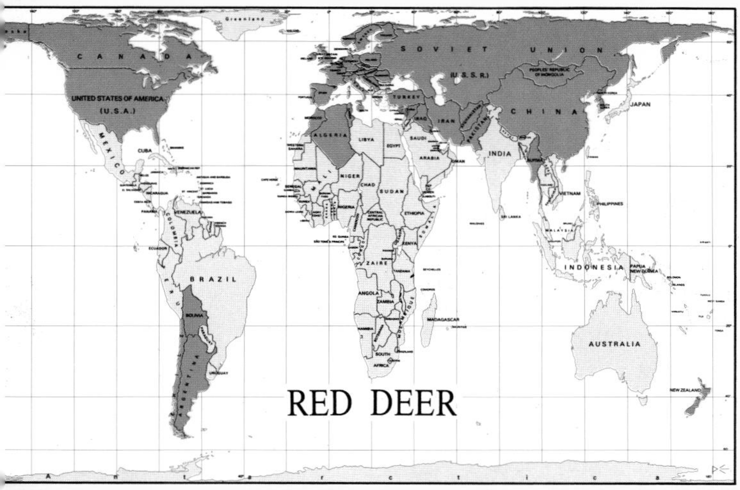

RED DEER

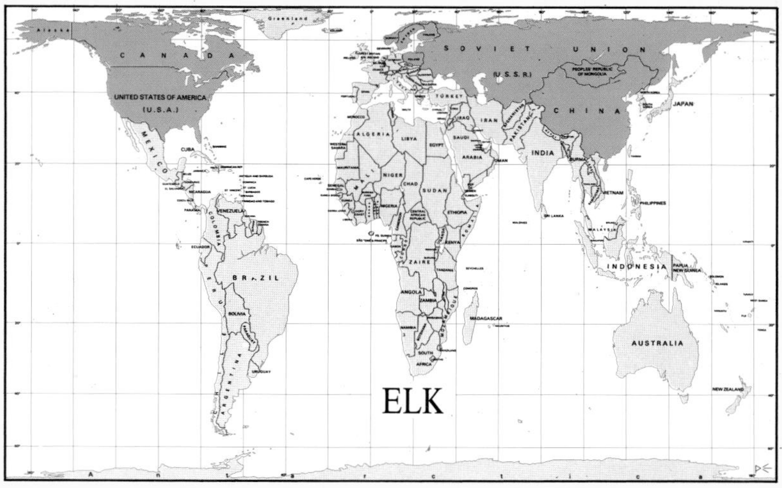

ELK

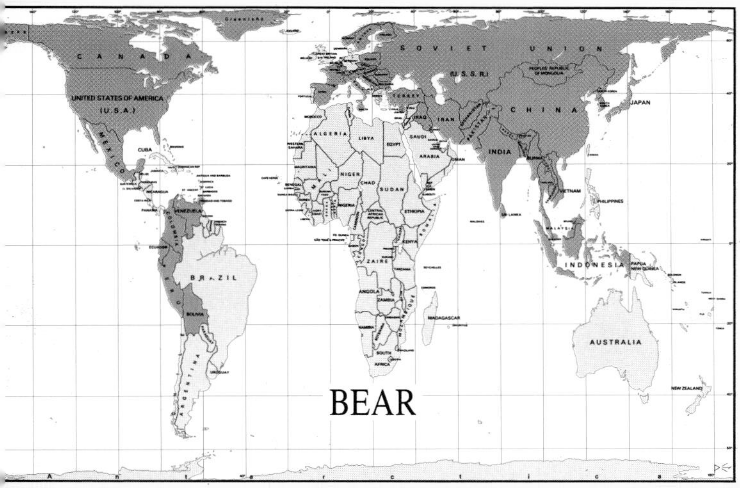

BEAR

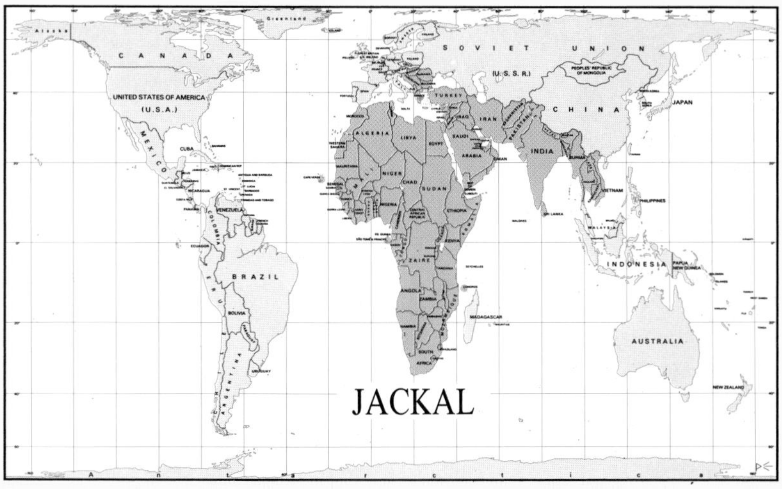

JACKAL

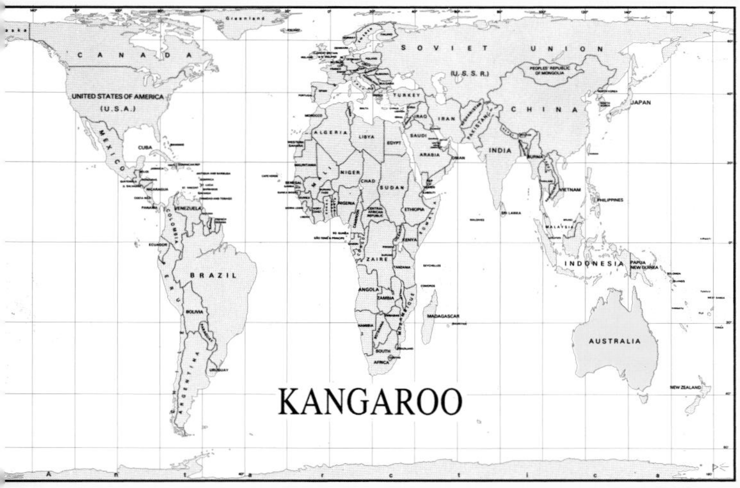

KANGAROO

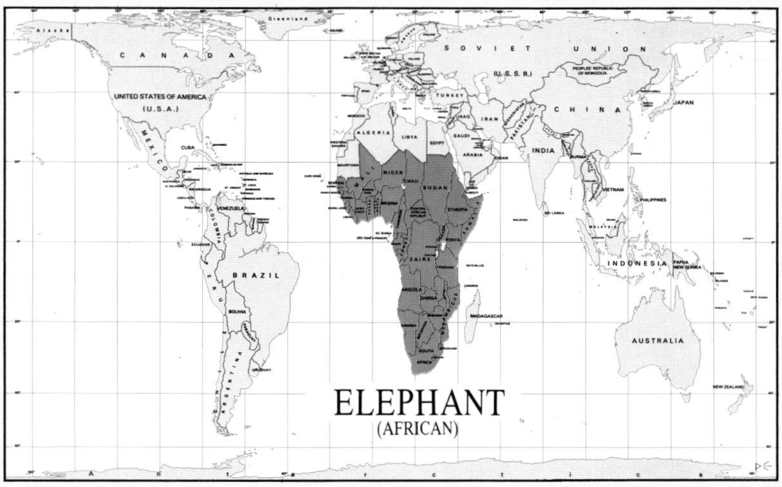

ELEPHANT
(AFRICAN)

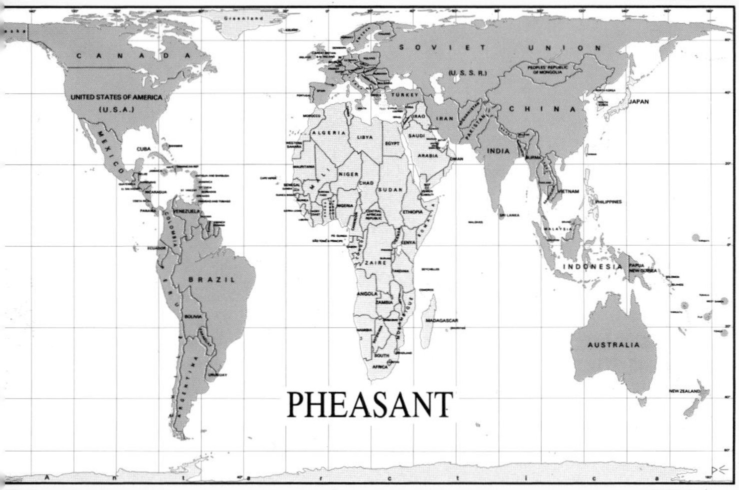

PHEASANT

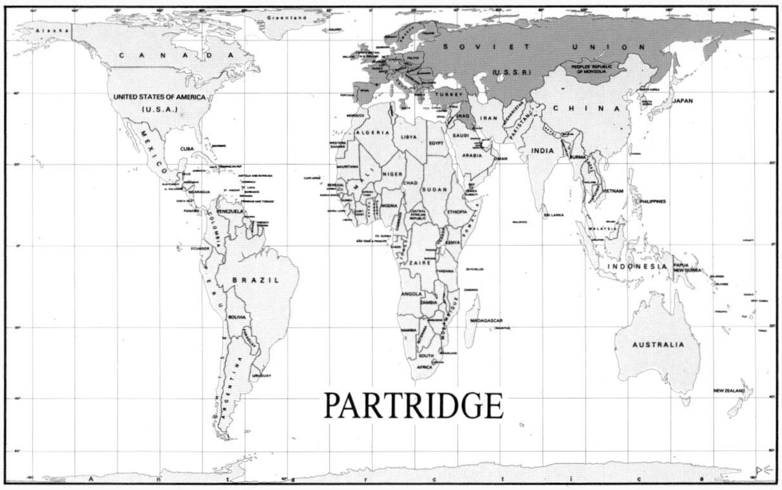

PARTRIDGE

TING

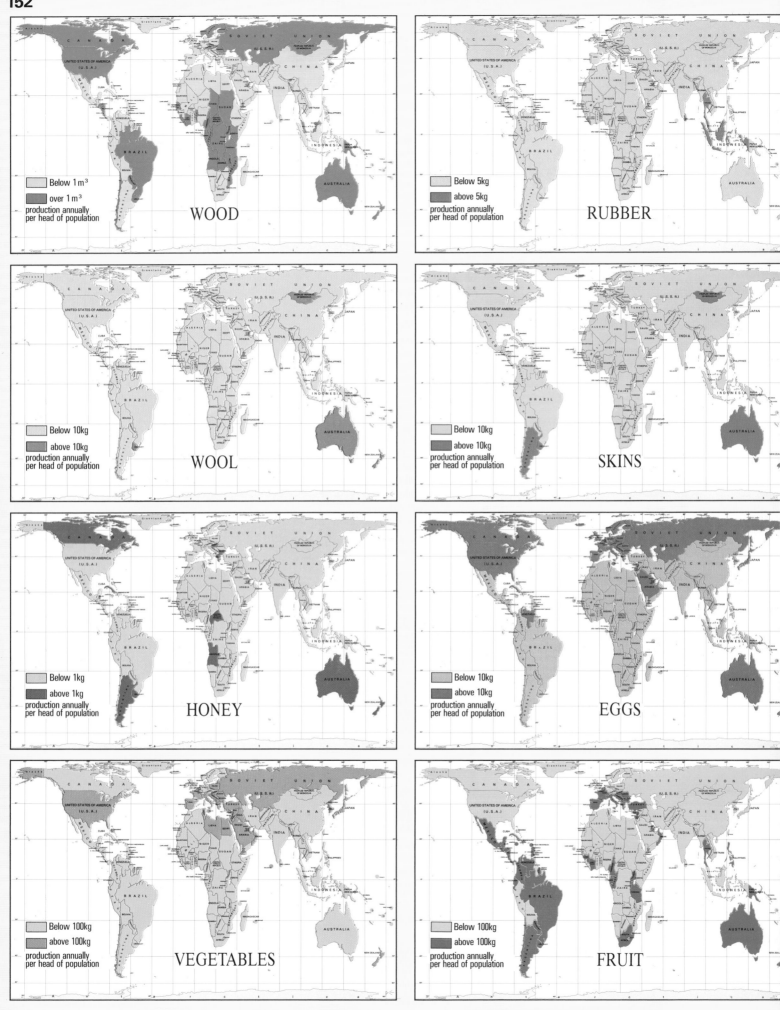

Below 1 m³

over 1 m³

production annually
per head of population

WOOD

Below 5kg

above 5kg

production annually
per head of population

RUBBER

Below 10kg

above 10kg

production annually
per head of population

WOOL

Below 10kg

above 10kg

production annually
per head of population

SKINS

Below 1kg

above 1kg

production annually
per head of population

HONEY

Below 10kg

above 10kg

production annually
per head of population

EGGS

Below 100kg

above 100kg

production annually
per head of population

VEGETABLES

Below 100kg

above 100kg

production annually
per head of population

FRUIT

NATURAL

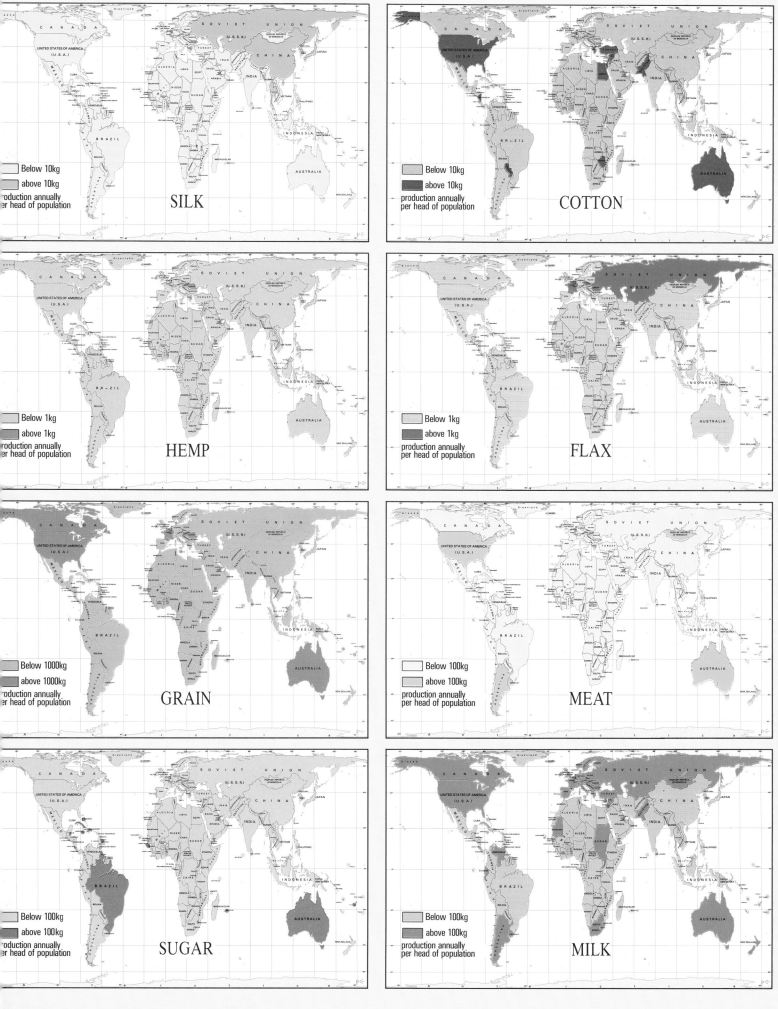

SILK
Below 10kg
above 10kg
production annually
per head of population

COTTON
Below 10kg
above 10kg
production annually
per head of population

HEMP
Below 1kg
above 1kg
production annually
per head of population

FLAX
Below 1kg
above 1kg
production annually
per head of population

GRAIN
Below 1000kg
above 1000kg
production annually
per head of population

MEAT
Below 100kg
above 100kg
production annually
per head of population

SUGAR
Below 100kg
above 100kg
production annually
per head of population

MILK
Below 100kg
above 100kg
production annually
per head of population

RODUCTS

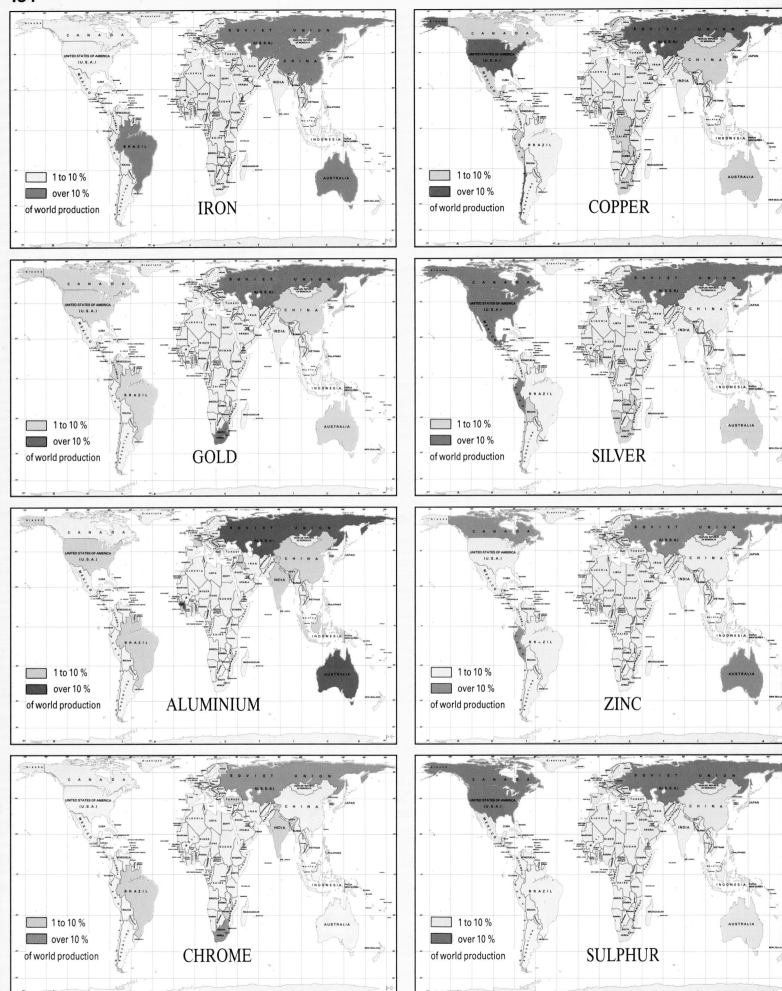

IRON

1 to 10 %
over 10 %
of world production

COPPER

1 to 10 %
over 10 %
of world production

GOLD

1 to 10 %
over 10 %
of world production

SILVER

1 to 10 %
over 10 %
of world production

ALUMINIUM

1 to 10 %
over 10 %
of world production

ZINC

1 to 10 %
over 10 %
of world production

CHROME

1 to 10 %
over 10 %
of world production

SULPHUR

1 to 10 %
over 10 %
of world production

MINERAL

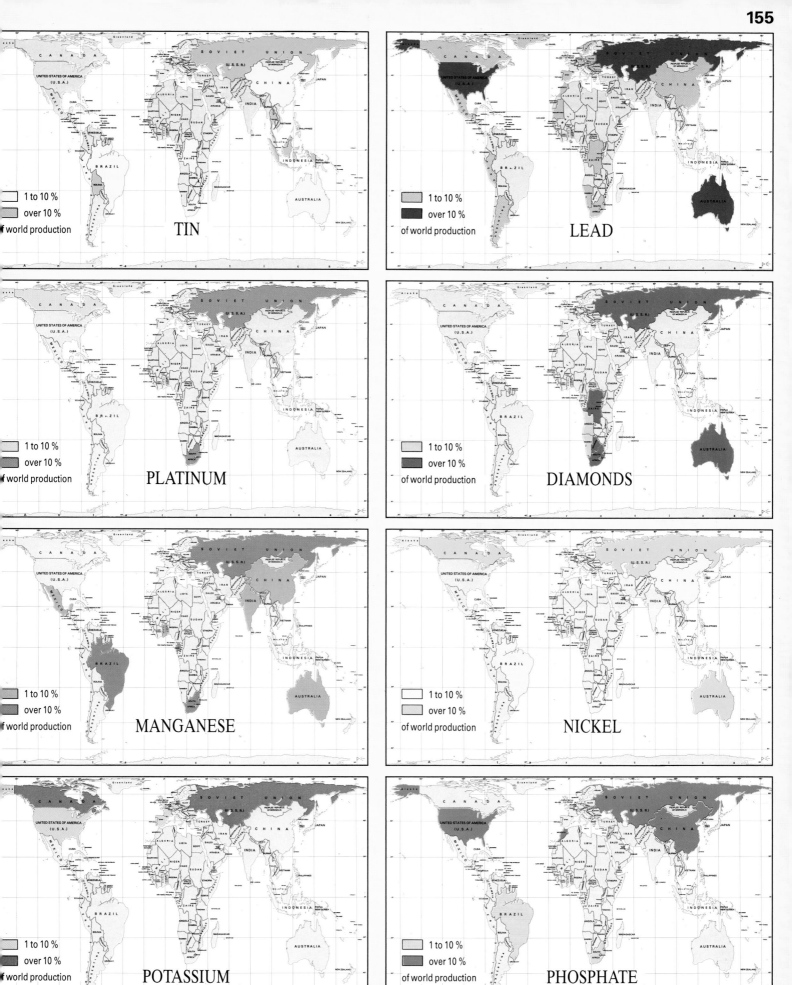

TIN

1 to 10 %
over 10 %
of world production

LEAD

1 to 10 %
over 10 %
of world production

PLATINUM

1 to 10 %
over 10 %
of world production

DIAMONDS

1 to 10 %
over 10 %
of world production

MANGANESE

1 to 10 %
over 10 %
of world production

NICKEL

1 to 10 %
over 10 %
of world production

POTASSIUM

1 to 10 %
over 10 %
of world production

PHOSPHATE

1 to 10 %
over 10 %
of world production

ESOURCES

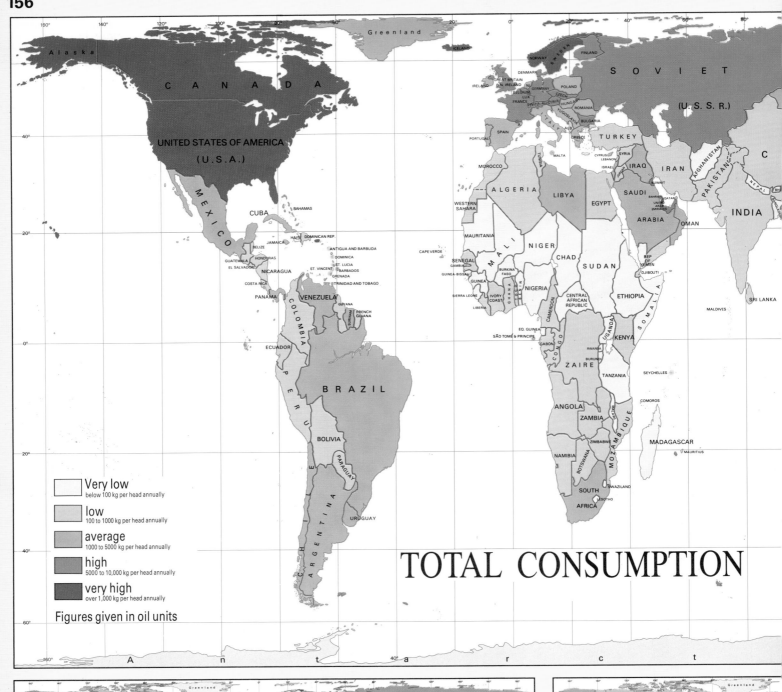

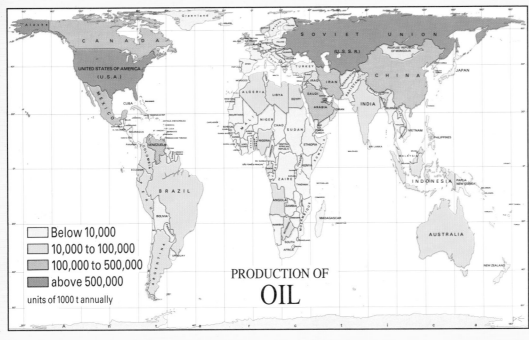

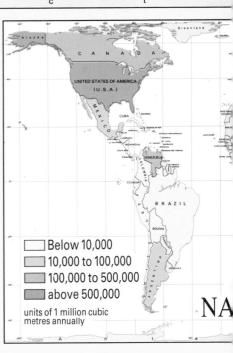

TOTAL CONSUMPTION

Very low
below 100 kg per head annually

low
100 to 1000 kg per head annually

average
1000 to 5000 kg per head annually

high
5000 to 10,000 kg per head annually

very high
over 1,000 kg per head annually

Figures given in oil units

Below 10,000

10,000 to 100,000

100,000 to 500,000

above 500,000

units of 1000 t annually

PRODUCTION OF OIL

Below 10,000

10,000 to 100,000

100,000 to 500,000

above 500,000

units of 1 million cubic metres annually

NA

ENI

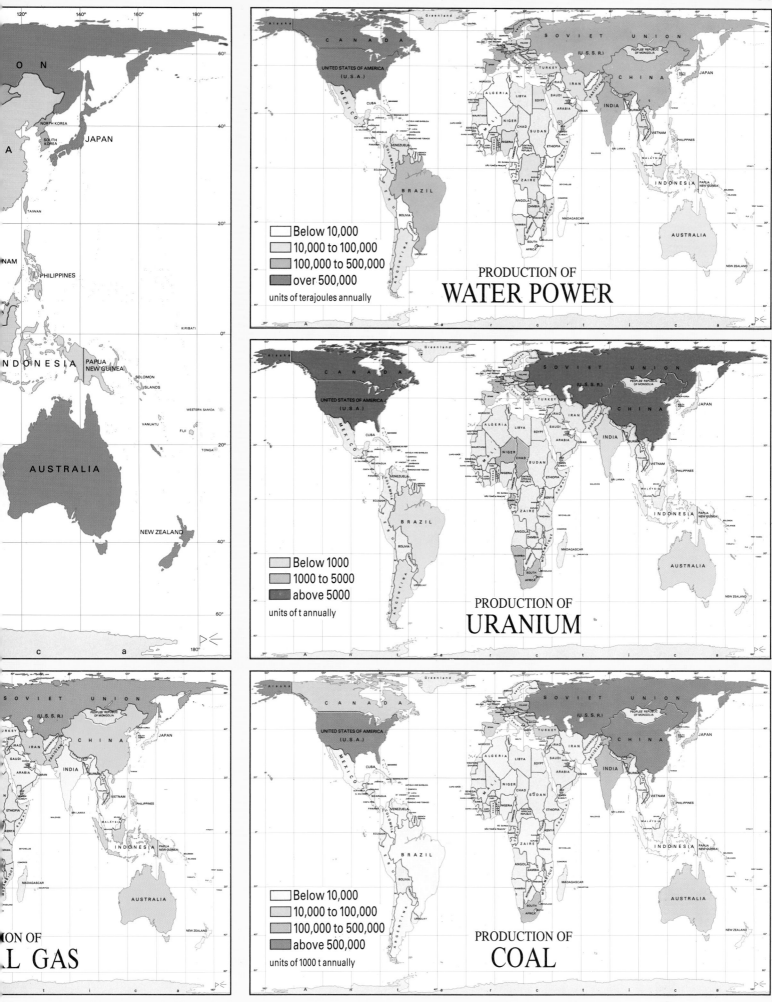

PRODUCTION OF WATER POWER

Below 10,000
10,000 to 100,000
100,000 to 500,000
over 500,000

units of terajoules annually

PRODUCTION OF URANIUM

Below 1000
1000 to 5000
above 5000

units of t annually

PRODUCTION OF COAL

Below 10,000
10,000 to 100,000
100,000 to 500,000
above 500,000

units of 1000 t annually

ON OF

L GAS

GY

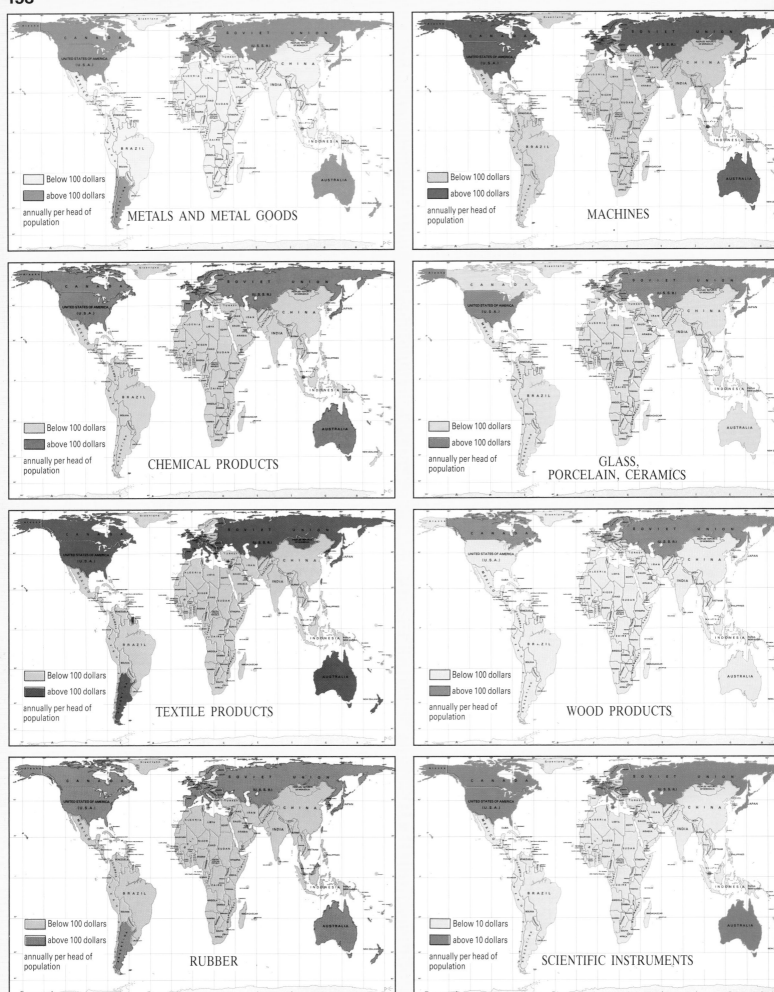

METALS AND METAL GOODS

Below 100 dollars
above 100 dollars
annually per head of population

MACHINES

Below 100 dollars
above 100 dollars
annually per head of population

CHEMICAL PRODUCTS

Below 100 dollars
above 100 dollars
annually per head of population

GLASS, PORCELAIN, CERAMICS

Below 100 dollars
above 100 dollars
annually per head of population

TEXTILE PRODUCTS

Below 100 dollars
above 100 dollars
annually per head of population

WOOD PRODUCTS

Below 100 dollars
above 100 dollars
annually per head of population

RUBBER

Below 100 dollars
above 100 dollars
annually per head of population

SCIENTIFIC INSTRUMENTS

Below 10 dollars
above 10 dollars
annually per head of population

INDUSTRIA

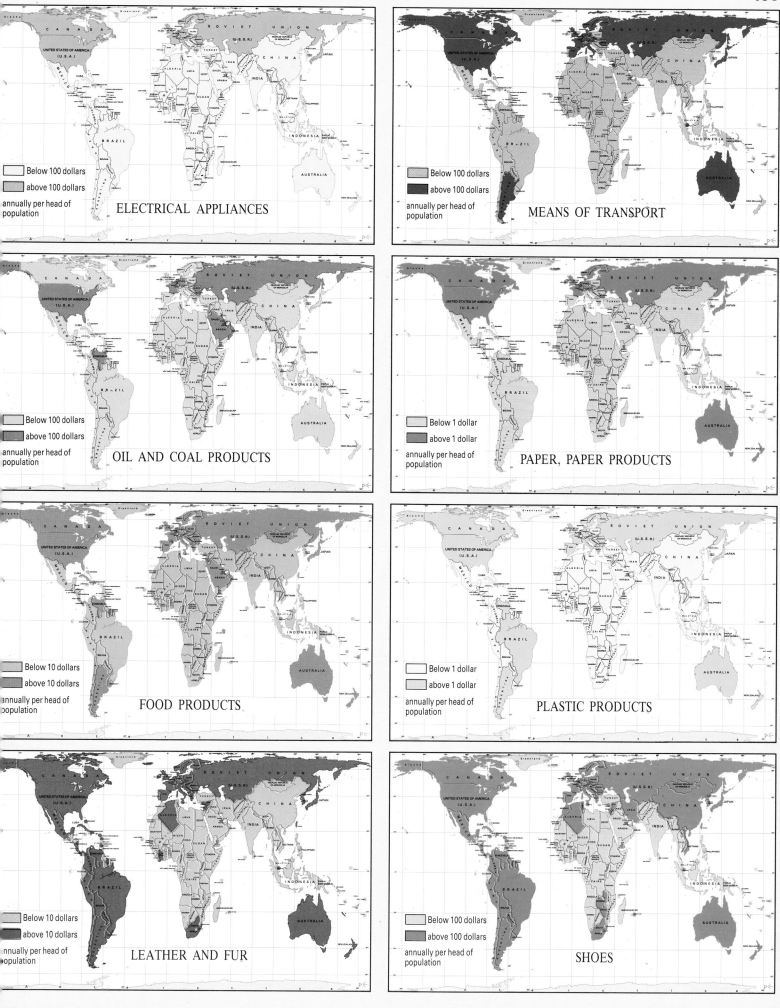

ELECTRICAL APPLIANCES

Below 100 dollars
above 100 dollars
annually per head of population

MEANS OF TRANSPORT

Below 100 dollars
above 100 dollars
annually per head of population

OIL AND COAL PRODUCTS

Below 100 dollars
above 100 dollars
annually per head of population

PAPER, PAPER PRODUCTS

Below 1 dollar
above 1 dollar
annually per head of population

FOOD PRODUCTS

Below 10 dollars
above 10 dollars
annually per head of population

PLASTIC PRODUCTS

Below 1 dollar
above 1 dollar
annually per head of population

LEATHER AND FUR

Below 10 dollars
above 10 dollars
annually per head of population

SHOES

Below 100 dollars
above 100 dollars
annually per head of population

PRODUCTS

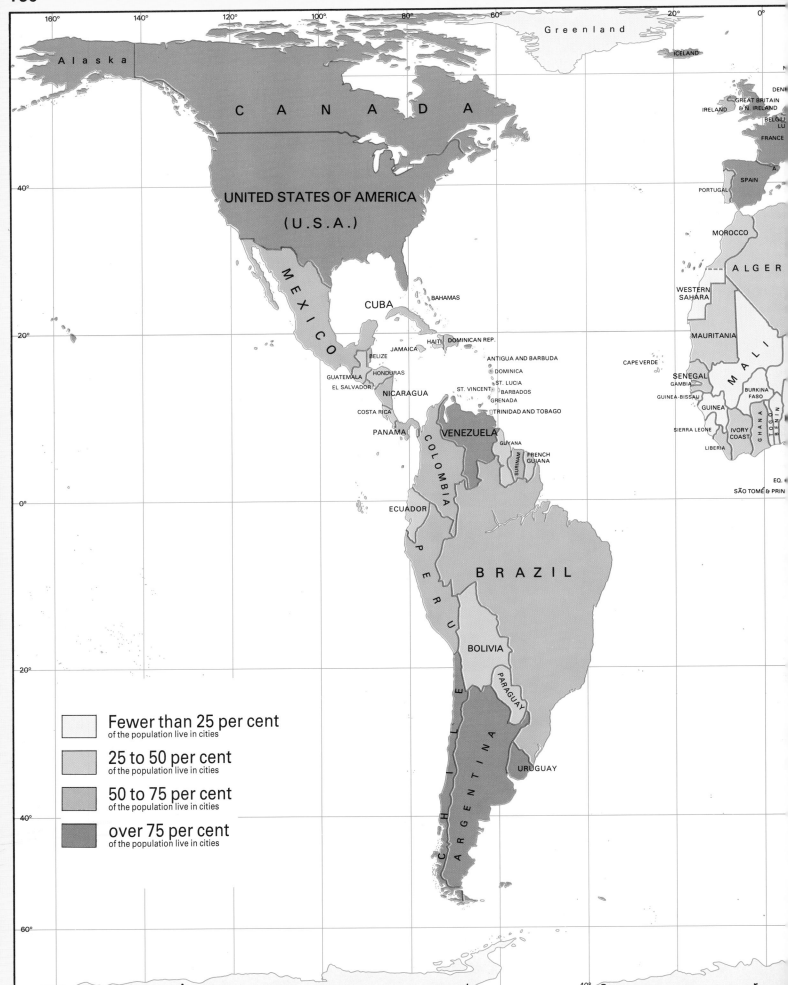

Greenland

ICELAND

DEN
GREAT BRITAIN
IRELAND & N. IRELAND
BELGIU
LU
FRANCE

Alaska

C A N A D A

SPAIN

PORTUGAL

A

UNITED STATES OF AMERICA

(U.S.A.)

MOROCCO

A L G E R

WESTERN
SAHARA

M
E
X
I
C
O

BAHAMAS

CUBA

MAURITANIA

MALI

HAITI   DOMINICAN REP.
JAMAICA

CAPE VERDE

SENEGAL

BELIZE

GAMBIA

GUATEMALA   HONDURAS
EL SALVADOR

ANTIGUA AND BARBUDA

DOMINICA

GUINEA-BISSAU

BURKINA
FASO

NICARAGUA

ST. LUCIA
ST. VINCENT
GRENADA

BARBADOS

GUINEA

G
H
A
N
A

T
O
G
O

B
E
N
I
N

COSTA RICA

TRINIDAD AND TOBAGO

SIERRA LEONE

IVORY
COAST

PANAMA

C
O
L
O
M
B
I
A

VENEZUELA

GUYANA

LIBERIA

EQ.

ECUADOR

SURINAM

FRENCH
GUIANA

SÃO TOMÉ & PRIN

P
E
R
U

B R A Z I L

BOLIVIA

PARAGUAY

C
H
I
L
E

A
R
G
E
N
T
I
N
A

URUGUAY

Fewer than 25 per cent
of the population live in cities

25 to 50 per cent
of the population live in cities

50 to 75 per cent
of the population live in cities

over 75 per cent
of the population live in cities

A   n   t   a   r

URBAN

SATION

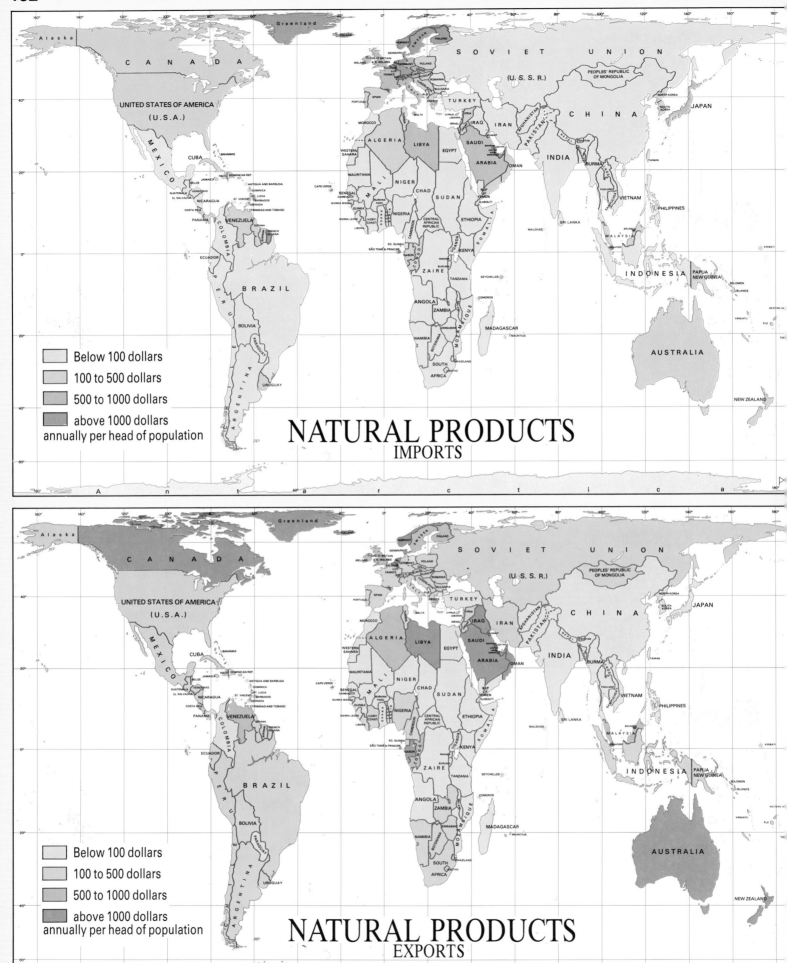

NATURAL PRODUCTS
IMPORTS

Below 100 dollars
100 to 500 dollars
500 to 1000 dollars
above 1000 dollars
annually per head of population

NATURAL PRODUCTS
EXPORTS

Below 100 dollars
100 to 500 dollars
500 to 1000 dollars
above 1000 dollars
annually per head of population

WORLI

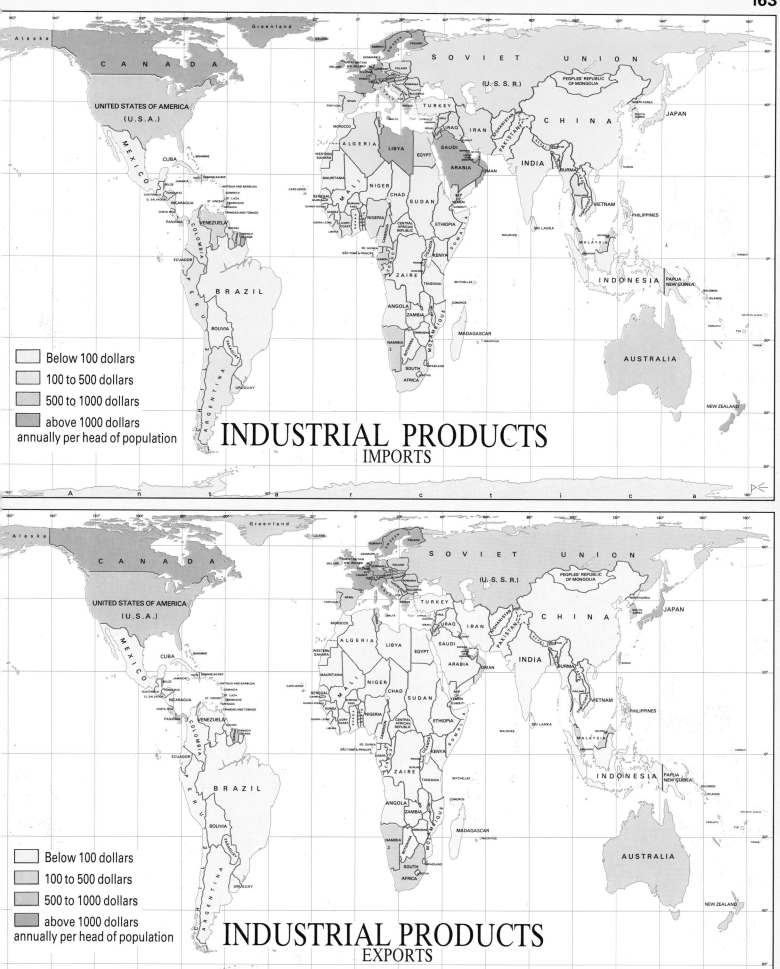

INDUSTRIAL PRODUCTS
IMPORTS

Below 100 dollars
100 to 500 dollars
500 to 1000 dollars
above 1000 dollars
annually per head of population

INDUSTRIAL PRODUCTS
EXPORTS

Below 100 dollars
100 to 500 dollars
500 to 1000 dollars
above 1000 dollars
annually per head of population

TRADE

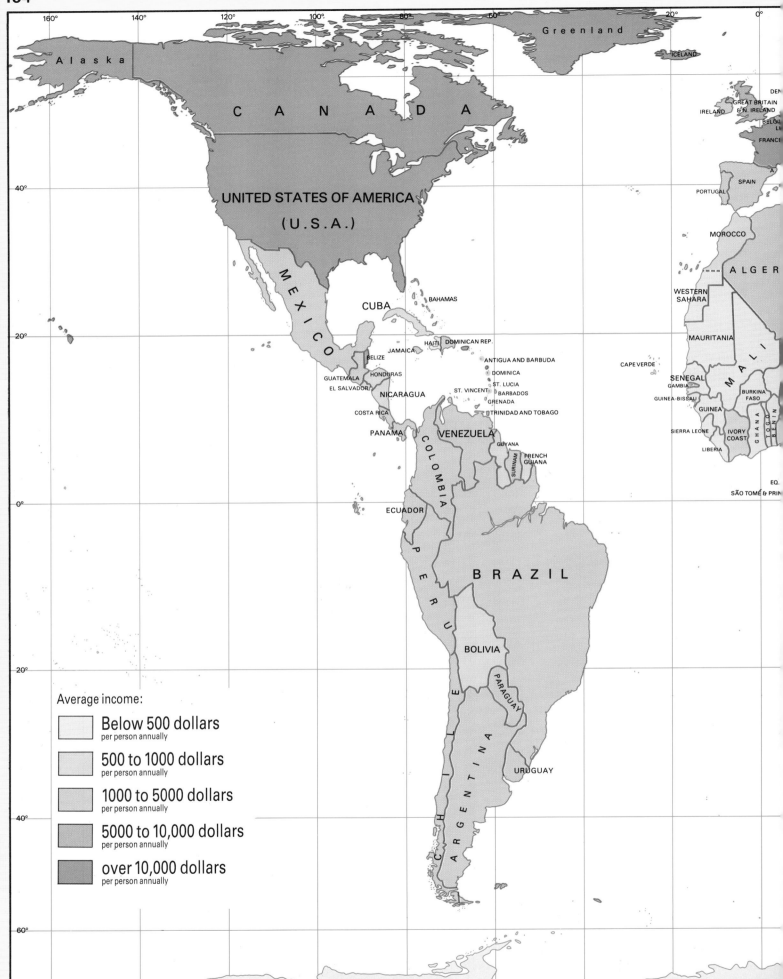

Average income:

Below 500 dollars
per person annually

500 to 1000 dollars
per person annually

1000 to 5000 dollars
per person annually

5000 to 10,000 dollars
per person annually

over 10,000 dollars
per person annually

POOR NATIONS

S O V I E T   U N I O N

(U. S. S. R.)

FINLAND

POLAND

CH
HUNGARY
ROMANIA
OSLAVIA
BULGARIA
ALB.
GREECE

TURKEY

CYPRUS
LEBANON
SYRIA
ISRAEL
JORDAN
IRAQ
IRAN

AFGHANISTAN

PEOPLES' REPUBLIC
OF MONGOLIA

NORTH KOREA

SOUTH
KOREA

JAPAN

C H I N A

PAKISTAN

NEPAL
BHUTAN

YA

EGYPT

SAUDI

ARABIA

KUWAIT
BAHRAIN
QATAR
UNITED
ARAB
EMIRATES

OMAN

I N D I A

BANGLADESH

BURMA

LAOS

TAIWAN

HAD

SUDAN

REP
OF
YEMEN

DJIBOUTI

THAILAND

KAMPUCHEA

VIETNAM

PHILIPPINES

CENTRAL
AFRICAN
REPUBLIC

ETHIOPIA

SOMALIA

SRI LANKA

MALDIVES

BRUNEI

M A L A Y S I A

UGANDA

KENYA

SINGAPORE

ZAIRE

RWANDA
BURUNDI

TANZANIA

SEYCHELLES

I N D O N E S I A

PAPUA
NEW GUINEA

SOLOMON
ISLANDS

KIRIBATI

GOLA

ZAMBIA

MALAWI

MOZAMBIQUE

COMOROS

MADAGASCAR

MAURITIUS

WESTERN SAMOA

VANUATU

FIJI

ZIMBABWE

IBIA

BOTSWANA

SWAZILAND

SOUTH
AFRICA

LESOTHO

AUSTRALIA

TONGA

NEW ZEALAND

c   t   i   c   a

RICH NATIONS

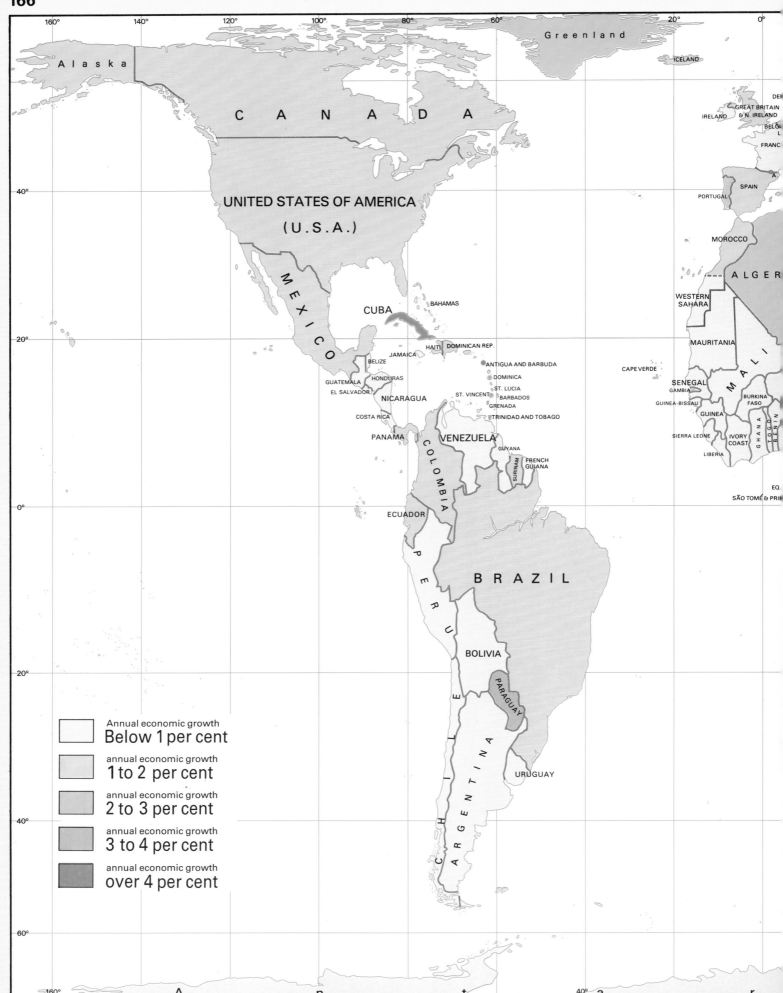

Greenland

Alaska

ICELAND

C A N A D A

DE
GREAT BRITAIN
IRELAND & N. IRELAND
BELGI
L
FRANC

UNITED STATES OF AMERICA

(U.S.A.)

SPAIN
PORTUGAL
A

MOROCCO

M E X I C O

A L G E R

WESTERN
SAHARA

CUBA

BAHAMAS

MAURITANIA

M
A
L
I

HAITI   DOMINICAN REP.

JAMAICA

CAPE VERDE

BELIZE

ANTIGUA AND BARBUDA

GUATEMALA

HONDURAS

DOMINICA

SENEGAL
GAMBIA

BURKINA
FASO

EL SALVADOR

ST. LUCIA

GUINEA-BISSAU

NICARAGUA

ST. VINCENT

BARBADOS

GRENADA

GUINEA

GHANA
TOGO
BENIN

COSTA RICA

TRINIDAD AND TOBAGO

SIERRA LEONE

IVORY
COAST

PANAMA

LIBERIA

VENEZUELA

GUYANA

EQ
SÃO TOMÉ & PRIN

COLOMBIA

SURINAM

FRENCH
GUIANA

ECUADOR

P
E
R
U

B R A Z I L

BOLIVIA

PARAGUAY

C
H
I
L
E

A
R
G
E
N
T
I
N
A

URUGUAY

Annual economic growth
Below 1 per cent

annual economic growth
1 to 2 per cent

annual economic growth
2 to 3 per cent

annual economic growth
3 to 4 per cent

annual economic growth
over 4 per cent

A   n   t   a   r

ECONOMI

GROWTH

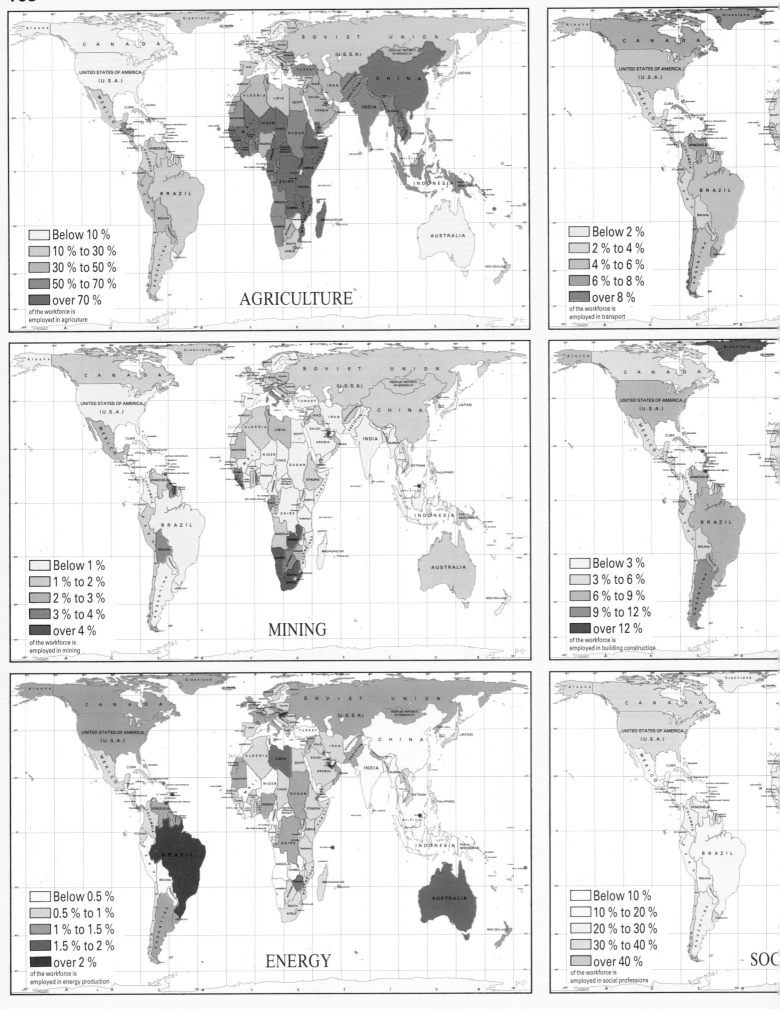

AGRICULTURE

Below 10 %
10 % to 30 %
30 % to 50 %
50 % to 70 %
over 70 %
of the workforce is
employed in agriculture

Below 2 %
2 % to 4 %
4 % to 6 %
6 % to 8 %
over 8 %
of the workforce is
employed in transport

MINING

Below 1 %
1 % to 2 %
2 % to 3 %
3 % to 4 %
over 4 %
of the workforce is
employed in mining

Below 3 %
3 % to 6 %
6 % to 9 %
9 % to 12 %
over 12 %
of the workforce is
employed in building construction

ENERGY

Below 0.5 %
0.5 % to 1 %
1 % to 1.5 %
1.5 % to 2 %
over 2 %
of the workforce is
employed in energy production

Below 10 %
10 % to 20 %
20 % to 30 %
30 % to 40 %
over 40 %
of the workforce is
employed in social professions

SOC

EMPLOYMEN

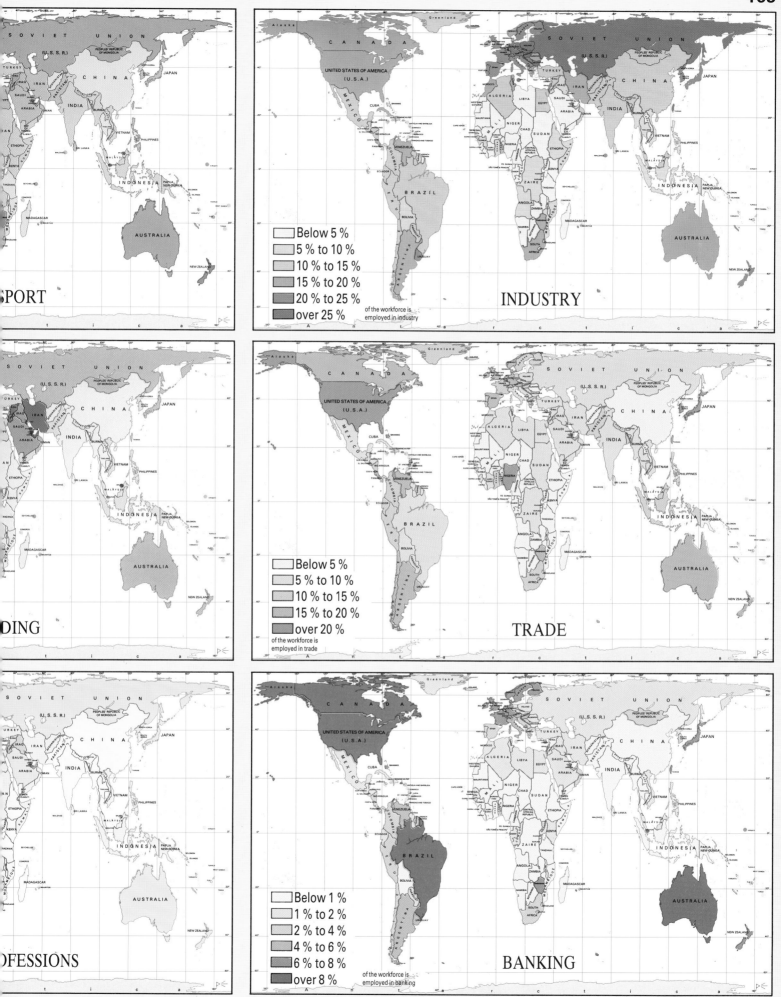

PORT

INDUSTRY

Below 5 %
5 % to 10 %
10 % to 15 %
15 % to 20 %
20 % to 25 %
over 25 %
of the workforce is
employed in industry

DING

TRADE

Below 5 %
5 % to 10 %
10 % to 15 %
15 % to 20 %
over 20 %
of the workforce is
employed in trade

OFESSIONS

BANKING

Below 1 %
1 % to 2 %
2 % to 4 %
4 % to 6 %
6 % to 8 %
over 8 %
of the workforce is
employed in banking

STRUCTURE

Capitalist

Marginal

Socialist

Situation as 1991

SOCIAL

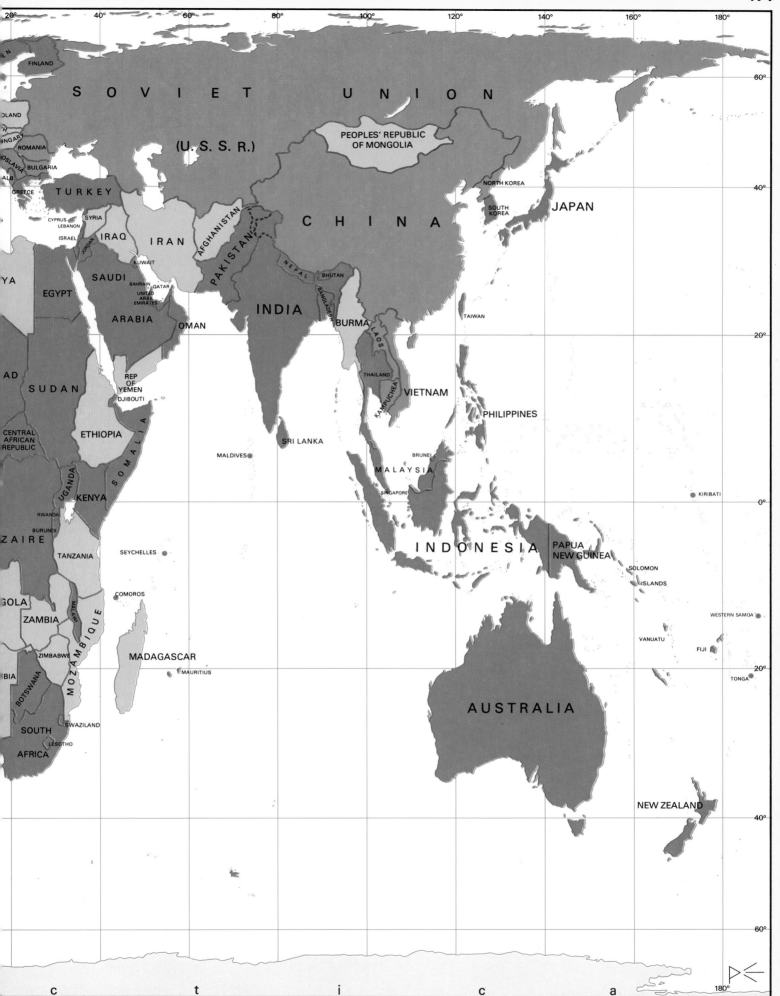

ORDER

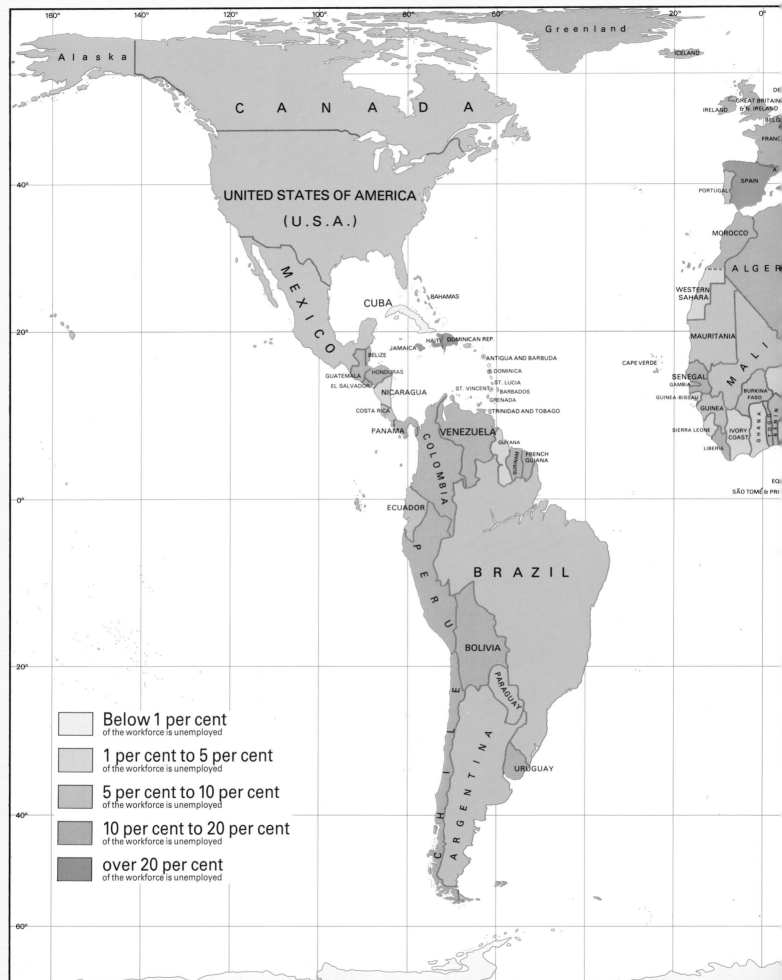

Below 1 per cent
of the workforce is unemployed

1 per cent to 5 per cent
of the workforce is unemployed

5 per cent to 10 per cent
of the workforce is unemployed

10 per cent to 20 per cent
of the workforce is unemployed

over 20 per cent
of the workforce is unemployed

UNEMPI

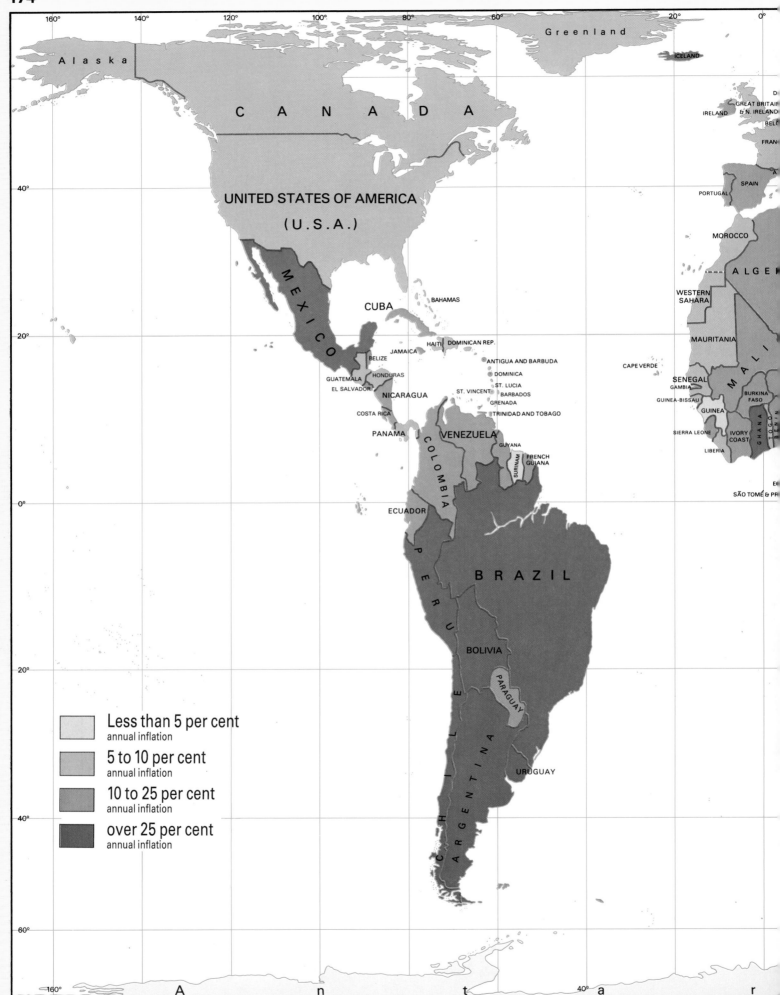

Less than 5 per cent
annual inflation

5 to 10 per cent
annual inflation

10 to 25 per cent
annual inflation

over 25 per cent
annual inflation

INFL

FINLAND

POLAND

HUNGARY
ROMANIA
YUGOSLAVIA
BULGARIA
ALB
GREECE

S O V I E T   U N I O N

(U.S.S.R.)

PEOPLES' REPUBLIC
OF MONGOLIA

C H I N A

NORTH KOREA

SOUTH
KOREA

JAPAN

TURKEY

CYPRUS
LEBANON
ISRAEL
JORDAN

SYRIA
IRAQ

IRAN

AFGHANISTAN

PAKISTAN

NEPAL
BHUTAN

BANGLADESH

TAIWAN

KUWAIT

SAUDI

BAHRAIN QATAR
UNITED
ARAB
EMIRATES

YA

EGYPT

ARABIA

OMAN

I N D I A

BURMA

LAOS

AD

SUDAN

REP
OF
YEMEN
DJIBOUTI

THAILAND

VIETNAM

CENTRAL
AFRICAN
REPUBLIC

ETHIOPIA

SOMALIA

KAMPUCHEA

PHILIPPINES

SRI LANKA

MALDIVES

BRUNEI

UGANDA
KENYA

M A L A Y S I A

KIRIBATI

RWANDA

SINGAPORE

BURUNDI

ZAIRE

TANZANIA

SEYCHELLES

I N D O N E S I A

PAPUA
NEW GUINEA

SOLOMON
ISLANDS

GOLA

COMOROS

WESTERN SAMOA

ZAMBIA

MALAWI

VANUATU

FIJI

ZIMBABWE

MADAGASCAR

BIA

MOZAMBIQUE

MAURITIUS

TONGA

BOTSWANA

SWAZILAND

SOUTH

LESOTHO

AUSTRALIA

AFRICA

NEW ZEALAND

c   t   i   c   a

TION

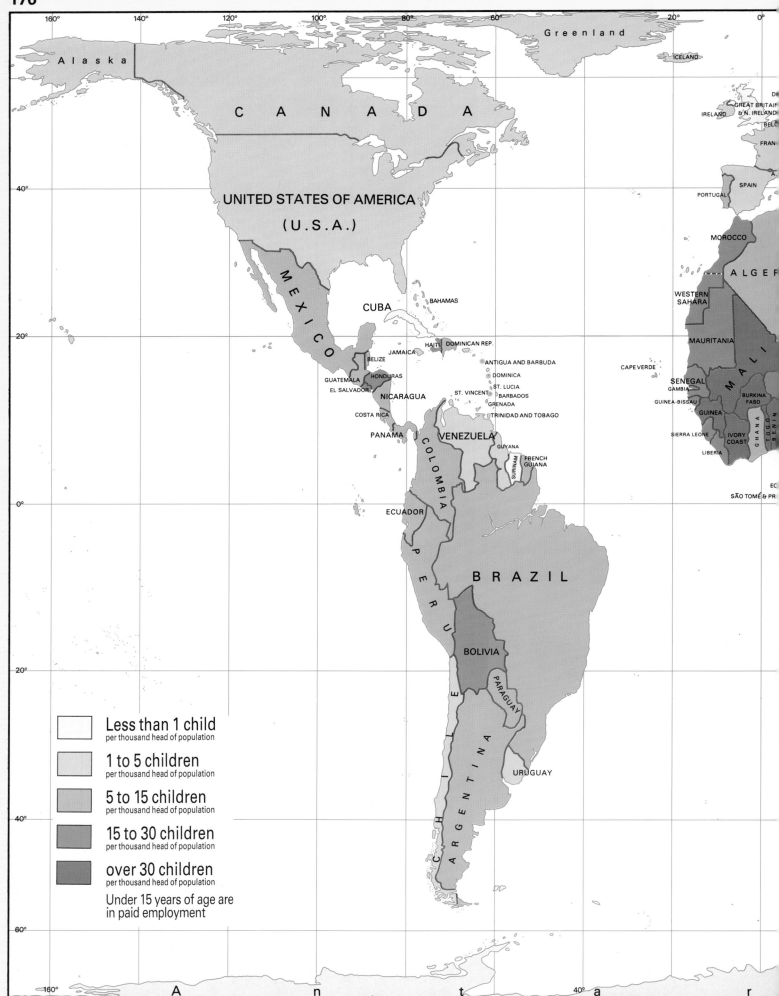

Greenland

Alaska

C A N A D A

UNITED STATES OF AMERICA

(U.S.A.)

ICELAND

GREAT BRITAIN
& N. IRELAND

IRELAND

FRAN

SPAIN

PORTUGAL

MOROCCO

A L G E R

WESTERN
SAHARA

M E X I C O

CUBA

BAHAMAS

HAITI

JAMAICA

DOMINICAN REP.

BELIZE

GUATEMALA

HONDURAS

EL SALVADOR

NICARAGUA

COSTA RICA

PANAMA

ANTIGUA AND BARBUDA

DOMINICA

ST. LUCIA

ST. VINCENT

BARBADOS

GRENADA

TRINIDAD AND TOBAGO

VENEZUELA

GUYANA

SURINAM

FRENCH
GUIANA

COLOMBIA

ECUADOR

P E R U

B R A Z I L

BOLIVIA

PARAGUAY

C H I L E

A R G E N T I N A

URUGUAY

MAURITANIA

CAPE VERDE

SENEGAL

GAMBIA

GUINEA-BISSAU

M A L I

BURKINA
FASO

GUINEA

SIERRA LEONE

IVORY
COAST

GHANA

TOGO

BENIN

LIBERIA

EC

SÃO TOMÉ & PR

Less than 1 child
per thousand head of population

1 to 5 children
per thousand head of population

5 to 15 children
per thousand head of population

15 to 30 children
per thousand head of population

over 30 children
per thousand head of population

Under 15 years of age are
in paid employment

A n t a r

CHILD

S O V I E T   U N I O N

(U. S. S. R.)

FINLAND

POLAND

CZECH

HUNGARY

ROMANIA

YUGOSLAVIA

BULGARIA

ALB.

GREECE

TA

CYPRUS

LEBANON

ISRAEL

JORDAN

TURKEY

SYRIA

IRAQ

IRAN

KUWAIT

SAUDI

BAHRAIN   QATAR

UNITED
ARAB
EMIRATES

ARABIA

OMAN

EGYPT

BYA

PEOPLES' REPUBLIC
OF MONGOLIA

C H I N A

NORTH KOREA

SOUTH
KOREA

JAPAN

AFGHANISTAN

PAKISTAN

NEPAL

BHUTAN

INDIA

BANGLADESH

BURMA

LAOS

TAIWAN

THAILAND

KAMPUCHEA

VIETNAM

PHILIPPINES

HAD

SUDAN

REP
OF
YEMEN

DJIBOUTI

CENTRAL
AFRICAN
REPUBLIC

ETHIOPIA

SOMALIA

SRI LANKA

MALDIVES

BRUNEI

M A L A Y S I A

SINGAPORE

UGANDA

KENYA

RWANDA

BURUNDI

ZAIRE

TANZANIA

SEYCHELLES

KIRIBATI

I N D O N E S I A

PAPUA
NEW GUINEA

SOLOMON

ISLANDS

COMOROS

GOLA

ZAMBIA

MALAWI

MOZAMBIQUE

WESTERN SAMOA

VANUATU

FIJI

ZIMBABWE

MADAGASCAR

MAURITIUS

MIBIA

BOTSWANA

SWAZILAND

SOUTH
AFRICA

LESOTHO

A U S T R A L I A

TONGA

NEW ZEALAND

ABOUR

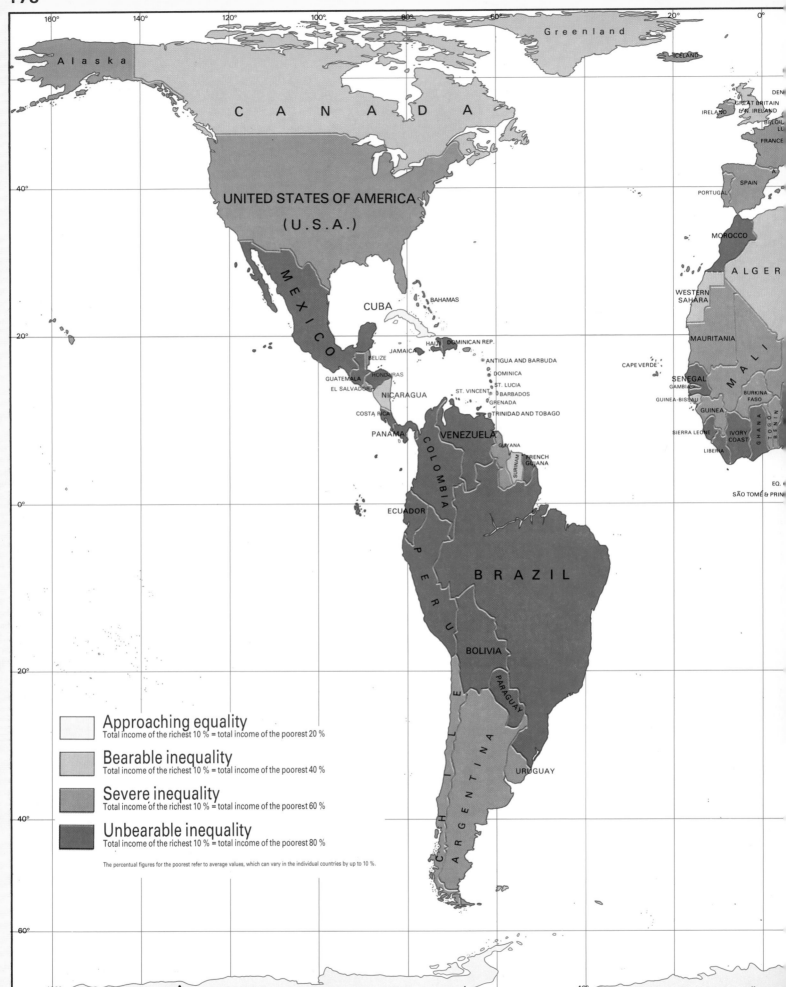

Approaching equality
Total income of the richest 10 % = total income of the poorest 20 %

Bearable inequality
Total income of the richest 10 % = total income of the poorest 40 %

Severe inequality
Total income of the richest 10 % = total income of the poorest 60 %

Unbearable inequality
Total income of the richest 10 % = total income of the poorest 80 %

The percentual figures for the poorest refer to average values, which can vary in the individual countries by up to 10 %.

INEQU

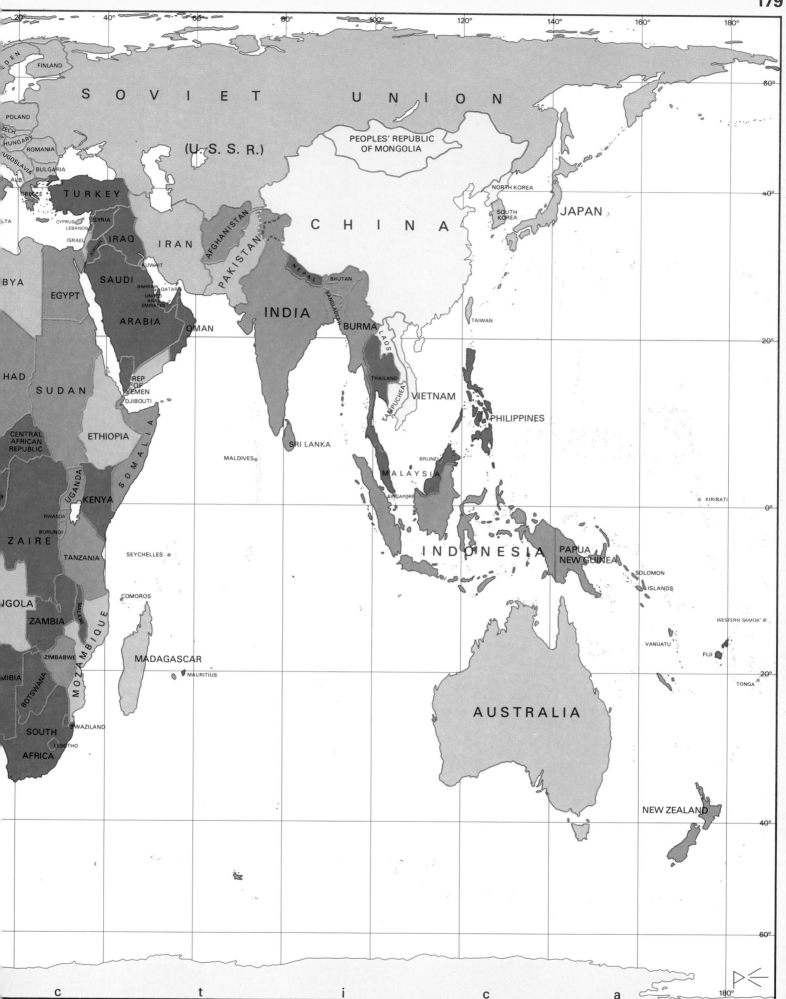

ALITY

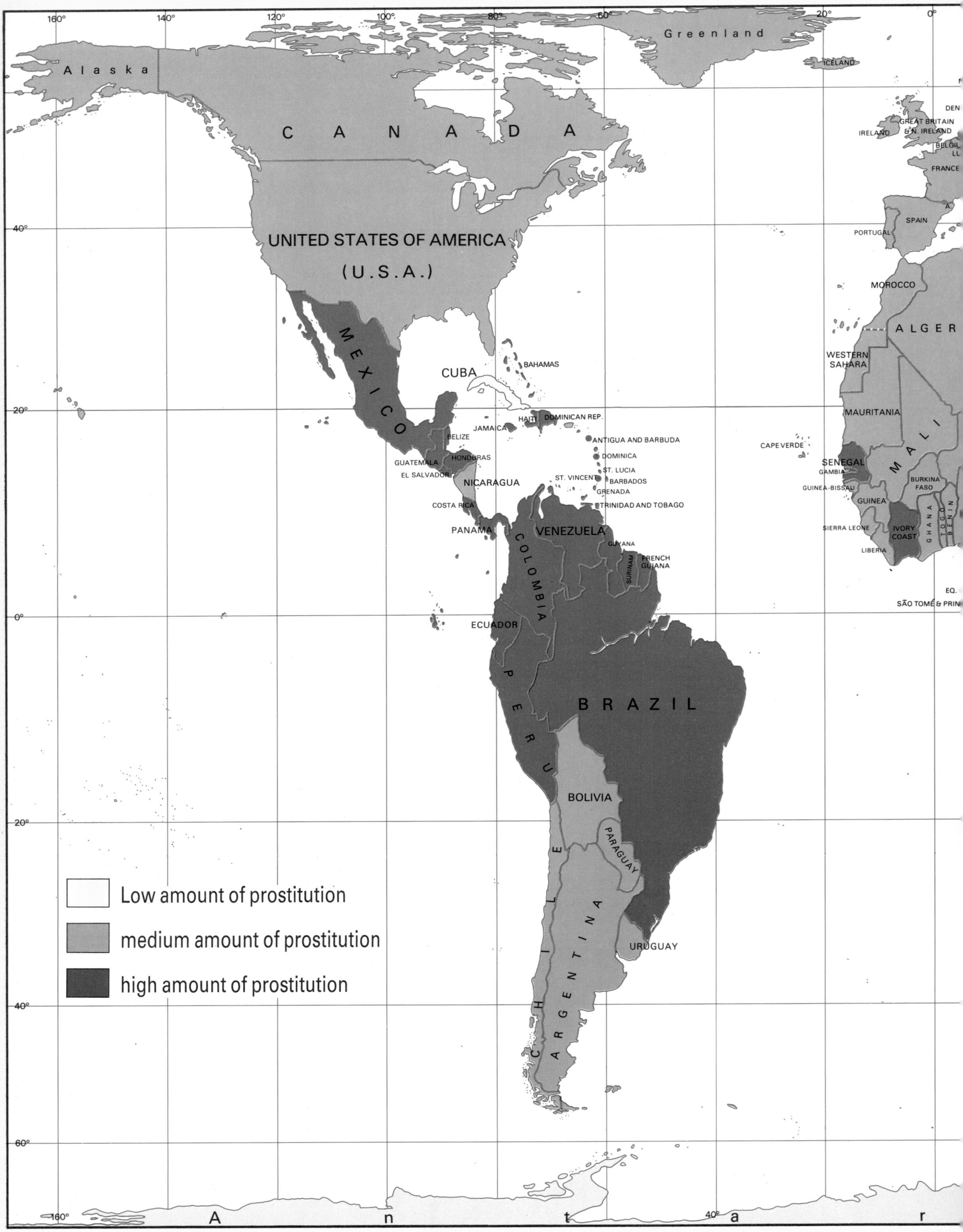

Greenland

ICELAND

Alaska

C A N A D A

DEN
GREAT BRITAIN
IRELAND & N. IRELAND
BELGIU
LU
FRANCE

SPAIN
PORTUGAL

UNITED STATES OF AMERICA
(U.S.A.)

MOROCCO

A L G E R

WESTERN
SAHARA

M E X I C O

CUBA

BAHAMAS

MAURITANIA

M A L I

BELIZE
JAMAICA
HAITI
DOMINICAN REP.
ANTIGUA AND BARBUDA
DOMINICA
GUATEMALA
HONDURAS
ST. LUCIA
EL SALVADOR
ST. VINCENT
BARBADOS
NICARAGUA
GRENADA
COSTA RICA
TRINIDAD AND TOBAGO
PANAMA
VENEZUELA

CAPE VERDE

SENEGAL
GAMBIA

BURKINA
FASO

GUINEA-BISSAU

GUINEA

SIERRA LEONE

IVORY
COAST

GHANA
TOGO
BENIN

LIBERIA

EQ.
SÃO TOMÉ & PRIN

C O L O M B I A

GUYANA

SURINAM

FRENCH
GUIANA

ECUADOR

P
E
R
U

B R A Z I L

BOLIVIA

PARAGUAY

C
H
I
L
E

A
R
G
E
N
T
I
N
A

URUGUAY

Low amount of prostitution

medium amount of prostitution

high amount of prostitution

A   n   t   a   r

PROST

S O V I E T   U N I O N

(U.S.S.R.)

PEOPLES' REPUBLIC
OF MONGOLIA

FINLAND

POLAND

CZECH

HUNGARY

ROMANIA

UGOSLAVIA

BULGARIA

ALB

GREECE

TURKEY

CYPRUS

SYRIA

LEBANON

ISRAEL

JORDAN

IRAQ

IRAN

AFGHANISTAN

PAKISTAN

KUWAIT

SAUDI

BAHRAIN   QATAR

UNITED
ARAB
EMIRATES

ARABIA

OMAN

NEPAL

BHUTAN

BANGLADESH

INDIA

BURMA

LAOS

THAILAND

KAMPUCHEA

VIETNAM

CHINA

NORTH KOREA

SOUTH
KOREA

JAPAN

TAIWAN

PHILIPPINES

BRUNEI

MALAYSIA

SINGAPORE

BYA

EGYPT

HAD

SUDAN

REP
OF
YEMEN

DJIBOUTI

CENTRAL
AFRICAN
REPUBLIC

ETHIOPIA

SOMALIA

UGANDA

KENYA

RWANDA

BURUNDI

ZAIRE

TANZANIA

SRI LANKA

MALDIVES

SEYCHELLES

COMOROS

GOLA

ZAMBIA

MALAWI

MOZAMBIQUE

ZIMBABWE

MIBIA

BOTSWANA

MADAGASCAR

MAURITIUS

INDONESIA

PAPUA
NEW GUINEA

SOLOMON
ISLANDS

KIRIBATI

WESTERN SAMOA

VANUATU

FIJI

TONGA

AUSTRALIA

SWAZILAND

SOUTH
AFRICA

LESOTHO

NEW ZEALAND

c   t   i   c   a

TUTION

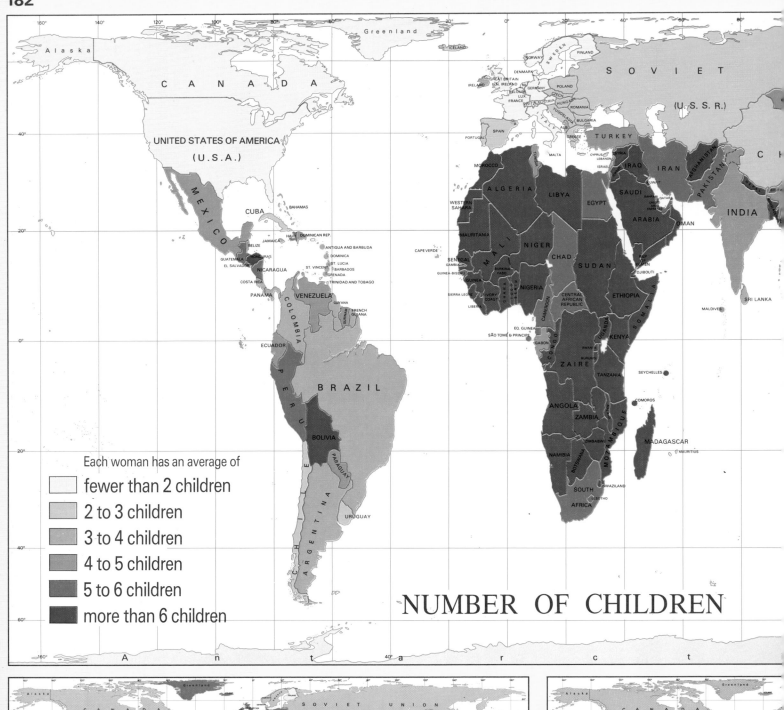

Each woman has an average of

- fewer than 2 children
- 2 to 3 children
- 3 to 4 children
- 4 to 5 children
- 5 to 6 children
- more than 6 children

NUMBER OF CHILDREN

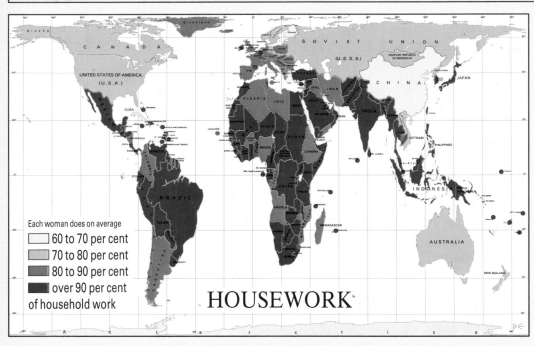

Each woman does on average

- 60 to 70 per cent
- 70 to 80 per cent
- 80 to 90 per cent
- over 90 per cent
of household work

HOUSEWORK

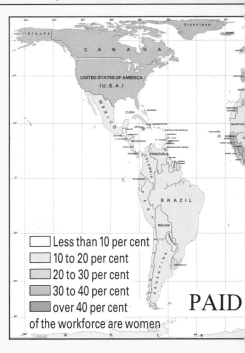

- Less than 10 per cent
- 10 to 20 per cent
- 20 to 30 per cent
- 30 to 40 per cent
- over 40 per cent
of the workforce are women

PAID

THE STATU

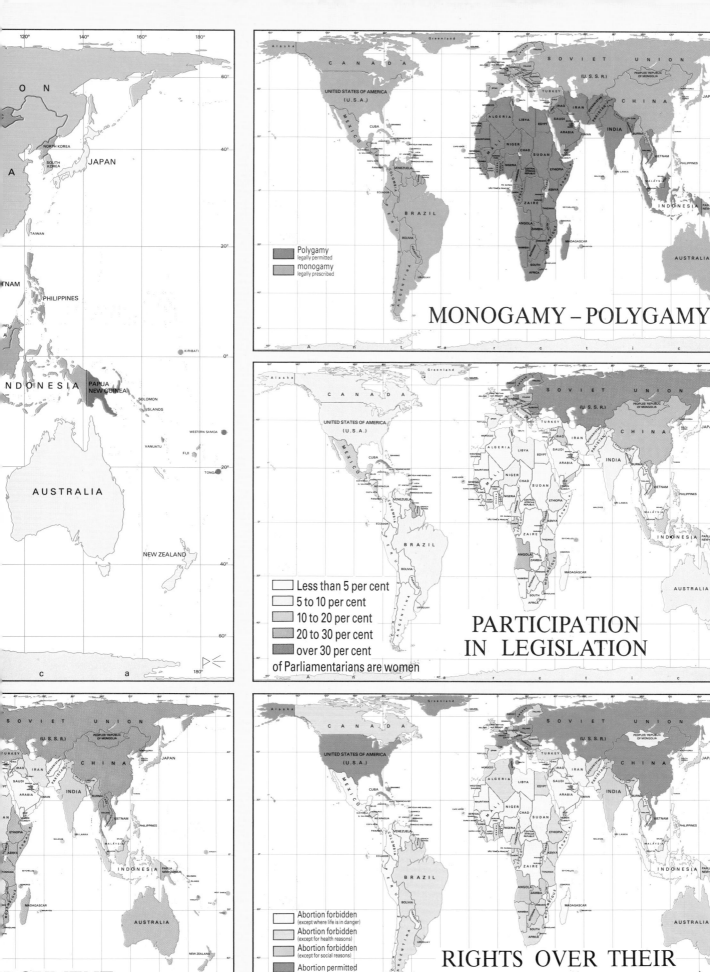

MONOGAMY – POLYGAMY

Polygamy
legally permitted

monogamy
legally prescribed

PARTICIPATION IN LEGISLATION

Less than 5 per cent
5 to 10 per cent
10 to 20 per cent
20 to 30 per cent
over 30 per cent
of Parliamentarians are women

RIGHTS OVER THEIR OWN BODIES (ABORTION)

Abortion forbidden
(except where life is in danger)

Abortion forbidden
(except for health reasons)

Abortion forbidden
(except for social reasons)

Abortion permitted

...LOYMENT

...OF WOMEN

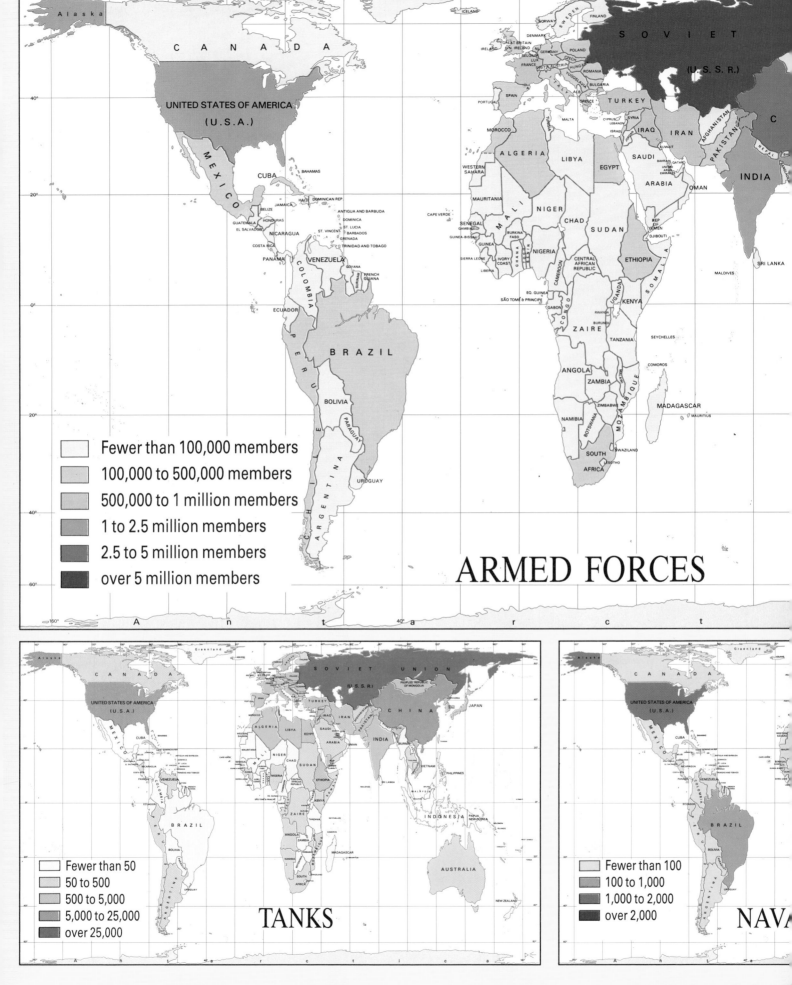

ARMED FORCES

Fewer than 100,000 members
100,000 to 500,000 members
500,000 to 1 million members
1 to 2.5 million members
2.5 to 5 million members
over 5 million members

TANKS

Fewer than 50
50 to 500
500 to 5,000
5,000 to 25,000
over 25,000

NAVA

Fewer than 100
100 to 1,000
1,000 to 2,000
over 2,000

RELATIVE MILI

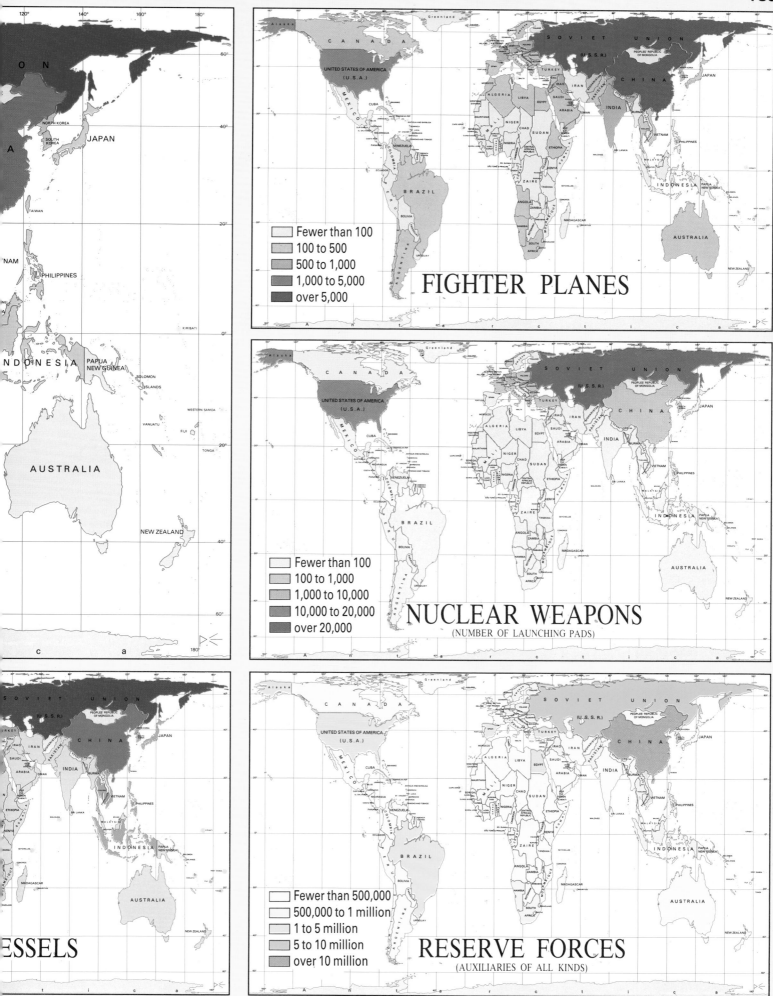

FIGHTER PLANES

Fewer than 100
100 to 500
500 to 1,000
1,000 to 5,000
over 5,000

NUCLEAR WEAPONS
(NUMBER OF LAUNCHING PADS)

Fewer than 100
100 to 1,000
1,000 to 10,000
10,000 to 20,000
over 20,000

RESERVE FORCES
(AUXILIARIES OF ALL KINDS)

Fewer than 500,000
500,000 to 1 million
1 to 5 million
5 to 10 million
over 10 million

ESSELS

ARY STRENGTH

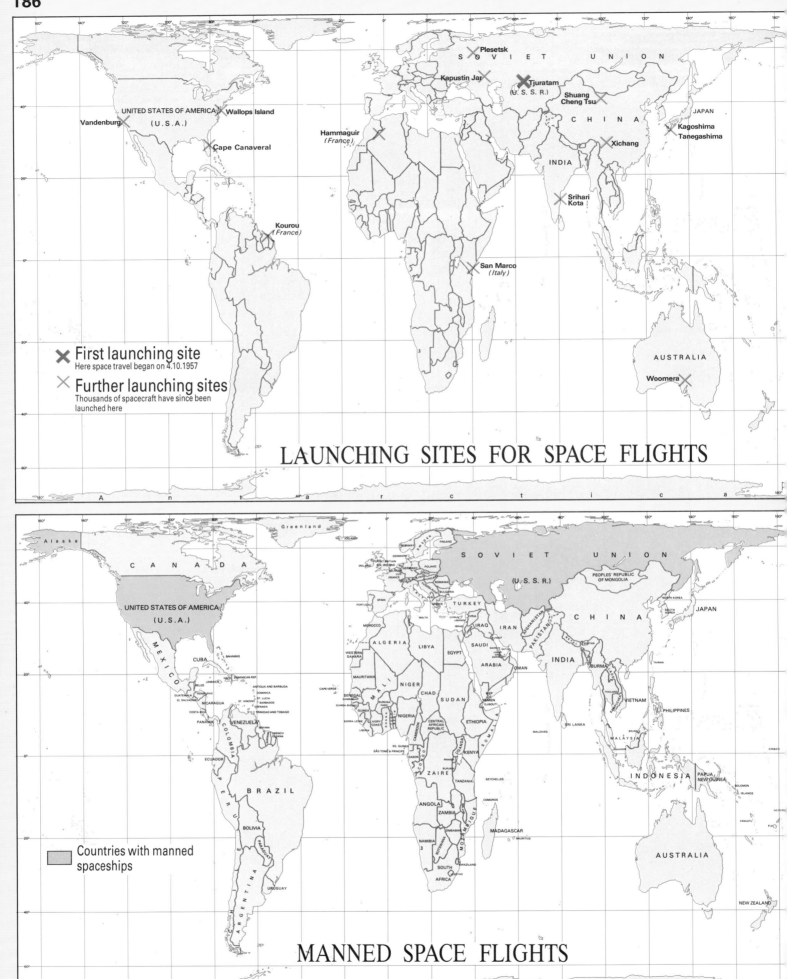

LAUNCHING SITES FOR SPACE FLIGHTS

✕ First launching site
Here space travel began on 4.10.1957

✕ Further launching sites
Thousands of spacecraft have since been
launched here

MANNED SPACE FLIGHTS

▨ Countries with manned
spaceships

THE CONQU

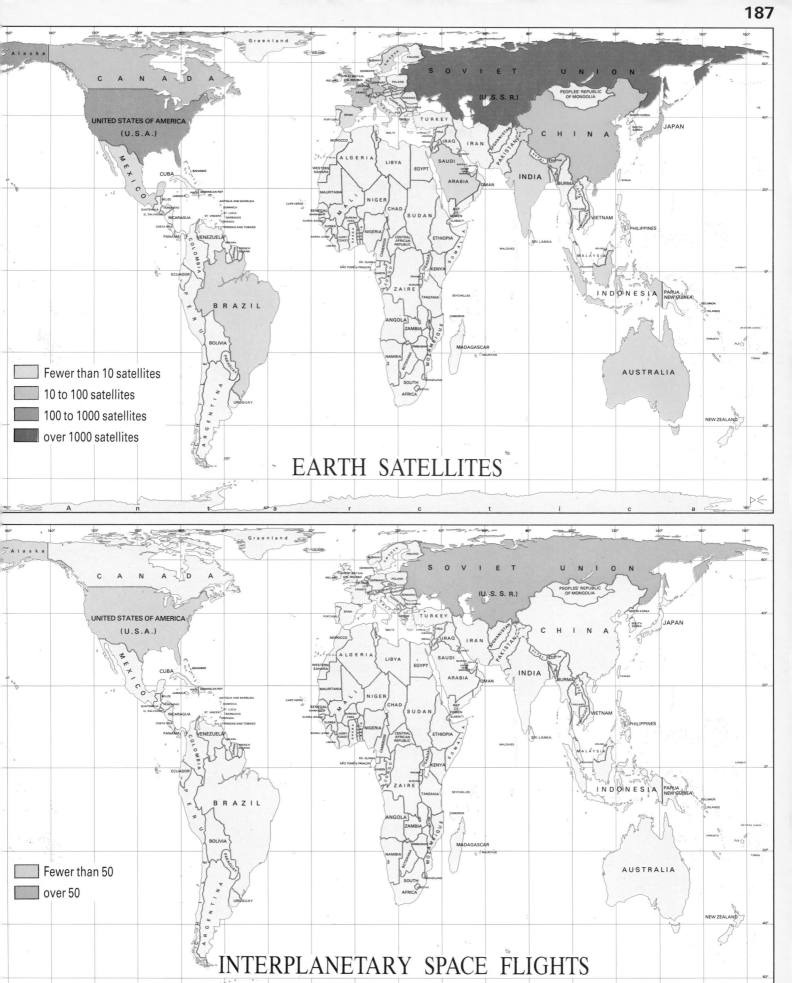

EARTH SATELLITES

Fewer than 10 satellites
10 to 100 satellites
100 to 1000 satellites
over 1000 satellites

INTERPLANETARY SPACE FLIGHTS

Fewer than 50
over 50

ST OF SPACE

INDEX

Each name in the index is followed by a page number and a letter. On the page referred to, the letter can be found either at the top or at the bottom of the map frame. In the first case, the place is in the upper half of the map vertically below the letter; otherwise it is on the lower half of the map vertically above the letter. If a name extends over several letters, the given letter indicates its beginning.

Names such as countries or oceans which cover a large area on the map are listed with their page number only. However, if they extend over two pages, two page numbers are shown – the left-hand and right-hand page numbers being linked with a dash. Names of countries, oceans, rivers and mountains that extend over more than a double page are listed under each separate page. A dash between two nonconsecutive page numbers means that the place appears on all maps between and including those two pages.

The headwords are in alphabetical order. Names with prefixes like "Saint" or "Bad" can be looked up under the initial letter of the prefix. Place names appear on the maps in their widely-used Anglicised form, or in their local spelling or a standard transliteration of that local spelling. The index also includes local forms of names where the Anglicised form has been used on the map. In these cases the local name is followed by the Anglicised name in brackets. This indicates that the place name appears on the map, at the reference given, in the form shown in brackets, not in its local form.

Aachen 33 n
Aaro 25 v
Aargub 36 o
Aba (China) 62 h
Aba (Nigeria) 41 s
Aba (Zaïre) 42 w
Abadan 39 g
Abadeh 39 j
Abadla 36 k
Abaeté 29 j
Abaetetuba 26 l
Abag Qi 57 v
Abakan 56 i
Abakan (River) 56 h
Abakan Mountains 56 h
Abala 41 c
Abalessa 37 o
Aban 56 l
Abancay 24 z
Abarqu 39 k
Abay 55 j
Abay (River) 43 b
Abaya, Lake 43 o
Abbabis 48 h
Abbe, Lake 43 e
Abbeville 32 x
Abbotabad 60 m
Abbot Ice Shelf 80 m
Abd al Kuri 43 m
Abdulino 54 m
Abéché 42 c
Abengourou 40 x
Abeokuta 41 p
Aberdeen Lake 12 y
Aberdeen (South Africa) 49 n
Aberdeen (South Dakota) 15 h
Aberdeen (UK) 32 x
Aberdeen (Washington) 14 x
Aberfoyle 74 o
Aberystwyth 32 w
Abez' 50 l
Abha 39 p
Abidjan 40 x
Abilene 19 b
Abingdon Downs 73 l
Abitibi 16 i
Abitibi Lake 16 j
Abiyata, Lake 43 c
Abkit 53 k
Abminga 77 d
Abomey 41 o
Abong Mbang 41 w
Abou Deïa 42 b
Abqaiq 39 h
Abra Pampa 28 f
Abrolhos, Archipelago dos 29 m
Abu al Abyad 39 x
Abu Dara, Ras 38 z
Abu Dhabi 39 x
Abu Habi 42 k
Abu Hadriyah 39 h
Abu Hamed 38 w
Abuja 41 f
Abu Kamal 39 b
Abu Madd, Ras 38 z
Abumonbazi 42 r
Abun 25 r
Abun (River) 25 q
Abune Yosef 43 c
Abu Shagara, Ras 38 z
Abu Simbel 38 v
Abu Tig 38 i
Abuye Meda 43 d
Abuyog 67 j
Abu Zabad 42 i
Acailandia 27 n
Acámbaro 19 n
Acampamento 26 i
Acampamento de Indios 25 w
Acaponeta 18 x
Acapulco 19 n
Acarai, Serra 25 l
Acaraú 27 f
Acarigua 23 d
Acatlán 19 p
Acayucan 19 r
Accra 40 z
Achacachi 25 p
Achénoumma 37 v
Achinsk 56 i

Achsu 54 w
Acklins 21 q
Acomayo 25 n
Aconcagua 28 p
Aconguija, Nev. de 28 s
Acre 25 p
Açu 27 u
Açu (River) 27 u
Acude Araras 27 s
Acude Orós 27 t
Ada 15 v
Adafer 36 s
Adak 10 v
Adale 43 v
Adam 60 u
Adam's Bridge 64 u
Adamaoua, Highlands 41 u
Adan 66 c
Adana 35 z
Adanac 15 b
Adapazari 35 j
Adarama 38 x
Adare, Cape 86 s
Adavale 74 o
Ad Da'ain 42 g
Ad Darb 39 p
Ad Dawadimi 39 r
Ad Dibdibah 39 f
Addis Ababa 43 c
Addis Zemen 43 b
Ad Diwaniyah 39 e
Ad Dueim 42 k
Ad Duwaid 39 c
Adelaide 77 g
Adelaide Island 82 u
Adelaide Peninsula 12 m
Adelaide River 73 c
Adélieland 87 o
Aden 43 h
Aden, Gulf of 43 h
Aderbissinat 41 g
Adi Arkay 43 b
Adigrat 43 d
Adi Keyih 43 d
Adilabad 61 q
Adi Quala 43 c
Adirondack Mountains 16 z
Admiralty Inlet 13 d
Admiralty Islands 71 n
Ado 41 q
Adoni 64 f
Adour 34 f
Adrar 36 l
Adrar of the Iforas 36 z
Adré 42 d
Adriatic Sea 35 a
Adwa 43 c
Adycha 53 c
Adygalakh 53 f
Adzhima 59 b
Adzva 50 k
Aegean Sea 35 t
Affolé, Montagnes de l' 40 g
Afghanistan 55/60
Afgoi 43 t
Afif 39 p
Afikpo 41 s
Aflou 34 t
Afmadu 43 s
Aftout 36 w
Afuá 26 l
Afyon 35 w
Agadem 41 j
Agadèz 37 r
Agadir 36 f
Agadyr' 55 k
Agailas 36 p
Agamor 41 a
Agan 51 q
Agapa 51 i
Agaro 43 a
Agartalā 61 z
Agassiz, Cape 82 w
Agassiz Ice Cap 13 h
Agata 51 j
Agboville 40 x
Agdam 54 v
Agdz 36 h
Agen 34 f
Agnew 76 g

Agnibilekrou 40 x
Agoare 41 c
Agra 61 c
Ağri 54 l
Agrigento 37 h
Agrínion 35 r
Agryz 54 m
Aguadas 22 z
Agua de Chale 18 e
Aguapei, Serra 25 w
Agua Prieta 18 i
Aguarico 22 y
Aguas Belas 27 u
Aguascalientes 18 z
Aguas Calientes, Sierra de 28 r
Aguaytía 24 x
Aguaytia (River) 24 x
Aguelock 36 z
Aguelt el Melah 36 s
Agueraktem 36 u
Aguilas 36 l
Agulhas 48 x
Agulhas, Cape 48 x
Aha, Mount 48 l
Ahaggar 37 p
Ahar 54 v
Ahmadi 39 g
Ahmadnagar 61 n
Ahmar Mountains 43 e
Ahmedabad 60 y
Ahnet 37 n
Ahome 18 h
Ahoskie 16 y
Ahuachapan 22 c
Ahwar 43 i
Ahwaz 39 g
Aibak 60 i
Aileron 73 r
Ailigandi 22 k
Aim 53 o
Aim (River) 53 n
Aimorés 29 k
Aïn Beïda 34 x
Ain Benimathar 36 k
Aïn ben Tili 36 s
Ain Oussera 34 u
Ain Sefra 34 s
Ain Sukhna 38 i
Aioun Abd el Malek 36 u
Aiquile 28 f
Aïr 37 r
Airo 25 h
Airy, Mount 16 w
Aitape 70 y
Aiwasedapur 51 r
Aix-en-Provence 34 j
Āizawl 62 o
Ajaccio 34 k
Ajaguz 56 c
Ajaguz (River) 56 b
Ajdabiyah 38 a
Ajmer 61 a
Ajni 55 u
Ajryk 55 m
Akabli 37 n
Akchar 36 o
Ak-Dovurak 56 i
Akelamo 69 m
Akespe 55 c
Aketi 42 r
Akhisar 35 v
Akhmîn 38 i
Akhtyrka 35 l
Akimiki Island 16 i
Akita 59 o
Akjoujt Faye 36 p
Akkabak 55 d
Akkani 10 k
Akkarga 55 d
Aklavik 11 k
Aknoul 34 q
Akobo 42 l
Akola 61 o
Akordat 43 b
Akoupé 40 x
Akpatok Island 13 x
Akqi 56 o
Akranes 32 b
Akreïjit 36 s
Akrerèb 41 g

Akritas, Cape 35 r
Aksakovo 54 m
Aksaray 35 y
Aksay 54 m
Akşehir 35 w
Aksu 55 j
Aksuat 55 f
Aksum 43 c
Aksumbe 55 u
Aktag 56 r
Aktau 55 k
Aktaz 56 s
Aktogaj (Kirgizskaya) 56 n
Aktogaj (Kazakhstan) 56 c
Aktyubinsk 55 a
Akulivik 13 s
Akure 41 q
Akureyri 32 c
Akwanga 41 f
Alabama (River) 19 j
Alabama (State) 19 k
Al Abyar 35 r
Alachakh 53 p
Al Adam 35 s
Alagoinhas 27 u
Al Ain 39 y
Alajuela 22 q
Alakanuk 10 m
Alakol', Lake 56 d
Al Alamein 38 g
Al Amarah 39 g
Alamogordo 18 k
Alamos 18 i
Aland Islands 33 h
Alanya 35 x
Al Aqaylah 37 m
Al Artawiyah 39 e
Alaşehir 35 v
Alashan Desert 57 p
Al Ashkhirah 60 q
Alaska 11
Alaska, Gulf of 11
Alaska Peninsula 11 o
Alaska Range 11 e
Al Aswaa, Ras 39 n
Alat 55 r
Ala Tau 55 z
Alatyr 54 i
Alausí 22 x
Al Awaynat 37 t
Al Aziziyah (Iraq) 39 e
Al Aziziyah (Libya) 34 z
Albacete 34 r
Al Bad 38 k
al Baida 43 h
Al Balyana 38 i
Albanel Lake 17 a
Albania 35 d
Albany (Australia) 76 e
Albany (Georgia) 20 j
Albany (New York) 16 z
Albany (Oregon) 14 g
Albany (River) 16 h
Albany Downs 74 q
Al Bardi 35 t
Al Batinah 39 z
Al Bayda 35 r
Alberga 77 d
Alberta 14 l
Albert, Lake 42 w
Albert Lea 16 o
Albert Nile 42 x
Alberton 17 e
Al Bir 38 l
Ålborg 33 p
Albuquerque 15 p
Albury 78 o
Al Busaiyah 39 e
Alcantara 27 b
Alcova 15 p
Alcudia 34 u
Aldabra Island 47 d
Aldama 18 k
Aldan 52 x
Aldan (River) 53 a
Aldar 56 l
Aleg 40 d
Alej 56 d
Alejandro Sekirk 30 c
Alejsk 56 d

Aleksandrovskoye 51 q
Aleksandrovsko-Sakhalinskiy 53 r
Alekseyevka (Kazakhstan) 55 j
Alekseyevka (Ukraine) 54 d
Alekseyevo 53 h
Além Paraiba 29 j
Alençon 34 f
Alenquer 26 h
Aleppo 54 q
Alert 91 g
Alert, Cape 89 k
Alerta 25 n
Alessandria 34 k
Ålesund 33 a
Aleutian Islands 10 u
Alevina, Cape 53 v
Alexander Archipelago 11 x
Alexander Bay 48 u
Alexander Island 82 w
Alexandra 79 r
Alexandra, Lake 77 t
Alexandra, Land 50 f
Alexandria (Australia) 73 k
Alexandria (Egypt) 38 g
Alexandria (Louisiana) 19 g
Alexandria (Minnesota) 15 h
Alexandria (Virginia) 16 y
Al Faiyûm 38 g
Al Farcia 36 f
Al Faw 39 g
al Fûla 42 i
Alga 55 a
Algarroho del Aguila 30 x
Algarve 34 n
Algatart 55 z
Al Gaydah 43 m
Algeciras 34 p
Algeria 34/36-37
Al Ghaydah 39 x
Algiers 34 u
al Hadd, Ras 60 q
Al Hadithah (Iraq) 39 c
Al Hadithah (Saudi Arabia) 38 m
Al Hajar al Gharbi 39 z
Al Hajar ash Sharqi 60 p
Al Hammâm 38 h
Al Hanakiyah 39 o
Al Hasakah 54 r
Al Hazm 39 r
Al Hijaz 38 m
Al Hillah 39 s
Al Hoceima 34 q
Aliabad 39 l
Aliança 25 f
Ali-Bagata 53 a
Alicante 34 s
Alice Springs 73 r
Aligarh 61 c
Alijos, Rocas 18 d
Alindao 42 q
Alipxa 51 q
Ali-Sabieh 43 e
Al Isawiyah 38 m
Aliwal North 49 o
Al Jabal al Akhdar 35 r
Al Jaghbub 38 d
Al Jalamid 39 b
Al Jawf (Libya) 38 p
Al Jawf (Saudi Arabia) 39 a
Al Jubayl 39 h
al Junayna 42 e
Aljustrel 36 g
Al Kamil 60 p
Al Karak 38 l
Al Khaburah 60 l
Al Khamasin 39 q
Al Khandaq 38 u
Al Khârga 38 u
Al Kharja Oasis 38 u
Al Khartum 42 k
Al Khaznah 39 y
Al Kut 39 f
al Kú, Wadi 42 g
Allahabad 61 q
Allakh-Yun' 53 c
Allegheny 16 w
Allegheny Mountains 16 w
Allende 19 a
Allentown 16 y

Sal'sk	54 f
Salta	28 t
Saltillo	19 a
Salt Lake City	14 z
Salt Lakes	76 g
Salto	28 y
Salton Sea	18 d
Salvador	27 t
Salvatierra	19 n
Salwa	39 v
Salween	65 h
Salzburg	35 a
Samagaltaj	56 l
Samar	67 j
Samara	54 k
Samara Reservoir	54 j
Samarga	59 a
Samarinda	69 d
Samarkand	55 l
Samatiguila	40 i
Samaumá	25 j
Samba	45 a
Samba (Maringa)	44 l
Samba Caju	44 g
Sambalpur	61 u
Sambas	68 l
Sambava	47 f
Sambhar	61 a
Samborombón Bay	31 d
Same	45 j
Samfya	45 q
Samirah	39 c
Sámos	35 u
Sampit	69 o
Samrong	66 g
Samsang	61 g
Samsun	35 m
Samui	65 j
San'a	43 g
San	40 j
Sanae	83 l
Sanaga	41 v
San Agustín de Valle Fértil	28 r
Sanandaj	39 f
San Andrés	22 i
San Andrés Tuxtla	19 r
San Angelo	19 b
San Antonio (Chile)	30 h
San Antonio (USA)	19 c
San Antonio de los Cobres	28 r
San Antonio Oeste	30 l
Sanaw	39 v
San Benedicto	18 u
San Bernardino	18 c
San Bernardo	30 i
San Blas	18 i
San Blas, Cape	20 l
San Borja	25 q
San Buenaventura	19 a
San Carlos (Colombia)	23 r
San Carlos (Luzon, Philippines)	67 f
San Carlos (Mexico)	18 g
San Carlos (Negros, Philippines)	67 i
San Carlos (Nicaragua)	22 g
San Carlos de Bolivar	31 a
San Carlos de Bariloche	30 i
San Carlos del Zulia	23 b
Sanch	57 b
Sanchakou	56 o
San Clemente	18 b
San Cristobal	75 a
San Cristóbal (Argentina)	28 v
San Cristóbal (Colombia)	24 m
San Cristóbal (Ecuador)	22 q
San Cristóbal (Venezuela)	23 b
San Cristóbal las Casas	19 t
Sancti Spíritus	21 n
Sandakan	69 e
Sanderson	18 m
Sandia	25 o
San Diego	18 c
San Diego, Cabo	30 y
Sandoa	44 y
Sandoway	62 p
Sandpoint	14 k
Sandstone	76 f
Sandusky	16 u

Sandy Bay	76 i
Sandy Cape	77 w
Sandy Lake	15 k
San Estanislao	28 z
San Felipe (Chile)	28 o
San Felipe (Lower California, Mexico)	18 e
San Felipe (Mexico)	19 l
San Felipe (Venezuela)	23 d
San Fernando (Chile)	30 i
San Fernando (Philippines)	67 g
San Fernando (Venezuela)	23 j
San Fernando de Atabapo	23 r
San Fernando de Apure	23 e
San Francisco (Argentina)	28 u
San Francisco (USA)	14 t
San Francisco de Macoris	21 t
San Francisco del Rincón	18 z
San Francisco del Oro	18 k
San Gabriel	22 y
Sangan	60 g
Sangareddi	61 p
Sange	45 c
Sanggau	68 m
Sangha	41 z
Sanghar	60 w
Sangihe	69 k
Sangihe Islands	69 k
Sangijn Dalaj Nuur	56 m
Sangli	61 n
Sangmelima	41 w
Sangre de Cristo Range	15 q
Sangyyakhtakh	52 x
San Guillermo	18 k
San Ignacio (Apere, Bolivia)	25 r
San Ignacio (Argentina)	28 y
San Ignacio (Bolivia)	25 v
San Ignacio (Peru)	24 i
San Ignacio, Laguna	18 f
San Ildefonso Peninsula	67 h
San Javier	25 u
San Joaquin	25 s
San Jorge	22 m
San Jorge, Gulf of	30 x
San Jose (USA)	14 u
San José (Mexico)	18 h
San José (Costa Rica)	22 g
San Jose (Philippines)	67 g
San José (Venezuela)	23 r
San José de Amacuro	23 j
San Jose de Buenavista	67 g
San José de Chiquitos	25 v
San José de Jáchal	28 q
San José del Guaviare	23 o
San Jose de Mayo	31 d
San José de Ocune	23 p
San Juan (Argentina)	28 q
San Juán (Chile)	24 x
San Juan (Dominican Republic)	21 s
San Juan (Puerto Rico)	21 w
San Juan (Venezuela)	23 s
San Juan (River, Colombia)	22 y
San Juan (River, USA)	15 n
San Juan (River, Argentina)	28 r
San Juan (River, Costa Rica)	22 g
San Juan Bautista	28 z
San Juan del Norte	22 g
San Juan de los Lagos	18 z
San Juan do los Morros	23 e
San Juan Mountains	15 p
San Juanico	18 f
San Julián	30 w
San Justo	28 w
Sankuru	44 m
San Lázaro, Cape	18 f
San Lorenzo (Ecuador)	24 h
San Lorenzo (USA)	18 j
San Lorenzo (Mount)	30 u
San Lucas	18 u
San Lucas, Cape	18 u
San Luis	28 s
San Luis de la Paz	19 o
San Luis de Tapajós	25 l
San Luis, Lago de	25 s

San Luis Obispo	14 v
San Luis Potosi	19 n
San Luis-Rio Colorado	18 e
San Malo, Golfe de	34 e
San Marcos	19 o
San Marino	34 m
San Martín (Argentina)	28 q
San Martin (Bolivia)	25 t
San Martín de los Andes	30 i
San Martin (River)	25/28
San Matías	25 w
San Matias Gulf	30 m
Sanmenhsia	63 a
San Miguel (Bolivia)	25 t
San Miguel (El Salvador)	22 d
San Miguel del Monte	31 c
San Miguel de Tucumán	28 t
Sanming	63 s
San Nicolas (Argentina)	31 a
San Nicolas (USA)	18 a
Sanniquellie	40 u
Sanouyah	40 f
San Pablo (Bolivia)	28 e
San Pablo (River, Bolivia)	25 u
San Pablo (Philippines)	67 g
San Pédro	40 v
San Pedro (Argentina)	28 t
San Pedro (Paraguay)	28 y
San Pedro (Paraná, Argentina)	28 w
San Pedro de Atacama	28 d
San Pedro de las Colonias	18 m
San Pedro de Lloc	24 h
San Pedro Sula	19 w
San Rafael (Argentina)	30 j
San Rafael (Venezuela)	23 b
San Ramón de la Nueva Orán	28 g
San Salvador	22 d
San Salvador (Island, Bahamas)	21 q
San Salvador (Island, Ecuador)	22 p
San Salvador de Jujuy	28 s
Sansanné-Mango	41 a
San Sebastián	34 e
Santa	24 v
Santa Ana (Beni, Bolivia)	28 e
Santa Ana (Bolivia)	25 r
Santa Ana (Serra de Santiago, Bolivia)	28 k
Santa Ana (El Salvador)	22 c
Santa Ana (Mexico)	18 h
Santa Ana (USA)	18 c
Santa Barbara (Mexico)	18 k
Santa Barbara (USA)	14 v
Santa Barbara (Venezuela)	23 s
Santa Catalina (Chile)	28 p
Santa Catalina (Island, USA)	18 c
Santa Catalina (Island, Mexico)	18 h
Santa Clara (Colombia)	25 b
Santa Clara (Cuba)	20 z
Santa Clotilde	24 l
Santa Corazón	25 w
Santa Cruz (Bolivia)	28 h
Santa Cruz (Brazil)	24 m
Santa Cruz (Chile)	28 o
Santa Cruz (Peru)	24 h
Santa Cruz (Spain)	36 b
Santa Cruz (USA)	14 u
Santa Cruz (Island, California)	18 a
Santa Cruz (Island, Ecuador)	22 p
Santa Cruz (River, Argentina)	30 v
Santa Cruz Island	75 d
Santa Elena, Cabo	22 f
Santa Elena de Uairen	23 v
Santa Fé (Argentina)	28 w
Santa Fe (USA)	15 q
Santa Filomena	27 o
Santa Helena	25 l
Santai	62 k
Santa Inés (Brazil)	27 b
Santa Inés (Chile)	30 t
Santa Isabel (Argentina)	30 k

Santa Isabél (Brazil)	25 v
Santa Isabel (Ecuador)	24 h
Santa Isabel (Peru)	24 l
Santa Isabel (Solomon Islands)	71 x
Santa Lucia	24 m
Santa Maria (Amazon, Brazil)	25 j
Santa María (Argentina)	28 r
Santa Maria (Brazil)	29 o
Santa Maria (Ecuador)	22 o
Santa Maria (Mexico)	18 k
Santa Maria (Peru)	24 l
Santa Maria (Venezuela)	23 e
Santa Maria da Vitória	27 p
Santa Maria di Leuca, Capo	35 p
Santa Marta	23 a
Santana	27 p
Santana do Araguaia	26 x
Santana do Ipanema	27 u
Santana do Livramento	29 n
Santander (Colombia)	22 y
Santander (Spain)	34 d
Santanghu	56 x
Santarém (Brazil)	25 m
Santarém (Portugal)	34 o
Santa Rosa (Argentina)	30 l
Santa Rosa (Brazil)	25 n
Santa Rosa (California)	14 t
Santa Rosa (Colombia)	23 p
Santa Rosa (Honduras)	22 d
Santa Rosa (New Mexico)	15 q
Santa Rosa (Island)	18 a
Santa Rosa del Conlara	28 s
Santa Rosalia	18 g
Santa Teresa	73 r
Santa Teresinha	26 x
Santiago (Argentina)	29 n
Santiago (Chile)	28 o
Santiago (Dominican Republic)	21 t
Santiago (Panama)	22 i
Santiago (River) (Mexico)	18 y
Santiago (River) (Peru)	24 i
Santiago de Chuco	24 v
Santiago de Compostela	34 b
Santiago de Cuba	21 p
Santiago del Estero	28 t
Santiago Ixcuintla	18 x
Santiago Papasquiaro	18 k
Santiago, Serra de	28 k
San Tiburcio	19 n
Santo Amaro	27 t
Santo Angelo	29 n
Santo Antônio	25 t
Santo Antônio (Negro)	25 i
Santo Antônio de Içá	25 d
Santo Antônio de Jesus	27 s
Santo Corazón	28 k
Santo Domingo	21 t
Santos	29 g
Santos Dumont	25 c
Santo Tomás	24 z
Santo Tomé	28 z
San Valentin	30 t
San Vincente	18 c
San Vicente de Cañete	24 w
San Yanaro	23 q
Sanyati	45 q
Sanyuan	62 m
Sanza Pombo	44 h
São Borja	28 z
São Carlos	29 e
São Félix	26 z
São Félix (Ilha do Bananal)	26 x
São Félix do Xingu	26 x
São Francisco (Island)	29 s
São Francisco (River)	29 i
São Francisco, Serra	27 r
São Gabriel	29 n
Sao Hill	45 h
São João de Araguaia	26 z
São João do Piauí	27 q
São José	29 r
São José (Negro)	25 d
São José do Anauá	25 h
São José do Egito	27 u
São José do Rio Preto	29 d

São José do Ribamar	27 c
São José dos Campos	29 g
Sâo José do Xingu	26 w
Saolat	69 m
São Lorenço	25 z
São Luis	27 b
São Luis de Montes Belos	29 c
São Marcos Bay	27 c
São Mateus	29 l
São Miguel de Guamá	27 a
São Miguel do Araguaia	26 x
São Miguel dos Campos	27 v
São Paulo	29 g
São Paulo de Olivença	25 c
São Pedro do Piauí	27 q
São Raimundo das Mangabeiras	27 n
São Raimundo Nonato	27 q
São Romo	29 g
São Roque, Cabo	27 w
São Sebastião	26 v
São Sebastio (São Paulo)	29 h
São Tomé	41 s
São Tomé (Island)	41 r
São Tomé and Principe	41/44
Sapele	41 r
Saposoa	24 j
Sapporo	59 c
Sapri	35 o
Sapt Kosi	61 i
Saqqez	54 v
Saquenay	17 b
Sarajevo	35 c
Sarakhs	55 q
Saraktash	55 a
Saran	55 j
Sarangani Islands	67 x
Sarangarh	61 s
Saranpaul	50 y
Saransk	54 h
Sarapul	54 m
Sarapulskoye	58 l
Sarar	39 z
Sarasota	20 k
Saratov	54 i
Saravan	60 e
Sarawak	69 b
Saraya	40 e
Saraysu	55 g
Sarbaz	60 e
Sarbisheh	60 d
Sarbulak	56 h
Sardinia	34 l
Sárek	33 g
Sarempaka	69 d
Sargasso Sea	21 d
Sargento Lores	24 l
Sargodha	60 l
Sarh	42 b
Sari Bulak	56 h
Sari-i Pul	60 h
Sarikei	68 m
Sarina	74 r
Sarkand	56 p
Šarlauk	55 n
Sarmi	70 v
Sarmiento	30 w
Sarmiento Peninsula	30 w
Särna	33 e
Sarnia	16 v
Sarolangun	68 l
Sarychik	54 l
Saryg-Sop	56 l
Sarykamysskoje, Lake	55 n
Saryozek	55 z
Sásabe	18 g
Sasaram	61 t
Sasebo	58 v
Saser	61 c
Saskatchewan (Province)	12/15
Saskatchewan (River)	15 e
Saskatoon	15 c
Saskylakh	52 f
Sassandra	40 v
Sassandra (River)	40 v
Sassari	34 k
Sasykkol', Lake	56 c
Satadougou	40 f
Satara (India)	64 d
Satara (South Africa)	49 f

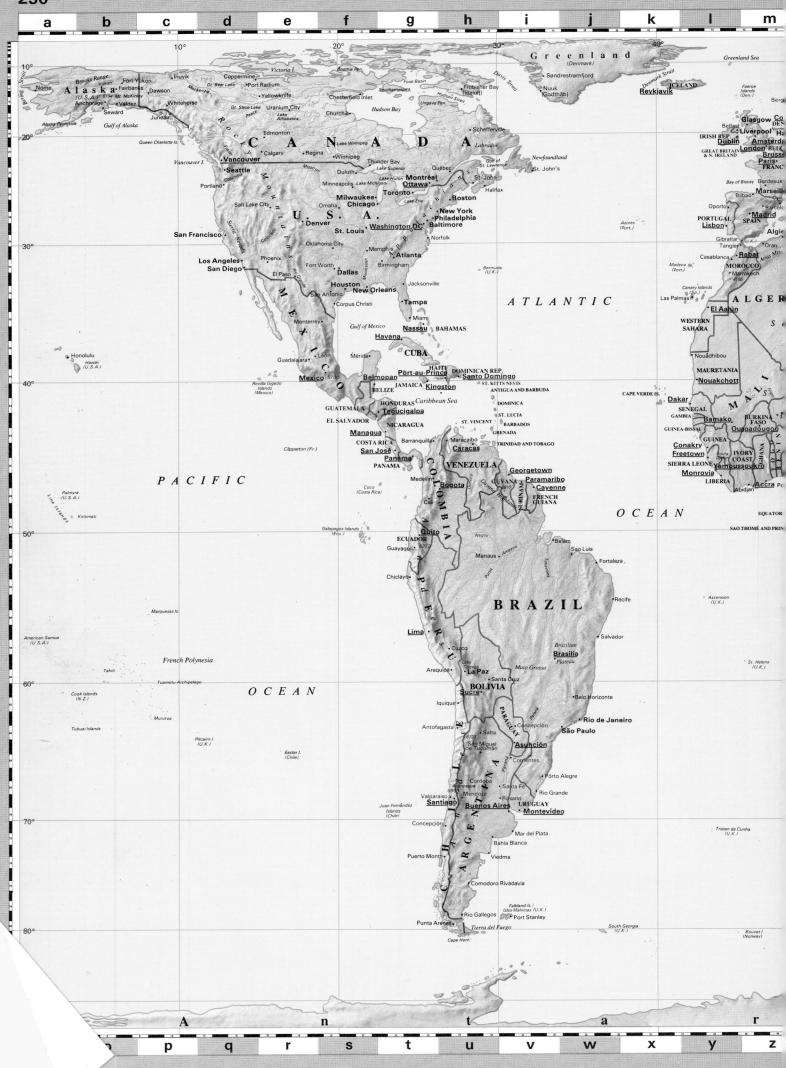

Greenland
(Denmark)

Greenland Sea

Søndrestrømfjord

Nuuk
(Godthåb)

Frobisher Bay
(Iqaluit)

Davis Strait

Denmark Strait

ICELAND

Reykjavik

Faeroe
Islands
(Den.)

Berg

Glasgow   Co
DEN
IRISH REP.   Belfast   Liverpool   H.
Dublin   London   BEL
GREAT BRITAIN   Amsterdam
& N. IRELAND   Bruss
Paris   FRANC

Alaska
(U.S.A.)   6194 Mt. McKinley
Anchorage
Valdez
Seward
Juneau
Gulf of Alaska
Alaska Peninsula

Brooks Range
Yukon   Fort Yukon
Fairbanks   Dawson
Whitehorse

Nome

Bering Strait

Inuvik   Coppermine
Mackenzie   Port Radium
Gt. Bear Lake
Yellowknife
Uranium City
Churchill

Victoria I.

Boothia Pen.

Southampton I.

Foxe Basin

Ungava Pen.

Hudson Strait

Chesterfield Inlet

Hudson Bay

Labrador

Queen Charlotte Is.
Vancouver I.   Vancouver
Seattle
Portland
Columbia
Calgary   Regina
Edmonton
Gt. Slave Lake
Lake Athabasca
Peace

CANADA

Lake Winnipeg

Winnipeg
Thunder Bay
Duluth
Lake Superior
Minneapolis   Lake Michigan

Scheffervville

Gulf of
St. Lawrence
Newfoundland

Québec

Montréal
Ottawa

St. John

Lake Huron   Toronto
Lake Erie

Boston

Halifax

St. John's

Salt Lake City
Milwaukee
Chicago

U.S.A.
Denver

Omaha
St. Louis

New York
Philadelphia   Baltimore

San Francisco

Oklahoma City
Memphis

Washington DC

Norfolk

Bermuda
(U.K.)

ATLANTIC

Azores
(Port.)

Bay of Biscay   Bordeaux

Bilbao   Marseill
Oporto
PORTUGAL   Barcel
Lisbon   SPAIN   MADRID
Gibraltar   Algie
Tangier   Oran
MOROCCO   Atlas Mts.
Casablanca   Rabat

Los Angeles
San Diego

Phoenix
El Paso

Fort Worth
Dallas

Birmingham
Atlanta

Rio Grande

San Antonio
Houston   New Orleans

Jacksonville

Tampa
Miami

Corpus Christi

Monterrey

Gulf of Mexico

Nassau
Havana
CUBA

BAHAMAS

Madeira
(Port.)
Canary Islands
(Sp.)
Las Palmas

WESTERN
SAHARA

Marrakech   4165

El Aaiún

ALGER

Honolulu
Hawaii
(U.S.A.)

Guadalajara   León
Mérida

Mexico   5700

Belmopan

MEXICO

Revilla Gigedo
Islands
(Mexico)

BELIZE
GUATEMALA
EL SALVADOR

Port-au-Prince
HAITI

JAMAICA   Kingston

HONDURAS
Tegucigalpa

Santo Domingo
DOMINICAN REP.
ST. KITTS NEVIS
ANTIGUA AND BARBUDA
DOMINICA

ST. LUCIA

Nouâdhibou

MAURETANIA
Nouakchott

Dakar
SENEGAL

GAMBIA
GUINEA-BISSAU

CAPE VERDE IS.

SENEGAL
Bamako
GUINEA

BURKINA
FASO
Ouagadougou
GHANA

MALI
Niger

PACIFIC

Clipperton (Fr.)

Palmyra
(U.S.A.)

Kiritimati

NICARAGUA
Managua
COSTA RICA
San José
Panama
PANAMA

Caribbean Sea

Barranquilla

Medellín

Maracaibo
Caracas

VENEZUELA

ST. VINCENT
BARBADOS
GRENADA
TRINIDAD AND TOBAGO

Georgetown
GUYANA
Paramaribo
SURINAM
Cayenne
FRENCH
GUIANA

Conakry
Freetown
SIERRA LEONE
Monrovia
LIBERIA

IVORY
COAST
Yamoussoukro
Accra

Abidjan

OCEAN

EQUATOR

SAO THOMÉ AND PRIN

COLOMBIA
Bogotá
Cali

Orinoco
Guaviare
Guainía   2810

Negro

Galapagos Islands
(Ecu.)

Quito
ECUADOR
Guayaquil   6272

Belém

São Luís

Fortaleza

Amazon
Manaus
Purus

Ascension
(U.K.)

Marquesas Is.

Chiclayo

Recife

BRAZIL

American Samoa
(U.S.A.)

Tahiti

French Polynesia

Tuamotu Archipelago

Lima

Cuzco

Lake
Titicaca
Arequipa

Andes Mountains

La Paz
Santa Cruz

Brazilian
Brasília   Plateau

Mato Grosso

Salvador

Belo Horizonte

St. Helena
(U.K.)

Cook Islands
(N.Z.)

Mururoa

OCEAN

Iquique

BOLIVIA
Sucre

PARAGUAY

Paraná

Rio de Janeiro
São Paulo

Tubuai Islands

Pitcairn I.
(U.K.)

Easter I.
(Chile)

Antofagasta
6723
Salta
San Miguel
de Tucumán

Concepción
Asunción

Corrientes

Pôrto Alegre

Juan Fernández
Islands
(Chile)

Valparaíso
Santiago

Aconcagua
6959
Córdoba
Mendoza
Rosario

ARGENTINA

CHILE

Santa Fé

Paraná

Rio Grande

Buenos Aires
URUGUAY
Montevideo

Tristan da Cunha
(U.K.)

Concepción

Puerto Montt

Viedma

Mar del Plata
Bahía Blanca

Comodoro Rivadavia

Puerto Montt

Punta Arenas
Cape Horn

Río Gallegos

Tierra del Fuego

Falkland Is./
Islas Malvinas (U.K.)
Port Stanley

South Georgia
(U.K.)

Bouvet I.
(Norway)